International Business and Governments

**CRITICAL ISSUES FACING
THE MULTINATIONAL ENTERPRISE**

Brian Toyne, Series Editor

Multinationals and
Canada–United States Free Trade
by Alan M. Rugman

International Business
and Governments:
Issues and Institutions
*by Jack N. Behrman
and Robert E. Grosse*

International Business and Governments:
Issues and Institutions

Jack N. Behrman
University of North Carolina

and

Robert E. Grosse
University of Miami

University of South Carolina Press

Copyright © 1990 University of South Carolina

Published in Columbia, South Carolina, by the
University of South Carolina Press

Manufactured in the United States of America

Library of Congress Cataloging-in-Publication Data

Behrman, Jack N.
 International business and governments : issues and institutions /
Jack N. Behrman and Robert E. Grosse.
  p.   cm. — (Critical issues facing the multinational
enterprise)
 Includes bibliographical references.
 ISBN 0–87249–696–1
 1. International business enterprises. 2. International business
enterprises—Government policy. I. Grosse, Robert E. II. Title.
III. Series.
HD2755.5.B414   1990
338.8′8—dc20   90–35691
                                                                     CIP

Contents

Contents

Series Editor's Preface

The purpose of this series is to explore the multifacted relationship of multinational enterprises (MNEs) with their global environment. Essentially, each book in the series is written by an expert and addresses a single issue of recognizable concerns to MNEs. Thus, the aim of each book is to draw together and present the views of the various groups interested in the issue in a way that presents constructive suggestions for multinationals, irrespective of their nationality and inherent interests. Towards this end, each issue will be placed in its historical setting and explored from the perspective of the MNEs, their home countries, and the host countries in which they operate—where they agree and where they disagree, and why. Of particular concern will be the differences that have emerged or are emerging, by region (even by country when necessary), and among multinationals from different parts of the world.

Thoughtful practitioners will find the series helpful in developing a better understanding of the organizations they work for, and interact or compete with. They will also gain a much better appreciation of the extent of the MNE's social, economic, and political influence. Specifically, the series is designed to provide a "library" of the many views taken toward the multinational by the governments, labor organizations, and the societies in which they operate or intend to operate, and the reasons for these differing views.

Educators will also find the series of value as a supplemental set of readers for topics in business administration, economics, international relations, and political science courses. Because of the scope of the series, and its historical perspective, students will eventually have access to an extensive and thorough analysis of the MNE, the role it plays, the influence it has on the global economic and political order, and thus the way it is viewed by other societal organizations.

It has become abundantly clear in the last few years that the economic activities of MNEs, as they strive for global integration of their activities and investments, irrespective of national boundaries, are increasingly of political concern to governments. This mounting concern by governments has resulted in demands being imposed on MNEs that are often heavily charged with political implications. In response, MNEs are finding it increasingly necessary to formulate and implement political strategies in addition to their economic strategies. Thus, *International Business and Governments: Issues and Institutions* by Jack N. Behrman and Robert E. Grosse deals with an extremely important and timely subject; namely, the relationship between business and government at the international, regional, national, and subnational levels. It is comprehensive, and contains a great deal of information and insights that should appeal to scholars, to those charged with developing the politically influenced demands of governments, and to those charged with responding to these demands.

Brian Toyne
Series Editor and
Professor of International Business
The University of South Carolina

Preface

One of the lessons we have learned in writing this book is that in the realm of policy, institutional memories are short, and lessons from abroad that might apply domestically are heavily discounted. Each country sees itself as unique or facing extenuating circumstances, so it seeks to choose its own way, without concern for consequences on other countries. Consequently, few countries entering the world economy garner the benefits of being a latecomer on the international scene, preferring instead to retrod the (often mistaken) paths of others. Instead of selecting from the "development smorgasbord" the technologies and strategies most appropriate to their future, they tend to follow some past model—even if inappropriate. The story of international business-government relations is one of varying progress and regress.

The relations of governments to international business are at three levels: local, national, and international. At the local level, most cities and states (provinces) seek to attract the foreign investor in order to gain more and higher paid employment and to increase the tax base. Few restrictive rules are imposed; rather incentives are offered. As competing candidate-locations offer incentives to the firm, the offers must be raised to keep the potential investor interested. The net result is that, in seeking to gain the investment, local hosts often lose by offering more than necessary to support the project; and the pattern is continually repeated.

At the national level, governments set the rules for the conduct of foreigners in their countries and sometimes for the conduct of locally based companies when operating abroad; they do so through constraints and incentives. Intergovernmental rules arise when nations agree as to behavior of transnationals moving within and across their borders. Efforts have been made to create a common body of rules for the world economy, but there is no single set of rules to which all countries have agreed in the treatment of international business. Between the national and international levels, there are some agreed rules among members of regional associations. These groups comprise countries in advanced stages of industrialization—the Organization for Economic Cooperation and Development (OECD); those in the beginning stages of industrialization—Association of Southeast Asian Nations (ASEAN); and those with a similar ideology underlying their economic systems—Communist Economic Council (COMECON).

Each of these governmental levels is addressed in the present book, but the major focus is on the national and intergovernmental levels where the concept of sovereignty comes into play. The fundamental issues underlying the treatment of international business and the conflicts between the objectives of business and those of government are reviewed, examining how these conflicts have been handled and why? What has been the process of dialogues? At what level they have occurred? What criteria have been applied in coming to accommodation? And finally, what appear to be the future prospects?

After an introductory chapter on the bargaining orientations of companies and governments, Part I examines the players in the dialogues. Chapter 2 delineates the characteristics of different transnational corporations (TNCs) in terms of their significance to government interests and, therefore, the differing treatment that might be expected because of these characteristics. Chapter 3 examines the relations with home governments, because they have been concerned with the extension of commerce overseas and the reactions in host governments to both costs and benefits of foreign investment. Part II examines the relations between TNCs and home governments. Chapter 4 surveys the issues and channels of communication between TNCs and host governments. Part III addresses the range of host-country policies toward TNCs, beginning with a summary in Chapter 5, followed by the policies of selected host governments in Chapters 6, 7, and 8, illustrating "open," "mixed," and "restrictive" approaches. Chapter 9 analyzes TNC responses to these divergent policies.

Part IV addresses intergovernmental policies concerning TNCs and the attempt to formulate rules of conduct. Chapter 10 treats the legal issues; Chapter 11 addresses the rules under regional associations, and Chapter 12 those of UN agencies and affiliates. Part V examines prospective (unresolved) issues in the sociopolitical and economic realms. Chapter 13 includes some of the ethical issues raised by the activities of TNCs. Chapter 14 examines the continued lack of solutions to basic economic questions of who should produce what for whom, where, and the extent of economic interdependence. The final chapter assesses the need for and sources of leadership in the international issues between TNCs and governments.

The materials in the book are based not only on extensive research but also on the direct experience of the authors in dealing with TNCs and governments in a variety of settings: as a government official, as advisors to government ministries and intergovernmental organizations, as consultants to companies, as educators in corporate management programs, as researchers on international issues, and as lecturers to foreign audiences. We have interviewed several hundred companies and thousands of business and governmental officials during the past forty years on issues related to international government / business relations and have published the results in a variety of media. This book, therefore, is an outgrowth of a long involvement in the issues and of multiple dealings with the various players. It is for the reason of extensive personal involvement that not all factual situations are cited as from secondary sources; where the material is official in nature or is drawn directly from a particular study, citations are given. Readings that are corroborative or supplementary in extending an examination of the issues are noted in a list of references. Although there were few direct contacts with corporate or government officials for the preparation of this book, each of us wishes to thank the myriad individuals who have contributed in the past to our understanding of these issues. Prof. Steve Kobrin read the manuscript carefully and offered important evaluations and corrections. Special gratitude is due the MBA students who offered extensive editorial advice during a semester course: Sidney Gause, Mary Ellen Goodall, John Patteson, Robert Shimp, Tom Stobbe, and Jun Yamamoto. We also wish to thank those who have assisted us in processing this manuscript, through several drafts, particularly Linda Wilson, Fontaine Hester, and Peggy Pickard at the UNC Graduate School of Business Administration.

Jack N. Behrman   Robert E. Grosse
Chapel Hill, North Carolina   Coral Gables, Florida

CHAPTER 1

Introduction

Problems of mutual trust between business and governments have long been the subject of analysis. Western businesses see the policies of governments largely as interventions, usually unwarranted in view of a preferred adherence to market principles in decision making. But, governments are "part and parcel" of the arena of international business. It is their existence that makes business become "inter-national," as opposed to "extra-domestic"—that is, merely an extension of domestic strategy and operation into another market.

No national policy toward domestic business and none toward foreign companies permits free markets or free trade, as prescribed by neoclassical economists. Governments are not elected to turn major decisions over to private corporations and certainly not to foreigners. The continued urging that the world's governments should avoid interferences in international business simply misunderstands the nature and purpose of government—which is to promote and protect *national* interests. We are, therefore, far from any supranational set of rules for treatment of international business, which continues to face diverse governmental policies.

It is the lack of recognition of the key role of government that has led to a virtually complete bias in theories on international business toward market, firm, and transaction explanations. In these theories, governments and cultures are left aside as mere "constraining parameters" that ought to be removed. A central theme of this book is the continuity and similarity of business / government problems *across* national boundaries and the diversity of and shifts in their treatment. Many countries remain tied to policies that are no longer effective as a result of changes in intercorporate relationships and in the world economy.

1

Even countries only recently coming into industrialization (e.g., China) have followed outmoded policies in making their way into the world economy. These new entrants complicate the problems of negotiation and accommodation between TNCs and governments, both by increasing diversity of choices and by their inexperience.

Countries at different stages of industrialization adopted foreign economic policies that were initially quite restrictive and relaxed them only after some time. Although Adam Smith argued that free trade and open economies were good for any country at any stage of industrialization, even if no other country adopted the same policy, he admitted that there were exceptions, particularly during the early stages of industrialization or in relations with so-called "natural enemies." The concept of a natural enemy has virtually disappeared from the international scene, even from the conflict between the United States and the U.S.S.R. The recognition of a natural enemy makes formation of policies between these two countries easy, since no advantage is to be given the other in any arena. However, in the nineteenth century, even the existence of a natural enemy did not prevent the continuation of trade or economic relations (as among the European countries), since each country thought it was gaining an advantage.[1]

Where there are no natural enemies to guide policies, relationships among nations in international business are more complex, simply because there is no agreed set of rules by which business is to be conducted or treated. It is, of course, the nature of the nation-state system that there are no supranational rules that can be enforced on national governments. Governments are free to treat foreigners as they wish, and it is this freedom to discriminate that gives rise to treatment of business in "foreign policies" that is different from the treatment of nationals. One of the U.S. objectives of a more rule-oriented relationship is to achieve "national treatment" for foreigners. This would not create a one-world economy, since it could mean merely a world of 145 (members of the UN) different national treatments, but at least there would be no discrimination between a national and a foreign company within a given country. Prior to World War II, the practice was to discriminate not only between nationals and foreigners but also among different types of foreigners depending on the various economic and political alliances among countries. Though less extensive, some such discrimination remains.

Two sets of players are directly involved in international business / government relations: national governments and transnational corporations (TNCs). But they are affected by several others: national (private and state-owned) companies, local governments, and intergovernmental and private international institutions. Each of the latter groups operates through collaborative processes, through legislators, or through the media to influence the two former, which have final authority, in that both TNCs and national governments have a unique arena of decision making. The national government has final power over all activities within its jurisdiction, and the TNC can decide whether to operate at all in that area and under those conditions. But the concept of sovereignty also means that no government can dictate to another, short of the use of force. Thus, accommodation between TNCs and governments and among governments is a matter of negotiation.

National governments have directed and interfered with business across national boundaries since the very beginning of such transactions, starting 2000 years ago with the trade of the Phoenicians and extending through the periods of the Hanseatic League (twelfth century), through the trade fairs of Europe (twelfth–sixteenth centuries), through the opening of China and Japan (nineteenth century), through the extreme protectionism of the 1930s, and into the present-day "industrial policies" of governments. The nature of the companies operating internationally has changed significantly from the early trading companies and the one-trip joint ventures to the highly complex (but not yet globally oriented) TNCs. An additional complication arises from overseas activities of the state-owned enterprises (SOEs), such as Renault or Petrobras, which sometimes are seen by host countries as introducing home-government policies directly into international business. Some studies have seen the SOEs as operating largely under market criteria; others, however, have argued that all the evidence is not yet in and that government / SOE ties differ among countries.[2] France and Italy have virtually substituted SOEs for private companies in some sectors. The U.S.S.R. and China did so nearly completely—only lately permitting joint ventures between SOEs and foreign TNCs. Many less-developed countries (LDCs) have SOEs—in extractive, manufacturing, and service sectors—with some noneconomic objectives as their rationale; the political goals of these LDCs are clearly to be furthered by the SOEs.

The SOEs cause private TNCs to face nonmarket competitive situations, since many are subsidized. However, there are limits to government support, and subsidies usually are given to offset un- or noneconomic responsibilities imposed by the government. The methods and scope of the SOEs' operations *abroad* under governmental aegis has not been adequately researched as yet.[3] Consequently, they are not a prime focus in this study, though their effect on TNC-host government relations is discussed, since the mere existence of SOEs tells much about the policies of a country, and they imply a willingness by the government to direct economic activity.

The concerns of governments over international business have expanded with the increase in number and complexity of worldwide activities. The procedures for alleviating these concerns have been expressed more extensively and intensively during the last few decades. The ability of TNCs to respond has also expanded, so there is always an intricate balancing of interference and response or avoidance. Many TNCs have taken initiatives to mitigate governmental concerns, but the specific concerns shift, causing continuing negotiations.

The locally owned companies have an interest in what is done with TNCs, since TNCs are both potential competitors and desired suppliers or customers. Local companies will often attempt to alter national policy by injecting their concerns and interests into the decision making so that the benefits of international business accrue more to them or they are protected from adverse results.

State (provincial) and local governments also adopt policies toward TNCs. They sometimes interfere in national policies and often compete with each other in attracting foreign direct investment (FDI). But, since state and local governments are subordinate to their federal authorities in the main, and since our focus is on inter-country comparisons of policies, we treat the issues at the lower levels of government only in passing.

The intergovernmental organizations (such as the World Bank, the International Monetary Fund and the International Labour Organization) have achieved a life of their own and an ability to take positions through resolutions or agreements that some governments at least would wish to avoid—such as the UN resolution on advertising to consumers. Therefore, pressures arise from this level of government which are sometimes rejected by national governments or the TNCs themselves. Since these organizations have no coercive power (i.e., lack sovereignty), they can make their wishes felt only through national governments, which have to approve both in principle and in practice the recommendations coming from the intergovernmental agency.

The subject of international business / government relations is approachable from several different perspectives. One is that of describing and assessing the policies of national governments toward international business, examining the various attitudes, orientations, and approaches; this viewpoint can be historical, or comparative among different governments, or detailed in its attention to the present specifics of regulations and laws. A second is to examine the process of negotiation between TNCs and governments in the entrance and operation of foreign business in each country; this would involve an examination of specific projects in different industry sectors, the performance requirements imposed by governments, the assessment by the TNC of the political and commercial risks, and examples of the actual bargaining process. A third centers on negotiation among governments themselves, both bilaterally in matters concerning international business and multilaterally in the formation and operation of intergovernmental associations; this approach would also involve an examination of laws and the historical development of various agencies, as well as their specific responsibilites. The fourth perspective focuses on the responses of TNCs to the requirements of governments, both unilateral and multilateral, emphasizing the bargaining positions and the operational responses of TNCs; case studies would be required to illustrate the actions of both governments and TNCs. The interplay of these four approaches is illustrated in Chart 1.1.

Chart 1.1: Focus of Thesis

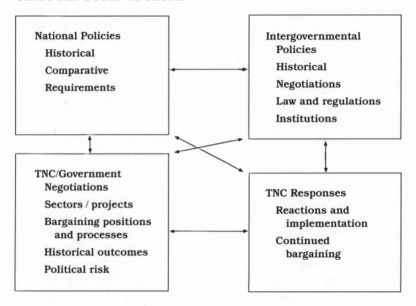

This book employs all four approaches because, as the diagram shows, these aspects are linked in a set of feedbacks running in both directions. The approaches are simply organized ways of looking at a single set of relationships. We attempt to provide as full an appreciation of the relations between TNCs and governments as is feasible in one volume. Rather than take a single focus, different issues are approached from one or more of the above perspectives. Some topics are developed historically, others in more current detail, others from an intergovernmental viewpoint, and some illustrations of TNC responses are included to show how the entire process works out through the bargaining relationship.

We have not hesitated to draw some policy conclusions despite the fact that we have not, in this volume, provided

all of the documentation that would be necessary to support every position. The proposals are included to stimulate
further thinking about the roles of TNCs and governments
in their mutual efforts to promote economic progress, both
nationally and internationally.

A BARGAINING VIEW

An underlying theme of the entire book is that relations
between home or host governments and TNCs everywhere
follow a bargaining pattern. That is, both government and
company seek to pursue their own goals, and each is constrained by the other, since their goals are not always con-
gruent; therefore, negotiation is required.[4] In some cases,
both government and TNC pursue similar ends (e.g., when
TNCs conduct research and development [R&D] in industrial countries and seek to achieve high incomes there, just
as those governments would like). In other cases, goals diverge dramatically (e.g., when firms seek to import into
countries with serious balance-of-payments deficits, or
when profitable business opportunities exist but the firm is
prevented from pursuing them through government action).
The international strategies of TNCs do not accord with
those of governments; if they did, there would be no need
for government regulations.

In all cases, the ability of government and TNC to persuade the other to accept its own preferred positions depends on the relative bargaining strengths of each in the
particular situation, often modified by cultural prejudices
and the personal agendas of the negotiators. Bargaining
theory can thus be applied to government / TNC relations,
focusing on the key strengths of companies and governments that enable each to get more favorable results. We
then can analyze the likely outcomes of negotiations and
other actions of either firms or governments, assuming various preconditions in the bargaining.[5]

A bargaining relationship implies that two (or more) parties seek through cooperation to achieve goals that each
cannot gain by themselves. Governments seek economic
development and balance-of-payments stability, for example,
and both goals can be pursued by attracting and channeling
the activities of TNCs. TNCs seek inexpensive sources of
raw materials and manufacturing sites as well as markets

for selling their products; they can pursue these by dealing successfully with host governments, which (by their sovereignty) control access to each of these factors. The full range of bargaining advantages possessed by companies and governments cannot be specified, since it depends to some degree on the idiosyncratic characteristics of specific countries and firms as well as the particular situation. Chart 1.2 presents a simple framework for examining bargaining strengths that are present for government and company in most contexts.

Chart 1.2: Bargaining Resources of TNCs and Host Governments

Strengths of TNCs	Strengths of Host Governments
1. ASSISTANCE IN IMPROVING HOST COUNTRY INTERNAL BALANCE (e.g., income, employment)	1. CONTROL OVER ACCESS TO THE HOST COUNTRY MARKET
a. proprietary technology including product, process, and managerial	a. control over access to the market in general
b. access to funds for investment in the host country	b. ability to offer an important market to TNCs when the government itself is a customer
c. managerial / marketing skills	
d. access to information	
2. ASSISTANCE IN IMPROVING HOST COUNTRY EXTERNAL BALANCE	2. CONTROL OVER ACCESS TO FACTORS OF PRODUCTION
a. access to low-cost inputs from abroad	a. natural resources such as minerals and metals, farmlands, forests, fisheries
b. access to foreign markets for exports	b. low-cost production inputs such as labor

The bargaining relationship between governments and TNCs has two major components: the *benefits* each player seeks, compared to the *contributions* (resources, markets, technology, and so forth) that the other is prepared to offer. Governments look for TNCs with abilities to <u>improve national income</u> (and concomitant employment) via use of their proprietary (product or process) technology and other skills, and also to improve the balance of payments by substituting local production for imports and / or offering access to foreign markets. These fundamental contributions can be subdivided into more specific bargaining chips. These include, for the company, proprietary technology that the government would only be able to obtain at a much higher cost otherwise; superior information about foreign sources of supply and markets; and access to capital, skilled management, key products, and R&D capabilities.

Companies look for countries that offer attractive market opportunities for the firm's products or services, and also for ones that can provide production locations through which the firm can reduce its costs or gain access to scarce factors of production. The government's bargaining chip related to the market may be simply that it has the sovereign right to set the rules of operation in that market—or, in frequent cases, the government itself or a state-owned company is the customer of the TNCs, so the government holds monopsony power over potential suppliers. This situation occurs around the world in the petroleum sector, where many countries operate SOEs with a wide range of oil exploration, refining, distribution, and transportation facilities. Governments also possess bargaining strength from their sovereign control over factors of production within their borders. If many TNCs are interested in a country's raw materials or other factors, the government's hand is strengthened in dictating conditions of TNC entry and operation.

The bargaining power of each party tends to shift through the stages of the project. The relative bargaining power of the TNC is greatest prior to entry, but that of the host country rises after plants are built, enabling it to hold those assets "hostage" to some degree. On the other hand, if the TNC structures its production with similar or tied activities in different countries, no host government can force the TNC to follow its direction completely, since the TNC has alternatives and the host government may want to be part of an international network. And, a government's interest in pressuring a foreign manufacturing affiliate usually wanes as the company becomes more closely associated or integrated with local companies.

In summary, the two fundamental bargaining resources possessed by host governments arise from control over the two usual targets of TNCs: either (1) the host country *market* or (2) host-country *factors of production* such as raw materials or inexpensive labor. Without either a desirable market or a source of supply, the host government does not generally offer any important opportunity to TNCs. Similarly, TNCs usually possess at least two attributes sought by governments: (1) assistance in raising host-country *income* through manufacturing or other activities such as extractive ventures or service provision which use the firm's proprietary technology and / or managerial knowledge; and (2) improvement of the host country's *balance of payments* through providing access to foreign markets and sources of supply that the firm has through its own affiliates or through its own information channels. In other words, TNCs offer host governments an additional tool for pursuing internal and external growth and balance in their economies.

The outcomes of bargaining between firm and government cannot be understood solely in terms of the relative bargaining resources of each of the sides. Another key dimension is the importance of the bargaining situation to each one. The *stakes* for a country may be the possible employment that would be foregone without a particular foreign direct investment project or other TNC activity that is being negotiated. The stakes for a firm may be access to a market that is viewed as desirable but which may be lost to another competitor if the initial firm does not negotiate successfully with the host government. Figure 1.1a depicts the two dimensions that we have now defined in the bargaining relationship.

In this two-dimensional space relating relative resources and relative stakes of TNCs and host-country governments, several cases can be identified. First, if the TNC's resources are relatively strong, as in the case of a computer company such as IBM or a biotechnology firms such as Pfizer, and the market is not great relative to other opportunities around the world (as in Costa Rica or Egypt, for example), the TNC can be expected to drive a hard bargain. This situation is noted by the point M in the graph, which is located on the lowest iso-regulation curve. Another extreme

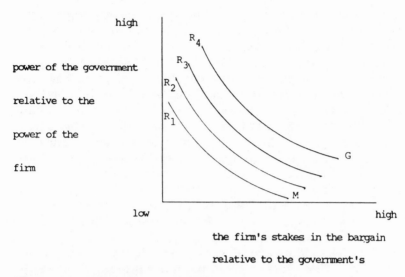

Figure 1.1a: Resources / Stakes

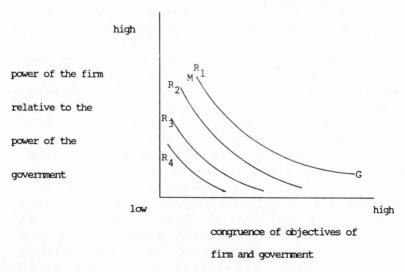

Figure 1.1b: Resources / Congruence

case exists when the host country possesses a very desirable production factor, such as oil in Indonesia or Mexico, and the TNCs are numerous and highly competitive among themselves. In this situation, denoted by point G in the graph, the host governments can be expected to have the upper hand in bargaining, and to obtain favorable results—such as a high degree of local ownership and control, high taxes on firms, and other restrictions on the foreign companies. Thus, point G is on the highest iso-regulation curve in the figure. The "iso-regulation" curves denote points where similar degrees of regulation can be expected in the resources / stakes space.

An example of the type M situation, where one of the TNC's bargaining resources dominates the relationship, is the case of mainframe computer production and software development. These products are made by a handful of TNCs (viz., IBM, Unisys, NEC, and a few others) primarily in their own countries, for sale there and export. No matter what interests the host country may have in attracting local production of these firms, the TNC's bargaining strength through proprietary technology and economies of scale permits it to retain centralized R&D and production. Because the technology continues to evolve, and the number of suppliers remains small, the TNCs dominate the bargaining relationships and are able to serve most foreign markets through exports.

In contrast, a type G situation existed in Colombia when huge coal resources were discovered in the 1970s and the government negotiated an agreement with Exxon to produce and market the coal jointly. Colombia had many foreign natural resource companies to choose from; but, given limited world coal reserves, Exxon had no comparable alternatives to play off against Colombia. The stakes were especially high for Exxon, which in the mid-1970s was looking actively for non-oil business in the energy field. This situation resulted in a 30-year turnkey venture in Colombia, in which Exxon receives half of the coal produced as its compensation for providing investment funds, managerial and scientific skills, and foreign marketing of the coal. Colombia maintains ultimate control over the project, employs thousands of people, generates major export earnings, and takes half of the coal produced for its domestic export use.[6]

A third dimension in the bargaining relationship is the degree of mutuality of interests between the foreign firm and the host government, i.e., their *goal congruence*. The greater the agreement of goals in the bargaining situation, the less the need for regulation or coercion to channel the TNC's activities into directions desired by the government. Figure 1.1b presents a view of the relationship between relative resources of the two sides and the congruence of their objectives. In this case, the iso-regulation curves increase toward the origin, as the firm's relative resources weaken and as the two sides' goals diverge.

Export-intensive manufacturing (i.e., offshore assembly typically in textiles and electronics) is an example of the type M situation. In this case, both TNC and host government have an interest in such employment in the host country and subsequent exports of the product. The firms have relatively greater power since they can choose among countries for the assembly location. To achieve its goals, the host government often offers incentives to TNCs that are willing to establish local manufacture for export to the United States and other foreign markets. Local ownership requirements are almost always foregone to attract such investment. Mexico has established a multibillion dollar industry of offshore assembly ("maquila") along the border from Texas to California, employing about 450,000 people. Foreign firms are permitted 100 percent ownership in such ventures, while Mexican law requires at least 51 percent Mexican ownership in most other cases.

In fact, it is necessary to combine both of these perspectives (Figures 1.1a & 1.1b) to draw useful conclusions about the likelihood of regulation in a given empirical context. Figure 1.2 depicts the full three-dimensional model, noting expected types of outcomes at each corner.

This figure captures the three main dimensions of the bargaining relationship between host governments and TNCs. The conditions that provide the greatest advantage to the firm are at point T, where the firm's relative resources are high and the government's, low; the firm has relatively little at stake, and the two sides have very similar interests in the situation. Offshore-assembly industries typify this set of conditions. At the other extreme, point G is the most likely to lead to conflict, since the government has rela-

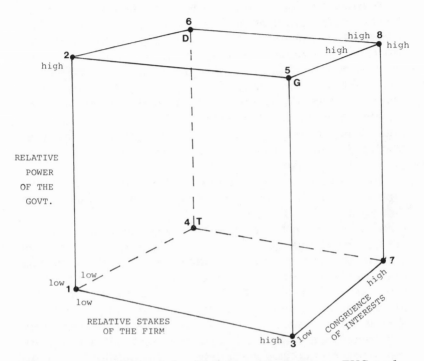

Figure 1.2: The Bargaining Relationship Between TNC and Host Government

tively great resources and the firm has a great deal at stake; in addition the two sides' interests are quite different. Extractive industries often fall into this category, when host governments seek more local processing and TNCs want to send raw materials directly to overseas (centralized) processing facilities. This model will be used throughout the book to depict the features of bargaining relationships in different situations.

ISSUES IN NEGOTIATION

The issues that form the relationships between TNCs and governments require continuous negotiation—from the entry stage to that of termination and withdrawal. The extent of negotiation depends on the degree of governmental intervention or the reliance of the TNC on assistance. Relevant negotiations may not always be between the TNCs and governments; they may also be between or among governments and at times only among TNCs through their various associations. But, in one form or another, the impetus toward negotiation is virtually continuous.

Throughout this assessment of the negotiation process, one or another of the following aspects are involved: the issues negotiated, the relative bargaining strength of the players, the negotiation mechanisms, the institutional settings of negotiations, the pressures or triggers that bring the parties to the negotiating table and urge a solution, the solutions themselves (oriented toward objectives of efficiency and equity), and the initiatives and leadership necessary to bring the solutions to fruition.

The issues involved are those raised by the concerns of governments and the strategic objectives of TNCs. These sometimes coincide but sometimes conflict, or they may differ in the intensity of interest on the part of one or the other player. The policies and strategies of each also change through time, not only because of the change of economic and political conditions in a country, but also because of greater familiarity with TNC operations and changes in the growth and objectives of TNCs themselves.

The processes and institutions through which negotiations take place are determined by the characteristics of the players themselves. For example, in the United States, negotiations tend to be at the state or local level, with the national government remaining aside. In China negotiations may take place at three levels of government—local, state, and central. The processes of negotiation are constrained by legislation and regulations in the host and home countries. In some instances, the home government enters the negotiations to attain more favorable treatment for the subsidiaries of its TNCs. Intergovernmental institutions are also important as forums for negotiations on policies and for supplemental financing. The United Nations Centre on Transnational Corporations (UNCTC), became a forum for discussion of some issues between governments and TNCs. The International Center for Settlement of Investment Disputes (ICSID) helps resolve problems between TNCs and governments, and the International Finance Corporation

(IFC) offers venture capital—both institutions are affiliated with the World Bank.

A number of factors can trigger a negotiation between TNCs and governments, and still others can press them forward to complete or terminate the negotiations. The road is not a smooth one. The trigger forces for negotiation may be as trivial as a visit of a CEO to a given country during a vacation, or the comment of a fellow member at the country club about prospects seen in a foreign country. The forces may be as serious as the necessity to reconstruct an area or industry after a natural disaster in a host country. They have been quite diverse in TNC experience.[7] During the 1950s and 1960s, the U.S. government sought to enhance developmental prospects in many of the former colonial countries by encouraging private FDI. It was not resoundingly successful. These initiatives were an extension of the U.S. Marshall Plan in the late 1940s and early 1950s, which helped reconstruct Europe and form the European Economic Community. In the 1960s, the Alliance for Progress (with Latin America) sought to give that area a similar boost, but with much less success. In the 1980s, the Caribbean Basin Initiative focused aid on a smaller group of countries, but with a similar lack of success. The U.S. government is still trying to find ways of encouraging private investment in support of its aid programs in LDCs.

Pressures to complete negotiations arise from impatience at the headquarters of TNCs, the desire to beat potential competitors, the desire to enter early into a foreign market with local production, and the desire to obtain a return from a particular asset (patent or technology) which may be declining in value elsewhere. Pressures from the host country can also stem from its desire to preclude the investor from going to a competing country.

Political stability may be dependent on economic growth, which can be fostered by foreign direct investment; national security may be dependent on foreign technology in the national defense sectors, and so on. A variety of pressures exist to bring otherwise reluctant negotiators to a successful agreement. Other pressures can cause a reopening of negotiations by either party, but this more frequently occurs at the instigation of a host government, who sees the prior agreement as inequitable, and its sovereignty permits it to force such a renegotiation.

The solutions to a negotiation are generally sought in terms of two criteria: efficiency and equity. There are other criteria, such as participation in the creative acts in enterprise (research and development), but these generally come to the fore later in the process. Efficiency and equity are the two most pressing criteria and must be satisfied on the part of both parties for the negotiation to be successful in the bargaining and implementation stages. If either party feels that equity is not achieved, they either seek to renegotiate or to implement the agreement in such a way as to achieve greater equity, whether or not the other one is informed. There are many arrangements that produce efficiency with equity; they are discussed in several chapters following.

Finally, in order to achieve a worldwide setting that makes the most efficient and equitable use of the capabilities of the TNCs, a fairly high degree of leadership is required on the part of both governments and TNCs. This leadership has been lacking (as discussed in Chapter 17). A greater willingness on the part of officials of both TNCs and governments to take a leadership position in the international economy is required; such willingness makes it easier to negotiate efficient and equitable arrangements between TNCs and governments. Some of the moves that can be made are delineated, in succeeding chapters, as well as some of the qualities which are required for effective leadership.

CRITERIA OF ACCEPTABILITY

The differences between TNCs and governments extend beyond the issues subject to negotiation into the criteria of acceptability of *any* given solution. From an examination of the results sought by governments in international negotiations and in their policies of economic development, six criteria of acceptability have been evidenced: *efficiency, equity, participation, creativity, stability,* and *autonomy*. Most recently, a concern for environmental protection has been raised by some host governments, adding a seventh criterion. Through meeting these criteria in various provisionsof the agreement, the parties become satisfied with the expected results—economically, politically, and ethically (reflecting value systems).

1. TNCs that base decisions on market signals stress the criterion of *efficiency,* claiming that this is the way in which they become competitive and in which they can make the most effective use of the world's resources for economic growth. Governments are also concerned with efficiency, and will provide a substantial leeway for the pursuit of market efficiency, but their concept is broader in that the entire system must be efficient; their criterion of efficiency (or effectiveness) is not competitiveness in a market. The objectives of governments are larger and wider than those pursued through a market; many resources are committed to purposes of national security, education, welfare, and environmental protection.

2. TNCs are concerned with the concept of *equity,* but this is usually interpreted as "fair and reasonable competition" and "fair return on investment," which seldom is seen as constraining the level of profits. In the view of governments, equity is a much wider concept, again, involving the distribution of benefits not only within a country (among the various claimants) but also among nations. Equity is pursued by governments through enhancement of trade positions and increases in employment, and in a better distribution of benefits from foreign direct investment and its contribution to economic growth.

It is a prime responsibility of governments to look after the interests of the citizens of the country, and this involves both an absolute and relative improvement in its wealth and power compared to other nations. In fact, the *relative* position is in many instances more important than the *absolute* level of wealth or power, in that national security is enhanced by a better relative position, whatever the absolute levels.

The efficiency criterion of the TNC is derived from signals in a "free and open" market; but, such markets do not really exist, since there are interferences from both oligopolistic characteristics of companies and government interventions. The criterion of efficiency is usually seen as one of physical production and distribution of products and services, with the markets determining the distribution of income and wealth resulting. But the criterion of equity raises the concern for the distribution of burdens and benefits both within the process of production and in the distribution of income and wealth. Therefore, governments are concerned with the distribution of gains among countries and between themselves and TNCs. The solution sought in any negotiation between TNCs and governments is *not* the "efficiency solution" of economists or even the "equity solution" of sociologists or political theorists. Rather it is an "effective-solution" that achieves acceptable tradeoffs or synergy between both efficiency and equity.

3. *Participation* is a desired result as seen by the TNCs, for this is expressed in the concept of "national treatment" under which the TNC is permitted to participate in economic opportunities in any other country—just as a local citizen would. But, in the minds of host governments, participation means two other things: participation in TNC activities through some local ownership of its affiliates, and participation in international rule making. Open participation to all foreigners could reduce the ability of the host country to participate effectively in the world economy. To be "taken over" by TNCs who direct the nature and extent of participation of the host country in the world economy would not be acceptable. It is assumed by governments that its officials should determine the way and extent of participation in domestic and international affairs. The post-World War II economies were organized internationally through the Bretton Woods Agreements in the late 1940s essentially under the guidance of the United States with the formal participation of a few major countries. The remaining countries were either left out because they were defeated or were seen as too insignificant to have a major input. Thus, both the traditional rules of international law and the post-war arrangements were established without participation of most of the countries of the present world economy.

Each government now insists on participation in the formation of future rules and arrangements. The fact that there are over 140 sovereign nations in the United Nations and some 160 in the world as a whole suggests the difficulty of obtaining worldwide agreement on a new set of international rules to guide economic policies or behavior.

Rather, the countries participating in any new agreements must be self-selective according to the scope and nature of the issues under consideration. The participants may range from two (under bilateral arrangements) to as large as 70 or 80 (under multilateral arrangements such as United Nations Conference on Trade and Development [UNCTAD] and the General Agreement on Tariffs and Trade [GATT]), but probably to no more than 15 or 20 in any regional association. Even the GATT has run into serious obstacles to further reductions in trade barriers, and the UNCTAD has been more successful in bargaining as a group with advanced countries than in establishing rules among its members.

4. The criterion of *creativity* (the creation and application of new knowledge) is clearly a part of TNC objectives, but it is sought within the TNC itself. The locus of such activities is determined by the parent company, selecting the site of R&D laboratories and the places where inventions will be innovated within the TNC and its affiliates.[8] A concern of governments with creativity is to have such activities within their own country, both offering opportunities and developing new capabilities so as to provide national wealth and power. Governments will not leave decisions as to the location, content, and application of R&D activities to TNCs. Here again conflicts arise among the means of implementing the common criterion.

5. *Stability* in the economy is sought by TNCs to enable them to make longer run investment decisions and to provide sufficient market stability to allow profitability. But, being involved in the economies of a number of countries simultaneously, the TNC is able to sustain instability in some arenas while enjoying stability in others.

National governments, on the other hand, are concerned with stability within their own economies and with the reduction of instabilities and uncertainties flowing from the world economy. This means that they also wish to protect against the vagaries of changes in TNC decisions on investment and trade. The TNC seeks a stable economic environment; the host government seeks some certainty and stability in the impacts of the TNCs on the national economy. The government is also concerned with the total stability of the economy, and will therefore make decisions to that end which will not necessarily favor the TNC.

6. The concept of *autonomy* arises within the TNC as it relates to the freedom of management decisions. The TNC wishes to be sufficiently independent of government interference to respond effectively to market competition. But the concept of autonomy sought by governments is one of independence from the pressures of other governments; and they are unwilling to permit an incursion on that autonomy through TNCs (as discussed more fully in Chapter 2). The governments wish to be in a position where they can exercise their independence by being sufficiently self-reliant in order to maintain their sovereignty and to enter international arrangements only at their own volition. There is, therefore, a continued reluctance to move strongly toward interdependence of nations despite the historical trend in this direction.

Conversely, the TNCs are advancing in the world economy through increasing interdependence of their affiliates and even with other TNCs through "strategic alliances" (as discussed in Chapter 3). A difference in the interpretation of the criterion of independence or autonomy arises in that TNCs are moving the world economy toward interdependence in seeking autonomy from governments, while governments are reluctant to see increased levels of economic interdependence and are seeking autonomy from the pressures of other countries and the burdens of adjustment to changes in the world economy.

All of the above criteria are involved in virtually any significant negotiation between TNCs and governments. But sometimes one or more are not expressed in the bargaining itself; they simply remain as parameters or constraints within which the negotiation takes place. Still they are intimately linked—sometimes conflicting and sometimes reinforcing.

NOTES TO CHAPTER 1

1. See Paul Kennedy, *The Rise and Fall of the Great Powers* (New York: Random House, 1987), Intro. and Chap. 4.

2. Yair Aharoni, *The Evaluation and Management of State Owned Enterprises* (Cambridge, MA: Ballinger, 1986); Y. Aharoni and R. Vernon (eds.)

State-Owned Enterprises in the Western Economies (London: Croom Helm, 1981); L. P. Jones, Public Enterprise in LDCs, (Cambridge, Eng.: Cambridge U. Press, 1982).

3. R. Vernon, "The International Aspects of State-Owned Enterprises," in W. A. Dymsza & R. G. Vambrey (eds.), International Business Knowledge (New York: Praeger, 1987), pp. 72–85.

4. The bargaining positions are examined by N. Fagre and L. T. Wells, Jr., "Bargaining Power of Multinationals and Host Governments." Journal of International Business Studies (Fall 1982), pp. 9–23.

5. See, for example, Gregory Smogard, "Intellectual Property Rights Protection: The Case of the Brazilian Informatics Sector," Discussion Papers, #88–3, University of Miami, International Banking and Business Institute, April 1988. Smogard uses the bargaining relationship to explore this issue.

6. See The Cerrejon Project (Bogota, Colombia: Exxon Corporation, Feb. 1982).

7. See Yair Aharoni, The Foreign Investment Decision Process (Boston: Harvard Business School, 1966); it is still the best account of the sequences in TNC decisions.

8. J. N. Behrman and H. W. Wallender, Transfers of Manufacturing Technology within Multinational Enterprises (Boston: Ballinger, 1976); and J. N. Behrman and W. A. Fischer, Science and Technology for Development: Corporate and Government Policies and Practices (Cambridge, MA: Oelgeschlager, Gunn & Hain, 1980).

PART I

Government Concerns and TNC Orientations

The concerns of national governments—both in terms of achieving a favorable contribution from TNCs and in guiding their behaviors so as not be be adversely affected—set the stage for their negotiating positions. The strategies of TNCs set their basic positions, but their goals also determine the nature of the companies' operations, their organizational structures, and their market orientations—all of which delineate their bargaining strengths vis-à-vis governments.

This section discusses these concerns and orientations in order to provide a preliminary understanding of the fundamental positions of the two major players in the world economy.

CHAPTER 2

Concerns of National Governments

Two fundamental issues underlie the concerns of national governments over the activities of TNCs: the location of economic activity among countries and the distribution of benefits from it. These are basic questions requiring answers in any economic system and are the first questions in economic theory: Who produces what? where, how and how much? Who receives the income? and Who consumes the output? These questions have not yet been successfully addressed among nations—and the answers continue to change even *within* those that have done so. Governments continue to argue not only over different solutions but also over the process of determining them. The answers are so difficult to agree on and even to conceptualize in different socio-political settings that neoclassical economic theory essentially avoided the distributional issues and focused almost all of its attention on the "laws of production." These involved the location of production, the most efficient combination of factors, and the physical distribution of goods to the markets. The much more difficult "laws" of distribution were left undiscovered. Although a theory of income distribution was formulated by David Ricardo in the 1820s, John Stuart Mill concluded in 1848 that though there are "laws of production" there are "no laws of distribution," since the distribution of benefits is a political (not an economic) problem. Despite many efforts, there is still no satisfactory theory of the distribution of gains or of how the distribution should occur.[1]

The problem of equitable distribution of benefits and costs is therefore at the center of international business / government relations, as it is in national economic policies. Few of the many actors in the economic systems around the world are satisfied with their absolute *or* relative share of the gains from economic development; all seek ways of en-

hancing their positions. This constant jockeying for a better share intensifies negotiations among TNCs, home, and
host governments. Not only do TNCs alter the location of
production and the patterns of the physical distribution of
goods, but also they substantially affect the level of the
gains and their distribution within and among countries.
And, since TNCs originate from abroad or operate in countries outside of their home base, they are seen in host
countries as external entities with considerable *power* to
contribute to and redistribute *wealth*.

Behind the questions of the location of production and
the distribution of benefits are the twin national goals of
wealth and power. Governments see these as closely linked;
power arises from wealth and wealth is acquired through
power.[2] The idea that wealth and power were gained through
the acquisition of gold was behind the mercantilist drive for
exports, colonies, and (pirate) plunder during the fifteenth
through seventeenth centuries. To gain gold, governments
dictated not only the kinds and quality of products but also
where they would be sold, at what price, and for what items
in exchange.

The mercantilist period was one of considerable government interference in and direction of economic life, including the storing of staple goods for purposes of war,
plus controls over prices, wages, interest rates, and gold
movements. International business was mostly trade but
was conducted primarily for the purpose of acquiring gold,
through an export surplus, which became known as a
"favorable trade balance." The consideration of an export
surplus as "favorable" is behind much of governmental
concern today over the trading patterns of TNCs.[3]

The period of colonialism followed, in which colonies
were sought as sources of gold and precious metals, jewels,
and staple commodities or as markets for exports so as to
achieve a "favorable balance" more easily. The colonies
were frequently controlled through royal trading companies,
set up not only to exploit the colony but also to govern it.
Because of this traditional use of foreign investment and
trade to buttress imperialism, TNCs in the 1960s and 1970s
were seen in some host countries as instruments of a new
imperialism.

Since the middle of the eighteenth century, the *concept* of worldwide free trade has been predominant in British and American economic theory, if not in practice. The argument over protectionism versus freer (never expected to be *wholly* free) trade and capital movements was won in the United States, *in principle*, by free traders; but, in most countries, *in practice*, by protectionists. That is, Western governments have continued to talk in favor of a freer world economy, reducing tariffs notably since World War II, while maintaining or increasing barriers to the movements of goods, people, capital, and technology. "Europe 1992" is an exception, as is the U.S. / Canada Free Trade Agreement, discussed in Chapter 12. Governments of developing countries and socialist nations have never accepted neoclassical economic theory, even if they allowed some "free-market" decisions in the economy.

The desire for power—particularly military—for the purpose of national security has caused governments to restrict the ownership and control of national-security industries, the foreign ownership of other key sectors of the economy, the import and export of technology, and reliance on foreign sources of supply of a variety of "key" items. The concept that wealth is greater in a country if employment is increased has led to an attempt to maintain employment in existing manufacturing sectors—rather than to permit shifts in employment to new endeavors—and to establish new projects to provide employment even if they are more efficiently (market-wise) situated abroad. Since TNCs can move their production, thereby altering the competitive positions of nations, all governments become concerned over TNC impacts on employment and wealth.

The concern for power would be mitigated if countries accepted a greater degree of economic interdependence, thereby reducing the frictions of attempting to remain independently powerful. Since the history of the world shows increasing integration, of communities into larger and larger units (despite stages of disintegration, as with the Roman, Hapsburg, Ottoman, and British Empires), it is conceivable that someday a worldwide structure will be erected on top of the nation-state system or based on regional associations. In this case, if conflict exists it would be within a "commonwealth" under a world federation and would be (potentially) controlled by an international police force. However, the world appears far from this position.

The development of the Bretton Woods Agreements in 1945 was an effort to move in the direction of creating a one-world economy, based on freer movement of trade and capital. It would be supported by a concept of "One World," politically ordered by "one-nation, one-vote" in the United Nations Organization. The underlying concept at Bretton Woods was that the location of production (who produced what, where, for whom) would be determined by market forces, with little or no interference on the part of governments. The objective was wealth without linking it to power. Wealth was to come through a much greater efficiency, based on market decisions, which would lead to more rapid economic development and a lessening of poverty around the world. Power was to be dispersed through the activities of the UN.

Many of the developing countries saw these agreements as a means of keeping them in subservient positions through perpetuating existing comparative advantages. Initially they did not participate fully in the World Bank, International Monetary Fund (IMF), and the GATT. The reluctance of many LDCs to join the GATT is evidence of their concern over the location of production and distribution of benefits. They saw benefits from access to loans from the World Bank and IMF, but they saw an opening of markets under the GATT as a means of perpetuating the dominance of the advanced countries through their stronger competitive trade positions. And, since many of the LDCs were seeking to develop their economies through policies of import substitution, they could hardly adopt freer trade policies.

The approaches of both the advanced and developing countries raised the question of the extent to which the world economy was to be characterized by national independence (autarchy), interdependence under TNCs, or self-reliance through governmental guidance. (Self-reliance is seen as the ability to determine the *nature* and *extent* of dependence and interdependence, as each nation sees fit.)

But, there are pressures to reduce the freedom to make such decisions. The continuing pressure throughout the world for closer international economic integration makes it costly for a country to disassociate itself from the rest of the group. There is clearly a greater efficiency in the use of world resources through closer international integration, but that closeness intensifies the issue of the distribution of the gains. If a nation is to give up some power and independence in exchange for wealth, it is clearly concerned with the amount of wealth it receives, and particularly in relation to what other countries obtain—that is, a concern for the equitable distribution of benefits. Unfortunately, almost every country sees equity as more than they presently have, especially relative to others.

The problem of equity is more readily handled inside a *national* community, because those who feel that they are inequitably treated on one issue have an opportunity to gain balancing benefits in another situation; this is the meaning of a "community of interest." Each member is committed to participation in the community and has a direct means of altering the processes of decision making. A similar situation seldom exists internationally; few countries are willing to compromise on *one* issue in the *hope* of getting more favorable treatment on some other issue at some later date. Thus, they see virtually every issue as independent; or, as has been often stated by U.S. government officials: "Each issue sits on its own bottom." This means that the opportunities for trade-offs among activities are few, and each is negotiated on a tight basis with an attempt to gain all benefits available. There are times in which several issues are being negotiated simultaneously, so a trade-off among them is possible—as between the United States and the Soviet Union on trade and Jewish emigration from Russia. But such linkages are rare; even in the instance noted, the link was imposed by the U.S. Congress but was rejected by the Soviets.

If the world is to move more towards international integration, some of the decision-making processes will have to be altered and criteria will have to be found for accepting different results.[4] There are continuing attempts to do so, as seen in the repeated calls at regional and world levels for a closer world community or, as one bumper sticker says "Reunite Godwanaland." (Godwanaland is the name given to the single earth-mass that apparently existed before its breakup into the present continental plates which are moving on the earth's molten core.) There are dreams of the unification of Latin America, closer association of all Asian states, of African federation, of union between the United States and Canada, of European unity, of a Pan-Arab community, of integration of socialist nations, and even world federation. These movements are eulogized, urged, or supported. Except for the continuing efforts in Europe and the U.S. / Canada agreement, no great progress has occurred in these directions.

The absence of cooperation has led to a reversion towards mercantilist orientations, with national governments being extremely concerned over trade balances and their *relative* positions in the world economy and the degree of national economic independence they can achieve. This is exemplified by their concern for independence economically, technologically and culturally.

The concerns of the host governments run both ways— that TNCs may not come into their countries or, if they do, will not bring enough benefits, and, alternatively, that they will come even if not needed or desired and will interfere or cause damage. The home governments, on the other hand, have attempted to use the TNCs to foster national objectives overseas—particularly through promoting private investment to accelerate development in selected countries—or have sought to constrain TNC activities so as to prevent support of countries that they see as potential enemies, or to prevent their movement of facilities overseas. Home governments are also involved in constraints on TNCs for social purposes—such as protection of the environment, safety, espionage, etc.

Host countries—both advanced and developing—seek contributions from TNCs to national employment levels, diversity of employment, technological advancement, increases in the level of wages, competitive strength, export volumes, a reduction of imports, new research activities, innovation, capital and management resources, and strengthening the national currency. Contrarily, host governments fear political interference, economic dominance, technological dependence, exploitation, and cultural shifts undermining social traditions and cohesion. Government policies move as emphasis shifts among these concerns.

During the 1960s, European countries were concerned about the technological dependence which might arise from reliance on U.S. FDI, and some were fearful of cultural penetration, but they also wanted the employment and the technology that TNCs held. Despite the agonies, they eventually opted for expanded flows of investment and became themselves a source of foreign direct investment, building their own TNCs.

In the 1970s, the developing countries were particularly concerned about the influences of TNCs, raising the issue to the highest levels of government and insisting on international rules through the United Nations. The problems of the 1980s—recessions, unemployment, inflation, disturbed economies, and large balance-of-payments deficits—have caused these governments to be more willing to receive foreign investors and to mitigate some of their concern about possible incursions. The contributions noted in Chapter 1 are sought. Nonetheless, the fears have not been removed completely, and there is a continued effort to balance the burdens and benefits. It is this continual balancing that colors the negotiations and renegotiations between TNCs and governments, forming the bargaining relationship between them.

HOST GOVERNMENT FEARS

Since host governments have taken responsibility for the level of economic activity, the level of employment, and the strength of national currencies, plus (in some countries) the structure of industrial and agricultural growth, they do not want any TNC activity to interfere with their economic objectives. Interference can occur, for example, when a foreign company seeks to locate in a region where there is already economic strain, wage inflation, and inadequate infrastructure. A TNC can see a market which it wishes to pursue from a specific location, but the government may consider that such expansion is undesirable for the sector involved or that the particular region is *relatively* crowded. Since a TNC often enters with substantial economic strength and financial ability, it can borrow readily from local sources of financing, either increasing inflationary pressures or pushing local borrowers aside. Also, the expansion of a particular sector in the economy, however much it may reduce the demand for imports of competing goods, can raise the demand for imports of capital equipment or of other goods, as incomes rise in the host country. The effect on the balance of payments can be destabilizing, weakening the international value of the currency. The demands of the new investor for infrastructure support can add to the expenditures of local, state, and federal governments, before there is adequate revenue forthcoming from the operations of the company. The crux of the problem is the differing assessments by the TNC and the host government of the most effective use of resources and the appropriate response to opportunities.[5]

Although the host country wishes to import technology, it is fearful of becoming technologically dependent on foreign sources of innovation and invention. It further fears the potential export of scientific talent back into the headquarters company, where most of the R&D of TNCs is performed. Even if some R&D is done in a host country, the results are sometimes innovated in another affiliate.

The very success of the new entrants can raise another problem in terms of industrial competition. The strength of the foreign-owned affiliate can reduce profits of existing companies, which provide support for political parties and for community development. Conversely, the success of the foreign entity can also put pressure on established marketing and managerial behavior and even on the capital markets, diverting funds from local companies to foreign-owned affiliates. The strength of such an affiliate can be attractive to local companies in the form of mergers and acquisitions, but this again may strengthen the foreign entity further. The reaction of the host government varies according to the sectors in which such mergers take place—for example, basic industry appears to be more critical than the light, consumer-oriented sectors. The fear of industrial dominance in key sectors is increased by the ability of the foreign company to shift operations among countries and therefore alter significantly the distribution of benefits.

The introduction of a different management style, different processes of manufacturing, different consumer products, different distribution systems, and different marketing techniques, all lead to a shift in demands and to product acceptance, which lead to cultural and social change in the host country—viz., "Coca Cola-ization." The introduction of the automobile (replacing the bicycle or moped), of fast foods, of blue jeans, of movies, and other changes shift the culture toward Western modes. In addition, the extended use of English begins to alter the use and the importance of the local language in at least some respects, making the local language appear inferior in some respects.

The spread of the TNC carries with it the spread of its ethical behavior, which embodies both management's values and the values of the home country. Home-country values may, in fact, be extended through law, extraterritorially, to the distaste of the host country. Social responsibilities are seen as different, including the willingness to make charitable contributions in a host country. Concepts of the role of women and of racial discrimination differ, leading to tensions, the most recent and excruciating being those in South Africa, as discussed in Chapter 14.

DO'S AND DON'TS FOR TNCS

From the foregoing discussion, one can draw up a number of prescribed and proscribed activities of TNCs in host countries. These set the stage for initial and continuing dialogues between the TNCs and governments, for they are not easily accomplished in precisely the way that the host government might wish. These activities can be summarized as contributions demanded by some host governments from TNCs that they:

- complement national investment and make a significant contribution to economic development, especially in raising living standards;

- do not displace national investors or enter into sectors adequately supplied by national companies;

- create positive balance-of-payments effects, adding to the capital inflows of the country, generating net increases in exports, and reducing expenditures for imports;

- increase employment at all levels and diversify employment opportunities, especially in the technical and administrative fields; train both technicians and managers;

- develop local resources and use local suppliers;

- help accelerate progress toward regional integration;

- stimulate activity in depressed regions;

- do not increase monopolistic tendencies in the market;

- do not cause a drain of local financial resources away from national companies;

- contribute significantly to local R&D efforts, both through a transfer of appropriate technology and in the building of a base of scientific and technical research;

- result in an improvement of quality of products and a lowering of prices;

- demonstrate "good corporate citizenship" and do not disturb the social and cultural values of the host country;

- result in a reduction of the ties of the local affiliate to decision centers abroad, so decisions arise from within the host country;

- expand credit to local customers and suppliers;

- assist local entrepreneurs in increasing their share of ownership and management of industry.

Each government has its own priorities and requests, as seen in subsequent chapters. These contributions have also been the basis for intergovernmental dialogues seeking to establish codes to guide the conduct of TNCs.

Added to these fears of host governments is a concern that they have to operate with inadequate information. They feel that TNCs and home governments have access to information that host governments and companies do not, leaving them in a poor negotiating position. Consequently, they have sought through direct negotiation and through intergovernmental agreements to foster the development and exchange of information (see Chapter 13), some of which the TNCs and the home governments consider is either proprietary or competitively sensitive. This matter pervades all TNC / government negotiations and is discussed throughout the remaining chapters.

NOTES TO CHAPTER 2

1. See Martin Bronfenbrenner, *Income Distribution Theory* (Chicago: Aldine-Atherton, 1971).

2. The relations between government goals and ideologies which support them are discussed by Robert Gilpin, *The Political Economy of International Relations* (Princeton: Princeton University Press, 1987).

3. Eli Hecksher, *Mercantilism* (London: George Allen & Unwin, Ltd, 1935).

4. For an assessment of the probabilities, see J. N. Behrman, "The Future of International Business and the Distribution of Benefits," *Columbia Journal of World Business*, vol. XX, no. 4 (1986), pp. 15–22.

5. José de la Torre, "Foreign Investment and Economic Development: Conflict and Negotiation," in Dymsza & Vambrey, *International Business Knowledge*, pp. 134–157.

CHAPTER 3

Orientations and Characteristics of TNCs

TNCs have been seen as both contributing to the wealth and challenging the power of host countries. But not all TNCs have the same impacts. They have different orientations and make different contributions and have different reasons and abilities to challenge national power. These diverse characteristics determine the form and substance of negotiations with governments. Each type of TNC seeks different situations or opportunities in the host countries. Each will be able to make singularly different contributions to economic development, balance of payments, technological advance, scientific inquiry, financial resources, and customer satisfaction. These differences set the scope and nature of negotiations between business and government. Not to understand these differences starts negotiations on a detour from which they may never successfully return.[1] If governments were unconcerned about FDI inflows, these differences would be unimportant. But there are no governments that are unconcerned about *all* activities of TNCs. Since the objectives, laws, and ethical systems differ among countries, an assessment of impacts of the TNC types is appropriate in preparation for negotiations.

TYPES OF TNCS

Foreign investment outflows are categorized in official statistics according to whether they are in agriculture, extractive (mining and petroleum), manufacturing, or services. This classification is useful for some purposes but it is not helpful in understanding and managing government / business relations. Distinctions are needed that show the different potential contributions of TNCs to governmental objectives. For this purpose, TNCs can be characterized according to their objectives, regardless of the sector to which they belong. The objectives stem from market conditions, from company strategy, from historical accident, and from reactions to government policies. The different objectives give rise to different organizational structures, ownership, and control, which set some parameters for negotiations with governments. There are four major types of TNCs: (1) those seeking a particular resource overseas, (2) those seeking to enter a foreign market and serve it from that location, (3) those seeking to establish production abroad that will be integrated internationally to serve a world market, and (4) those seeking to establish networks with other TNCs to enhance their competitiveness or minimize government intervention. The first three have been called resource seekers, market seekers, efficiency seekers, and the last can aptly be called network seekers. Each of them can be divided into subcategories, according to their market orientations and objectives.

Resource Seekers

Some TNCs invest abroad for the purpose of obtaining production inputs that are not available in the home country. Others seek to establish a specific functional activity in a low-cost production area, increasing productivity and lowering cost for the entire product. The two major attractions to such investment are *natural resources,* which cannot be found or are more costly to develop at home, and *low-cost* but sufficiently productive labor to permit moving a particular task overseas. Investment for these purposes leads to what is known as "foreign sourcing," although such purchasing may also be done through simple imports of materials or components produced by companies that are indigenous to that foreign country. That is, foreign sourcing need not be from an affiliate of the TNC, but this type of FDI does create foreign sourcing. (When an activity is relocated abroad, with the operation in the home country being closed, the transfer is often called a "runaway plant." Such a movement of investment shifts employment and gives rise to complaints over foreign [low wage] labor by workers in the home country.)

Natural-Resource Seekers. Companies seeking natural resources are generally in the agricultural and extractive

sectors, looking for fertile land, mining, or petroleum resources. These resources do not exist at home, *or* are much
too costly to develop compared to foreign investment, *or* the
firms may seek additional sources of supply. The location
of the least-cost resources dictates the place to invest
(aside from risk), as far as the TNC is concerned. The host
government may prevent such investment to keep control
over its "heritage," but TNCs can contribute to their development. Such investments have arisen often over the past
two hundred years, and quite a few large international enterprises were formed—such as, Cerro de Pasco, Rio Tinto
Zinc, AMAX, United Brands, Lipton, and Aramco.[2]

The market which is to be served by the foreign sources
is usually abroad—in the home country or in third countries. The host country is not the primary market in this
particular kind of investment. A TNC invests in tropical areas for the purpose of producing foods not found in the
home country; or, it invests in mining to bring minerals
back to the home country for further processing; or it
seeks petroleum resources, to be exported to the home (or
a third) country for refining. The final consumer market in
the host country is of little significance in affecting the location, scope, or size of the investment in such resources.

The activity is so loosely coupled to the host-country
market and so intimately tied to the parent company's operations at home or in third countries that the criteria for
decision making are the same as those for the parent company, though treatment of workers and government relations will be different. Consequently, the management style
of the foreign affiliate is likely to be a mirror image of that of
the parent company, that is, "ethnocentric." (Such "ethno-
centricity" arises even within a nation since corporate cultures differ and do not always mix well, as in mergers or
joint ventures.)

At the extreme, this type of activity has been called "en-
clave investment," meaning that the operation is really an
extraterritorial production site intimately tied to the home
country, offering few "dispersion benefits" (spillover) to the
host country. In some cases, the tie was so close to the parent that the laws and customs of the host country were dis-
regarded, with the management of the affiliate virtually

becoming the local government—as with United Fruit in Honduras after World War I, oil companies in rural Venezuela, and Firestone in Liberia.[3] Production sites were frequently far away from the center of government in the host country, and it could not or did not care to exercise its authority in outlying locations. Today central governments are more in control, but the historical dissatisfaction with enclaves is still a factor in present negotiations. It is for this reason that host governments insist on activities that integrate the investment site with the larger community, requiring the TNC to build roads, hospitals, schools, and other links with the surrounding communities.

Human-Resource Seekers. Companies seeking low-cost, skilled labor are looking for an opportunity to reduce the cost of a particular stage of production, such as component manufacturing or assembly; or, they may be looking for a supply of scientists who can assist in R&D activities, thus expanding the scope of R&D for the company as a whole and at lower cost than would be done through expansion at home. The investment in R&D activities overseas is similar to the natural-resource seeker in that, once made, the investment is firmly in place and is very difficult to move. Large sunk costs make it unlikely that the company will decide to shift location readily. In many of those situations, there are few alternatives to the existing location, since either the resources are scarce or they have been acquired by others. But in the search for low-cost labor, it is relatively easy to move the location of production because there are many countries with low wages and fairly well-trained labor and the facilities are relatively easy to set up (or expand in alternative locations where some facilities exist), and most such capital costs are quickly amortized.

As with the natural-resource seeker, the human-resource seeker will use these production locations to serve the market in the home country, or less frequently, that in the countries of other affiliates. Thus, a foreign source that is supplying components will ship these directly to the parent company or to other affiliates for further processing, as with Fairchild, Texas Instruments, and Motorola assembling semiconductors in South Korea and Malaysia. The host-country market is usually not served at all or only insignificantly. For example, cut-and-sew operations in textile affiliates overseas sell little of the product in the host country but ship nearly the entire output to the parent or one of its affiliates, as do the suppliers of Blue Bell, Levis and other blue-jeans makers. Even the technological advances of an R&D institute overseas are frequently innovated in the home country, though they may be used later in the foreign affiliate.

Again, as with the natural-resource seeker, the decision criteria and the management style are very much dictated by the close ties to the parent company and again are designated as "ethnocentric," meaning that they are derived from the customs and traditions of the parent company. The parent company's management style is more readily extended to the affiliate when it is 100 percent owned. However, some "border plants" ("maquiladoras" in Mexico) are owned and run by locals under host-country styles, rather than being mere extensions of the parent company. When 100 percent owned, the affiliate tends to operate essentially as though it were located in the United States. A high-tech affiliate will also operate under U.S. management guidelines.

Structure and Organization. The organizational structure of the natural-resource seekers is dictated by the fact that the affiliate's product is tied into the rest of the TNC at an early stage of processing or assembly; the labor-resource seekers may be tied in to any stage, including final marketing network of the parent. In the case of components, they are imported for further processing or for packaging and distribution by the parent or another affiliate; these ties dictate that this foreign affiliate be controlled by the divisions which it serves. For example, the cut-and-sew operations in Mexico of a U.S. textile company would be controlled by the product division served by that operation, with the bulk products being shipped back for final inspection, packaging, and distribution to various retailers. Similarly, the parent-company unit that is responsible for production of components overseas, processes those components further, and has the capacity to inspect for quality. It also determines production schedules and often supplies materials for processing from itself or another affiliate.

If one were looking at an organization chart of a company with affiliates abroad that are of the resource-seeker type, it is unlikely that these affiliates would be found on any of the summary (overall) diagrams; rather, they would be found far down in the company, representing their status as mere suppliers. Consequently, the CEO typically does not pay much attention to a foreign affiliate that is a resource seeker, unless it is being pressed hard by a government to alter its behavior or is threatened by expropriation. Those in the parent most closely tied with its operations are responsible for seeing that its activities are carried out efficiently. Of course, when the affiliate is large (such as Exxon's $4 billion coal mine joint venture in Colombia) or critical (such as the only supply of bauxite to an aluminum producer), much more attention is paid to it by the home office.

A further consequence of these relationships is that such a TNC does not care what country it is investing in so long as it can obtain the results that it wishes. It does not seek an investment, therefore, because of close ties with a host country, nor does it necessarily develop close ties if it is a human-resource seeker. A TNC seeking natural resources is quite likely to develop long-term and close ties because the investment is so firmly implanted and can be so significantly affected by government policies.

A final consequence of this type of investment is that the affiliate is tightly integrated with the parent company in operations in the home country, but the integration is at a low level. It is so tightly integrated that the operations of the parent company or other affiliates are highly dependent on the supply from the resource affiliate—as with semiconductors supplied by an affiliate abroad. The labor-resource affiliate that operates with relatively high technologies supplied by the parent will be kept under tight surveillance, guidelines, and schedules. This is done to prevent leaks and to contain costs; otherwise, the parent company and its affiliates cannot remain competitive.

Market Seekers

A second type of TNC activity arises in the establishment of a production facility in a foreign country for the purpose of serving the market in that country. This opportunity is attractive when it is too costly to export to that country or there are governmental restrictions (trade barriers or prohibitions) which force local production. The market may already exist or it may have to be developed through market research and sales promotion. In any event, the precise country location is determined by the TNC's assessment of the profitability of the market, its growth, and the competitive situation. An assessment will then be made of the ability to obtain necessary materials, labor, and other factors of production. This has been the typical investment in manufacturing overseas for over a century. Affiliates of DuPont, Kodak, Ford, Caterpillar, Siemens, Ciba-Geigy, Fiat, Nissan, Honda, Mitsubishi, ICI, Pfizer, Unilever, and so on are investments of this type. They are all intimately related to the host country and, therefore, the criteria of decision making tend to be dictated by conditions in the host country, modified by whatever is necessary to gain the continued financial, technical, and managerial support of the parent company.

The management style tends to be closer to the host country's, frequently because the managers are local nationals. Given that each such TNC usually establishes many foreign affiliates, management styles are called "polycentric"—meaning each affiliate is managed similarly to local companies. The use of local nationals is particularly common in long-established affiliates in more advanced countries. In the early stages, expatriates or officials of the parent company are sent to the foreign affiliate, and in LDCs the parent's management style is transmitted to the host country. In more advanced countries, some management techniques may be transmitted, but the overall *style* remains local.[4]

This type of investment is found not only in manufacturing but also in retailing, banking, and a variety of other service activities, such as insurance, tourism, law firms, accounting firms, architectural firms, construction firms, movie distribution, hotel chains, auto rentals and so on. Organizationally, these affiliates are hardly integrated at all with the parent company or other affiliates—though the reservation systems in international hotel chains auto rental agencies, and other tourist activities provide a formal linkage. But when the local market is to be served, there are frequently sufficient distinctions in the type of product that make it less suitable for export or distribution to other affiliates. If production in a host country was forced by government action, costs are generally so high that it would not be competitive enough to export. Consequently, the organizational structure is decentralized, with the affiliates generally being run out of an international company or division located in the company headquarters—or, in some cases, through a regional office located in another city in the home country (as with Exxon's Central American / Caribbean Division and Texaco's Latin American and West African activities, located in Coral Gables, Florida, or for the Asian activities of several TNCs located in Honolulu).

Efficiency Seekers

Since the 1950s, trade barriers have been reduced and the flow of funds and movement of people made easier, so a third type of TNC has arisen, based on multinationality. Internationally oriented companies began to seek the best structure of production around the world so as to serve worldwide markets. This opportunity arose when a number of countries reached the level of industrial advance under which they demanded the same types of technically advanced products—consumer and industrial—so that major national markets were not significantly differentiated. It became possible to manufacture components in several locations, assemble in others, warehouse and distribute in still others so as to achieve least-cost production and distribution for all markets. Interaffiliate integration is far more extensive than the simple offshore assembly of the labor-resource seekers. (If the TNC is *also* concerned to reduce risks from foreign exposures, it will duplicate investment projects in other countries, thus minimizing the ability of any one government to interfere with worldwide operations.)

As markets opened to products from a number of countries, international competition to serve them was increased, and it became even more necessary to keep costs down. The markets themselves already existed; it was simply a question of which TNCs would be able to serve them better. The competition for market share spread internationally, though this has been primarily in the advanced (northern) countries of Europe, North America, and Asia. The Southern Hemisphere is represented only by Australia and South Africa in being linked through this type of TNC, though more recently, Mexico, Brazil, and South Korea have joined the ranks of "newly industrializing countries" (NICs) that *could* be linked in this way, and the other three of Asia's "Four Tigers" are emerging into such an opportunity.

Not all companies operating overseas can adopt this form, because it depends on the customer's acceptance of standardized products—those which have similar (or readily distinguishable) characteristics in major markets.[5] This acceptance generally depends on the technology desired or on particularly competitive designs. In addition, there must be relatively low transport costs and economies of scale in production and marketing to permit worldwide distribution.

We find this type of operation in companies such as ASEA of Sweden, Brown-Boveri of Switzerland (these two are now merged), IBM throughout the Northern Hemisphere, Ford of Europe, UNISYS, Hewlett-Packard, Xerox, Philips, and so on. The Japanese companies moved into this form of operation only in the late 1980s, tending primarily to be market seekers (in the United States and Europe) or resource and market seekers (in Asia).

The efficiency seeker has a different structure of organization. The elements of operation that can be integrated tend to be tied together in the most efficient manner. Control is centralized, and the decision criteria are set and applied by headquarters. The management style tends to be "geocentric"—meaning brought together at a center where all elements of the periphery are considered and weighed to form a corporate strategy. (This pattern is quite distinct from the polycentric management of the market seeker, which implies that each of the affiliates has its own distinct style, influenced by its host country, or the ethnocentric management of the resource seeker, which implies a home-country style.) Even *local* managers of foreign affiliates will be brought together periodically to help them learn and assimilate common management approaches. The efficiency seeker may accept ideas and management patterns from the host country, but such transfers are often thwarted because headquarters seeks standardization for ease of centralizing decisions and integrating activities of affiliates.

The first functional activity that is centralized is that of finance, where even the cash flow may be managed from the center, as well as various types of investment. This is done in order to *force* the affiliate to *ask* the center before reaching major changes; all else follows. Marketing research and sales promotion follow for *some* companies; then harmonized pricing, so as to regulate competition among the affiliates. Production of components and schedules of supply and quality control generally come next, including the determination of the location of production of specific products in the line and the location of assembly activities. Centralized purchasing follows next. Conversely, *R&D* is initially tightly held at the center and only slowly dispersed through the affiliates in satellite labs.

The only two activities that are likely to be significantly determined by the affiliate in the host country are its external relations (communications with the host government) and personnel policies, plus sometimes an independent marketing activity. Both tend to have significant local differences. Not all efficiency seekers have the same degree of integration nor the same degree of centralization among or within these different functions. The trade-offs depend on the competitive structure, the economies of scale achieved by integration, and the management style at headquarters.

Not all TNCs can adopt the efficiency-seeker form, either because they are in product lines that are not standardized or that cannot be transported easily, or their products do not require meshing with operations of other affiliates in order to achieve economies of scale. It is unlikely that one would find companies using this form that were in the production of cement, steel, shipbuilding, or furniture because of high transport costs. Some sectors are quite appropriate for efficiency seeking, though a TNC may not use the form simply because of corporate strategy (rather than government pressure). Thus, Volkswagen integrated some of its worldwide (including U.S.) operations, only to pull back later; many of the French and German companies have been slow to adopt the efficiency-seeker form, and British companies operating abroad are mainly market seekers, as are the large Japanese conglomerates.

The suitability of the efficiency seeker to the U.S. TNC derives from the fact that U.S. companies have historically been multidivisional and multilocational, spread through a conglomerate of products and regional locations. Although European companies have historically been in a number of product lines, they have tended to have all production facilities within a single location, or at least only minimally dispersed geographically. The historical concentration of production by major companies in a single location—as practiced by Bayer, BASF, Siemens, Philips, Pechiney, Rhône-Poulenc, Hoffman-La Roche, Fiat, ICI, Ericsson and other European TNCs—is in striking contrast to the earlier dispersion across the United States of plant locations by one company.[6]

The locational decisions of the efficiency seeker are related not only to least-cost production but also to the size of a local market, since this indirectly affects the cost of production through assuring economies of scale in both production and marketing. If the local market in a host country is of significant size, it is likely that the affiliate in that country will produce the particular product most suitable to that market, exporting to other countries that have relatively less demand for that product. Or, alternatively, the particular product may require large inputs of labor compared to capital or technology, which makes it suitable for a host country where labor is relatively low-cost but productive.

Network Seekers

With the increasing interest of governments in guiding the developments of industrial and service sectors of their economies and the growing concern over control of the financial markets and banking institutions, pressures have increased to form cooperative groups among foreign affiliates of TNCs and between them and local enterprises.[7] The push to more cooperative forms—joint ventures, consortia, joint projects, and other more or less permanent associations—has been stimulated also by the spread of technological and financial resources around the world leading to formation of a network of TNCs linked both functionally and geographically. These alliances are generally impermanent (compared to a joint venture) and often relate to a single project or function (such as R&D).

Until the 1980s, the United States remained the major source for international technology transfers, for FDI capital, and even for management that would serve overseas. Other countries were involved after the 1960s, but only at a low level compared to the flow coming from the United States. But the decline of the dollar relative to other currencies (notably the Japanese yen and the Deutschmark), caused firms from other industrialized countries and NICs to accelerate their expansion overseas. With the progressive reduction of tariff barriers after World War II, the markets of the advanced countries have become more accessible; while trade rose dramatically, it was tied to international production, which is larger in volume than international trade.

To satisfy the desires of governments for involvement of national institutions and individuals in international production *within* the country and to tie into local capabilities and resources of management, technology, capital, and marketing / know-how, a network of affiliated companies and cooperative projects has arisen, particularly in the northern hemisphere—Europe, North America, and Japan. IBM alone is reported to have some 140 ties with other TNCs and locally owned companies. The U.S.S.R. and China are not yet significantly included in such networks, though they eventually probably will be as they open their economies.

An extreme example of network seekers is the formation of Airbus Industrie, a European consortium of aircraft manufacturers that joined in 1966 to begin design and production of a passenger aircraft capable of competing with Boeing, Lockheed, and McDonnell-Douglas in the international market. The four European firms—Aerospatialle (France), Messerschmitt (West Germany), British Aerospace, and Construcciones Aeronauticas (Spain)—individually did not have the capital base needed to design, test, produce, and sell large passenger aircraft in competition with the U.S. giants. By pooling their financial and technological resources, as well as by obtaining guaranteed orders from government-owned airlines in Europe, Airbus Industrie was able to begin selling wide-bodied jets in the early 1970s. Although the consortium has not yet reached profitability (losses are estimated at about U.S. $10 billion through 1987), by 1989 the firm had taken almost one-third of the wide-bodied segment of the market with its A300, A310 and A320 planes. Because the Airbus planes served a market segment that had not been met by the large U.S. manufacturers at the time (viz., wide-bodied planes for 250–300 passengers on short and medium hauls), the firm carved out a short-term competitive advantage. The advantage has been eroded with the development of the Boeing 767, but Airbus had captured several major sales commitments of more than U.S. $1 billion in the late 1980s, so it appears that the consortium may become a viable competitor against the U.S. producers. The governments of each of the European partners in Airbus Industrie have judged that the technological, political and other benefits of a locally owned and managed aircraft manufacturer outweigh the continuing financial burden that the firm has placed on them since the early 1970s. They have been satisfied to have a *piece* of the total since each realized its own economy was not large enough to sustain commercial aircraft production.[8]

Other examples of network seekers include the major automotive firms, which operate joint ventures, coproduction facilities, and various cooperative arrangements around the world. Perhaps the most visible U.S. alliance is the General Motors-Toyota joint venture called New United Motor Manufacturing, Inc. (NUMMI) in Fremont, California. In addition, Ford and Volkswagen operate the largest manufacturing venture in Latin America called Autolatina in Brazil and Argentina. Many other similar ventures exist—and beyond this, the firms often own significant portions of foreign competitors: GM owns 25 percent of Isuzu, Ford owns 25 percent of Toyo Kogyo, and Chrysler owns 15 percent of Mitsubishi.

Strategic alliances (networks) are not limited to industries that require huge economies of scale and production. Most major pharmaceutical companies have "tolling" agreements with competitors, using one firm's production facilities to formulate proprietary drugs for two or more companies. This type of arrangement is common in smaller markets, where potential sales do not justify complete production facilities for each firm, but a shared factory can be operated quite profitably.

At the R&D stage, quite a few joint research efforts have been established among competitor firms over the past years. The main European computer firms (Bull, ICL, Siemens, and Ericsson) have formed a joint research venture called ESPRIT to compete with IBM and other international computer manufacturers by developing both hardware and software jointly. Indeed almost 40 percent of 839 collaborative agreements among TNCs (as reported in a study by INSEAD covering the years 1975–86) were at the stage of R&D—much more than at any other stage of production.[9]

No one TNC is likely to be of only one type; different operations will fall into different categories. For example, Ford of Europe operates like an efficiency seeker, but Ford of Brazil more like a market seeker—similarly for DuPont in Europe and some of its products in Mexico. The distinction arises from the ability and profitability of linking operations, interferences by governments, and high-cost production in protected markets. Some TNCs include all three types, as Exxon—a natural-resource seeker in petroleum, a market seeker in oil refining and distribution, an efficiency seeker in petrochemical products, R&D, and distribution facilities. TNC organizational structures reflect the existence of these different orientations.

SIGNIFICANCE OF TNC CHARACTERISTICS

The significance of the different TNC characteristics for business / government relations is that each type offers some, but not all, of the contributions that governments seek from TNCs. Each also gives rise to different governmental concerns or fears. Characteristics of the four TNC types also differ in the extent to which particular remedies can be successfully applied through government intervention. As indicated earlier, these differences are significant in the scope and success of negotiations between business and governments over the investment process.

However, much of what the TNCs want in overseas investment is not different among the various types. On the contrary, there is a significant similarity among TNC requests
of host governments. For TNCs to find an overseas opportunity attractive, host governments and their national economies need to be seen as having the following attributes:

- economic and political stability
- certainty in the rules affecting foreign investors
- low barriers to trade and financial movements (though
  not for market seekers)
- a significant role for domestic private enterprise (versus SOEs)
- little intervention in business operations and
  decisions
- sufficient protection (for market seekers) against foreign competition
- industrial policies providing appropriate infrastructure
  and priorities for development
- acceptance of international law concerning business
  and investment

Only the host government can guarantee these conditions. But, if it did so, its role would be increased, raising a
fear that other avenues of interference might be opened.
Thus, a conflict of TNC desires arises—for free markets but
also for protection. A second conflict arises between the desires of the TNC for non-interference and the concerns of
government over improper conduct by TNCs.

Since the concerns of government embrace the fears of
economic dominance, of technological dependence, of cultural penetration, and of dominance in key sectors, the different TNC types lead to complex resolutions of diverse
interests of governments and companies, requiring careful
and skillful negotiation.

Economic Dominance

The fear of economic dominance by foreign investors
has led many host governments to insist on the creation of

joint ventures between TNCs and local investors. This policy, however, does not take into account the differences in the types of TNCs that we have discussed above. The differences in orientations, market objectives, technology, and degree of integration of operations alter the ability and willingness of TNCs to enter joint ventures. Further, the degree of mobility of the affiliate changes the power held by the TNC and negotiating strength with the host government, which it will use at times to offset pressure from the government to accept certain constraints.

The resource seeker that is looking for agricultural or mineral resources finds that, once the investment is made, the host government has considerable power vis-a-vis the TNC and can insist on the addition of local partners at critical decision junctures. For example, a prospective investor may be so attractive that the host government will permit 100 percent ownership, but once operations are established, a later request for permission to expand may reopen negotiations; the host government will then insist on the formation of a joint venture as a prerequisite, this time successfully, since the future of the affiliate is held hostage. Studies of the obsolescing bargain between TNCs in natural resource sectors and host governments demonstrate that the TNCs strength declines significantly over time.[10] However, not all industry sectors are similarly affected.

What the government is seeking in joint ventures is a reduction in the influence of the foreigner and a greater distribution of the benefits to its citizens. This desire for joint ventures is enhanced by the fact that local investors see foreign-owned enterprise as more safe and more profitable than one owned wholly by locals, so they often put pressure on the government to require that local equity owners be brought into the enterprise. Local businessmen also do not want the economy to be dominated by foreign interests.

The willingness of the TNC to accept joint ventures is greater when the investment is immobile—as with natural resources. There is very little choice but to accept. The human-resource seeker will also have little reason to refuse a joint venture partner, if the technology is relatively unsophisticated and sufficient control is left with the foreign investor to be able to guarantee quality, schedules of production, and reasonable prices.* All that a natural-resource or a human-resource seeker really desires is a continuous, high quality, low-cost supply of materials of components. But 100 percent ownership appears to give a stronger guarantee of performance. Yet, virtually any ownership relation will be acceptable, so long as the goal of stable supply is met.

However, a human-resource seeker that also is supplying high technology to the affiliate is likely to want to keep complete control over the technology and therefore will insist on 100 percent ownership. This insistence is supported by the relatively high mobility of the affiliate, for it can be moved readily from one country to another if need be since it generally has a low level of capital investment. Thus, a TNC seeking a supply of semiconductors from abroad, manufactured by an affiliate, will want to make certain not only of the supply but also of the continued secrecy of the technology. If the host government insists on joint ventures, which might permit the technology to leak out into the host country, the TNC simply locates the operation elsewhere. This can be done fairly readily, since the investment is usually not large, it is not tied to the local market, and it can readily redirect the flow of materials to another affiliate and cut off the shipment of components.

The host country is so interested in maintaining employment that it is not likely to press such an affiliate to the point of its leaving. Many a host government has failed to distinguish among the characteristics of the TNCs only to find that it has lost desirable investment through companies leaving or not entering. Once government constraints are announced on TNCs entering and operating in the country, it is difficult for the government to retract them without appearing to give greater control to the foreigner, opening itself to criticism from the political left, which has been pervasive in many developing countries. Therefore, government officials should assess carefully the type of

---

*According to our bargaining model, the human-resource seeker (for offshore assembly) will be weak because several or many other firms could provide the same benefits to the country; however, the government's position is also weak, because the TNC could choose other countries for the same activity. More needs to be known about the particular bargaining situation before conclusions could be drawn as to comparative strengths.

TNC with whom they are negotiating before they establish policy precedents.

Citizens' perceptions of foreign economic dominance in many countries is much greater than in fact exists. This is a result of a surfeit of advertising—large billboards, logos, neon signs flashing company names and products—so that perceived economic control is highly inflated. (When asked how much of Mexico was owned and run by foreigners, a taxi driver replied "80 percent"; government statistics at that time indicated that about 18 percent of Mexican industry was owned by foreigners with much smaller percentages of agriculture and services.) The desire of TNCs to be known for their contributions and products feeds this perception. There is, therefore, a conflict between the desire of the TNC to keep a low profile (to avoid criticism of economic dominance or becoming a scapegoat) and at the same time to have a high profile (in order to sell more profitably). The TNC would like to have market dominance but cares nothing for overall economic dominance. Consequently, it would like a situation in which it controlled a significant position of a sector in a host country but the aggregate of FDI did not disturb its reception. This is a difficult balance to achieve, especially since foreign dominance of any *key* sector becomes generalized in the minds of media professionals and the public.

The market-seeker TNC has much less power against the host government in terms of negotiating satisfactory conditions than the human-resource seeker using proprietary technology. This is so, again, because of relative immobility. If the investor leaves, he loses that market. This is a strong deterrent when it comes to rejecting government requests, especially in a renegotiation. At the same time, if the government forces the foreign investor out, the country loses employment, payrolls for suppliers, service to customers, and some additions to its technology and management skills. Although local companies might pick up the slack, they probably cannot do as well as the foreigner. That means that a company such as Sears is needed by the host country, since the country needs marketing skills; yet Sears is not in a position to leave readily, so the negotiation between the company and the government is more one of equals. Since the market seeker does not require 100 percent ownership and control to achieve market share, it can accept joint ventures of various percentages and can more readily accept ownership conditions requested by a host government. It may not like the precedent that would be set by accepting such joint ventures, but it is likely to consider them as a price not too high and comply.

The efficiency seeker, however, finds it exceedingly difficult to accept joint-venture partners because of the high degree of integration and centralization needed. Further, it has the power to reject such requests by governments since it also can move plant facilities without losing a significant portion of the market. The efficiency seeker cannot accept interference by joint-venture partners in the determination of what part of the product line to introduce in the host country, the pace of expansion, the payout of dividends, the intracompany flow of funds, the pattern of trade among the affiliates, or the transfer of technology. All of these must accord with the least-cost operation of the company worldwide in order to be internationally competitive. Particular interests of joint-venture partners in a single country are likely to upset the objective of cost-minimization. The host government simply has to decide the trade-off between having this particular type of TNC and the consequent influence from abroad resulting from the integration of company operations across national borders versus losing that TNC entirely.

The conditions leading to acceptance of joint ventures of various sorts noted above help in assessing the creation of cooperative linkages. Where a market can be differentiated —as with small cars—TNCs may link production and distribution of a model that does not compete directly with the major line of either partner yet fills a niche for both (e.g., Mitsubishi's production of the Colt for Chrysler). Or, joint efforts may be needed in basic research because of high costs or special knowledge of the partners. Any functional activity—e.g. joint development of a natural resource—that can be separated from similar activities by the individual TNCs is appropriately a subject for networking. And these ties have included several TNCs of different countries, making governments feel that each country shares more equitably in the benefits. In fact, governments have, on occasion, promoted these linkages by "suggesting" ties with specific companies.

Technological Dependence

Western nations have repeatedly asserted that man's destiny is to be creative, leading to higher forms of himself and to progress towards perfection. In the industrial realm, this creativity is seen in science and technology and their innovation into new products and processes. The advanced economic position of the Northern Hemisphere has been built on industrial technology, and the rest of the world has fed at this trough. To achieve greater progress, LDCs seek to achieve a degree of technological independence. They are, therefore, quite concerned about the flow of technology from advanced countries and the ties that are created by that flow, leading to continued dependence of local enterprises on foreign technology. Some flow is necessary, but many countries wish to reduce dependence as soon as possible (e.g., Brazil, China, and Korea). This desire has led to a series of governmental restrictions on technologies transferred, on provisions in licensing agreements, on patent protection obtainable, and pressure to set up R&D laboratories. At the same time, incentives are offered to accelerate the inflow of technology.

The natural-resource seeker brings technology into the host country as necessary to carry out the processes of production. While some of this technology is fairly sophisticated and proprietary, it is licensed to the host country or to a joint venture affiliate if that is necessary. But, as noted above, some of the labor-seeking TNCs will refuse to release ownership and control over proprietary technology for fear of losing their competitive advantages. Any insistence by the host country that this be done simply causes the withdrawal of the affiliate.

The market seeker also brings some technology, and the degree of sophistication will vary substantially among different manufacturing sectors. In the case of services, little proprietary technology is brought, but know-how exists in such lines as insurance, hotel management, banking, accounting, and so forth. Given the number of companies that can be attracted from a variety of foreign countries, it is not likely that the host country will feel technologically dependent on a single foreign country (though long-standing ties with France by some African countries have continued such dependence). But most will remain dependent on some foreign supplier until they are able to develop their own bases of science and technology—for some this is decades away. Once again, this is an arena for continuing negotiation between the TNC and governments, as well as the firm receiving the technology.

The efficiency seeker is generally a TNC that does have significant proprietary technology, and this is one of the reasons why it is circumspect in accepting joint ventures. When a TNC does accept joint ventures, even though it might appear to be an efficiency seeker, it is likely to be found that this particular activity is not one that is tightly integrated into the operations of the total company. TNCs are usually quite eager to advertise their advanced technology and their rapid innovation into new products. This is done for competitive purposes, and yet that very success is both attractive to host governments and a source of concern, since it demonstrates their relative dependence on the foreigner. An uneasy balance is all that is achievable for this type of company.

The network seeker is melding technologies or other abilities across national borders and is, thereby, enhancing capabilities in both countries. It is this result that leads governments not to interfere in such alliances, so far, and even to encourage them—as with the "Economic Interest Groups" in Europe.

Cultural Penetration

Although there is considerable concern voiced over the undesirable alteration of cultural traditions and customs in host countries, most countries desire the new products, fashions, and diverse modes of living offered in the advanced countries. Soft drinks, fast foods, rock music, blue jeans, stereos, VCRs, and motor bikes are readily sought by consumers in the newly industrializing countries. One discussion, in a UN advisory group where this issue was raised, elicited an outburst from a representative of a developing country: "I do not understand all of this discussion about cultural penetration. We know that industrialization will change our culture, and we are ready for it." However, a number of complaints of "cultural imperialism" arise in host countries, and many are seeking to prevent their language from being pushed aside by insisting that it be used in business dealings. Yet in the 1980s, young Chinese were eagerly learning English, which they saw as the language of business and as opening employment opportunities in foreign-owned affiliates in China.

Although activities of TNCs that change the local culture are not usually a subject of negotiation with the host government, they do color the negotiations and alter the final result. A lack of cultural understanding on the part of TNC officials will make the results of negotiations less successful for them—a most significant point, which is too broad to develop here. (Besides government relations with sovereign nations, cultural differences are the second distinction between international and domestic business. These differences require a volume of their own.)[11]

Industrial Dependence

Akin to both economic dominance and technological dependence is the question of industrial dependence, or the reliance on foreign companies for the development of a key industrial sector—such as autos, electronics, nuclear power, pharmaceuticals, surgical instruments, or photographic and optical equipment. These sectors are usually classified as high tech; therefore, this issue is related to that technological dependence, but it is also different because industrial dependence can arise from oligopoly in a sector. Even though the technology may be available from several countries, the product itself will frequently be developed only by a few *foreign* companies investing in the host country. This leaves the sector controlled by foreigners, with little opportunity for local enterprises to participate. The question involves both market and efficiency seekers.

Governments can insist on local suppliers being brought into the process, with the hope that they will acquire an understanding of the technology and participate in at least part of the benefits. Such insistence can be accepted by market seekers but not readily by efficiency seekers. The necessity to use local suppliers frequently raises costs to the foreign investor, limiting his ability to export into competitive markets abroad, and raises costs to customers in the host country, limiting market growth there as well. Once again, governments have to make the necessary trade-off, while the TNC finds itself negotiating for its own interests.

Negotiation and Renegotiation

The first concrete relationship between international business and the host government is the negotiation surrounding the entry of the foreign investor. The negotiation includes the determination of the location, the scope of operation, the product line, and a number of so-called "performance requirements" set forth by the government, including the use of local suppliers, joint-venture partners, export requirements, import constraints, percentage of local content in production, imports of capital, price controls, production controls, distribution requirements, technology inflows, licensing agreements, dividend policy, reinvestment of earnings, and R&D facilities. (These are described in Chapters 6–9.)

Each of these may turn up in subsequent negotiations on any changes in TNC operations or as the government's development plans change. In many situations renegotiation occurs with changes in the government, new economic conditions, or merely a desire to shift the benefits. It is this process of renegotiation that has led to the concept of the "obsolescing bargain," in which the TNC finds itself in a progressively weaker bargaining position as it integrates into the host economy and renegotiations take place. Its position is weakened because of the deep roots that the TNC spreads into the host economy; this absorption is desired by the host government and is used by it to exact a higher proportion of benefits from the TNCs. Therefore, the TNC is itself ambivalent about becoming a long-term "good corporate citizen" and looking after the national interest of the host country, since this process also weakens its ability to pick up its marbles and leave if a government presses particular issues. As it grows the foreign affiliate becomes a greater hostage to government pressures. On the other hand, the greater the mutuality of interests and the greater the integration into the host economy, the less there is to negotiate and the more readily is agreement reached when conflicts do arise. It is this status that the long-term investor seeks in becoming a "good corporate citizen."

The continuous interest of the government as well as local business groups and labor unions in the presence and activities of private enterprises means that there is a high involvement of TNC managers in host-government relations (whether locals or expatriates). Many a managing director of a foreign affiliate in a host country has found that rather than 15 percent or so of his time being spent in external relations, it is more on the order of 75 percent, particularly in LDCs, where the government plays a larger role in the economy. Yet, very few parent companies send managing directors out with a job description that stipulates that 60 to 75 percent of their time is to be spent in cultivating and negotiating with government officials. This gap leads to considerable misunderstanding between the manager of a foreign-owned affiliate and the headquarters company, which is more likely to insist on greater attention being given to production, sales, profits, and remittances. In addition, there is a concern at headquarters that a local manager would favor host-government requests more than would a person from the home office, but even the latter has been known to "go local."

Legal Jurisdiction

One of the main demands of host governments is that foreign companies abide by the laws of the host country. Yet, the TNC and its affiliates are subject to the laws of their home countries and of each host country where affiliates exist. Multiple legal jurisdictions apply. Frequently, in one transaction, three jurisdictions may be involved: the home country, the host country, and the host country of another affiliate when the transaction is between two affiliates of a single TNC. Thus, technology developed in the past and innovated in one affiliate in a host country may be transferred to another affiliate in a second host country, with funds flowing back in the opposite direction, creating a three-party involvement if questions are raised by the last government or by the second recipient concerning the provisions of the contract. If the courts are involved, an important decision is to establish the appropriate jurisdiction.

Of more concern to the host country, however, is the extension of the law of the home country into the host's jurisdictions, as is sometimes done by the U.S. government through its tax code, antitrust rules, or export controls. Jurisdictional conflicts usually require the TNC to step aside in favor of negotiations between officials of governments. Still, the TNC may urge either the position of the host or home government. It is this ability to call on support from one or both governments that has increased the desire of the host country to stipulate that the jurisdiction will always be within its courts, in an attempt to cut off intervention from the home country.

The U.S. government has sought to avoid the conflict of laws by obtaining an acceptance by host countries of the jurisdiction of international law. It has been a primary objective of the U.S. government to extend the application of international law (customary and agreed) so as to provide greater protection to U.S. companies operating abroad. However, because few of the developing countries were involved in the formation of this law, they do not feel bound by it. The U.S. government has attempted to gain its acceptance through treaties on investment or on friendship, commerce, and navigation (the so-called FCN or FCI treaties) with varied success. These attempts by the U.S. government and the issues underlying legal jurisdiction are of sufficient importance to require fuller treatment in Chapter 11.

Mutual Interests

The different types of TNCs have interests that are more or less close to those of host governments. Though governments do not make formal distinctions in their policies toward TNCs, they do recognize in negotiations that they receive differential contributions from these TNC types. However, the extent of mutuality of interests between TNCs and governments varies according to both the type of TNC and the particular issue. Chart 3.1 illustrates the convergence and divergence of interests, according to type of TNC (compare to Chart 1.2). A 10 indicates intense interest and a

Chart 3.1: Mutuality of Interests

Government Concerns:	Natural resource seekers	Labor resource seekers	Market seekers	Efficiency seekers	Network seekers
Higher Employment	2 / 10	10 / 10	10 / 10	10 / 10	2 / 10
Higher Wages & Skills	6 / 10	5 / 10	10 / 10	10 / 10	10 / 10
Exports up; Imports down	10 / 10	10 / 10	1 / 10	5 / 10	10 / 10
Technology Inflows	6 / 10	5 / 5	5 / 5	5 / 10	10 / 10
Less Local Borrowing	1 / 10	5 / 10	3 / 10	6 / 10	5 / 5
Capital Inflows	2 / 10	5 / 10	3 / 10	5 / 10	3 / 5
Local Mgt. & Supplier	5 / 10	5 / 10	5 / 10	5 / 10	5 / 10
Ownership & Control	4 / 10	3 / 7	5 / 10	1 / 5	10 / 10

Note: Numbers indicate the relative intensity of interests on the part of each player (TNCs in upper-right-hand corner and governments in lower-left-hand corner), from a low of 1 to a high of 10. Obviously, quantities are suggestive rather than being precise for all parties to any negotiation.

The interests of each type of TNC are affected by the fact that they are responding to different market, government, and environmental conditions: Natural-resource seekers to the location of resources fixed by nature; Labor-resource seekers to the necessity to meet competition with low costs; Market seekers to government interventions, costs, and customer demands; Efficiency seekers to worldwide competition requiring cost reduction; Network seekers to governments and increasing international integration.

1 low interest in the given issue, with the upper right number being the TNC interest and the lower left under the diagonal that of the host government. The closeness of the numbers indicates mutual stakes in a given outcome and, therefore, greater ease in reaching bargaining agreements.

The resource seeker will completely satisfy a host government only in its orientation to exports, and a labor seeker only in respect to employment and exports. The market seeker is also intensely interested in employment and upgrading labor skills (and usually wages), as is the efficiency seeker. But, the network seeker offers the greatest coincidence of interests simply because that part of the network in the host country is usually local, will be upgrading skills, exporting new components or products, importing new technologies, and will enhance local management. Consequently, network seekers will have easier negotiations with governments, which will see their contributions as bringing both efficiency and equity.

NOTES TO CHAPTER 3

1. The discussions in this chapter are focused on the large, multiproduct, multilocation manufacturing and service corporations. For a comparison of experiences of smaller and medium-size companies operating abroad see the McKinsey & Co. report on the American Business Conference, "Winning in the World Market," Nov. 1987.

2. A careful assessment of government policies and TNC responses in the mineral / petroleum sector is provided by Raymond F. Mikesell and John W. Whitney, *The World Mining Industry: Investment Strategy and Public Policy* (Boston: Allen & Unwin, 1987).

3. See the studies sponsored by the National Planning Association in the 1950s and 1960s on United States business performance abroad, especially Theodore Geiger, *The General Electric Company in Brazil* (Washington, DC: NPA, 1961 [New York: Arno Press, 1976]); and Galo Plaza and Stacy May, *The United Fruit Company in Latin America* (Washington, DC: NPA, 1958).

4. Lars Otterbeck, *The Management of Headquarters–Subsidiary Relationships in Multinational Corporations* (Hampshire, Eng.: Gower, 1991).

5. Ted Levitt's article on "The Globalization of Markets," *Harvard Business Review* (May / June 1983), pp. 92–102, sparked a debate as to whether there were in fact any such worldwide markets.

6. See J. N. Behrman, *Some Patterns in the Rise of the Multinational Enterprise* (Chapel Hill: School of Business Univ. of North Carolina, Research Paper 18, Mar. 1969), chap. 2. See also, L. Franko, *The European Multinationals* (Stamford, CT: Greylock, 1981).

7. The development of more complex "International Corporate Linkages" is the focus of the entire Summer 1987 issue of *The Columbia Journal of World Business*. See also, Howard V. Perlmutter and David A. Heenan, "Cooperate to Complete Globally," *Harvard Business Review* (Mar.–Apr. 1986), pp. 136–152; Peter Fleming and Farok Contractor, *Cooperative Strategies in International Business* (Lexington, MA: Lexington Books, 1988); Kenichi Ohmae has detailed some of these cooperative arrangements in *Triad Power: The Coming Shape of Global Competition* (New York: The Free Press, 1985); "The Global Logic of Strategic Alliances," *Harvard Business Review*, (Mar.–Apr. 1989), pp. 143–154.

8. See Badiul Majumdar, "Upstart or Flying Start? The Rise of Airbus Industrie," *The World Economy* (Sept. 1987), p. 497–518.

9. C. Deigan Morris and Michael Hergent, "Trends in International Collaborative Agreements," *Columbia Journal of World Business*, (Summer 1987), p. 21.

10. S. Kobrin, "Foreign Enterprise and Forced Divestment in the LDCs," *International Organization*, vol. 34 (1980), pp. 65–88.

11. There are few single books that cover a range of business cultures and management styles around the world. One attempt is by Raghu Nath (ed.), *Comparative Management* (Cambridge, MA: Ballinger, 1988). Also, see Vern Terpsta (ed.), *The Cultural Environment of International Business* (Cincinnati: South-western, 1978).

PART II

TNCs and Home Governments

In the nineteenth century a major debate over the activities of foreign investors arose around the concept of imperialism—whether the home governments were using the companies to advance their colonial interests, or whether the governments were being used by the companies to advance their commercial interests. "Finance imperialism" was the term used to describe the process of exploitation of foreign countries through the power of both direct and portfolio investments—that is, investments by trading companies, agricultural companies, extractive companies, and manufacturers as well as banks and other financial institutions lending for the overseas development of railroads, new lands, commercial enterprises, canals, and so on. A symbiotic relationship existed between business interests and national interests in terms of expansion overseas—whether for developing or exploiting foreign resources and markets. There is, therefore, a long tradition of governmental support for and promotion of investment overseas by national companies and financial institutions. This promotion has continued to the present through a number of incentives to investment, sometimes tied to economic aid to foreign countries.

However, home governments have also adopted policies that are nonpromotional in purpose and have at times restricted foreign investment outflow. The relationships between a home government and TNCs are more complex than in nineteenth-century international finance. Of singular significance is the fact that no home government has adopted policies that treat the TNC as a single integrated entity comprising multiple economic activities. Rather, every government tends to treat the *separate* (functional) activities of the TNC according to its own interests, and therefore frequently establishes contradictory policies.

Governments have provided export incentives and also have adopted monetary policies (to "deflate" or strengthen the currency and raise the exchange rate) which make exports difficult. The export of capital and the establishment of direct investment enterprises is sometimes fostered, while technology transfers are constrained. Or, investment is fostered in LDCs to help raise their exports, while trade policies restrict imports into the home country of the same products. Exports, technology transfers, investments, imports, patents, competitive efforts, and employment activities are treated separately, rather than collectively; the unique capabilities of the TNCs cause impacts on the economy that call for an integration of foreign economic policies. This lack of perception of the TNC as an important international institution in itself has hindered both host and home governments in adopting more cooperative and effective international policies.

CHAPTER 4

Home-Government Policies

The home countries of over 90 percent of the TNCs are the United States, the United Kingdom, the Netherlands, West Germany, Japan, France, and Canada. Figure 4.1 shows the proportion of foreign direct investment (FDI) by TNCs arising from these countries.

Figure 4.1: Distribution of the World Stock of Foreign Direct Investment, by Major Home Country (percentage)

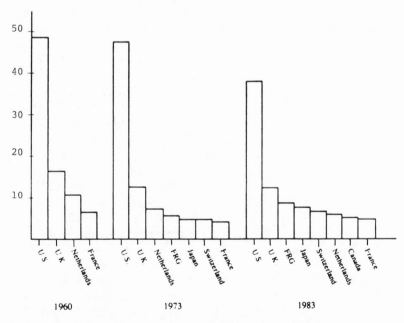

Source: United Nations Centre on Transnational Corporations, *Trends and Issues in Foreign Direct Investment and Related Flows*, New York: UNCTC, 1985.

The policies of these countries on outward direct investment have been similar, but the U.S. government was in the forefront of FDI promotion from 1950 to 1980. U.S.-based TNCs accounted for more than half of worldwide FDI, until inflows surged into the United States in the 1980s. Historically, other governments have been less directly involved in TNCs going abroad than has the U.S. government. Until the 1980s, the other advanced countries were more concerned about *incoming* direct investment. In the 1980s, the roles reversed; U.S. policy concerns shifted to incoming FDI, while the others shifted more to outgoing FDI, attracted by a cheaper dollar and a growing and stable U.S. economy.

PROMOTIONAL POLICIES

From the mid-1940s to the mid-1980s the U.S. government sought to encourage the outflow of direct investment from the private sector to foreign countries in the free world. A primary objective of U.S. post-World War II economic planning was to stimulate the contribution that private foreign direct investment could make to the reconstruction of the war-torn economies in Europe. Direct encouragements were included in the European Recovery Act of 1948, which legislated the Marshall Plan.

The desire to encourage private direct investment was enunciated also in the Articles of Agreement on the International Bank for Reconstruction and Development (World Bank) signed in the late 1940s, but the provision to guarantee FDI flows against certain risks has not been used because it was easier to borrow in the world's money markets than to bother with FDI.* As a result of the political and economic instability during the 1940s and 1950s, little private direct investment flowed abroad. Private direct investment to Europe began to accelerate as growth was stimulated through the U.S. Marshall Plan and the formation of the Organization for European Economic Cooperation (OEEC) to help distribute the funds and guide industrial cooperation. FDI was boosted again by the establishment of the European Economic Community in 1957,

---

*This gap was filled in 1988, with the creation of the Multilateral Investment Guaranty Agency in the World Bank.

which threatened to curtail U.S. exports to Europe. Only with the development of the Point IV Program for economic aid to developing countries in the 1950s did private direct investment also flow significantly to them. Thus, market conditions had to be sufficiently attractive before any other stimuli could be effective. Once that base existed, however, support was found effective—such as provided through the investment guarantees.

Besides mere persuasion of potential investors, the government provided some guarantees against currency devaluation and expropriation or confiscation by a foreign government. This initial program was restricted to Europe, but was later expanded through the Overseas Private Investment Corporation (OPIC) to cover all countries that accepted mutual responsibilities in such coverage. These responsibilities included assurance of appropriate return of any earnings, nondiscrimination against U.S. investors, and prompt and equitable compensation in cases of expropriation. Another caveat was that the host country accept the U.S. government as the creditor in lieu of the TNC when an affiliate was expropriated.

During the debates on these encouragements to private investment, Congressmen expressed concern that this investment would lead to production overseas that was competitive with U.S. exports or even be imported back into the United States. Some Congressmen and labor groups sought unsuccessfully to require provisions to prohibit this. Although organized labor in the United States has long been supportive of a more open world economy and of assistance to the developing countries to stimulate their economic growth, it has more recently been concerned about potential encouragement to "runaway plants" and the loss of American jobs. Labor has, therefore, been ambivalent in its support of economic assistance before Congress, private direct investment, technology transfers, and a reduction of import barriers. Its concern would have been greatly alleviated if the U.S. economy had maintained full employment throughout the period, as projected by the Full Employment Act of 1945. However, the periodic rise of unemployment meant that labor sought ways of maintaining jobs; discrimination against the foreign competitior was a ready technique. Therefore, support from the unions was conditioned upon government assistance to workers harmed by imports.

The U.S. government also encourages what are known as "branch plant" (offshore assembly) operations in developing countries. These are the "cut-and-sew" activities discussed earlier. They ship materials to a foreign affiliate for processing or assembly and return them back to the parent company. The tariff code was amended (in Sections 806.30 and 807) so that the duty is applied only on the value added overseas rather than the total value of the product as returned. This means that it is economical for a U.S. manufacturer to split production processes between those done in the United States and those that can be done more cheaply abroad (often mere assembly), thereby exporting jobs, at least in the eyes of unions. From the standpoint of those concerned to aid the developing countries, it was simply a matter of placing investment opportunities where the resources are most effectively used—that is, following the law of comparative advantage.

The U.S. government also, historically, gave considerable encouragement to companies that sought resources abroad, especially petroleum. In particular, antitrust exemption was given to the major oil companies (the "Seven Sisters") to form joint ventures abroad for the exploration and exploitation of petroleum in the Middle East. This was the origin of Aramco (Arabian-American Corp)—begun as a partnership of Socal, Exxon, Mobil, and Texaco.[1]

No special encouragement has been given to any other sectors in manufacturing, banking, or agriculture for investment abroad. Home-country governments have generally been indifferent as to which sectors are developed abroad. However, during the late 1960s into the 1970s, considerable encouragement was given to the developing countries to accept private direct investment, contrary to strong advice by some economists (in both advanced and developing countries) that it was more beneficial to borrow than to accept private direct investment.[2] The argument was that the (anticipated) fixed-interest rates on debt would make it easier for the developing countries to manage their balances of payments; they would know with certainty what their liabilities were from year-to-year. The unpredictable amounts that would be paid out as dividends from affiliates to TNCs were, seen as too great an uncertainty for the developing countries to accept. It was argued, further, that the levels of such payments would be greater than warranted and certainly greater than interest payments on debt. Finally, government planning of the use of the funds supposedly would be more effective in promoting desired economic development than would the decisions of the private sector, especially by foreign TNCs. These arguments seemed valid for a few years; but, during the oil crises, borrowings rose precipitously to pay for needed petroleum imports. The ease of borrowing (from recycled funds earned by the oil-exporting countries) permitted governments to undertake some uneconomic projects; the funds were not used to enhance the ability to repay debt. Interest rates rose and debtors sought to refinance the debt; payments due rose faster than foreign exchange earnings, leading to potential defaults. And governments found that they could restrict outflows of profits easier than they could reschedule debt or adjust interest rates.

The debate on debt versus investment should have flowed the other way—to the effect that the fixed payments required under debt would be more burdensome if the projects did not lead to higher foreign-exchange earnings; still worse, government debt put the creditworthiness of the entire nation at risk. Whereas, if the funds had been received as private direct investment, the remission of dividends would have arisen only when earnings were made, and they could have been restricted by the government when foreign exchange earnings were not adequate, without harming national creditworthiness. But, the 1960s was a period in which considerable antipathy arose among developing countries against (all) private enterprise. This attitude remained through the 1970s—until the recessions of the late 1970s and early 1980s forced a recognition that the private sector had to be relied upon for encouragement to economic development. Further, the absence of effective exchange controls allowed the foreign exchange to be used for capital flight (to Switzerland or Miami, etc.) reducing the *net* capital inflows to a fraction of the gross inflows. Private investment inflows would have been in the form of capital equipment and components necessary for generating productive activities and eventually raising the ability to repay the borrowings.

All through these decades, the U.S. government continued to encourage an outflow of private direct investment to the developing countries. It restricted the outflow to advanced countries only during 1965–1973 to improve the balance of payments. It also encouraged the international transfer of technology and continued to lower barriers to imports from nonsocialist countries.

The U.S. government, during the 1960s and 1970s, gave unofficial encouragement to joint ventures in developing countries. It was considered that joint ventures would stimulate private enterprise activities within the host countries, many of which seemed to be leaning toward socialist models of development. It was further considered that the opportunity to join local capital with that from the United States would tend to keep host-country capital resources in that economy, since there would be attractive investment outlets, instead of the funds being invested in Europe or the United States through capital flight. The magnitudes of such capital flight at times rose to levels higher than the inflow of funds from the advanced countries.[3]

Finally, the promotional activities of the U.S. government have not extended to an appreciation of the capabilities of the efficiency-seeker type of TNC in integrating the world economy, despite its existence since the 1960s. Free trade was seen as integrating the world economy through reliance on comparative advantages, generating the most efficient use of world resources and therefore raising prospects for growth. Given the internationalization of business through the TNC, it has the capacity to restructure comparative advantages through the movement of factors of production and relocation of plants, altering the channels of intracompany trade as well as intercompany and international trade. Not to use the efficiency seekers as a means of achieving the most effective use of the world's resources is not to pursue the objectives of free trade with the techniques at hand. This position is probably the result of the governments continuing to treat functional activities of companies—exporting, importing, patenting, licensing, investing, transferring technology—as separate activities, without seeing the significant linkages among them. Since this is not the case and companies are integrating activities for their own objectives, it would be desirable, *if* worldwide integration is an objective of governments (as often espoused), that they adopt policies toward TNCs that would promote this end, since in this respect they would have parallel interests.[4]

RESTRICTIVE POLICIES

Home governments seek to channel the activities of TNCs so that they gain an increase in national income, in employment, and in the trade surplus (or reduce a deficit). Incentives and restrictions are used to try to induce the firms to invest or keep business in the home country. Incentives are not directed at TNCs preferentially, but to all companies—both in the United States and abroad—to encourage new or expanded investment in the home country.

Restrictive policies to force more economic activities to be carried out in the home country include labor laws that create barriers to a TNC's ability to move production overseas, import limitations that discourage foreign sourcing, constraints on technology transfers, and tax laws that add differential taxes to foreign income.

Restrictive policies used to improve the balance of payments include import restraints of all kinds—not only tariffs and quotas but also nontariff barriers such as licensing requirements, restricted access to foreign exchange to pay for imports, orderly-marketing agreements, bureaucratic red tape, and many others that cause importing to be more costly and difficult. In the 1960s, the U.S. government concluded that the outflow of FDI would not be recouped in any form through the balance of payments for 15–20 years;[5] it then *imposed* a policy of a Voluntary Capital Restraint (1965) on potential foreign investors and then mandatory controls (1968). Others calculated that returns would occur within 3 to 5 years through several items in the balance of payments surpassing the value of the outflow.[6] These returns would arise not only from dividends but also from exports of capital equipment, of technology, of headquarters contributions (management fees, R&D fees, training fees, etc.), plus components and final products. Rather than displace exports only, the FDI would both displace and expand a variety of credit items in the balance of payments, to the short-term net benefit of the home country. Japan found this to be the case with its FDI in the United States in the late 1980s, and U.S. TNCs have maintained a net balance-of-payments surplus and a surplus in trade, mainly through intracompany activities.

Employment Maintenance Rules

Policies to maintain employment usually take the form of limitations on the firm's ability to lay off workers. The rules typically originated to protect labor against capricious layoffs by management, but they have become an important factor in limiting firms' abilities to move production overseas when costs or other conditions make such moves attractive. For example, to lay off workers in France, the firm must pay severance benefits of up to 6 months' salary.

Taxes

Tax policies in the industrial nations have primarily sought to achieve fairness in distribution of tax revenues; that is, applying taxes to jurisdictions where income is really earned. Most of these countries credit taxes paid on income that is earned abroad by TNCs and taxed in host countries before arriving at the parent company. In West Germany, income earned abroad is taxed when earned; whereas most of the other home countries defer taxation on foreign source income until the income is repatriated. These and other basic rules of the home countries of TNCs, are shown in Table 4.1.

It may be argued that any double taxation of foreign source income is a disincentive to FDI. However, if the double taxation only occurs when funds are actually remitted to the parent firm, then the tax laws can encourage FDI through the retention of (untaxed) profits abroad *if* local taxes are less than those in the home country. If the TNC intends to return the earnings to the home country and the foreign tax rate happens to be higher than the home-country rate, then a country with a foreign tax credit is neutral toward FDI versus domestic investment.

Table 4.1: Taxation of Foreign Source Income in Selected
Home Countries

Country	Credit or Deduction for Foreign Income Taxes Paid	Taxes Deferred until Profit Remitted	Domestic vs. Foreign Income	Other Issues
France	credit if global income is consolidated	yes	consolidated	
West Germany	credit	no	consolidated	LDC income is taxed less; foreign losses deductible against income
Japan	credit	(na)	(na)	
Netherlands	(na)	(na)	consolidated	
Sweden	credit	yes	consolidated	
United Kingdom	credit	yes	consolidated	
United States	credit	yes	no	all foreign income may be consolidated; domestic income taxed separately

Source: Business International Corporation. *Investing, Licensing, and
Trading Conditions.* New York: Business International Corp.,
1989 edition.

Tariffs and Quotas

Tariffs and other import restrictions are primarily imposed by *host* countries against foreign firms. But they are
also important constraints on home-country firms as well,
principally because these firms can and do at times shift
some of their activities offshore, then import components
and products back into the home country.

While the tariff rules of the United States and other industrial countries do *not* discriminate between foreign-owned or U.S.-owned imports, they directly affect the decision making of domestic TNCs that are seeking low-cost and low-risk strategies in FDI. Exceptions to the broad tariff policy of the United States show how important tariffs may be in the case of offshore assembly. The Tariff Code's Sections 806.30 and 807.00 permit reimport of goods that are exported partially assembled from the United States and imported back fully assembled, with duty paid only on the value *added* overseas. Under these provisions, literally billions of dollars of manufacturing takes place in the four leading Asian NICs (Hong Kong, South Korea, Singapore, and Taiwan), the Caribbean islands, and in Mexico across the U.S. border from Texas and California. These "maquiladoras" are considered runaway plants from U.S. labor's point of view.

Any limitations on import access to the U.S. market push domestic as well as foreign TNCs to reconsider their location decisions. The more restrictive the quota or Voluntary Export Restraint (VER), the greater the pressure to locate production within the United States. The VER on Japanese auto imports, while relieving pressure on the producers, also caused them problems, since General Motors owns 25 percent of Isuzu Motors, Chrysler owns 15 percent of Mitsubishi Motors, and Ford owns 25 percent of Toyo Kogyo Motors (Mazda). When these domestic manufacturers want to benefit from lower Japanese costs, they are constrained just like Toyota and Nissan by the VERs.

Capital Controls

One U.S. policy to ease balance-of-payments pressures was to limit capital outflows by TNCs. Historically, few limitations have been placed on foreign investment into and out of the United States. But, concerned over the continuing payments deficits in the early 1960s, the government imposed an Interest Equalization Tax (1963) and Voluntary Capital Restraint (VCR) under Foreign Direct Investment Regulations during 1968–1974. Both of these policies were attempts to dissuade U.S. investors from financing their overseas operations with U.S. funds. U.S. TNCs were thus encouraged to borrow overseas, to the annoyance of some host countries.

In the case of the Interest Equalization Tax, the policy was directed toward *any* U.S. investors, individuals or firms, buying foreign long-term securities. The tax was on the purchase of foreign securities by a U.S. resident from a foreign resident, and it was set sufficiently high as to make yields on similar domestic securities 1 to 1½ percent higher. This tax was eliminated in 1974 because it was seen as an ineffective nuisance and contrary to free-market principles; in addition, other countries objected strongly, threatening retaliation.

The Foreign Direct Investment Regulations were established by the U.S. Department of Commerce in 1964. The largest U.S. TNCs were requested to improve their individual company's balance of payments by cutting capital outflows, raising exports, decreasing imports, or increasing net inward capital flows (interest and repatriations). In 1968 the rules became mandatory, calling for each U.S. firm to limit its direct investment to an annual amount of US $2 million, with an additional US $4 million allowed in less developed countries. Alternative limitations were permitted, based on each firm's recent rate of outward FDI, but the constraints were most stringent on investment in industrial nations (the main targets of FDI) where alternative financing was available. Canada was excluded from these limits—resulting in much financing of European expansion indirectly by TNCs through their Canadian affiliates. Australia retaliated by prohibiting U.S. TNCs from borrowing locally in substitution for former dollar-flows. The restraints were continued for nearly a decade, before the government realized that the returns on FDI through many activities of TNCs passing through the balance of payments were, in fact, positive and should be encouraged. The United States, consequently, damaged its future balance-of-payments position by damping FDI in the 1960s. A Department of Commerce official, recognizing these relationships, tabled a Presidential request in 1963 to encourage European FDI into the United States as a short-term means of easing the U.S. deficit. The continued lack of understanding of the relation between capital outflows in FDI and returns led to further misguided policies in the 1980s under which dollar devaluation was encouraged to increase U.S. exports; the result *will* be *larger* outflows of dollars as a consequence of the new trade patterns of foreign affiliates in the United States.

In addition, the Federal Reserve Board "imposed" a Voluntary Foreign Credit Restraint in 1965 that limited U.S. financial institutions from extending additional credit to overseas borrowers. At its inception this program set ceilings on increases in foreign claims for each bank of 105 percent of the amount of foreign assets outstanding in 1964. Subsequently, this limit was adjusted, but it continued to restrict extension of U.S. bank credit to foreign borrowers during the short life of the program.

Other Constraints

The U.S. government has used other constraints affecting TNCs for special purposes. Technology and export controls have been used since 1949 to limit sales of strategically sensitive high-tech products to Communist countries. Antitrust rules have been implemented in the domestic market which affect the decisions of U.S.-based TNCs in international competition. In addition, industrial policies select certain key sectors for special treatment.

Restrictions on exports of strategically sensitive, high-tech products and technology have been imposed by the Department of Commerce, in concert with Defense and State (and in consultation as needed with the CIA, the Department of Energy, Department of Agriculture, U.S. Trade Representative [USTR] and others) to prevent potential adversaries from acquiring capabilities detrimental to the security of the United States. Sales are generally permitted to such countries only if the end-product cannot be reverse engineered, it has little military significance, and its secrets cannot be extracted to permit development of countermeasures against U.S. equipment.

Not only are parent companies in the United States under these controls but also their foreign affiliates if 51 percent or more U.S.-owned. These controls also apply to any licensee receiving U.S. technology, and any foreign importer of controlled products is enjoined from transferring either goods or technology to "prohibited destinations"—directly or embodied in other products. Where the host country does not accept such constraints on trade with the Soviet Union, the TNC is faced with conflicting pressures from governments. In the case of projected sales by Italy to the Soviet Union of large dimension (48") pipeline for oil distribution back to Europe in the mid-1960s and again in the early 1980s, substantial technology was to be transferred from other European countries to help build pipeline for gas distribution back to Europe. U.S. affiliates in Europe had also agreed to supply some components and technology but were prevented from doing so by the export controls. Attempts were made by the U.S. government to use its export and technology controls to prevent European licensees of U.S. TNCs from participating. This effort was rejected by European companies and governments. The U.S. affiliates reportedly lost other orders because of a concern over possible U.S. intervention through export controls.

The antitrust laws in the United States are the strictest in the world. Beginning with the Sherman Act of 1890 and continuing with the Clayton Act of 1917, plus many subsequent court rulings and clarifications, the U.S. government has taken a position against restraint of (domestic) trade through operation of large, monopolistic firms or cartels. This position has extended to international business for the most part, except that export associations (formed under the Webb-Pomerene Act of 1918, and amended in 1976) are permitted among U.S. competitors to combine export activities of members. This exception exists to enable these firms to compete successfully in foreign markets against their foreign rivals, some of which may receive subsidies from their governments. Further, the Export Trading Company Act was passed in 1982, also providing exemption from antitrust provisions for the purpose of permitting a single company to handle multiple export accounts even of competitors— similar to Japanese trading companies. Banks were also permitted to join in the ventures to provide financing.

The main effect of these restraints—originally having nothing to do with foreign investment—lies in preventing U.S. TNCs from engaging in cartels (or monopolistic practices) with foreign enterprises *if* they adversely affect U.S. commerce (exports or imports). Some U.S. TNCs are so fear-

ful of antitrust prosecution that they will hardly go to a
meeting with foreign companies—even if sponsored by the
host-country government.

Other home-government policies affecting TNCs are
those under the name of "industrial strategy or targeting."
The objective is to encourage advancing or to protect declining sectors. The techniques used are extensive, including subsidies, government purchasing, low-cost loans, tax
rebates, R&D grants, and so on. They can significantly alter
TNC strategies in FDI and their overseas operations. These
policies are still under debate in advanced countries; they
are discussed more extensively in Chapter 15.

REACTIONS ABROAD TO U.S. INTERVENTION AND PROTECTION OF TNCS

The U.S. government (more than any other home-
country government, at least overtly) has intervened in host-
country policies related to treatment of private TNCs. It has
done so for two reasons: (1) to prevent the frustration of its
own policies toward the foreign activities of its corporations
and (2) to protect U.S. TNCs from unacceptable treatment by
host countries. Despite the different intentions, the result
is intervention in activities *abroad*, which most host countries consider to be solely their own jurisdiction.

Intervention

U.S. policies that intervene in TNC activities overseas
give rise to reactions by foreign governments. To counter
the extraterritorial reach of U.S. antitrust law, some foreign
governments have limited the intervention of U.S. courts
and prevented the transfer of information desired by the
U.S. Attorney General. U.S. policy at times, therefore, puts
the U.S. TNC between the two governments.

The application of U.S. export and technology controls,
as extended to U.S. affiliates abroad and to licensees of U.S.
patents and know-how, is frequently not matched by other
governments. Therefore, U.S. companies could supply customers in "prohibited destinations" through their foreign
operations or licensees, frustrating the objectives of U.S.
regulations. Consequently, U.S. companies are themselves
legally bound to prevent affiliates owned 51 percent or more
and licensees (whether affiliates or independent companies)

from shipping products under the export control list or technology to "prohibited destinations." A violation exposes U.S. executives to criminal punishment and foreign companies to "black-listing" by the U.S. Department of Commerce, prohibiting them from receiving exports from the United States. Host countries consider this an unwarranted intervention in their own policies, especially since many have agreed under a Coordinating Committee (COCOM) not to ship certain products to "enemy" countries. The U.S. regulations extend beyond this agreement, however.

In the tax arena, during the time when the U.S. government was seeking to encourage private foreign direct investment to developing countries—particularly in the 1960s under the Alliance for Progress with Latin America—host governments offered tax incentives through reduced or zero taxes to U.S. investors for a negotiated period of time. The U.S. tax code permitted U.S. companies with affiliates abroad to consolidate their affiliates on accounts into the parent company for the purpose of paying U.S. taxes. TNCs were given credit for taxes *paid* abroad by affiliates. But, they were not given credit for taxes that were waived in the foreign country, thereby nullifying the incentive given by the host country. (However, so long as the earnings were retained abroad, no U.S. taxes were paid.) To the extent that the U.S. tax was greater than the foreign tax, the U.S. company had to pay the difference between the tax in the host country and that in the United States, essentially taking revenue out of the developing country and transferring it to the United States. The developing countries requested the United States to "spare" these taxes which were waived, thereby making the incentive effective. The U.S. Treasury Department refused to permit such tax-sparing, much to the chagrin of the host countries and other departments of the U.S. government. It refused to do so simply because it would encourage the waiving of taxes abroad, or increase of taxes in the host country which could then be waived; this would reduce taxes paid to the United States, making this reduction an effective incentive to invest in the host country.

The United States has been in the forefront of protecting human rights abroad, and several pressure groups have insisted that the same protection be extended through Amer-

ican TNCs into foreign countries. The requests focus principally on racial discrimination—primarily in South Africa,
with its policy of apartheid. Through several years of protracted negotiations both in the United Nations and by the
U.S. Congress, the Reagan administration eventually
adopted a policy of urging U.S. companies to divest in South
Africa, for the purpose of putting pressure on the Afrikaaner government to remove the apartheid laws. These
were not successful, even though many TNCs did withdraw,
and the practice raises a serious question of "ethical imperialism," which is an attempt to extend the ethics of one
country into another by means stronger than persuasion.

Protection

The U.S. government has attempted to protect the interests of its companies investing abroad through four different routes: (1) the negotiation of "investment treaties" (as
discussed in Chapter 11), (2) the attempt to achieve "national treatment" for all foreign investors through the OECD
Code, (3) the passage by Congress of the Hickenlooper and
Gonzalez Amendments to the AID program, and (4) in bilateral negotiations with host-country governments.

"National treatment" covers the entire range of business activities, including the "right of establishment"—
meaning incorporation on the same basis as a citizen. It
means also that no distinction in national laws will be
made between firms locally or foreign owned, including expropriation. However, expropriation by host countries introduces a discrimination in the form of payment, for the
foreign investor contributed foreign funds. The U.S. government accepts the right of any host country to expropriate
whatever assets it considers necessary in the national interest; the issue is over the amount and type of compensation—(see Chapter 11). Many of the governments in
developing countries have found U.S. requirements unacceptable, since they come from a traditional international
law that these countries did not help form. They insist that
compensation be determined by the courts of their country,
which simply defers the dialogue with the U.S. government.

The Hickenlooper Amendment provided that U.S. aid
could be cut off to any developing country that nationalized

an affiliate of a U.S. company without providing proper compensation, and the Gonzalez Amendment that U.S. representatives in international lending agencies should oppose loans to such countries. The Hickenlooper Amendment was overtly applied to Ceylon (Sri Lanka) when it would do no serious damage, and there was considerable discussion of whether it had been covertly applied to Peru in the case of the International Petroleum Company (IPC)—an affiliate of a Canadian company that was wholly owned by Standard Oil of New York (Exxon; Esso at that time). The Peruvian government objected to the intervention of the U.S. government, which simply refused the objection and continued its negotiations to obtain proper treatment of the U.S. parent company.

In order to avoid some of the problems of expropriation or damage to U.S. companies operating abroad, the U.S. government established an insurance program in AID—later made independent, as the Overseas Private Investment Corporation (OPIC). It has the ability to insure foreign investments and licensing contracts against expropriation, riot, or war risks. To be a party to OPIC's programs, the host country has to agree to accept, in case of an expropriation that is not given adequate, prompt or effective compensation, the substitution of the U.S. government for the American parent company as claimant. In that instance, the claim of the company becomes a claim of the U.S. government, and will be settled through direct bilateral negotiations at the government level. The U.S. company is compensated by OPIC, which has Congressional funding and guarantees.

Despite the claims from the left that international companies have drawn governments into "Capitalistic Imperialism," there is no evidence publicly available that the U.S. government was seduced into diplomatic negotiations with host countries simply because of acts of U.S. companies seeking to exploit foreign economies—save possibly in the petroleum sector in earlier decades. Even in the petroleum case, however, there is evidence that the companies were used for national security purposes on behalf of the U.S. government as much as vice versa.[8] In all other situations, the evidence indicates that the U.S. government has been very deliberate in its representations of U.S. companies

abroad and has been seldom drawn into investment disputes with host countries. When it has, it was representing
a matter of principle relative to the concept of "equal and
equitable treatment," which it generally interprets as "national treatment"—i.e., the same as offered a local company.
This is a principle that it has sought to expand internationally with reference to all foreign direct investment. This
concept is more than most LDCs can accept; and even Canada has had a great deal of difficulty swallowing it, insisting
on differential treatment of foreigners compared to domestic companies.

These policies indicate that the TNCs must be prepared
for a variety of negotiations, involving also the participation
of the home government and its embassies abroad. The
structure of embassies around the world for assistance
in government relations varies widely from country to
country, both from the standpoint of the country represented and the country in which the embassy is located.
Thus, the instructions to U.S. embassies as to the extent
and intensity of support for the positions of U.S. affiliates
abroad are different from instructions given by the French,
German, Japanese, Dutch, British, and other governments
to their embassies. In fact the instructions given by each of
these governments is likely to differ from others in significant ways. The U.S. government, for example, is wary of
making representations on behalf of a single company in
terms of bids for projects overseas, though it will represent
the interests of all U.S. companies simultaneously if they
are bidding on a project. Other advanced countries have
taken more active roles in promoting the trade interests of
their TNCs abroad.

The U.S. government enters into the relations between a
U.S. TNC and a foreign government only where interests
critical to the United States are involved—either in security
or economic areas or where precedent is being broken under international law. If for any of these reasons the interests of the United States are being adversely affected, the
government will decide to represent the company case
through the U.S. embassy in the host country or even directly through the State Department to the foreign embassy
in Washington. The extent to which the U.S. government

supports TNC positions will depend also on the willingness of particular ambassadors or ministers in the U.S. embassies to make such representation. Some are uncomfortable in this role; others find it much easier to carry out. The U.S. State Department has on occasion sent out instructions that its embassies should be more supportive of the positions of U.S. affiliates in foreign countries, helping countries locate, negotiate, and improve relations with the host country. A large number of economic/commercial reports are sent in from these embassy posts to help U.S. companies in their operations overseas. These reports go through the State Department and the Commerce Department, with the latter sending them to companies that have so requested.

NOTES TO CHAPTER 4

1. See Anthony Sampson, *The Seven Sisters* (New York: Viking Press, 1975).

2. Raul Prebisch, *Reflexiones sobre la Cooperation Internacional en el Desarrollo Interamericano* (Washington, DC: Pan American Union, 1968).

3. Donald Lessard and John Williamson, *Capital Flight and Third World Debt* (Washington, DC: Institute for International Economics, 1987).

4. For a historical assessment of U.S. interests compared to that of TNCs, see Donald E. Neuchterlein, "U.S. National Interest and National Strategy: Are There Parallels with U.S. International Cooperate Interests?" in Herbert L. Sawyer (ed.), *Business in the Contemporary World* (Lanham, MD: University Press of America, 1988), pp. 197–220.

5. G. Hufbaer and M. Adler, *Overseas Manufacturing Investment and the Balance of Payments* (Washington, DC: U.S. Treasury Dept., 1968).

6. J. N. Behrman, *Direct Manufacturing Investment, Exports and the Balance of Payments* (New York National Foreign Trade Council, 1968).

7. Dismissal rules are discussed conveniently for many countries in Business International Corporation, *Investing, Licensing and Trading Conditions* (New York: Bus. Int. Corp., 1989), sect. 12.

8. Sampson, *The Seven Sisters*, chap. 4.

CHAPTER 5

Organization for Communication

The structures of communication between TNCs and their home governments differ from country to country, and the channels for dialogue between foreign TNCs and host governments often differ from those available to local companies. Communications between TNCs and the U.S. government are not organized in any formal fashion. Rather, each has a number of entities or channels through which to communicate with the other in an ad hoc fashion. Over 80 agencies within the U.S. government have something to do with international activities of TNCs—from the major departments with their many bureaus and offices to independent units such as the Small Business Administration (SBA), the Export Import Bank (EIB), the Food and Drug Administration (FDA), the Overseas Private Investment Corporation (OPIC), the Maritime Commission, and so on. For their part, the TNCs work through representatives in Washington which contact Congress and the Administration, as well as communicating jointly through trade and industry associations.

Complex structures are found in other countries, but in a few countries the dialogues are more formalized, both as to channels and the periodicity of consultation. There is a history of closer government-business relations on the European Continent and in Japan than there has been in the United States and United Kingdom, which sought a limited government. And, the extent to which governments of advanced (OECD) countries support or protect operations of business abroad varies significantly in form and intensity, somewhat reflecting their colonial experience in cooperating with companies overseas. To describe adequately the complex patterns and mechanisms of business-government relations even in a few major home countries would require several chapters; the focus of this chapter is on U.S. patterns of communication, with some contrasting illustrations from other countries.

BUSINESS ORGANIZATIONS

Communication of TNCs with the home governments has developed essentially out of a broader domestic pattern of business/government relations, which in the United States has grown up in an adversarial mode. U.S. business has not trusted the U.S. government to look after the interests of business; nor has the government felt that business was concerned with the interests of society or the nation. Each has felt it necessary to oppose and persuade rather than to cooperate. Cooperative activities have taken place, but these have been ad hoc and temporary rather than part of a pattern of convergent interests.[1]

The U.S. TNC makes itself felt through direct communications with government officials—administration and Congress—and through trade and industry associations. The use of either the direct or joint mode depends on the issue and whether or not the company believes that the efforts of more than one company are needed to be successful in persuading the appropriate government officials.

Internal Units

There are a number of units internal to the TNC that make representations to the U.S. government. They begin with the CEO himself, and it is his direct representation to appropriate high government officials that is likely to be most persuasive. If he considers the issue significant enough to become directly involved, and if the firm is sufficiently important, government officials at the highest levels will listen. Whether or not they agree with the CEO is another matter, but the communication does exist.

To give effect to communications by the CEO, the major U.S. TNCs have representatives in Washington (called Washington reps). These offices have from 1 to 30 professional staff, who determine what issues have serious impacts on the company and which warrant the time of top company officials in dialogues with government officials. These issues are signaled back to the company through the headquarters' external relations department (sometimes, the

public relations department or personnel or legal departments) and sometimes directly to the office of the president
itself. A screening process is used inside the company to
determine the level of representation required and the intensity and the presentation of data, supporting documents,
and the number of government officials that need to be targeted. Arrangements are made by the Washington reps for
these dialogues, and they usually accompany the corporate
officials so as to follow up more effectively.

The Washington reps trace legislation through the Congress, examine cases that are before the Supreme Court,
keep track of and make representations on regulations
coming out of government departments, follow the activities
of the regulatory agencies, help to prepare cases for presentation before any of these bodies (plus the World Bank or
Inter-American Development Bank, both in Washington),
monitor the passage of applications and approvals required
by various regulatory agencies, and arrange for appropriate
meetings. These representatives have an association for
exchange of information among themselves as to the significance of particular issues. They frequently invite government officials to make presentations at these meetings on
current issues. This provides them the opportunity for
open dialogue without company commitment.

Behind the Washington reps are the external relations
departments of the TNCs, which gather information not
only from the Washington reps but also from various state
jurisdictions within the United States, for example—where
a major plant is located, such as in California, Texas, Illi-
nois, North Carolina, or wherever. This is because the state
governments also apply regulations and taxation affecting
the future of the company here and abroad. The most pressing issue in TNC relations with state governments in the
1980s was the effort to tax TNCs on a unitary basis; that is
to tax the worldwide profits of the company on the percentage of business done in the state where a plant was
located.[2] Thus, if 1 percent of the production of the company came out of California, 1 percent of the worldwide
profits would be taxed as though earned in California. This
raised the possibility of double taxation of the same income—within the United States and abroad. With these

taxes added to prior ones, the entire profits of the company worldwide could be eaten up in taxation. It was the job of external relations departments to discover the views of the several state legislatures and seek to offset the pressures for such taxes. TNCs and foreign governments persuaded U.S. officials to get several of the states to remove pending legislation. The California statute was upheld in the courts but mitigated in the regulations.

A further means of persuading legislators are the Political Action Committees (PACs), through which U.S. companies are permitted to collect funds to support Congressional campaigns. The record raises some doubt as to the effectiveness of these PACs on specific legislation; there are a number of other sources of support, and the legislator simply trades off one source against another. Congressmen also are invited to give speeches to corporate gatherings for substantial sums (and some Congressional families have been entertained at corporate expense at plush resorts). The company hopes these favors will be remembered when laws are being considered that might have adverse impacts on it. Such "compensation" is supposedly beyond accepted modes of ethical conduct in the United States, but it still occurs.

External Associations

There are some 800 industry and trade associations in the United States, each of which seeks to promote the interests of its members. Many of these associations are headquartered in Washington, for ready access to government officials. The associations sponsor meetings of key members with key government officials on significant issues to represent corporate interests. Only 15 to 20 of the associations are highly successful in representing these interests simply because of inadequate budgets or a lack of high-priority issues before Congress. The most successful represent some of the key industries in which TNCs are prominent—e.g., electronics, automobiles, chemicals, pharmaceuticals, machinery and allied products, tobacco, and textiles—and to which Congress gives high priority.

Some associations cut across both companies and trade associations—such as the Business Roundtable, the Com-

mittee for Economic Development, the Council on Foreign
Relations, and the Trilateral Commission. And a variety of
business advisory committees, more or less permanent,
have been appointed by the various departments or agencies of the government.

There is no formal business organization with close ties
to government agencies that provides for a continuing dialogue on specific subjects. The advisory committees to the
State Department and the Commerce Department are set
up for discussion of policy issues and even for recommendations on implementation, but had limited success. In
some, membership rotates; in others, no provision was
made for follow-up implementation. One exception is the
National Export Council (later the President's Export Council) attached to the Department of Commerce, which has
been active for 25 years. However, it is not charged with issues related to investment, but with the expansion of U.S.
exports and, in the 1980s, improvement of international
competitiveness.

Communications in Other Countries

Communication between the TNCs headquartered in
other advanced countries and their home governments follows different channels. For example, in Japan, a network of
industry associations (comprised of Japanese companies)
have regular meetings with their opposites numbers in the
Ministry of International Trade and Industry (MITI). A MITI
official exists for every major industry and subsector; he is
responsible for knowing the problems and opportunities in
that sector. Meetings are held frequently during the year
with representatives of the industry to determine what support is needed from the government, such as tax incentives,
research funds, trade protection, export promotion, financing, and so on. These needs are then given priorities, with
key sectors given the largest support. Beyond the dialogues
there is an indicative plan called "A Vision;" industry is not
required to follow it, for it is not precise as to each sector.
But there is sufficient dialogue so that sectoral needs for
local development or penetration of world markets are determined by industry and government. The four major Japanese asociations are the *Keidanren* (the National Associa-

tion of Manufacturers), *Shoko Kaigesho* (Chamber of Commerce), *Keizai Doyukai* (Committee for Economics Development), and the *Neikiren* (Employers' Association) which sets the terms of bargaining with labor unions. In addition, there is a 24-member group known as the *Zaikai*, which is composed of the CEO's of major companies and heads of the above industry organizations. These groups have supported the Liberal Democratic Party (the only one in power since World War II), which in turn sets policies through the parliament (Diet), which are to be carried out by the various ministries in discussion with the companies. Business-government relations in Japan are channeled through formal organizations, which have the long-term purpose of maintaining harmony between business and government for the survival and growth of Japan as a nation.

In France, dialogues with the government are also through industry associations differentiated by sector; these, too, have their opposite number in the Ministry of Industry. A national plan is developed every five years to indicate the directions of industrial development. It is periodically discussed with the representatives of each industry sector, *before* and *after* the enunciation of the plan. The government can then encourage a response by providing specific support through finance, tax relief, export production, investment guarantees, etc.

In Germany, the dialogue also takes place through the industry association (Bundesverband fur Deutsche Industrie) but probably more importantly through the banks, which have ties to the Central Bank and the Ministry of Finance and which also have officials sitting on the Boards of the major corporations. Bank officials, therefore, are a channel for mutual expression of concerns and objectives by both TNCs and government officials.

In Britain, the dialogue is much less structured, with no direct formal, periodic dialogues between industry and the Board of Trade. These communications arise on *ad hoc* issues or when either party feels the need for such consultation. The Federation of British Industries (originally, Confederation) is composed of various industry associations that are willing to get together on significant issues for representation to the government. It has developed a strong central management and leadership, which is willing to take initiatives on its own, apart from the interests of specific members.

Fairly close ties exist between the major companies in Sweden, Denmark, Norway, the Netherlands and their governments. The strongest is in the Netherlands, where a few companies dominate the economy: Philips, Shell, AKZO, Unilever, and KLM (government-owned).

Compared to any of the other advanced countries that are home for TNCs, the United States has the least structured channels of communication between TNC and home government. The possible exception is Italy but even there there are major SOEs to reflect government objectives. Frequent calls were made in the 1980s for closer government-business communication on major issues affecting the U.S. economy both at home and abroad. But under the "Sunshine laws," this can be done in the United States only if the dialogues are open to the public so that citizens can witness the process; such openness hinders some useful exchanges or shifts them to private conversations.

U.S. GOVERNMENT ORGANIZATIONS

The major organization responsible for U.S. government policies on the international activities of U.S. TNCs is the State Department, followed by the Department of Commerce and the Treasury. Each of them has representatives in U.S. embassies overseas to whom businesses can turn for counsel and information. The Department of State has an Economic/Business Bureau which is responsible for forming government policy on economic issues abroad and business problems with which its embassies are involved. This bureau, for the past decade, has had an Advisory Committee on International Trade, Investment, and Development, composed principally of business officials, with some representatives from academia, labor, the legal profession, and a few policy-research groups. What started out in the 1970s as fairly close deliberations on policy matters became in the 1980s an amorphous sounding board, more given to listening to government pronouncements than offering detailed critiques. It does provide an entrée for members of the Advisory Committee to talk informally with State Department officials, but this has gradually diluted the concerted effort that was made by the business sector initially to offer constructive policy suggestions.

Overseas, some of the U.S. embassies have established advisory councils to the Ambassador or the Economic Minister, composed of managers of U.S. TNC-affiliates in that country, both to inform them of U.S. policies and representations to the local government and to find out what problems the affiliates face. On occasion, the embassy and the TNC-affiliate managers have combined to make formal representations to the host government and sometimes to the executive branch in Washington. The embassies are charged with reporting back to Washington on developments in the host country for dissemination to other interested agencies, and some of that information is culled from the local managers.[3]

The Department of Commerce has both industry and country desks within its offices concerned with international and domestic business. These officials combine their resources when a specific industry problem arises in a specific country abroad. They are in touch with companies in a given sector, and the country desks are in touch with the embassy personnel abroad, especially the commercial attachés, who are responsible for gathering commercial information and assisting American businessmen abroad.

The responsibilies of the Department of Commerce include export promotion, technology exchanges, export controls, patents, industrial promotion, the exchange of scientific information, and the development of a broad range of economic information and statistics both in the United States and abroad. The department attempts to keep the U.S. business community apprised of changes in policies, and emerging problems overseas, and to be an information source on specific business opportunities for export, licensing, or investment.

The Treasury Department has responsibility for tax policy and its application to TNCs at home and abroad as well as for customs services on U.S. imports and negotiations with other countries on customs problems.

All three departments provide support through informational and policy counsel to the U.S. (Special) Trade Representative (USTR) in the White House. The USTR is a negotiating arm responsible for tariff reductions, seeking to open the world economy to the trade of all companies and countries. It has recently focused on the removal of nontariff barriers to trade and on barriers to trade in services. The approaches in this office do not in any direct way recognize the existence of the TNC or the volume of intracompany trade that has arisen in the world. Given that over 25 percent of all U.S. trade, and between 45 and 50 percent of U.S. trade in manufactures, occurs between affiliates of U.S. TNCs, the natures and the demands for protection and the ability to reduce barriers is altered from what would occur in free-market decisions.

An interagency committee between the State, Commerce, and Defense Departments has charge of policy concerning the control of U.S. exports and technology to destinations that might use it to harm U.S. interests. The export controls are themselves administered by the Department of Commerce under delegation from the President; they are most stringent on exports to the U.S.S.R., Eastern Europe, and Cuba. However, some Eastern European countries are treated much less severely than the U.S.S.R. itself. This differential was applied for the purpose of drawing some of these countries more into the Western orbit. TNCs are not directly involved in the formation of policy on export controls, but they do testify before Congress during the time of the renewal of the legislation, and there is frequent communication from the Washington reps when particular cases have become stuck in the approval process.

Among the independent agencies of the government, two are most important for TNC relations. The first is the Export-Import Bank, which is primarily responsible for funding exports from the United States and is, therefore, interested in the export policies of the TNCs. The Ex-Im Bank has also offered loans to foreign governments in connection with projects in which a U.S. TNC would be involved.

Of more direct relevance to FDI is the Overseas Private Investment Corporation (OPIC), which arose out of U.S. policies supporting direct private investment. This agency was spun out of AID in 1969; AID had a group promoting private enterprise abroad and had urged the establishment of an insurance/guarantee program that would reduce the risks of FDI in developing countries. Since OPIC's establishment, a number of developing countries have signed bilateral investment treaties, which the United States requires for each to be eligible for guarantees, TNCs have found the guarantees attractive enough to pay the small fees required for coverage of commercial and political risks.

No one government agency has a scope of responsibility or the coordinating authority to utilize the unique capabilities of the TNC; the TNC encompasses *more* of the various activities to which U.S. foreign economic policy is addressed than does any government unit. The lack of coordination is itself an obstacle to the formation of sound policies on the part of the U.S. government and has also contributed to the difficulty of continuing dialogues between business and government—as will be discussed further in Part V.

COOPERATION BETWEEN TNCS AND HOME GOVERNMENTS IN HOST COUNTRIES

Although the prevalent attitude between U.S. companies and the U.S. government is adversarial, they have cooperated to achieve mutual goals on a number of international business issues and situations abroad. Such cooperation is found more frequently, however, in European and Asian countries, where the government often supports the activities of selected companies. The promotion of exports and large projects in a foreign country is often undertaken by top officials in the home government, even to the Prince of the Netherlands making representation on the behalf of a major Dutch company on a project abroad. U.S. ambassadors have also supported the bids of U.S. companies and have urged favorable treatment of applications for investment in particular host countries, but seldom for a specific U.S. company (when only one was involved). The U.S. Government has also made representations to host countries about tax issues, patent issues, exchange restrictions, advertising regulations and so on—all in the hopes of freeing up the choices and decisions of business and gaining at least national treatment for U.S. TNCs abroad.

There are times when U.S. TNCs seek support from embassies of other governments in a host country. For example, a U.S. TNC with an affiliate in Germany may seek help from the German embassy in Brazil in order to support its activities there that emanate from the German affiliate; the TNC might consider that German influence would be more direct and acceptable than any from the United States in this particular case. Also, embassies of other countries abroad are found to have different information than that gained from a U.S. embassy, so TNCs seek out all services available. Formal links are unlikely to exist between the U.S. TNC and these other embassies, but a network of informal channels does exist.

NOTES TO CHAPTER 5

1. The experience of the 1960s is recounted in J. N. Behrman, *U.S. International Business and Governments* (New York: McGraw-Hill 1971). Examples of specific and extensive cooperation are found in Anthony, *The Seven Sisters*, and his study of *The Sovereign State of ITT* (New York: Stein & Day, 1973). The internal memoranda of ITT are found in *Subversion in Chile: U.S. Corporate Intrigue in the Third World* (Nottingham, Eng.: Bertrand Russell Peace Foundation, 1972). See also, Laton McCartney, *Friends In High Places: The Bechtel Story* (New York: Simon & Schuster, 1988). In the latter two instances the TNCs were in the service of government, even though it also served their interests to do so.

2. See, "Global Profits Slip Away from the States," *Business Week* (Sept. 16, 1985), p. 116.

3. For an assessment of these relationships as they developed in the 1960s, and early 1970s, see J. N. Behrman, J. J. Boddewyn, and A. Kapoor, *International Business Government Communications* (Lexington, MA: Lexington Books, 1975).

PART III

TNCs and Host Governments

The major frictions between TNCs and governments over the post-World War II decades have been with the *host* governments, but the locus of friction has shifted according to the stages of development of the host country and the length of time in which the governments have become used to the presence of TNC affiliates. The position of host governments has been influenced by the attitudes of local business sectors as well; some of them welcome the foreign company eagerly while others are reluctant to see it enter, and still others hope to profit from it through partnerships of one type or another.

Host-country policies toward TNCs are distinguished as being relatively "open," "mixed," or relatively "restrictive." No country is completely open nor completely closed, but the differences along the continuum are significant. This openness or restrictiveness relates to trade, technology transfers, investment, ownership, financial flows, pricing, production levels, R&D, protection of patents and trademarks, and the movement of technicians and managers.

The relationships between TNCs and host governments are not dictated by governments alone, since the TNCs have an ability to respond in more or less cooperative ways in negotiation, in strategies, and in operations. Their strategies form the basis of continuing negotiations between business and governments and help, therefore, to determine the final orientations of the host country towards being "open" or "restrictive."

Range of Policies

The world economy is characterized both by increasing volumes of trade and by increasing protectionism in some countries and openness in others. These opposing moves are matching in the investment arena by desires in some countries for greater inflows and in others for tighter constraints on sectors open to investment, and on ownership and behavior of affiliates. The advantages of more "open" policies are evidenced by the relatively more rapid growth in countries adopting them. But openness subjects the host country to the impacts of structural adjustment, the international mobility of industrial (and agricultural) production, and shifting financial flows as more countries develop their financial institutions.

In both advanced and developing countries, a constant friction exists between "restrictive" approaches aimed at domestic economic objectives and more "open" policies aimed at gaining benefits from larger and wider international exchanges of goods, technology, and investment. "Restrictive" policies seek to solve the question of the international division of labor by developing or attracting import-substituting industry. More "open" policies rely on export-driven development. But neither the results of more "open" policies nor the costs of "restrictive" policies are sufficiently known to make uncontested economic judgments. Consequently, the policies are more politically than economically motivated.

Once again, the political rationale has to do with perceptions of power (national security) and of an equitable distribution of benefits. These concerns raise a problem of international balance—that is, a balance *among* countries as to the structure of agricultural and industrial development, the risks borne in the process of worldwide production and distribution, the rewards received, the burdens of adjustments, and the degree of national control that can be exercised over economic growth and financial flows directed to enhancing national wealth and power (or security).

These issues have taken on increased importance in the high-tech sectors of industry, for some stages of these are relatively mobile, and governments see them as important to international competitiveness. Achieving a balanced growth of the high-tech sectors among countries is exceedingly difficult, but highly unbalanced growth is excessively costly, through duplication of investments leading to overcapacity. Mercantilist policies produce an imbalance in development as each nation seeks its own economic interests over others. The goals are similar for each country, but the approaches taken are different, and the mechanisms used are often conflicting, even internally, and are not necessarily efficient for the pursuit of the goals intended, either nationally or internationally.

POLICY ISSUES

Not all countries—not even all the advanced countries or the newly industrializing countries (NICs)—have agreed on what constitutes the best foreign economic policies. Even so, almost all of them have adopted measures for the stimulation of industry, ranging from support of general industrialization, to aid for specific industrial sectors, to treatment of foreign investors, and even to deeming specific companies as "national champions."[1] These national champions are frequently the state enterprise in a given sector—such as in petroleum or telecommunications.

The range of policies demonstrates the complexity of objectives among countries, in turn, affected by divergent economic and political situations or interests. These differences are explainable and justifiable—that is, there are rational and acceptable reasons for the positions taken—based on the government's acceptance of responsibility for national *wealth* and *power*. Not all countries are concerned with relative national power. Some are simply too small to be able to protect themselves effectively, while others have declared neutrality or are protected by another country. Such countries are concerned, therefore, not with those industrial sectors necessary to maintain national security but only with those basic to growth. The degree to which a national government accepts responsibility for the generation and level of national wealth, as well as its distribution, depends on a variety of cultural, social, and political factors, each of which has historical roots.

A concern for national *power* leads to a desire for economic independence so as to reduce potential damage from an interruption of supply in time of war. (Classical free-trade doctrine is based on an assumption of peace, or the identification of a "natural enemy" who could be isolated.) This independence focuses principally on national-security industries, but the argument is also used to justify protection or support of agriculture and petroleum (as by the United States, European countries, and Japan) and a host of secondary and tertiary sectors that supply the defense establishment.

In the last few decades, the high-technology sectors have become of critical importance for national defense. Some "key" sectors are also deemed critical even though they are not high tech (e.g., steel, automotive, heavy motors, electrical machinery, earth-moving equipment, and even textiles), because of their contributions to growth of other sectors, or to employment (levels and skills), or to sustaining depressed regions. Some of these key sectors have high-tech stages within them (e.g., high-tech fabric-cutting processes within the textile industry). And all the high-tech industries have substantial low-tech activities. High-tech is, therefore, less an industry classification than a characterization of a "stage" of production, or an "end product." All countries seek to increase high-tech opportunities and to enlarge them within their economies. Further, to assure the existence of national sources for the supply of defense-related products, certain sectors (high-tech or not) are either closed to imports or foreign-owned local production, or are provided with sufficient support to maintain them in the face of foreign competition.

Governments have accepted responsibility for the generation of national *wealth*, leading to their concern over the level and composition of GNP and the stability of economic activity. These can be guaranteed *only* if the international sector is controlled—as France learned in the early 1980s when it tried to stimulate the domestic economy without paying attention to the international repercussions. Disturbances from the international economy upset the structure and level of a nation's economic growth and stability. For these reasons, governments have injected themselves into the structure of domestic industry—including efforts to catalyze advancing industries, to ease the decline of particular sectors by facilitating shifts into other sectors, or to maintain a given sector in the face of international competitive pressures. Governments have also intervened in international trade both by stimulating exports to assist particular sectors and by restricting imports to provide breathing space to domestic producers. These efforts constitute what are called "industrial policies"—discussed in Chapter 16.

Similarly, governments have stimulated or constrained foreign direct investment (both inward and outward). The aim is to reduce pressures on the international balance of payments, or on foreign exchange rates, and therefore on domestic industry. The policies adopted on international trade and foreign direct investment reflect the degree to which the country is willing to become dependent on (or interdependent with) other countries. The nature and extent of these ties determines the degree to which national wealth is, at least in part, a result of development in other countries.

Given the desire in all countries not only for greater absolute wealth but also for greater *relative* wealth (a tenacious mercantilist concept), the emphasis on high-tech competition that stems from the concern for *power* is augmented by the concern for *wealth*. The high-tech sectors are seen as necessary not only for defense but also for gaining income and wealth, because they increase the value added in manufacturing and the skill-levels of workers more than other sectors. Since all sectors are seeking similar patterns of growth, multiple trade-offs will be required to achieve balance among national economic policies.

Finally, wherever there is intervention or regulation *or* monopsony in buying (as with government or preferential procurement), there is the opportunity to alter decisions or implementation through bribes, payments, or favors. In some countries, favors are given *after* the completion of transactions and are customary "courtesies" which cement long-term relationships. But large payments can also be expected (even asked for), and bribes are often offered successfully. Business in *most* countries is *not* done at "arm's length," relying *only* on market signals. How TNCs respond is a matter of law and ethics, as discussed in chapters 11 and 14.

COUNTRY INCENTIVES AND PERFORMANCE REQUIREMENTS

Almost every country receiving FDI has offered incentives of some sort and at the same time imposed some requirements on the performance of the foreign affiliates. There are few countries that have remained freely open in all respects in terms of incoming FDI. Still, there is a substantial difference in the extent to which each is practiced. Some countries, as discussed in the succeeding chapters, have standing policies regarding both incentives and performance requirements; others simply offer incentives on an ad hoc basis during negotiations, and these and others impose various performance requirements during negotiations or even afterwards.

Information concerning the various practices is, therefore, not always commensurate when one is looking at policies or actual practice. Policies as enunciated are not always followed in negotiations. Still, there is enough information to get a rather full picture of the approaches taken by various countries. A variety of business services provide information on policies, statutes, and regulations on investing and licensing; and the U.S. Department of Commerce surveys the experience of U.S. TNCs every five years to see what actual practices have been in the provision of incentives and the requirements of performance.

In its 1977 Benchmark Survey, the Department of Commerce questioned 23,641 U.S. non-bank affiliates of non-bank parents as to incentives and performance requirements. And a 1982 Benchmark Survey questioned 17,213 such affiliates, comprising virtually all U.S. FDI by value.

The two surveys showed that some 25 percent of all affiliates received one or more incentives; however, only about one in ten of the incentives were available only to foreigners. The two surveys, respectively, showed 20 and 24 percent receiving tax concessions, 8 and 10 percent tariff concessions, 9 and 14 percent subsidies, and 5 and 7 percent other incentives. The use of incentives varies widely, with Ireland granting 70 percent of U.S. affiliates some incentive, South Korea over 50 percent, but Hong Kong only 5 percent. Affiliates in manufacturing showed some 40 percent receiving incentives, compared to less than 30 in mining, and only 12 in the service sectors.

As to performance requirements, the two surveys showed some 15 percent of U.S. affiliates subject to one or more interventions, with 8 percent subject to local labor and local content requirements, and less than three percent subject to export/import and foreign exchange requirements. Only 6 percent of the affiliates were limited in the proportion of equity held by the U.S. parent.

Table 6.1: Incentives and Performance Requirements, 1982 (number of U.S. TNC affiliates affected)

Incentives	Developed Countries	Developing Countries
Tax concessions	2671	1483
Tariff concessions	738	923
Subsidies	1912	490
Other	738	491
Total	6055	3387
Performance Requirements		
Local Labor	434	866
Technology Transfer	200	414
Local ownership	149	579
Exports	122	152
Foreign exchange	70	171
Imports limited	56	192
Local suppliers	42	120
Total	1073	2494

Source: Bureau of Economic Analysis, *U.S. Direct Investment Abroad*, (1982 Benchmark Survey), Washington, D.C.: U.S. Department of Commerce, Dec. 1985, Tables II.I, 1–4.

A major difference was exhibited between the advanced and developing countries in the application of performance requirements. Some 30 percent of affiliates in LDCs were subject to such requirements, compared to only 6 percent in the advanced countries (in the 1977 survey; data for the 1982 survey were not provided, so a comparison cannot be made). India's percentage was the highest worldwide—60 percent. Hong Kong was lowest, again, at 2 percent, with Singapore close behind at 11. In the advanced countries, the poorer imposed the most such requirements—Portugal and Turkey at 37 percent of the cases. The sector most constrained was mining (27 percent in 1977) with manufacturing at 19 percent, though transportation equipment matched that of mining. Comparative data from the 1982 survey are given in Table 6.1, along with comparative use of incentives. The advanced countries offered incentives 1.7 times those offered by LDCs, but the developing countries imposed performance requirements 2.4 to 1 compared to advanced countries. The use of performance requirements by individual countries is shown in Table 6.2.

Virtually all countries employ some form of performance requirement when it suits their objectives; however, as indicated above, the incidence on all affiliates reporting shows less than one-third of U.S. affiliates affected. Still, over 20 different requirements have been imposed by one or more countries on the entry and operations of TNCs.[2] Although the five requirements shown in Table 6.2 are the most frequently used, others are used to guide location of plants to depressed or developing areas of the host country, to limit local borrowing by the foreign affiliate, to induce FDI into priority sectors or limit entry into others, to limit remittances of profits or capital to the parent, to limit the number of foreign employees, and to restrict mergers and acquisitions. The relative frequency and stringency of use of these requirements signals the extent to which a host country is "open" or "mixed" or "restrictive" in its approach to FDI.

The grouping of countries into one of these three categories is somewhat arbitrary, as one gets close to the borders of the "mixed" group. It is easy to place countries at the extremes, but a classification based on laws and regulations would not produce the same selection of coun-

Table 6.2: Performance Requirements for FDI During 1980s (selected countries)

Country	Local Content	Local Equity	Local Emp.	Export Forex	Technology Transfer
Argentina	*	*	*	*	*
Austria	*		*	*	*
Belgium	*	*	*	*	*
Brazil	*	*	*	*	*
Canada	*	*	*	*	*
Chile	*	*	*		*
China (PRC)	*	*	*	*	*
Colombia	*	*	*	*	*
Denmark			*		
Egypt	*	*	*		*
Finland		*	*	*	
France	*	*	*	*	*
Greece	*	*	*	*	*
India	*	*	*	*	*
Indonesia	*	*	*	*	*
Italy		*	*	*	*
Israel	*	*	*	*	*
Japan	*	*	*		*
Malaysia	*	*	*	*	*
Mexico	*	*	*	*	*
Netherlands	*	*	*		*
Nigeria	*	*	*	*	*
Peru	*	*	*	*	*
Philippines	*	*	*	*	*
Portugal	*	*	*	*	*
Singapore	*	*	*	*	*
South Korea	*	*	*	*	*
Spain	*	*	*	*	*
Sweden			*	*	*
Switzerland		*	*		
Taiwan	*	*	*	*	*
Turkey	*	*	*	*	*
U.K.	*	*	*	*	*
U.S.	(a)		(a)		
U.S.S.R.	*	*	*	*	*
West Germany	*	*	*	*	*

(a) By insisting on FDI inflows in autos, for example, the United States has implicitly required local content and employment; the Congress has considered more explicit requirements.

Note: The indications of practices are *not* necessarily statements of policy positions; they merely show that some TNC affiliates have had to give assurances of performance in these aspects.

Sources: U.S. Department of Commerce, *Incentives and Performance Requirements for Foreign Direct Investment in Selected Countries*, 1978; and *Overseas Business Reports*; and *the Use of Investment Incentives and Performance Requirements by Foreign Governments*, October 1981; also, *U.S. Direct Investment Abroad: 1982 Benchmark Survey Data*, December 1985.

tries as one based on actual practice in negotiation. Nor are words of officials and acts of departments or ministries the same. The subsequent classifications are, therefore, impressionistic and subject to change as conditions and government orientations shift, what is important is *not* the classification but the caution to be prepared for negotiation on specific issues and to be relieved if difficult ones are not raised.

POLICY APPROACHES

Policy approaches can be categorized, somewhat indistinctly, as "open," "restrictive" or "mixed." No economies have ever been completely closed or completely open, though for a time in the 1950s thru 1970s, Albania, Burma, and China were closed to FDI, and during the 1860s Britain was virtually completely open to trade and investment. Thus, national policies are along the continuum between the extremes.

The policies toward FDI tend to follow the basic development strategy of each country. Since World War II, three different strategies of economic development have been proposed and practiced: autarchy, import-substitution, and export-driven. Autarchy is a strategy of self-contained growth, or growth wholly from within. It is the oldest, having been employed by China for hundreds of years prior to its opening to the West, as well as by Japan prior to the mid-nineteenth century. In fact, many countries or regions were relatively isolated until forced to join the expansion of the Western countries as colonies, at which time they were drawn into international trade as an engine of growth. Since World War II, autarchy has been the principal strategy for socialist states, though the U.S.S.R. included within its "trading bloc" the Eastern European countries and China(at least for a time). China also remained virtually self-contained during the Maoist period—save for its ties to the U.S.S.R.—until 1978. Under this overall strategy, there was virtually no place for FDI inflows or outflows.

During the 1950s and 1960s, the import-substitution strategy was adopted by many developing countries, especially in Latin America. Its attraction was the ease with which the gaps in comparative advantage could be identi-

fied. Since comparative advantage is essentially static ex-
plaining what a country should produce and trade but not
how it ought to develop, governments do not see it as a
guide to growth. Growth leads to *changes* in comparative
advantages, and guided growth requires the management of
changes in factor endowments and their use. The fact of imports shows that the country does not presently have an advantage in those items and that there is a domestic
demand, which might be satisfied through domestic production. The developmental strategy is to establish, develop
or improve the local ability to produce import-substituting
items. FDI inflows could be used to develop such industry—
as was done with autos in Brazil and Mexico. But not all FDI
inflows will be welcome, since only those that lead to import substitution are given priority or permission.

The export-driven strategy relies on an expansion of international trade to stimulate the economy. It has been
used mostly by countries whose internal market is relatively small and which require the larger markets in other
countries to permit expansion of industrial production. As
has been recognized since Adam Smith, economic growth is
limited by the size of the market. Quite large countries
could employ autarchy, if done efficiently; they and even
some medium-sized countries (such as Mexico) have unde-
veloped resources that could be used to stimulate internal
growth. But the small countries—such as Taiwan—require
access to the demand in larger countries to reach economies of scale and competitive costs that will raise living
standards. Thus, the strategy seeks to identify niches in
world markets that can be met from their countries—initially the low-cost, mass-consumption goods such as textiles, toys, paper products, etc.—with gradual upgrading.
The upgrading occurs through the entry of TNCs, seeking
low-cost human resources. The TNCs provide market access needed by the developing country, plus the technology
and managerial skills required to reduce costs. Thus, FDI
inflows are welcomed; an ability to participate in FDI outflows follows later. South Korea has been through all
phases of the export-driven strategy in the last decades,
emerging with its own TNCs operating even in the more advanced countries.

Open Countries

Not only are major countries (the United States and the United Kingdom) among the more open economies but also small states such as Chile, Switzerland, Singapore, Hong Kong, the Netherlands, and Denmark are included. The smaller countries have relatively little concern for power or national security guaranteed by their own abilities; and they have small national markets, requiring them to trade internationally in order to raise their productivity and therefore their wealth. All seek to attract sectors of industry with advanced technologies and high value-added, to export the product, and thereby achieve economies of scale. Switzerland, for example, exports as much as 95 percent of the production of some of its major industry sectors (watches, pharmaceuticals). The Netherlands is dependent on international trade for about 60 percent of its GNP. The primary concern of governments in this group of countries is to raise living standards, leading to open policies on trade and foreign direct investment.

The potential economic dependence that results from open policies is mitigated by spreading the economic ties among many countries. The strategy adopted seeks, further, to create *inter*dependence so that other trading partners are as concerned for the smaller countries as the latter are to generate contacts abroad. These countries are willing to experiment with a number of different mechanisms and arrangements in order to establish appropriate ties. The government will frequently, support new initiatives and innovations on the part of companies and will promote a high level of flexibility for rapid adjustment to international economic and market changes. They recognize that they are too small economically to dominate any market or even to force negotiation at any given point. They have to "live by their wits" and are not particularly doctrinaire in their support of free trade and investment (apart from Switzerland). They are much more pragmatic in working out whatever arrangements they can to further their objectives. Any country deciding not to concern itself significantly with national defense could adopt a similar policy, but not all do.

The most open economies also include some of the larger, advanced countries. Canada, the United Kingdom,

Germany, and the United States have held to a more generally open foreign economic policy but have, for key and high-technology sectors, provided governmental support through research grants, preferential purchasing, export assistance, and other techniques. Only exceptionally have they closed off their own markets, and their levels of protection against import competition are deemed "reasonable." It is this group of countries that is most agitated by the closing off of markets in the high-tech sectors by the group of countries that is "restrictive," for they see the burdens of adjustment being thrust upon themselves.

Mixed Countries

The mixed economies include countries such as Brazil, Colombia, France, Kenya, South Korea, Malaysia, Mexico, Sri Lanka, Thailand, Turkey, and Venezuela. This group requires further differentiation because within it are some who are legitimately concerned with national power positions, which they perceived as requiring restrictions. Others are concerned with national power, even though they might be more easily protected in another way but cannot bring themselves to do so. A third group is not concerned with national power but still seeks to guide or support key sectors, so as to maintain a national presence in them. Not all of the mixed economies are concerned with high-tech sectors, but virtually all of the large ones are. Even some of the smaller ones have carved out niches in a few of the high-tech sectors—such as Malaysia in electronics, Colombia and Venezuela in petrochemicals. Each has sought to stimulate and protect these sectors through governmental policies.

The restrictiveness of these countries is seen in their intervening in TNC decisions or activities. In doing so, they will often be open to one type of TNC or to certain activities. Thus, *if* a TNC is willing to accept a joint venture, the host country market will be open to it. Or, *if* a TNC is willing to export, it may find a welcome in a host country. It is the "ifs" which lead to a classification of mixed. Across *all* countries there are *some* "ifs"; the difference is the number and their significance for TNC activities. Thus, a lack of protection of proprietary information and industrial property rights is characteristic of many LDCs in the mixed category, though not all; and some "open" countries (Taiwan) provide little protection on proprietary rights.

Further, some of these are highly dependent on world trade for national progress, while others are *relatively* unaffected by world trade in industrial goods at least. One might disagree with the way in which the governments assess their concerns and responsibilities and with the way in which they implement their policies, but so long as the effects of their decisions are on the domestic economy *alone*, they should not be the subject of intergovernmental dialogue. The problem, of course, is that it is very difficult to keep economic impacts within national boundaries. This transference leads again to the question of international balance and distribution of benefits and burdens.

Restrictive Countries

The restrictive economies include both advanced and developing nations: China, U.S.S.R., Egypt, Poland, Hungary, India, East Germany, and Cuba. Not only are all of these significantly concerned with national defense, but they are also imbued with recent or long-standing traditions of government intervention in the economy. Domestically, they have established (or bought) state enterprises; the foreign affiliate is guided or controlled. In the Soviet-bloc countries, SOEs dominate all sectors. India has numerous SOEs and is seeking to promote local activities in high-tech sectors other than its established government-controlled sectors. China, despite its shift to greater openness in the 1980s, remains "restrictive" and mainly reliant on SOEs. Thus, the countries in this group shift from time-to-time, and various gradations exist within it. But all have a bias toward heavy government intervention in the location and control of foreign affiliates.

Policies to free or restrain national economic activities have varied over the decades, with almost all countries intervening during the early 1800s when wars were waged on the European Continent and the United States was pulling away from Europe, and in the 1930s during the Great Depression. But for the past 40 years, as shown in Table 6.3, the *overall* trend has been toward greater openness for trade, investment, and technology transfers—as was sought in the Bretton Woods agreements.

Presently, a world of nations closed to each others' economies is not seen as desirable, and most countries are attempting to open. Only Albania and Burma remain nearly completely closed to FDI. With the opening of China in 1978 and its progressive moves to join the world economy, the pressure has risen on the U.S.S.R. and Eastern Europe. But these countries differ considerably in their new policy pronouncements, with the U.S.S.R. proclaiming to the Group of

Table 6.3: Policy Shifts in Selected Countries

Country	1960s	1970s	1980s
Argentina	M	M	M
Brazil	M	M	M
Canada	O	M	O
China	R	R	R
France	R	M	M
Germany	O	O	O
India	R	R	R
Indonesia	R	R-M	M
Italy	R	M	M
Japan	R	M	M-O
Korea	R	M	M-O
Mexico	R	M	M
Singapore	R	M	O
Taiwan	R	M	M
U.K.	O	O	O
U.S.	O	O	O
U.S.S.R.	R	R	R
Eastern Europe	R	R	R-M

O = Open

M = Mixed

R = Restrictive

Note: Variations exist even within each classification both between countries and over time.

Seven in July 1989 that it wishes to "join the world economy and assume its responsibilities in it," followed by the
fall of the Berlin Wall in October 1989. This contrasts with
China in June 1989 asserting that it will accept wholly
owned FDI affiliates, but attacking student marchers,
thereby isolating itself from the world community and causing FDI inflows virtually to stop.

EFFICIENCY OF POLICY TECHNIQUES

Any governmental policies towards TNCs will affect their
efficiency and profitability. And interventions can be made
at greater or lesser costs to TNCs—both in terms of final
effects and of techniques used. Pursuit of any objective—be
it national autonomy or international interdependence—
raises the question of appropriate means. What techniques
will, in fact, achieve the goals sought? In a world in which
the level of international economic interaction was low,
techniques that were isolationist in nature and internally
oriented appeared appropriate, and lower absolute growth
was acceptable. But, once the world economy was opened,
through Western expansion, the desire for *relative* growth
became primary.

Consequently, all but a few nations have given up closed
positions. Burma chose to close itself off to protect its culture and lifestyle; and the U.S.S.R. imposed a relatively
closed system on Eastern Europe (members of the communist economic bloc, or COMECON) until 1989. However, Japan, China, and some of the Eastern European countries
have recognized—at different times—the advantages of a
more open system in achieving growth and have determined
that they cannot reach their goals in an autarchic system.

Even from the standpoint of national power and security, such economic isolation is viable only if other nations
will leave that country alone. This detachment has not been
afforded all of the restrictive economies; military, commercial, or diplomatic pressures have been applied to open up
their resources or markets to more aggressive nations. But
few countries have historically chosen *complete* isolation.
The question is always one of the extent of openness—a
balancing of costs and benefits.

This same question of extent must be answered even by the relatively open economies, since none is *completely* open. The reason for rejection of total openness is that it entails complete dependence on what *all* others are doing and makes the country subject to exploitation by others *without* adequate assurances of an appropriate distribution of the benefits. The high-tech sectors raise this question even more strongly, for openness implies dependence— such as the present dependence of the United States on Japanese components for electronic systems for the military. Therefore, even open countries impose constraints to protect their security and economic rewards, despite the fact that the precise costs and benefits are not known. The optimum level of constraints and the means used depend on the trade-offs made among security, industrial or agricultural growth, urban/rural development, technological advance, cultural changes, income distribution, ownership and control, employment levels and skills, inflationary pressures, and so forth.

The lesson of economics is that there is a *cost* of everything gained. National policy should seek to maximize choices and minimize costs so as to increase national welfare. Choices can be maximized only through open systems, assuming that national security can be assured at the same time. In the present world, however, national security requires a more open economy since military strength for many depends on foreign sources for weapons systems, energy, and even training of armed forces. Further, national defense establishments alone are seldom strong enough to guarantee the security of a nation; ultimately, alliances are necessary, forcing interdependence even to achieve pursuit of power for security.[3]

Therefore, from standpoints of both economics (wealth) and security (power), the more rapidly advancing countries (whether large or small, industrially developed or newly industrializing) have found it desirable to move towards interdependence. The smaller countries—Taiwan, South Korea—while maintaining substantial defense establishments, recognize their dependence on the United States *in extremis*. Japan has accepted dependence on others for its security. And the NATO countries have recognized the necessity of mutual dependence both for armed forces in the field and technological support in weaponry and strategies.

Dependence is increasing and even mandated in some of the high-tech, national-security sectors, and it brings greater economic interdependence in its wake. But problems of *balance* and *degree* remain. The United States is reluctant to rely on Europe or Japan for critical weapons systems, and Europe is reluctant to rely wholly on a U.S. nuclear umbrella or trip-wire strategy. Both are careful to maintain a balance of costs and benefits in production and trade of their national-security industries in pursuit of mutual security.

In the economic realm, the increase in national welfare has been greater for those countries that have had relatively open and interdependent systems internationally—most countries of Western Europe, and North America, plus several in the Far East. Those that have chosen more "restrictive" systems internationally have not advanced as rapidly—Eastern Europe, the U.S.S.R., China, and several countries in Latin America, South Asia and Africa. (It is, of course, illogical to focus on a single factor to explain development patterns, for culture, organization, climate, etc. are also causal elements, but a strong correlation exists between "open" economic policies and national growth.) The reasons are straightforward:

1. Growth is a function of the size of the market, and both large and small countries can reach desired economies of scale in many sectors only by serving foreign markets.

2. Trade is merely a means of raising productivity through specialization, and the more choices in exchange the greater the potential productivity.

3. Foreign direct investment employs all necessary factors of production and potentially increases their efficient use still more when factors are melded also across national boundaries.

4. Science and technology are increasingly the basis of economic advance (surpassing both markets and capital in critical significance since these are *relatively*

more accessible to all). *National* sources are simply inadequate; access to foreign sources of invention and innovation is required to maintain competitive strength by making modifications and advances that lead to international specialization, at least at the margin.

Therefore, for objectives of *both* wealth and power, open policies are increasingly necessary; yet, the greater the openness the less there is need for *national* security and the greater interdependence that results. Interdependence is unavoidable in a world that assumes that material progress is required to achieve its goals of vanquishing poverty, squalor, disease, and ignorance—unless a country is willing to live wholly from the resources within its own boundaries and accept the low levels of growth that result.

The difficult question remains of the distribution of the benefits in a world that is being forced into interdependence but has not yet formed (or even recognized the necessity to form) a global *community of interests*. Until such a community is formed, each nation will *seek* to alter the international division of labor and distribution of benefits in its favor—and do so *not* by general rules but by specific interventions, each of which is likely to affect TNCs.

Policy approaches to the high-tech sectors of electronics, informatics, telecommunications, aircraft, aerospace, nuclear energy, petrochemicals, pharmaceuticals, new materials, biogenetics, and others reflect this lack of community. Many of the advanced countries and even some of the newly industrializing countries have decided that their future economic growth and competitiveness internationally depends on their ability to gain a strong position in these sectors. Many of these countries have, therefore, provided various forms of support or stimulation to companies within these sectors so they can carve out a market niche internationally or at least to retain the national market for their chosen company or companies.

Japan, for example, is providing substantial assistance to the electronics industry in the form of grants for cooperative research on very-large-scale-integrated (VLSI) circuits. France, Brazil, and Britain have subsidized their infor-

matics sector and chosen a "national champion." Japan,
Britain, Germany, and France are subsidizing telecommunications companies within their countries and giving them
preferential positions in government purchasing; France
and Germany, with other European countries, have established subsidized aircraft production; aerospace activities
are subsidized by all advanced governments having such a
sector. Nuclear energy has been supported by preferential
government purchasing or by developmental financing. Petrochemical production is subsidized particularly in the
NICs. National pharmaceutical industries are supported
through large-scale purchases by national health programs,
though prices may be controlled or negotiated. The discov-
ery and application of new materials is supported in many
countries by defense research, as is biogenetics. The Soviet
Union and China, as they begin their more open policies are
stressing the high-tech sectors in attracting foreign investment and technology transfers.

On top of these efforts, one must add the further support by state or provincial governments that are seeking to
become centers of electronics production, biogenetics,
medical instrumentation, or whatever. These subsidies are
frequently more effective in stimulating industrial activity,
or at least at redirecting its location than are national incentives. But what is gained by these policies?

Policies that control ownership, impose local-content
requirements, restrict technology transfers, control prices,
require exports, limit local borrowing, and encourage R&D
activities are aimed at increasing the gains from international production and trade. *But*, there is no firm evidence
that they achieve the *larger* objectives of industrial development. The evidence lacking is in the hidden trade-offs in the
responses by corporate investors, exporters/importers, and
foreign exchange dealers to mitigate these constraints.
Thus, ownership requirements alter technology transfers,
trade patterns, and capital flows in unknown ways in each
case. Insistence on R&D activities may produce a new laboratory, but unless the requisite conditions exist, little
comes out of it—with no resultant stimulation to local innovation. The unknown trade-offs can be multiplied. To

trace them requires research not yet done, and to make better policy requires a degree of business/government cooperation and dialogue that does not yet exist.

EFFECTS ON HIGH-TECHNOLOGY SECTORS

The effects of relatively open or closed policies on high-tech sectors depends on the reasons for the policies. If they are restricted because they are involved in national-security industries, several impacts follow: The development of the sector is likely to be subsidized through research and other financial grants as well as through government purchasing. Many of the products and techniques developed are not transferable to other sectors. Even worker skills may not be transferable. Technologies developed are restricted in terms of their transfer internationally—whether for military or commercial purposes because of their potential military use. Foreign direct investors are not encouraged in the sector; even when they are permitted, they are excluded from military-type production or sales. There is a pressure to export products in order to achieve economies of scale—even of military equipment—and this is frequently done through export subsidies of various types. There is a further impact on other countries in terms of their political/strategic position through "choosing sides in choosing a supplier." In sum, the pressure to develop high-tech, national-security industries affects the competitive position and security of all countries involved in that sector.

Apart from national-security interests, governments that have mixed policies are seeking to insure that their high-tech companies retain their national market. Their objective is to develop the economy through support of what they consider to be "key" sectors. They are seeking to upgrade workers' skills and achieve a degree of economic independence. They impose constraints on FDI in selected sectors and seek to acquire technologies that enhance local production and reduce technological dependence. Mixed-policy governments enhance this ability through subsidies to R&D activities or inducement to foreign companies to establish R&D labs within the national borders. Once again, there is pressure to export in order to achieve economies of scale and thereby reduce prices and obtain foreign exchange earnings through high value-added manufacturing.

If a government reserved the national market for a high-tech sector and did nothing more than that, announcing its intention clearly, others could adjust around it and seek an appropriate balance of risks and rewards in the remainder of the world economy. But when a government stimulates a particular sector, closes it to foreigners, even partially in both trade and investment, and then seeks to penetrate foreign markets through exports and possible investment, it shifts the burden of adjustment to other countries who are unwilling to accept those adjustments. The government is then forced to respond in like kind or to seek some accommodation with other countries to achieve appropriate balance. The dynamic aspects of high-tech sectors make achieving such balance a difficult and continuing process.

Given the dynamic nature of the high-tech sectors and the high uncertainty involved, even the adoption of international-market orientations by the more open economies raises some problems. The move to such an orientation arises from a recognition of the necessity of a world-market perspective to achieve desired efficiency and to have a market area large enough to accommodate the continuous adjustments necessary in high-tech sectors. Such an orientation leads to widespread technology exchanges and to a high degree of interdependence in the sectors involved. Unless there is a role for all potential players in each of these high-tech sectors, it is unlikely that such an open-market orientation will be achieved. To do so, intergovernmental cooperation at high levels is required, as discussed in parts IV and V.

STATE AND LOCAL GOVERNMENTS

The federal or central government is not the only level of government to have policies toward foreign investment. While it is the only one that has policies toward outflows of foreign investment, state and local governments have adopted their own policies toward FDI inflows.[4] For example, Quebec has sought foreign investment, particularly from the United States and Europe much more avidly than has the Canadian central government, which has attempted to put constraints on such inflows. Within the province of Quebec, Montreal has sought investment from English-speaking companies, while Quebec City has also sought it from French-speaking companies, though the province has imposed use of the French language on all foreign affiliates.

Within the United States, there is a constant competition among states to attract foreign investment with various incentives. (Such incentives are available to domestic companies as well.) In countries such as France or Brazil, where central government policy is somewhat constraining on foreign investment, the most vocal support for a particular project often comes from the locality in which the investment is likely to be made—both the city and province. The desire for higher employment levels, for higher-skilled employment, for a larger tax base, and for the ancillary employment and economic growth likely to be stimulated by foreign investment, causes the local or state government to use whatever political or other influence it has to push the central government into a more receptive posture.

Many of the states in the United States have promotional offices abroad—especially in Europe and Japan—which seek to attract potential investors into the state. To enhance these contacts, many governors have undertaken a variety of missions to advertise their state's opportunities. The Southeastern states have a formal association with officials stationed in Japan, which sponsors annual meetings for the purpose of discussing closer ties and greater investment by Japan in that region.

The incentives that the various states and municipalities offer are not regulated by the central government, leaving these entities to counter the restrictions imposed by the central government with some benefits of their own. These incentives include not only low-cost loans or grants, but also provision of plant facilities, offers of land, construction of infrastructure such as roads, railway sidings, airport facilities, convention centers, plus training of workers in special or generalized programs, and a wide variety of cultural attractions including sports and theater as well as educational opportunities for the families.

There is hardly a locality around the world that does not seek the contributions of foreign investors. There are a few—Paris, London, and other cities that are already crowded beyond the ability of the infrastructure to sustain the growth—that do not encourage any new industry to locate there. However, there are some such as Mexico City and São Paulo that are already overburdened but into which industry still flows. Where dispersion away from such centers is desirable, the province or state simply raises the incentives to locate some distance from these centers but still within the same province.

There is considerable disagreement as to the usefulness of such incentives. Few states or local governments have developed specific plans for their industrial growth, and generally the attractions are non-specific in terms of industrial sectors desired. However, a few states or localities have attempted to emphasize certain types of sector or industry. Such selectivity is usually not so specific as to constitute an industrial policy. The closest that states or local governments come to such planning is in the formation of industrial parks, which sometimes are centered on particular kinds of industry or merely "high-tech" companies, or "research-based" companies, or "clean" industries. These programs of development generally do not focus on a particular sector but simply on the desirability of raising the skills and wage levels of workers and the income base of the region. Successful industrial parks enlarge the community of similarly-minded managers and workers, which is a generalized enticement to other corporate investors.

General incentives such as low-cost loans, infrastructure, tax relief, or subsidies, which are as readily offered by one locality as another, introduce competitive giveaways that tend to cancel out. Still, like advertising, no locality can afford *not* to offer such incentives for fear of losing a potential investor to another locality that does offer them. In the main, this is self-defeating for all local governments, since the benefits that should accrue are greatly reduced through lower revenues and higher expenditures to support the new facility. But, knowing the eagerness of the local government to acquire the investment, the TNCs play on this desire to increase the incentives offered, negotiating for the best deal that they can so as to enhance the project's profitability.

Any efforts by the Organization of Economic Cooperation and Development (OECD) or any other intergovernmental agency to eliminate incentives offered by national governments will run into the inability of the organization to stop or mitigate the offer of such incentives by the local or state governments. These activities are, therefore, a critical part of government/business relations in the international arena and have significant consequences for the distribution of benefits.

NOTES TO CHAPTER 6

1. The UN Centre of Transnational Corporations publishes a series of documents on *National Legislation and Regulations Relating to Transnational Corporations* (New York: United Nations, 1978–).

2. See the report compiled by LICIT, *Performance Requirements* (Washington, DC: The Labor-Industry Coalition for International Trade, Mar. 1981).

3. This view is comparable to that of Paul Kennedy in *The Rise and Fall of the Great Powers*.

4. See John M. Kline, *State Government Influence on U.S. International Economics Policy* (Lexington MA: Lexington Books, 1982).

CHAPTER 7

Open Policies

The selection of an open policy by a government is not the consequence of an advanced level of development. It is more a result of decisions as to *how* growth is best achieved—i.e., through ties to international markets. The countries that are most open to the activities of foreign TNCs are those that believe that they will develop or gain from the international specialization, exchange, and profitability of TNCs. Most of these countries are "home" to TNC parent companies. They are joined by some small newly-industrializing countries that seek to attract specific activities of TNCs to assist in their economic development; to do so, these governments either identify specific sectors (e.g., textiles or electronics) and seek to attract offshore assembly or merely let TNCs identify what they can do in the host economy.

Openness to foreign TNCs is related also to host-country policies toward the domestic private sector. The greater the role of the private sector (relative to state-owned companies[1]) and the less government intervention or control, the greater the role and freedom likely to be permitted to foreign business. The portion of GDP expended by the government does not appear to be a significant factor in forming policies toward foreign TNCs; as shown in Table 7.1. Some of the smallest government sectors appear in LDCs, some of which are restrictive and others open. Conversely, most Western European countries have large public sectors—constituting about half of GDP—but "open" policies toward TNCs and their own private sectors. Thus, *policies* toward the private sector are more important than government *size* in determining the reception of TNCs.

The specific policies affecting foreign TNCs relate to FDI entry conditions, tariffs and nontariff barriers on imports, export subsidies, controls on international financial flows,

Table 7.1: Central Government Expenditure out of GDP
1985 and FDI Policy Positions

Country	Percent	Position	Country	Percent	Position
Israel	68	O	Venezuela	26	M
Netherlands	57	O	Singapore	26	O
Belgium	56	O	United States	25	O
France	45	M	Costa Rica	25	O
Kuwait	43	M	Brazil	21	M
United Kingdom	41	O	Argentina	18	M
Chile	36	O	Japan	18	M/O
Spain	32	M	Korea	18	M/O
Germany	31	O	India	17	R
Canada	27	O	Philippines	11	M
			Yugoslavia	7	R-M

O = Open
M = Mixed
R = Restrictive
Source: Expenditures from World Bank, World Development Report,
          Washington, D.C., 1987. pp. 246–247

local-content rules, buy-national regulations, and others.
Open countries impose few limitations on TNC activities
and offer treatment to foreign firms equal that of domestic
companies—that is, provide "national treatment."

COUNTRY POLICIES

Along the continuum of policies, the United States and
Canada present the least restrictive approach to TNCs, followed by West Germany and the United Kingdom. Among
NICs, two of the Four Tigers of Asia (Hong Kong and Singapore) have very few limitations on foreign business entry,
though they provide guidance to enterprise in general. In
addition, a few other LDCs have established highly market-
oriented regimes in an attempt to attract more foreign capital and technology to their economies (e.g., Chile). Finally,
there are several countries that have created unrestricted
legal environments to attract specific kinds of business
such as banking and finance (e.g., Panama, the Bahamas,
the Cayman Islands, and the British Channel Islands). However, even the most open countries have tight controls over

some sectors for reasons of national security or protection of health and the general welfare.

United States

The United States has chosen to maintain a "free-market" or "free-enterprise" system as a critical element in its economic development. In a belief that this system would be good for others and is good for itself even if others do not adopt it, the United States since 1933 has espoused the *principle* of freedom of trade and captial movements; it has argued against protectionism in foreign trade and investment, the use of direct controls, and state-owned enterprises (SOEs). It has been more liberal in capital movements than in trade.

U.S. rules on foreign firms are virtually identical to the rules facing domestic U.S. firms. No discrimination is practiced toward foreign business in general, though some restrictions do exist on firms that supply products and services to defense-related business. That is, some activities such as designing, producing, and installing military equipment are limited to domestic firms (although components used in this equipment many times *are* imported or made by foreign-owned firms in the United States.) Ostensibly for "national security" reasons, the U.S. government blocked the Japanese acquisition of Fairchild Semiconductor in March 1987; however, it was viewed in the business press as a tactic of "industrial strategy" to protect some new initiatives taken to stimulate U.S. technology in semiconductors—especially since Fairchild was owned by Schlumberger (a French corporation).

However, some exceptions to these open policies do exist with reference to certain foreign countries. The United States disallows the purchase of U.S. businesses by agents of several Communist countries (viz., Cuba, Kampuchea, Nicaragua, North Korea, and Vietnam). But Communist government agencies from the Soviet Union, China, and other countries operate in U.S. markets, particularly in international banking and trading activities though they have not set up industrial plants. Restrictions also exist on firms from other countries deemed unfriendly to the United States, such as Iran and Libya.

The U.S. government also owns a few businesses. The Postal Service is a government-owned company, which has been granted monopoly rights to provide first-class mail delivery. Even the scope of this business has been curtailed, since the government permits others to provide express mail, regular package delivery, and other forms of document transmittal, such as telex and telefax. (The governmental Post-Telephone-Telegraph (PTT) in many other countries holds a monopoly over postal and telecommunications service.)

The U.S. government also owns and operates a major electric power utility (the Tennessee Valley Authority) in the southeastern part of the country and Amtrak passenger rail service in the northeast. Beyond these examples, the Federal government operates only in a regulatory capacity in businesses—such as telecommunications, electric power provision, and transportation service—that are often government-owned in other countries.

The U.S. government also reserves some business activities to domestic providers, such as the press, radio and television transmission, freshwater shipping (Great Lakes and major rivers), and domestic air transportation. Each of these industries is limited to firms owned at least 75 percent by U.S. interests. In addition, operation of nuclear power facilities, development of federally owned lands, and work on classified U.S. government contracts is restricted to U.S. firms only.

But there are no Federal limits on foreign firms buying U.S. real estate, financial institutions, industrial companies, or other direct or portfolio investments. (Some individual states do restrict a few activities, such as foreign ownership of state-regulated commercial banks, and some are seeking to impose restrictions on land purchases and on timber.) The U.S. government provides national treatment to non-national firms in virtually all sectors.

There are no limits on percentage ownership by foreign firms, nor on methods of market entry such as acquisition, joint-venture, or start-up. Mergers and acquisitions that would create monopolies or near-monopolies are usually not permitted, without regard to the nationality of the firms involved. Thus, any foreign firm from a "friendly" country has only to follow the incorporation steps for any domestic company in order to begin "doing business" in the United States. Some difficulties with visas for foreign managers and engineers appear as unnecessary obstacles to others.

The Committee on Foreign Investment in the United States (CFIUS) was established in 1975 within the executive branch to review FDI inflows that might adversely affect U.S. interests. The concerns arose largely due to investment from OPEC countries, who, it was feared, could use the growth in petrodollars to enter and perhaps control important segments of U.S. business.[2] CFIUS reviews investment trends, provides guidance on prospective inflows, and considers proposals for new legislation or regulations on FDI. It has no authority to approve or disapprove FDI inflows.

Despite its open policy, which has been reaffirmed by both the Reagan and Bush administrations, as a result of the increasing inflow of FDI and the rising frequency of mergers and acquisitions from abroad, Congress added a provision to the 1988 Omnibus Trade Bill restricting FDI inflows that were determined to adversely affect "national security." This provision, known as the Exon-Florio Provision, expands the authority held through several other avenues, but using different methods, to restrict FDI inflows. Thus, there are individual statutes restricting foreign ownership of nuclear energy and communications; the Defense Production Act maintains domestic ownership of the production of some military materiel; a review process (required under Hart-Scott-Rodino and other antitrust laws) treats anticompetitive mergers and acquisitions; and *in extremis*, the International Emergency Economic Powers Act could be used to impose restrictions on foreign investment or operations in the United States.

The Exon-Florio provision arose out of the projected purchase by Fujitsu (Japan) of the Fairchild Semi-Conductor Corp., previously bought by a French company, Schlumberger. Since the Emergency Powers Act requires declaration of a national emergency relative to the foreign country, it was not useful in this case. Congress considered that additional and wider authority was needed by the President to block such a takeover if he desired. This new provision authorized the President to block or suspend

mergers, acquisitions or takeovers by foreign persons that
he determines might threaten to impair national security.
The administration accepted the provision as proper and
within the generalized "open policy," though the legislative
history shows that the term "national security" is intended
to be broadly defined and not confined to any specific industry sector. A review and presidential decision is to be
completed within 90 days.

The process of review and recommendation was dele-
gated to CFIUS, with the Treasury implementing the regulations. But, the new regulations do put a burden on potential
new projects or mergers to notify CFIUS of the intended investment. Since the regulations went into effect, some 40
proposals have been submitted voluntarily to CFIUS; three
investigations were instituted, with one completed in which
the President chose not to intervene. If CFIUS decides not
to investigate, no further action can be taken against the
proposal, but if it does, the matter must proceed to a presidential decision.

Canada

Canada presents a similar perspective to foreign firms
seeking to operate there, with some notable exceptions. The
economy under the current Progressive-Conservative government is broadly open to participation of foreign firms, in
contrast to the restrictive policy of the Liberal government
from the mid-1960s until 1984. In the post-World War II period, the private sector has accounted for most of GNP as
each of Canada's national governments has adopted free-
market principles.

However, a Foreign Investment Review Agency (FIRA)
was used from 1973–1985 to screen FDI proposals and to
permit only those that clearly offered net benefits to the
country. This agency varied in its openness to FDI according to the party in power—refusing very few FDI applications under the Conservatives; and rejecting many under
the Liberals. In 1985, FIRA was replaced by a new agency,
called Investment Canada, to attract more FDI.

With its tight ties to the United States—interdependent
both economically and militarily—Canada has elected to
maintain an open policy. Given the demonstrated employment, income, and balance-of-payments benefits from allow-

ing U.S. firms to operate in Canada for production that is sold in both countries, Canada is unlikely to change this basic orientation. However, there is an underlying current of nationalism that can be played upon by a charismatic leader, so the question is not closed. Access to Canada by U.S.-based TNCs is likely to increase significantly under the new U.S.-Canada Free Trade Agreement, discussed in Chapter 12.

The range of government-owned companies in Canada is much larger than in the United States. The national government owns or controls 62 crown corporations; these profit-seeking firms are mostly involved in public utilities, finance, and energy. The largest of these is Petro-Canada, the national oil company. Another highly-visible crown corporation is Air Canada, the national airline. The combined assets of all crown corporations in 1987 was approximately U.S. $40 billion, compared to a GNP of about U.S. $354 billion.[3]

Limits on foreign firms' activities in Canada are fairly few. Most of the rules affecting non-Canadian investors are aimed at service industries such as banking, the media, advertising, airlines, and coastal shipping. In addition, fishing rights are restricted to Canadians, and real estate purchases by foreigners are subject to various restrictions by the different provincial governments. The provinces, analogous to the American states but with greater autonomy, establish rules that sometimes discriminate against foreign investors in many or all sectors and at other times provide incentives to attract them. Thus, Quebec encourages FDI inflows (to strengthen itself against English-speaking Canada), but Alberta and Saskatchewan have been generally opposed to TNC incursions.

Also similar to the United States, Canada does not impose restrictions on a foreign affiliate's access to foreign exchange, nor does Canada's government restrict the foreign exchange market in general. Dividends, royalties, fees, interest payments, etc., may be paid abroad with no special permission, although withholding taxes do apply.

United Kingdom

After Canada, the United Kingdom has remained the second largest recipient of U.S. FDI. Its growth was strongly stimulated during the 1960s and 1970s. The United Kingdom differs from the United States in its receptivity toward foreign TNCs mainly through its operation of state-owned enterprises. That is, many large and significant U.K. companies are government-owned, and they are given preference in government purchasing, somewhat limiting the opportunities for foreign competitors. Despite the government policy in the 1980s to privatize many SOEs, the number and importance of government-owned firms remaining cannot be ignored.

Major examples of SOEs include: British Leyland (BL), British Rail, British Steel, British Nuclear Fuels, and the National Coal Board. Each of these firms is majority or wholly owned by the British government, and each one is a dominant competitor in its industry. In the past four years, a number of other key SOEs have been sold to the private sector—e.g.: British Gas, British Airways, British Telecom, and British Petroleum—in an effort to reverse socialism. The net result is that state ownership of industry remains a fact of life in British business, but the opportunities open to foreign TNCs are widening. In all, British government expenditures account for 41 percent of GDP and those of SOEs for 11 percent more.[4]

British restrictions on incoming FDI are virtually non-existent. A few exceptions exist in that some industry segments are restricted to domestic providers; for example, ownership of media such as television and radio broadcasting. Also, the acquisition of an existing British bank or securities firm by a foreign TNC requires that the parent country permit similar acquisitions by British investors there. Finally, the British government has established limits on foreign shareholding in some of the privatized SOEs, such as British Gas and British Airways.

No government agency monitors FDI activities in the United Kingdom, and no reporting requirements exist for foreign investors different from domestic investors, except in the cases of acquisition of financial institutions, as mentioned above. The single legal consideration that could preclude a foreign investment from being undertaken via acquisition of an existing British firm is the impact on competition, i.e., the antitrust implications. Both domestic and foreign firms are precluded from abusing monopolies, dominating markets against the public interest, and operating cartels. Thus, acquisition of a British firm must be reviewed by one or more government agencies before receiving final permission.

Money and capital markets function freely in the United Kingdom, with no exchange controls, no limits on foreign or domestic holdings of securities, bank accounts, or other financial instruments. There are no limits on profit remittances, royalties, interest payments, or other international financial flows.

The British government also offers incentives to attract capital investment in depressed areas of the country—as in Scotland and Wales.[5] The incentives involve low-cost loans, plant construction, tax waivers, and so forth; they are offered to both domestic and foreign investors.

Since the United Kingdom belongs to the European Community (EC), trade policy clearly favors firms from other EC countries. There are no tariffs on industrial goods traded within the EC, while imports from outside the region face varying tariffs, quotas, and other (generally low) barriers.

West Germany

Policies of the Federal Republic of Germany are quite similar to the other open economies. While West Germany belongs to the EC and places some barriers on international business from non-EC countries, it nonetheless follows a free-market regime. Among the EC countries, West Germany has the smallest government sector, accounting for only 31 percent of GDP compared to the EC average of about 50 percent. Consequently, West Germany has policies toward domestic and foreign business that are more similar to those of the United States than to those of its continental Common Market partners.

There are almost no industries reserved to the government or government-owned firms, with the two major exceptions of the postal service and railroads. Even in industries where SOEs exist, foreign firms are permitted to operate freely. Foreign firms may incorporate and do business in Germany just as domestically-owned firms—i.e., national treatment is provided. There is no foreign investment board or agency and no separate approval process for establishing a foreign-owned business. The regulatory environment facing foreign investors is virtually identical to that in the United States, though differences do exist in regulations on all firms (foreign or domestic) on such aspects as environmental protection, illicit payments, product liability, and discrimination.

State-owned companies do play a larger role in West Germany than in the United States. Several major industrial companies are government owned, including Salzgitter (a steel firm 100 percent owned) and Saarbergwerke (a mining firm 74 percent owned). Certain, major service firms such as Lufthansa airline and the telephone company (PTT), are also state owned. To increase industrial competitiveness, the government embarked on a privatization campaign in the mid-1980s that has led to sale of its 20 percent share of Volkswagen and its 25 percent share of VEBA, the country's largest industrial firm. In the late 1980s, state ownership of business continued to decline.

No limits on international financial flows exist. Foreign firms may invest freely in wholly owned or joint-venture affiliates, in new ventures or acquisitions, and their earnings may be remitted without limit. No restrictions exist on royalty payments, capital repatriation, foreign loans, etc. But, any financial (or other) practices that serve to restrict competition are prohibited, for domestic as well as foreign firms.

The government does seek to channel foreign and domestic investment into selected industries and locations. Incentives are offered by the federal government and by state (laender) governments within Germany to attract capital investment into depressed areas. So extensive are these federal grants, that other EC countries have demanded a reduction in the level of financial subsidy offered. In addition to regional incentives, several programs offer assistance to businesses established in West Berlin*. A federal R&D program offers substantial support to development of new technology, though it limits most of the assistance to small and medium-sized firms. Thus, it is fair to conclude that

---

*This assistance will be expanded to firms in East Germany, upon reunification, but the process is not yet clearly defined.

West Germany offers a wider range of incentives to attract foreign business than do the United States, the United Kingdom, and Canada.

Restrictions on imports are few, other than the comparative preference for EC imports relative to those from outside countries. The EC's common external tariff structure is generally not prohibitive, and few quotas exist. Imports from other EC countries enter duty-free. However, a number of nontariff and nonquota barriers are the focus of reduction or removal by 1992 within Europe and under GATT negotiations with the rest of the world.

Sweden

Sweden is one of the few remaining countries in Western Europe that has not joined the European Community, though its business system and government policies are quite similar to those in the EC, and it has a preferential position in the EC, as do other members of European Free Trade Association (see Chapter 12). Free enterprise is a fundamental part of the economy, and SOEs coexist with private companies in many industries. Sweden is home to a number of large TNCs (e.g., Electrolux, ASEA, SAAB, Alfa-Laval, Volvo and L. M. Ericsson; ASEA has recently merged with Brown-Boveri of Switzerland into ABB). It views both incoming and outgoing FDI favorably.

For the most part, foreign TNCs seeking entry into Sweden receive equal treatment with domestic firms. Investments in newly formed firms require registration with the Swedish authorities, but the process takes only a few days, and problems seldom arise. When the FDI enters via acquisition of an existing Swedish firm, the process is somewhat more complicated, since the Ministry of Industry must approve acquisitions and mergers. In addition, many Swedish firms have an "alien ownership clause" in their bylaws, which stipulates that at least 60 percent of their shares must be held by Swedish nationals. This common practice makes acquisitions by foreign TNCs relatively difficult, though both the shareholders and the government may consider a particular contribution important enough to warrant an acquisition of more than 40 percent and thereby extend approval.

Only a few activities are precluded from foreign TNCs' participation—including utilities, munitions, and ownership of Swedish-registered ships. Also, foreign firms are limited to 20 percent ownership of natural resource ventures in Sweden, unless special permission is obtained. Beyond these limits, foreign firms receive the same treatment as domestic firms in the same industries.

One aspect of the Swedish business system that differs notably from those of other European countries (except West Germany) is the participation of labor in company management. The concept of codetermination that was introduced in West Germany in the 1950s has also been followed in Sweden, with the result that labor has an important say in decisions such as plant openings and closing, acquisitions, and profit distribution. For example, unions must be notified in advance in the event of a plant closing. Also, an acquisition must be approved formally by the trade union(s) involved before it may take place. The participation of labor in company decision making is much greater in Sweden than in most other countries.

The government functions mostly as regulator of the private sector economy, though SOEs are important. These account for about 9 percent of GDP, and they exist in a wide range of industries. Basic public utilities are all state owned and operated. In addition, SOEs exist in banking, chemicals, food products, construction, engineering, hotels, and many other businesses. The government in recent years has functioned as an investor of last resort in companies facing financial crisis when bankruptcy would lead to serious unemployment. In practice, when such firms have been placed on viable footing after the government investment, they were often resold to the private sector. In 1987, one-third of the state-owned conglomerate, SAAB, was sold to the public, as was a 19 percent share in the state holding company, Precordia.[6]

There are no local-content requirements (though informal persuasion does exist in major government purchases), only occasional price controls, and no limits on technology transfers or financial transactions. Repatriation of capital is subject to permission from the central bank, but this is usually a formality. Incentives to attract capital investment apply equally to local and foreign firms, and such incentives are generally given to attract firms to depressed areas and industries.

Trade restrictions are minimal, with low tariff rates and few nontariff barriers. Except for agricultural products, all merchandise trade with EC and European Free Trade Association member countries is free of tariffs. Sweden is as open as the other Western European countries in international trade.

Hong Kong

Hong Kong and Singapore are two Asian city-states whose economic viability has been based on broad acceptance and even active promotion of free-market capitalism. Each of these states actively promotes incoming FDI and places few restrictions on the activities of foreign-owned firms within their territories. As a result of these policies and the availability of low-cost, hard-working labor forces, both are classed among the handful of NICs that are positioned to influence the industrial patterns of the future—despite their small size.[7]

Hong Kong faces probably the most difficult task of any of the NICs in achieving full industrial status. With the impending reversion of this British colony to Chinese rule in 1997, its future remains uncertain. While this situation has not led to any massive disinvestment from the colony, such outflows have occurred, and wealthy citizens are seeking homes in Canada and the United Kingdom. Also some reduction in the volume of incoming FDI has occurred and will likely continue. The other side of this coin is that Hong Kong after 1997 will have even closer ties to China, which (with a population of 1.1 billion) offers a large potential market and opportunities for FDI. Firms in Hong Kong may find easier access to the rest of China at that time, and some are already taking advantage of the relaxation by China to establish a number of ventures there using low-cost labor. Many of these arrangements are for "contract manufacturing," which has been singularly important as a means of Japanese, U.S., and European investment in Hong Kong.

Hong Kong treats FDI inflows as though they were domestic investment. Public utilities are limited to government ownership, but the rest of the economy is open to private-sector, domestic, and foreign firms. This policy is even less restrictive than those of the industrial countries discussed previously, mainly because Hong Kong has no key sectors in manufacturing that the colony could protect (such as national defense industries or domestic automobile companies). Since the entire colony is quite small geographically, the opportunities for large-scale manufacturing or other land-intensive ventures are few. Much of Hong Kong's FDI inflow is in real estate, banking, and other financial services, because of its long history as an entrepôt.

No restrictions exist on international capital flows; on the contrary, one of Hong Kong's main industries is the offshore banking sector. Profit remittances, interest payments, royalties, and other international financial flows are freely permitted.

Chile

Chile has been the most open country in South America since the overthrow of the leftist Allende government in 1973. Still, it has not received a large inflow of FDI. This result shows that, to be effective, open policies must be supported by sound economic and political conditions. The government, led by General Augusto Pinochet, pursued a liberal economic policy through the 1980s, with few restrictions on the activities of foreign firms and an increasing willingness to privatize many of the state-owned firms. The economy was opened to stimulate growth and to overcome the negative perceptions by TNCs of Chile (due to the nationalization of the copper companies by Allende's government and the generally antagonistic view of that regime toward foreign firms). After more than a decade of openness, Chile shows no signs of changing its approach. In late 1988, General Pinochet himself was rejected in a plebiscite by the voters, but he remained in office until early 1990. Policies of the freely elected government of Patricio Alwyn have preserved the free-market economy and appear likely to continue in this direction in the future.

Despite its promotion of free enterprise and openness toward foreign firms, Chile continues to leave a large portion of the national economy in the hands of the state. As a legacy of socialism and of strong government control under Pinochet, the central government and SOEs account for almost half of GDP and control more than three-fourths of the shares of the largest 100 firms in the country.

On the other hand, Chile's privatization program is proceeding in earnest to divest partial or total shares in dozens of major SOEs. Controlling ownership in the national railroad system plus several electric power companies and telecommunications networks (Ental and Telex Chile) is being sold to private investors. Many more manufacturing firms have already been sold and are being offered to private sector purchasers. Despite an orientation toward private-sector growth and a free-market system, the importance of the government sector as a producer of income and employment will remain significant in the future.

FDI is regulated under Decree Law 600, which was passed in 1974 as a measure to attract more foreign firms to the investment-starved economy. This law largely offers the TNCs access to the Chilean market under conditions similar to those available to domestic Chilean firms. The Foreign Investment Committee, charged with approving applications for FDI projects, has rejected few proposals during its 15-year history.

The only sectors expressly prohibited to foreign investors are television broadcasting and industries that could affect national security. FDI is permitted, even in the copper mining industry, though the state firm, Codelco, had controlled most of the mines since the nationalizations between 1969 and 1973. The petroleum sector is open to foreign firms, but all oil produced must be sold to the state-owned oil company, ENAP. Finally, the insurance industry is only opened to minority ownership (up to 33 percent) by foreign firms, though they may operate freely as joint ventures.

Few restrictions exist on company operations. Local-content requirements are placed only on automotive products, where the minimum is 13 percent local value-added (compared to the 50 to 100 percent required in many other Latin American countries). Price controls are used only on basic utilities at present.

There are no limitations on remittances of profits, interest payments, royalties, etc.—except that access to foreign exchange requires approval from the Central Bank. Permission is routinely granted without significant delay. Initial capital investments cannot be repatriated for three years, though they face no limits after that time. In sum, the foreign exchange regime is open at present, but it could be restricted easily, since permissions from the Central Bank to buy foreign exchange could be delayed.

International trade policy is liberal, with a uniform tariff of 15 percent ad valorem on most products. An import license from the Central Bank is required on all imported goods, though obtaining the permit has not presented important problems for importers during the Pinochet regime. All import shipments are subject to Chile's value-added tax, which currently carries at a rate of 20 percent of the landed value of the goods in Chile.

Chile's attraction to FDI was principally to resource seekers (copper). With that door closed, it has not yet shown an ability to attract market seekers and is too remote to attract efficiency seekers.

Policy Review

The policies of the open countries are compared in Chart 7.1. (pp. 140–41). They form a clear contrast with the more restrictive environments present in the mixed and restrictive countries, described in chapters 8 and 9. Except for reserving some public services such as telephone, air transportation, and the media to local and/or government enterprises, the open countries do not restrict FDI entry or exit. Tariffs are quite low in these countries, and (with a few exceptions) other import restrictions such as licensing requirements are not used. International financial flows are largely unrestricted. Intellectual property protection is greatest in these open countries. Local-content requirements, price controls, and other competitive restrictions are seldom used. In all, the open countries are significantly more receptive of and attractive to TNCs than those with mixed and restrictive policies.

TNC RESPONSES

Given that the rules on foreign business are least restrictive in the open countries, and that many of the world's

Table 7.2: Foreign Direct Investment. Selected Countries. 1977 and 1987 (millions of U.S. dollars)

| COUNTRIES | 1977 | | 1987 | |
	FDI OUTFLOWS	FDI INFLOWS	FDI OUTFLOWS	FDI INFLOWS
U.S.A.	11,897	3,724	44,171	41,960
U.K.	3,291	2,309	25,745	9,401
Canada	1,505	1,031	5,069	4,146
W. Germany	2,218	969	9,207	1,953
Chile	5	21	8	105
Hong Kong	n.a.	145	n.a.	203

Source: International Monetary Fund, Balance of Payments Statistics, 1988. (U.S. Dollar/SDR Rate: 1977 = 1.16752, 1987 = 1.29307)
(Note: the balancing of FDI inflows and outflows of the United States during the past decade, as firms from other countries have rapidly expanded their transnational business. Also note the continuing net FDI outflows that characterizes Europe's two largest economies, West Germany and the United Kingdom.

largest economies are included among them, it is not surprising to see that a large portion of total international business takes place among them. Table 7.2 offers a view of the value of inward and outward FDI for the open countries discussed above.

Examples of TNC investments in the open countries demonstrate the responses of these companies to open policies, the significance of such business, and the nature of the bargaining relationships involved.

Japanese FDI in the United States

The openness of the United States to FDI permitted a rapid inflow of investment from Japan in the 1980s, raising a series of issues. A major inflow occurred in the auto sector, but large investments were made in other manufacturing and service sectors as well. As a result of the dramatic increase in U.S. imports of cars made by Nissan, Toyota, and Honda (and to a lesser extent Isuzu, Subaru, and Mazda) during the oil crises of the 1970s, American car manufacturers found their profits and market shares dropping rapidly. This demand for imports arose from the Japanese

Chart 7.1: Summary of Policies

RESTRICTIONS	U.S.A.	Canada	West Germany	United Kingdom	Sweden	Hong Kong	Chile
1. FDI entry and exit	Open. Some limitations on defense-related business. FDI coming even from communist countries.	Some limits on foreign equity in banking, real state, transportation, media, and securities firms.	Transportation, postal, banking & insurance activities subject to special licensing. All other areas open to FDI.	Ownership restricted on television and radio stations.	Prohibited in domestic air transportation, Swedish-registered vessels, municipations (large scale), and credit-record agencies.	No fields are off limits to FDI except those reserved for SOEs: public transportation & media, waterworks and airports.	Prohibited in TV stations and industries affecting national security. Only 1/3 foreign equity in insurance companies.
2. Import limitations	4.2% average industrial tariff. Quotas on cotton & fibers and some dairy products. Banned: certain narcotics and fur skins.	From U.S.:tariffs on publications, computer parts, semiconductors. From Asian Countries: clothing & automobiles.	For certain items from Taiwan, Japan, Korea, Hong Kong and the GDR.	Mainly those imposed by the EEC: iron & steel, textiles & fibers.	Banned all imports from South Africa and major agricultural products. Quotas for textiles from Asian countries.	Licenses required for textiles, rice, & frozen meats. Duties on beverages (alcoholic & non), tobacco & cosmetics.	15% ad valorem tariff. Forbidden: caviar, pearls, gems and synthetic fur clothing.
3. Financial flows	Restrictions only to nationals or authorities from Cuba, Vietnam, North Korea, and Cambodia.	No limitation, although a withholding tax applies on dividends.	No restrictions.	No restrictions.	Free, without limits. Formal approval from central bank.	No restrictions.	Original capital can be repatriated after 36 mo.; net profits at any time. All FX transactions need approval from Central Bank

4. Intellectual property	Highly developed system of patent & trademark licensing. Trade policies linked with IP protection in investor's country.	Patents are 93% foreign-owned. Patents & trademarks highly protected with the exception of pharmaceuticals.	Patent & trademark laws satisfactorily enforced. Penalties are roughly equivalent to what a license would have cost	Complex law and procedures but meticulously observed & enforced by U.K. Licensees and courts.	Infringements are rare and solved by exchanging rights. No regulation on licensing or royalties: commercial negotiation.	With the exception of computer software, effective brand & trademark protection.	Liberal policy on licensing agreements; all types of arrangements are authorized.
5. Local content requirements	None	Only indirectly to qualify for tariff rebates (U.S.-Canada auto pact) or for export insurance or credit	None	Only indirectly to qualify for incentives, export insurance and licenses.	None	No local-content requirements	Reduced but still effective for the automotive sector.
6. Price controls	None	None	Maximum prices on rent, minimum prices for agricultural products (EEC), price-calculation ordinances for utilities.	Some public utilities and milk.	Some to cope with devaluations and wage agreements.	On public transportation charges and electricity monopolies.	Only for postal services; water, electricity & telephone rates; and long-distance overland mass transportation rates.

Source: Investing, Licensing, and Trading, New York: Business International Corp., 1988

design of small, fuel-efficient cars and the low cost of Japanese cars due to high productivity and the "overvalued" dollar. But high imports continued through the 1970s, even after the dollar devaluation and American production of new smaller cars.

The success of Japanese cars in the U.S. market led to pressure from domestic companies to protect them against the Japanese. By 1981, orderly marketing agreements (Voluntary Export Restraints) were negotiated between Japan and the United States that limited the number of Japanese cars imported. The Japanese were later told they "should" invest in the United States to produce cars locally, under threat of further barriers to imports; but, no local-content requirements were imposed. To avoid losses of market share, the major Japanese auto firms made substantial investments in production facilities in the United States during the 1980s. Several states competed for these new entrants, and the Southeast states set up a joint commission with the Japanese (governments and companies) to attract new investors. Some U.S. auto companies welcomed joint ventures in U.S. plants with the Japanese, hoping to reduce cost and raise quality through Japanese technology.

The Japanese TNCs preferred to export from their home country, but when forced to invest abroad, to gain raw materials or access to markets, they responded readily. The attraction of Japanese FDI into the United States was also enhanced by the devaluation of the dollar from 280 yen in the early 1980s to 120 yen in the late 1980s, making American assets cheap in Japanese terms. Japanese companies consequently invested in a wide range of manufacturing and service sectors including chemicals, light machinery, light trucks, tires and rubber products, plastics, toys, as well as banks, brokerages, and investment firms. They also bought land and real estate and set up a number of "green field" operations (new plants) in regions around the country. Following these investments were many supplier companies which did not want to lose their position with the parent companies, particularly those related to the auto industry. As a consequence, some U.S. labor shifted from employment in American companies to Japanese affiliates—sometimes from one component supplier to another in the same sector. Japanese also invested in tourism and hotels, developing tourist packages sold for yen in Japan and keeping all the revenue in Japan except the necessary expenses in the United States. The existence of Japanese-owned supplier companies in the United States kept the business "within the family." The lack of requirements in the United States on joint-venture ownership permitted this kind of "wholly owned" and vertically and horizontally integrated investment, with the profits of the entire complex flowing back to Japan.

The moves by Japanese auto producers into U.S. manufacturing were principally a response to U.S. government policy (enforced through Voluntary Export Restraint by the producers in Japan), which sought to reduce the trade deficit with Japan. Given the huge U.S. market and the ready availability of alternative suppliers of autos, the Japanese firms had a weak bargaining position and great deal at stake in the potential loss of market share. (Their situation would be located in Figure 7.1. on point J between corners R_4 and R_3 at the back.)

While Japanese auto investment was clearly stimulated by the Voluntary Export Restraint, direct investment from most major countries surged into the United States during the 1980s. Table 7.3 shows the trend in FDI inflows.

The government's position in fostering an open economy has precluded barriers to incoming FDI. Consequently, as the dollar weakened in foreign exchange markets after 1985 and as more non-U.S. TNCs expanded their operations, a flood of direct investments entered the United States, attracted by the world's largest national market.

Debt/Equity Swaps in Chile

The highly open policy environment facing TNCs in Chile since 1974 has attracted far less FDI than hoped by the government, due initially to lack of confidence in the policy's permanence and due later to the Latin American debt crisis. However, the Chilean government succeeded in attracting more FDI than others in Latin America in the late 1980s by permitting "debt/equity swaps." These swaps permit foreign bank lenders to sell their problem loans back to the government in exchange for local currency that must be invested in equity projects. Generally, these deals involve a bank that sells its loan to another foreign firm for cash in

Figure 7.1: The Bargaining Relationship Between TNC and
Host Government

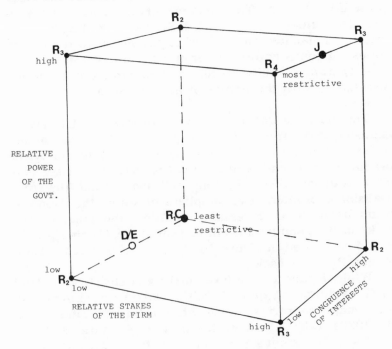

Regulation levels			Point(s)	level (X+Y+Z)
	low	high		
Firm Stake (X)	0	1	R_1 (M)	0
Govt Power (Y)	0	1	R_2	1
Congruence (Z)	1	0	R_3	2
			R_4 (G)	3

dollars (at a large discount on the order of 50 percent of
face value) and a direct investment by the other foreign firm
in some project such as a manufacturing company or other
type of business venture in Chile.* Chile's open policy has

---

*The Central Bank then redeems the loan *in pesos* to the direct investor
at a value somewhere between 50 percent and 100 percent of the original
loan value.

Table 7.3: Cumulative Foreign Investment in the United
States by Select Countries, 1980–1987 (in billions of
dollars)

	1980	1981	1982	1983	1984	1985	1986	1987	Percent Change 1986 to 1987	1980 to 1987
U.K.	14.1	18.6	28.4	32.2	38.4	43.6	55.9	74.9	34	431
Netherlands	19.1	26.8	26.2	29.2	33.7	37.1	40.7	47.0	15	146
Japan	4.7	7.7	9.7	11.3	16.0	19.3	26.8	33.4	25	611
Canada	12.2	12.1	11.7	11.4	15.3	17.1	20.3	21.7	7	78
West Germany	7.6	9.5	9.9	10.8	12.3	14.8	17.3	19.6	13	158
Switzerland	5.1	5.5	6.4	7.5	8.1	10.6	12.1	14.3	18	180
France	3.7	5.9	5.7	5.7	6.6	6.7	7.7	10.2	32	176
Subtotal (7 countries)	66.5	86.1	98.0	108.1	130.4	149.2	180.8	221.1	22	232
Total	83.0	108.7	124.7	137.1	164.6	184.6	220.4	261.4	19	216

Source: 1986, 1987: Bureau of Economic Analysis, Department of Com-
merce, unpublished data. 1982–1985: Survey of Current
Business, Aug. 1987, p. 96, 97. 1980, 1981: Survey of Current
Business, Aug. 1985, p. 63.

provided more opportunities and attraction for such swaps
than in other debtor countries, but it required a substantial
discount to overcome other unfavorable factors. By the end
of 1988, over U.S. $2 billion of debt/equity swaps had been
carried out in Chile, reducing the total foreign debt by about
10 percent and resulting in a rise of FDI by more than 50
percent over previous years. In this case, the government
had a relatively weak bargaining position with much at
stake. (The situation would be located in Figure 7.1 at the
point between corners R_1 and the lower left R_2.)

U.S. TNCs' Ownership of Canada

Although Canadian policy has been something of a
roller-coaster ride with respect to FDI, the net result has
been long-term ownership of Canadian firms by U.S. investors plus establishment of new affiliates. That is, a large
percentage of key industries in Canada is owned by foreign

interests, typically U.S.-based TNCs. Despite the use of the Foreign Investment Review Agency to screen new FDI projects during the 1970s and early 1980s, Canada never reversed this aspect of its economy.

The broadly welcoming environment has resulted in substantial development of manufacturing and extractive industry in Canada, though with foreign control over decision making in these firms. Policy debates have shown dissatisfaction among the Canadian public, despite the desired growth. The concerns were raised to the level of party differences in the election of 1988, in which the U.S./Canadian Free Trade Agreement became a matter of national referendum. The agreement itself was a recognition of the extensive and intimate ties across the border. Victory in the 1988 general election by the Progressive-Conservative Party headed by Brian Mulroney was viewed as a vote of confidence in the Prime Minister's open policy and support for the U.S./Canada Free Trade Agreement. In terms of the bargaining model, the Canadian government apparently feels that the position is somewhere near point C (Figure 7.1) at which the TNCs offer substantial benefits and the government has a great deal at stake, while government and TNC interests are quite similar.

POLICY ISSUES

Although the countries discussed above have adopted open policies, there are continuing debates as to the appropriateness of these policies, given the flow of FDI and trade. The continued large annual trade deficits of the United States, one-third of which were with Japan during the last half of the 1980s, raised intense political debates over protectionism and reciprocity in rules and regulations concerning trade. Bills were introduced into Congress requiring the application of protective measures, particularly against Japan (unless the Japanese opened up their markets in the same fashion that the United States maintained). The 1988 Trade Act authorized the President to impose restrictions unless reciprocity was granted in his view, and in May 1989 the President invoked these provisions against Japan.

An additional issue had been raised with Japan, relating to technology. Toshiba, under license from a U.S. TNC, violated U.S. prohibitions against the export of defense-related products or technology to Soviet bloc countries. Its subsidiary in Norway shipped high-tech milling equipment to the U.S.S.R. for production of submarine propellers that would be too quiet to be detected by sonar. Toshiba began extensive and costly lobbying (calculated at over $4 million) under the auspices of MITI's office in New York and through U.S. law firms to prevent imposition of sanctions by Congress. It was so successful that a further concern arose over the potential influence (if not dominance) of Japanese interests in the United States. In the Toshiba affair, U.S. importers of Toshiba products were encouraged by Toshiba to make strong representations to Congress as to the value of continuing the inflows of its products. Through this lobbying effort, Toshiba was able to reverse the position of Congress and eliminate the proposed punitive measures. Though the policy of the U.S. Administration has remained unchanged in terms of maintaining relatively open trade, the Congress is not wholly supportive of that position and the question of protectionism remains.

The concern over the growing dominance of Japanese interests was fed also by the Japanese purchase of banks in California and some other states. Strong incursions into the automotive industry, the electronics industry, into investment and brokerage firms, and projected incursions into the consumer goods and services sectors increased the number of commentaries on the size and extent of Japanese ownership and control—despite the fact that it is only the third-ranking holder of FDI in the United States— behind the United Kingdom and the Netherlands. Added to this was extensive purchasing of farm land and cattle ranges, the produce of which was exported to Japan, again returning the profit from such transactions to that country.

This issue of dominance was repeated in Canada, but with reference to the U.S. position in that economy. U.S. companies own and control something over half of Canada's manufacturing and extractive sectors—much more than Japan holds in the United States. The Canadians have attempted to differentiate between treatment of Canadian-owned firms and U.S.-owned affiliates, thereby *not* extending "national treatment." The U.S. government has long insisted

on similar treatment of both sets of companies, but the Canadian government has refused to accept the principle,
though it has altered its policies more or less favorably in
this direction according to the party in power. However, the
issue remains high in Canadian policy discussions, particularly as a result of the U.S./Canada Free Trade Agreement,
which will open more doors to foreign investment.

Both the issues of protectionism and dominance reflect
a concern over the nature and extent of economic integration across national borders. The United States has continued to support free-market determination of the location of
economic activities and has practiced free movement of foreign investment, encouraging the same policies for others.
Yet, neither it nor the rest of the world have been prepared
for the extensive integration of the world economy that has
resulted from foreign investment and intracompany trade.

The most critical issue is the distribution of the benefits of economic advance resulting from this integration. It
is not simply a question of dominance but a question of
who decides the distribution of benefits as well as who receives them. The benefits are seen to be increased employment, particularly in depressed areas, enhanced incomes,
the acquisition of advanced technology, and ownership and
control of enterprises (obviously preferred, by host countries, to be in the hands of nationals). Each of these aspects—raised to high levels in the Europe in the 1960s and
the 1970s and in Latin America particularly in the 1970s—
surfaced in the United States in the late 1980s as objections
to the substantial inflows of FDI. They are addressed at
some length in Chapter 15.

This concern over integration is probably too late to have
any policy impact in the area of financial markets, which
have been progressively integrated around the world through
the meshing and merging of financial firms. At the end of
1980s, the only question was how to *adjust* other policies
to this fact of worldwide financial integration. It is not yet
clear how the major economies will react through monetary
and fiscal policies to protect themselves from the significant shifts in international financial conditions and their
impacts on interest rates, exchange rates, and funds flows.

Hong Kong, for example, cannot avoid its future integration with China. To enhance its bargaining position with

China, Hong Kong has sought a closer integration with the rest of the world through a continuing open policy. It appears unlikely that the Chinese government would force restrictive policies on Hong Kong, since it seeks to use that city as a window to the world, as well as a listening post, and a means of learning the techniques of dealing with the rest of the world.

In the United States, one policy that has been repeatedly pressed in Congress is that of obtaining more information on the inflow of FDI. There is substantial information on the outflow through the balance of payments and the gathering of census data on manufacturing. But no regulation exists requiring foreigners to register their investments or an intention to invest with any agency of the U.S. or state governments. Consequently, it is possible for substantial investment to be made directly or through intermediaries without public knowledge of the fact until somewhat later, if at all. There is a concern that lack of knowledge will permit situations to arise later that are deemed undesirable, which could have been prevented with adequate foreknowledge. Virtually every other country, including Canada, has instituted such a registration procedure, but the U.S. government still considers this discriminatory against the foreigner and, therefore, incompatible with "national treatment," which it continues to press on other governments.

However, the activities of TNCs are becoming more complex in the variety of cooperative arrangements, both within the domestic economy and with foreign companies in and outside of the United States. The complexity makes it more difficult to obtain adequate information, except where special efforts are made to do so in the examination of the cooperative arrangement of a single firm or within a single industrial sector. Much more observation and analysis is required before policy shifts in the open countries can be adequately substantiated.

NOTES TO CHAPTER 7

1. On the international implications of the existence of SOEs, see Raymond Vernon, "The International Aspects of State-owned Enterprises," in Dymsza and Vambrey, *International Business Knowledge*, pp. 438–446.

2. A survey of "American Attitudes toward Foreign Investment," in *The International Economy* (May/June, 1988), pp. 28–33) shows that FDI is welcomed but is seen as needing monitoring.

3. Mary Shirley, *Managing State-Owned Enterprises* (Washington, DC: World Bank, 1983), p. 95.; and World Bank, *World Development Report* (Washington, DC: World Bank, 1987), p. 247.

4. *Loc. cit.*

5. For a review of TNC experience in Scotland the public policy implications of inflows and outflows of U.S. direct investment, see Neil Hood and Stephen Young, *Multinationals in Retreat: The Scottish Experience* (Edinburgh: University Press, 1982).

6. See Business International Corporation, *Investing, Licensing, and Trading Conditions*, 1988, (Sweden section).

7. An inside assessment of the policies of the "Four Tigers" is provided by Richard Hu, "We NICs Earned our Slice of the Pie," *The International Economy* (Mar./Apr., 1988), pp. 80–85.

CHAPTER 8

Mixed Approaches

Some countries have intervened in FDI in an effort to limit levels and patterns of investment by TNCs and to guide their behavior. Such an orientation is often the result of significant government responsibility for the economy. However, as seen in the previous chapter, some countries of Western Europe have large public sectors and relatively open policies, while some LDCs with relatively small government sectors have mixed policies toward TNCs (see Table 7.1). The restrictions seem to reflect nationalistic positions in advanced countries but more ideological influences in LDCs.

France, Italy, Spain, and Portugal, among the EC countries, have traditionally followed economic policies that reserve large areas of activity to the government. This statist tradition may be difficult for U.S. managers to understand and cope with, but it is a continuing central aspect of many European and all Latin American countries. When problems arise in private sector activities that are deemed important to national interests, these governments have repeatedly stepped in to protect the jobs, income, and competitive positions of local companies. At the extreme, some companies have been nationalized. Thus, when financial crises struck St. Gobain, Thomson, and CII-Honeywell-Bull, they were taken over by the French government. Because of a long history of governmental guidance to industry (arising with Colbertism in the seventeenth century), France views government intervention through ownership or control of economic/commercial activities as more appropriate than most advanced Western countries do. Reliance on SOEs signals more frequent interventionist policies toward foreign companies as well.

151

COUNTRY POLICIES

The majority of governments employ a mixture of restraints on TNCs, and the mixes vary considerably among advanced and developing countries. Several major NICs are also firmly in the mixed group, though the city-states of Hong Kong and Singapore are quite open. The country policies described—France, Italy, Japan, Sweden, Mexico, and South Korea—provide ample illustrations of policy responses to the concerns of governments over corporate behavior (as discussed in Chapter 2). The relative positions of these countries in FDI inflows and outflows for 1977 and 1987 are shown in Table 8.1. The fairly strong increases in FDI outflows by France and Sweden are not surprising for 1987, but the greater increase (absolutely and relatively) by Japan reflects its new position in the world economy. Still, Japan's small inflows, compared to the European countries, shows a continuing reluctance to accept FDI.

Table 8.1: Foreign Direct Investment. Selected Countries. 1977 and 1987 (Millions of U.S. dollars)

	1977		1987	
COUNTRIES	FDI OUTFLOWS	FDI INFLOWS	FDI OUTFLOW	FDI INFLOWS
Japan	1,635	35	19,396	1,190
France	999	1,890	9,080	5,083
Sweden	737	82	3,138	294
Italy	551	1,138	2,335	4,077
South Korea	21	93	185	595
Mexico	n.a.	556	n.a.	3,229

Note: (US Dollar/SDR Rate: 1977 = 1.16752, 1987 = 1.29307)
Source: International Monetary Fund, *Balance of Payment Statistics*, Washington, D.C. 1988.

France

France has long had mixed policies toward TNCs, regardless of the party in power or the macroeconomic situation. With the election of a Socialist government, the entire banking sector was nationalized in 1982. (Exchange rate instability and massive capital outflows were the proximate cause, though the three largest banks were already state-owned.) Business is broadly open to private-sector participation, but the government employs "indicative planning" for each sector, using its financial resources and some incentives to obtain some compliance from French companies. TNCs are less susceptible to such guidance since they have other sources of finance. Over half of GDP is generated by the government sector, and state-owned companies account for about 15 percent more. With this high level of government participation in the economy, the roles of foreign firms are expected to be coordinated with government plans, but foreign firms do not always respond as wanted. As governments change and as economic conditions vary, the rules facing foreign firms have been tightened or relaxed, but direct dialogues are always expected on TNC expansion, contraction, and operations. This necessity to negotiate and the uncertainty are themselves "restrictions."

The potential use of SOEs as "national champions" is one of the most important aspects of French policies toward foreign TNCs. The petroleum sector is dominated by Elf-Aquitane, the coal business by Charbonnages de France, the auto industry by Renault, and the steel industry by Sacilor —all SOEs. Major SOE competitors exist in the chemical industry (Rhône-Poulenc and EMC), the electrical equipment industry (Thomson-Brandt), and aircraft industry (Snecma and Aerospatiale). Foreign firms are permitted to operate in each of these industries, but their opportunities are constrained by the government's support of these competitors, including preference in government purchases.

Privatization of many of these SOEs began in the late 1980s, with the sale of St. Gobain in 1986, of Compagnie Financière de Paribas in 1987, and of Compagnie Generale d'Électricité later in 1987. Literally dozens of SOEs were scheduled to be sold to private investors during the rest of the decade. This shift toward greater private-sector participation in the overall economy reflected a recognition that international competitiveness had waned and that success in the EC of 1992 would require more innovative and aggressive firms.

The drive for greater competitiveness *within* the EC provided a greater opening for foreign TNCs that can add to this goal. Domestic ownership is required, however, in public utilities, national-defense industries, stockbrokerage, highway transportation, and life insurance. In addition, acquisitions of French firms by foreign interests are sometimes restricted by bureaucratic approval procedures, made more complex by the fact that French regulations are written so they permit varying interpretations. The approval commissions can switch positions, when the government changes its views on foreign ownership, for whatever reasons. Even the restriction on foreign participation in national-defense industries is relaxed when no French company has the ability or the technology to supply acceptable products or services.

No local-content requirements are imposed on TNCs, but contract negotiations to supply the French government often include assurances of local production and the use of local suppliers. There are no limits on remittance of profits, interest, or royalties to a parent, though until 1986 many exchange controls affected foreign financial flows. Price controls have also been used in some sectors, notably pharmaceuticals, tobacco, and books.

Policies selectively affecting foreign investors in France are generally ad hoc, resulting from varying interpretations by French ministries of the standing regulations. The vagueness of statutes and regulations reserves both authority and flexibility for government officials. Thus, the foreign firm needs allies in contested situations. One of the best sources of support is a provincial or municipal government, which can strongly represent TNC and local interests in the project before the Paris bureaucracy.

Foreign investors must register all proposals with the Ministry of Economy and Finance, though the process is generally a formality for EC-based companies and not usually a serious constraint even for non-EC firms—though it could be so used. Firms from outside the European Community must file detailed economic impact estimates and other information about proposed projects. The approval process usually takes one month to complete. FDI proposals that are rejected are normally those that seek to enter sectors deemed sensitive by the government, or involve acquisitions that do not appear to add any important financial, technological, or other capabilities to the French firms.

The extent to which the process has deterred FDI has varied
with different governments in France and with different economic conditions.

Italy

The Italian government views the private sector and FDI
as important elements in the economy. While major SOEs
do exist, most sectors are open to foreign investors under
national treatment. Acquisitions as well as new investments
are permitted, with a variety of restrictions largely arising
from the reservation of activities to selected SOEs. Permissions are required for initial direct investment, construction of facilities, remittances of funds, and many other
aspects of company operations in Italy. While the national
governments have changed frequently in the post-World War
II period, the attitude toward private business has always
been tolerant in principle; but it is curious that no foreign
auto company has *established* a manufacturing affiliate in
Italy, though Chrysler did purchase Lamborghini in 1988.
As in France, there are informal obstacles that can arise for
any given project.

Initially, FDI projects must be approved by the Ministry
of Foreign Trade, following the foreign investment law (Law
No. 43 of 1956). Large industrial investments must also be
approved by the Interministerial Committee for the Coordination of Industrial Policy (CIPI). Although permission to
invest is not difficult to obtain, classification of the investment project is critical. All projects classified as "productive enterprises" are covered by Article I of Law 43, while
the rest are covered by Article II. If a firm qualifies for Article I coverage, it is guaranteed unrestricted remittance of
funds at the official exchange rate and several other privileges. Most investments that add capital, technology, and
jobs can gain classification under Article I. Acquisitions of
existing Italian firms without major capital expansion fall
under Article II, which does not offer preferential treatment.

FDI is precluded in several sectors: insurance, banking,
air transportation, and shipping. These service sectors are
seen by many countries as adequately provided by local enterprises—i.e., they do not need foreign capital, management, or technology; therefore, they can be reserved for
nationals without harm to the economy and with some sav-

ing to the balance of payments. Beyond these prohibitions, foreign firms may enter the Italian market and compete with local firms on a fairly even footing.

As in France, competition in many sectors is affected by the presence of SOEs. Two major SOEs (IRI and ENI) dominate the Italian economy, though many smaller ones also exist. IRI is the largest; it is a public utilities monopoly but also owns subsidiaries in several other industries. Its main business is the operation of the Italian telephone system (Italtel) and the production of telecommunications equipment. In addition, IRI controls the major steel producer (Finsider), the radio and TV broadcasting company (RAI), and the major airline (Alitalia), among others. During the past few years, the Italian government has privatized several of the parts of IRI, including its auto manufacturing subsidiary (Alfa Romeo) in the hope that they will become more competitive. Such a return to the private sector does not seem to imply a similar welcome to FDI in these key sectors.

In addition, most petroleum-related business is either limited to the national oil company, ENI, or is done in cooperation with ENI. ENI is also a holding company. It owns the national oil firm (Agip) as well as several other petroleum-related and energy-related firms, such as Agip Carbone (coal), and Enichimica (petrochemicals). Italy is almost completely dependent on imports for its energy requirements, so the sector has been considered critical since the 1930s. As noted above, foreign firms interested in the oil sector in Italy must generally come to terms with ENI to obtain a place in the market.

The other SOEs are dispersed throughout the manufacturing, service, and extractive sectors. These firms are independently incorporated, just as private-sector companies, and tend to operate without significant government guidance. Obviously, the risk for foreign TNCs interested in the Italian market is that the SOEs do have government support, at least as a last resort. Since the Italian government has assisted the private sector in providing employment and in coping with macro- and microeconomic problems, it is likely that the SOEs will not soon fade away.

Operating rules for foreign firms are roughly the same as for domestic firms. No local-content rules apply, though approvals for FDI inflows are more readily obtained when the firm carries out local production. Transfers of funds abroad must be approved by the Ministry of Foreign Trade, though access to foreign exchange has not been a problem in recent years. Domestic and foreign firms also must obtain approval from the Treasury to borrow abroad, though once approval is given, there is no interference in repayments despite a scarcity of foreign exchange.

Japan

Japan presents the most changed policy environment toward foreign TNCs of any industrial country in the past two decades. Historically, Japan has been highly protectionist, with steep tariffs and many nontariff barriers to imports, as well as severe limitations on incoming foreign investment. It was only with its Foreign Exchange and Trade Control Law of 1980 that Japan moved dramatically *toward* becoming an open economy. The changes have been so rapid and so large that it is difficult not to classify Japan in the late 1980s as nearly open. But, because of the remaining nontariff barriers and the limitations still placed on incoming FDI, it is still classified as mixed. If Japan continues to open domestic business to foreign participation, by 1990 it should qualify as an open economy in its official *policies*. But, unofficial practices and procedures (custom and culture) are likely to keep it somewhat more restrictive than other advanced countries.

In the 1980s, foreign direct investors in Japan were required to obtain official permission by informing the Finance Ministry and the Foreign Exchange Council, as well as other government agencies that may be relevant to the specific investment, and by waiting 30 days for approval. During that period the government evaluates the potential impacts of the investment on existing Japanese firms and on antitrust concerns, either of which may lead to rejection of the application or demands by the government for alteration of the project. Further, opposition by Japanese competitors to a foreign firm's application for permission to invest in Japan still is likely to lead to important practical limitations, if the firm finds it possible to invest at all. Foreign construction firms have faced delays from local suppliers, inspectors, and other groups necessary for successful operations and have eventually "gotten the message" that domestic companies are preferred.

Since the Japanese business environment is so different from that in Western Europe or North America, it is difficult to discuss government policy without also raising cultural issues. For example, though the rules on foreign firms have greatly changed since 1980, the business system has not. This means that the traditional forms of cooperation between Japanese firms and the government have not changed notably. The Ministry of International Trade and Industry (MITI) continues to support development of Japanese exporters and overseas business if considered important for the Japanese economy. Information is shared between MITI and Japanese firms, so that serious competition from foreign firms can be avoided or blunted by restrictions on foreigners or support for the local firms. It is difficult for a foreign-owned affiliate to participate in this collaboration—though IBM has done so through being managed *completely* by Japanese; it is also the first foreign affiliate to be permitted membership in the *Keidanren* (Japan's NAM).

In addition, the trading system of Japan is highly concentrated under the control of some 60 of the over 2,000 trading companies (the Sogo Shosha), with the 10 largest handling 30 percent of imports. Foreign firms seeking access to the Japanese market typically find themselves constrained by unavailable or inadequate channels of distribution; the alternative is to take on a Japanese partner that already has dealings with one of the Sogo Shosha or is tied into some other means of successful distribution.[1] For this reason, as well as to assure good government relations, many foreign direct investors take Japanese joint venture partners to participate in their Japanese business.

The Japanese government participates in business mainly through a process of dialogue and regulation, rather than through direct ownership of industry. There are few SOEs, and even some of these have been privatized in the past few years. Since 1985, government monopolies in telecommunications (Nippon Telephone and Telegraph), tobacco (Japan Salt and Tobacco Corporation), and railroads

(Japan National Railways) have been sold to private investors. This leaves public utilities such as electric power, the postal service, and water provision as the main SOEs remaining in Japan today.[2]

Although the government has not retained ownership of much of Japanese industry, it has precluded foreign firms from entering many activities. Until 1980, these restrictions were written into the law. Foreign firms were prohibited in agriculture, oil, and mining, among the largest industries. Since then, Japan has opened legal doors to foreign firms in these sectors, but entry is closely watched by the government. Entry through *acquisition* is basically unacceptable because it removes a Japanese company from its place in the society. In any case, it is difficult because little of the stock is publicly held; most is held by banks and other (competing) companies. An American TNC would not want Japanese companies holding shares in its affiliate, and a buy-out would thus involve multiple companies.

When the various "bureaucratic" constraints on FDI and the problems of access to local distribution channels are accounted for, it appears that de facto the most viable way to enter the Japanese market for a foreign direct investor is through a joint venture—with at least 50 percent ownership by the Japanese partner. This situation is largely a result of the continued antiforeign attitudes that slow Japan's adjustment to a more open role in the world economy.

Once a foreign firm is established in Japan, the operating rules are not particularly onerous or discriminatory. Financial transfers to foreign parent companies are subject only to normal taxes on dividends, and access to foreign exchange is free unless specifically restricted. Some restrictions on financial dealings do remain, particularly with respect to the issue of new securities abroad by Japanese entities or in Japan by foreign entities, both of which require special permission.

Limitations on imports were reduced dramatically, beginning in 1980. Today the average tariff in Japan is about 3 percent ad valorem, and quotas exist mainly on a range of agricultural products. While it is true that Japan's agricultural market is still tightly protected, other sectors are principally unrestricted by official regulations. However, Japan continues to have difficulties dealing with foreigners in Japan. Its historical isolation is still a strong influence in its mix of policies toward FDI inflows.

Mexico

Among the major Latin American countries, Mexico and Brazil present the most restrictive policy environments toward foreign TNCs, though FDI exists and continues to expand. With a market second only to Brazil in the region and a border with the United States, Mexico is an attractive location and thus has a strong bargaining position in its dealings with foreign firms. For the past half century, the Mexican government has played an active part in the economy: the government's operations account for about 25 percent of GDP; SOEs account for another 7.4 percent of GDP;[3] and extensive regulations guide both local and foreign private enterprise.

Mexico's rules in the 1980s on incoming FDI have been the strictest in the region, other than Cuba's. During the period since the 1973 Foreign Investment Law, all foreign direct investments have required at least 51 percent Mexican ownership, unless an exception was granted. Foreign firms that had established operations in Mexico before that time were granted an exemption, but requests to expand facilities or relocate subject the firm to the joint venture requirements. In practice, this has caused most FDI in Mexico to be constituted as joint ventures between foreign and local private investors.

The Foreign Investment Law requires approval from the Commission on Foreign Investment for any new FDI. Permission is given fairly routinely for investment projects that have majority Mexican ownership. The projects that sometimes are rejected are ones that would compete directly with existing Mexican firms that are deemed to serve the market adequately already. When foreign firms seek majority ownership of FDI projects, they must prove that substantial benefits would accrue to Mexico through the investment. The final decision is made on an individual basis for each project. But the debt crisis beginning in 1982 caused the Mexican government to approve most of the TNC requests to invest, including those with majority foreign ownership, in order to obtain the inflows of needed foreign exchange. Once the pressure of the debt is removed, Mexico can be expected to return to its pattern of an "on again, off again" welcome to TNCs.

A high degree of government participation in the economy is present in Mexico, especially through SOEs, which play a major role in Mexico's economy. The government enterprises are in commercial banking, petroleum, nuclear energy, electricity, railroads, and telecommunications— generally encompassing *all* firms in each activity. But there are exceptions, such as Citibank's commercial banking operation and the activities of several petrochemical TNCs. And, both domestic and foreign firms can operate in other parts of these sectors—as in petrochemicals and pharmaceuticals.

The largest company in the country is the national oil monopoly, Pemex. This firm has expanded its activities downstream into petrochemical production—a section it also largely controls. The government development bank, Nacional Financiera, owns significant shares in a wide range of manufacturing businesses—such as Diesel Nacional, Mexico's main producer of trucks and buses. The existence of literally hundreds of SOEs has meant that foreign TNCs entering the Mexican market often find themselves competing with government-supported firms, restricting the attractiveness of FDI inflows.

The limits on foreign equity do not apply to foreign-owned, offshore assembly operations ("maquiladora" plants of labor-seeking TNCs), which may be established in most parts of the country to assemble manufactured components or goods for final sale outside of Mexico. They encompass a variety of sectors—textiles, plastics, electronics, toys, etc. These operations may be 100 percent foreign owned, as long as their sales are exported; or they may be merely manufacturing contracts, or any arrangement in between. The "maquiladoras" have grown dramatically in the past decade, especially along the borders with Texas and California. In the late 1980s, offshore-assembly plants in these areas employed about 400,000 Mexicans in a wide range of manufacturing industries. Most of the output of these plants is sold to U.S. contractors.

Mexico also places numerous constraints on FDI projects that seek to market in Mexico; some are applied to domestic firms also and some only to FDI ventures. Most products sold in Mexico are subject to some degree of price control. Foods and drugs are tightly controlled, with price increases forbidden except by decree. Other products face less extreme controls, but all price increases must be approved by the economic ministry, Secofi. Many, though not all, industries are required to achieve specified percentages of local content in their output. Firms in automotive assembly must have at least 60 percent local content; in auto parts the minimum is 80 percent; and in pharmaceuticals the minimum is 64 percent.

Restrictions on financial transfers are more complicated because of Mexico's foreign debt crisis. It is very difficult to obtain dollars at the official exchange rate (which holds down the peso price of dollars), although dollars and other foreign exchange are available through the free foreign exchange market at a higher exchange rate. In general, transfer of funds overseas in the form of dividends, royalties, etc., is restricted more by the inadequate availability of dollars than any specific policy to prohibit access to foreign exchange.

Imports are substantially restricted, though trade policy has become more open in the 1980s than previously in order for Mexico to join the GATT. Many, though not all, imports into Mexico require licenses. Tariffs on fully assembled manufactured goods are generally high, ranging from 20 to 45 percent ad valorem. Tariffs on raw materials and production inputs tend to be much lower, and imports into "maquiladora" plants enter duty free. Thus, the policy environment toward imports is similar to that toward foreign firms in general, broadly restrictive, but with many exceptions that permit imports of selected products without major constraints. This import policy stimulates FDI to jump the barriers and gain access to the important Mexican market.

South Korea

South Korea, along with Taiwan, is one of the larger of the so-called "Four Tigers" of Asia, i.e., the newly industrializing countries that are growing rapidly and whose products are competing successfully in advanced-country markets. Both of these countries historically implemented extensive policies that guided business into desired channels, particularly favoring domestic firms over foreign ones. More recently, Taiwan has become more open since its domestic companies have not become as strong as those in South Korea. (The other "Tigers," Hong Kong and Singapore, are city-states that do not possess the leverage of large domestic markets, and which consequently have opened their economies far more to foreign firms so they can tap into the world market.)

South Korea is a very attractive market to foreign TNCs, because of its relatively high standard of living and large population (estimated at 45 million in 1990), yet a continuing lower wage structure than in the United States or Japan. The government is aware that its acceptance of foreign business in manufacturing for overseas sales (offshore assembly of textiles and electronics, principally) has provided an engine of economic growth. Nonetheless, it also realizes the strong attraction of South Korea's domestic market to foreign firms, and thus it has been able to gain greater benefits for the country by imposing a number of controls on TNCs.

The most notable constraint on FDI in South Korea probably is the de facto difficulty of obtaining any more than 50 percent ownership of an affiliate in the country. Under the Foreign Capital Inducement Law, all new direct investments must be approved by the Ministry of Finance, which generally permits projects that involve at least 50 percent South Korean ownership. While 100 percent foreign ownership is not precluded by law, the approval process has been interminable for most such applications. Sectors in which foreign participation is limited to joint ventures include: construction, insurance, transportation equipment, textiles, and others. Acquisition of existing South Korean companies is prohibited. In addition, FDI projects are more likely to be approved the more they involve exporting from South Korea. (In fact, projects that do not result in the projected levels of exports are penalized with additional taxes for the time periods of nonperformance.)

Another major constraint on incoming FDI is that many sectors are reserved for local investors or SOEs. These include more than a dozen agricultural products, publishing and printing, wholesale and retail trade, public transportation and communication, several financial services, public broadcasting, tobacco, and electric power and water; several commercial banks are also state owned. The main constraint on FDI, however, is through limits on foreign ownership. Thus, entry into the South Korean market for foreign direct investors results in a proliferation of joint ventures and other contractual forms of participation.

The independent licensing agreement, which requires no direct investment, is the most frequent arrangement; it was strongly promoted by the government in the 1960s and 1970s, following Japan's example in the 1950s and 1960s. Historically, South Korea has raised problems for foreign licensors because of inadequate intellectual property protection; but since 1980 patent laws and other protection of proprietary rights have been improved significantly. To reduce capital risks, the most attractive form of licensing has been contracting with South Korean firms to produce manufactured goods for sale to the licensor in industrial countries. This arrangement is desirable because it permits the TNCs to reduce their production and assembly costs, and it permits South Korea to maintain local ownership.

In contrast to the extensive restrictions on entry of foreign TNCs, once the firms are operating, they are treated on a relatively nondiscriminatory basis compared with local firms. Financial transactions are essentially unrestricted, including profit remittance, interest and royalty payments, and capital transfers. This open environment for international financial transactions has followed from South Korea's success in balancing its trade flows and avoiding foreign exchange crises during the 1980s, despite a large foreign debt.

Trade barriers do exist, in the form of mandatory licensing requirements for all imports. Limits are then placed on obtaining the licenses to protect domestic firms when desired. Foreign direct investors involved in offshore assembly have had few problems obtaining the necessary import licenses to support their production for export.

Policy Review

As in the case of the open countries, the mixed countries can be compared along six policy dimensions. Chart

8.1 shows this comparison, which identifies an increasing restrictiveness from France to Mexico. All of these countries present more limitations on FDI entry than did the open ones, and in the present group the policies tend to become more restrictive as the level of economic development decreases. The members of the European Community are least restrictive in this group, though both France and Italy are significantly more restrictive than West Germany and the United Kingdom. Both France and Italy limit FDI in banking—France nationalized the entire banking system in 1982. Price controls on various products are common in the mixed countries, as are strong SOEs; both are infrequent in the open group.

RESPONSES OF TNCS

Three TNC investments illustrate the strategies in response to the mixed policies of France, Japan and Mexico.

Digital Equipment Company in France[4]

U.S.-based Digital Equipment Company has operated sales offices in France for many years, importing its minicomputers, components, and office systems from production facilities elsewhere. Its main competitors have been IBM and Machines Bull, both of which produce computers locally; Digital ranks third in market share behind the other two. In the early 1980's Digital's management decided to seek permission to establish a production facility in France.

The French government historically has been concerned about foreign dominance of the economy, evidenced notably in the mid-1960s when Jean-Jacques Servan-Schreiber made his claim that American TNCs were becoming a force as powerful as European governments in the European economies.[5] As a result, French policy toward foreign TNCs has been relatively restrictive compared to its European neighbors. Especially in high-visibility industries, the French government has often sought to stimulate local firms and to keep out foreign competitors. Thus, in the computer industry, the French government supported the local firm, Machines Bull, and pursued other pro-domestic

Chart 8.1: Summary of Policies

RESTRICTIONS	France	Italy	Japan	Mexico	Korea
1. FDI entry and exit	Regulated: utilities, insurance, banking, stock brokerage, travel agencies, oil, and transportation.	Precluded: insurance, banking, oil, shipping, and air transportation.	Controlled: agriculture, oil, fisheries, mining, leather. Implicit rule: 50% foreign ownership ceiling.	Prohibited: electricity, oil & derivates, nuclear energy, banking, and communications. Most FDI is in joint ventures.	50% ownership implicit limit. Closed for 13 agriculture products, finance transport & communication printing, tourism, etc.
2. Import limitations	Airplanes, ships, steel, textiles and energy products. Stiff for Asian countries; relaxed for OECD and EEC.	Quotas on imports coming from Japan or any central-planned economy—especially automobiles and electronics.	Quotas on agricultural products; 3% ad valorem tariffs.	8% of imported products require licenses. Higher protection for locally produced goods & those with greater value added.	Imports require licenses. Prohibited: luxury items, few local produced goods. Limitations relaxed for export-oriented firms.
3. Financial flows	No limits if properly justified.	Restrictions eased in last 3 years. Capital repatriation after 2 years of investment.	Only simple formalities required for authorizations.	Controlled rate: exports, imports, royalties. No limits on dividends via free market Repatriation subject to FX availability.	Unlimited at the prevailing exchange rate.

4. Intellectual property	Full patent and trademark protection.	Fairly weak protection.	Still a major weakness, in particular, application of antitrust concepts to industrial property rights.	Clear process patents for pharmaceuticals, chemicals, alloys. Harder penalties for trademark piracy. Legal red tape & corruption.	Substantial penalties for patent & trademark violators especially in the chemical & pharmaceutical industries.
5. Local-content requirements	Only indirectly, when supplying government organizations.	None	Not explicitly, but sometimes FDI approval contingent on the use of local materials or components.	64% in pharmaceuticals. 60%–90% range in transportation sector. Less requirements for export oriented firms.	High for heavy transportation equipment. Waived for high-tech imports.
6. Price controls	Pharmaceuticals, tobacco, and books.	Controlled (30): energy resources, utilities, basic foods. Supervised (12): schoolbooks, oil products, pharmaceuticals	Mostly lifted.	Three-tier price surveillance system: frozen & negotiated (basic foods, drugs), controlled (90% inflation), and reported.	Virtually all prices decontrolled except for 110 "of low competition" items: home electric appliances, steel products, & textiles.

Source: Investing, Licensing and Trading, N.Y.: Business International Corp., 1988.

alternatives, rather than let IBM and other U.S. and German firms dominate the industry.

In this environment (in 1976), Digital Equipment Company made its first application to the French foreign investment review agency--the Ministry of Economy, Finance, and Privatization. The proposal to construct a new plant in Valbonne, near the French Riviera, was denied at that time. Evidently, the French government judged that the political costs outweighed the economic benefits of the planned 300 jobs to be created.

Eight years later, after Digital had set up a major research facility employing 130 scientists and technical staff in Valbonne, the request to build the production facility was made once again. Given DEC's response to French interests, the 1981 recession that struck Europe, and French unemployment well over 10 percent of the labor force, permission was granted. Realistically, competition in the industry had not changed drastically, but the underlying economy had deteriorated to the point where new foreign direct investment, especially in high-tech sectors, was being welcomed by 1984.

The bargaining outcome results from a situation in which the firm has relatively weak bargaining resources but the stakes have increased greatly for the government; additionally, the two parties have similar interests—as at point F in Figure 8.1.

Novo Industri A/S in Japan.[6]

Dealings with the Japanese government since World War II were extremely laborious for foreign TNCs until the mid-1980s. Until that time, FDI was prohibited in many sectors and limited to joint ventures in others. Many bureaucratic rules contributed to the hostile environment facing the foreign firms. Because of Japan's rise to challenge the United States for economic leadership of the noncommunist countries, it has been forced to open its domestic market to competitors from abroad. The pressure became intense in the 1980s, and the Japanese government responded with a dramatic reduction in restrictions on entry and operations of foreign TNCs. Japan's regulatory environment approached the open category.

Figure 8.1: The Bargaining Relationship Between TNC and Host Government

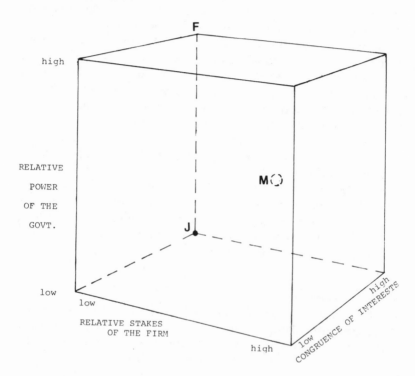

One TNC that has dealt with the Japanese government as a foreign direct investor in both periods is the Danish pharmaceutical company, Novo Industri A/S. Novo entered Japan in 1955 through an agreement with Kodama Ltd, to export insulin to it. In the 1960s, Novo began supplying industrial enzymes to Kodama for sale in Japan. In 1980, the agreement was expanded into a 50/50 joint venture, Novo Yakuhin KK. During this entire period, Novo was limited in its ability to operate in Japan, first by proscription of foreign direct investment, then by health and safety standards that effectively discriminated against firms that produced drugs overseas.

In 1982, Novo received permission to open a 100 percent owned subsidiary to manufacture its industrial enzymes locally in Japan. The facility opened in 1986 and gave Novo a solid base for selling both in the domestic Japanese market and throughout Asia. The long experience of dealing with the Japanese government unquestionably helped the company in its negotiations to establish the wholly owned plant; and Novo's plans to export a significant part of the production also contributed to the positive reception by the government. This bargaining outcome probably resulted less from the company/government interface than from Japan's overall strategy of becoming more open (in legal and regulatory terms) during the 1980s. In the bargaining framework, the Novo 100 percent owned venture would appear approximately at point J (Figure 8.1), where the firm has relatively great strength through its technology and access to foreign markets, and where the government has an important stake in demonstrating its openness to rest of the industrial countries, and also where government and company interests are similar.

IBM in Mexico[7]

IBM has operated in Mexico as an importer of mainframe and minicomputers since the 1950s. Manufacture of minicomputers was begun near Guadalajara in 1981; at the time, all IBM facilities abroad were wholly owned by the company. Mexico is a relatively small market for IBM, accounting for annual sales of only 90,000 PCs in 1986, valued at approximately U.S. $200 million. On the other hand, Mexico's proximity to the United States and the availability of low-cost labor presented an important opportunity to IBM for reducing production costs of its computers that are sold elsewhere.

Mexico has, since 1973, required that all FDI projects accept a minimum of 51 percent local ownership. But, as with IBM in Guadalajara, this rule has been broken when the government found compelling reasons to permit greater foreign ownership (typically due to the investment's introduction of new technology, creation of many jobs, and/or generation of significant exports). Nonetheless, the Mexican government has largely held to the minority joint-venture law, even during the 1980s foreign debt crisis.

Mexico passed legislation in 1981 to require foreign computer manufacturers to meet the 1973 rule on 51 percent minimum local ownership and to increase their Mexican local content beyond rules established for most other industries. The stated goal was to achieve 70 percent local supply of the nation's computer needs by 1986. In addition, computer manufacturers were required to meet minimum export requirements to generate foreign exchange for Mexico.

In 1984, IBM proposed to construct a PC plant at the site of its existing minicomputer facility near Guadalajara, to invest about U.S. $40 million, and to produce about 100,000 personal computers per year, 75 percent of which would be exported. The firm sought 100 percent ownership of the plant, presenting its case that the project would create many major benefits for Mexico (namely, about 80 direct new jobs and over 800 indirect ones; transfer of high-tech job skills into Mexico; new direct investment of U.S. $7 million; and exports of 75,000 personal computers per year). The government initially rejected the proposal, on the grounds that IBM did not propose to use sufficient local content in the plant, and thus would be importing too much in parts and materials. It appears as well that the other foreign firms that were producing PCs locally successfully lobbied the government to refuse 100 percent ownership to IBM, since they all had accepted minority positions.

A year later, with Mexico increasingly hobbled by its more than U.S. $100 billion indebtedness to foreign banks and other foreign lenders, IBM twice more resubmitted the proposal, each time increasing its commitment to purchase local inputs, to increase investment more than tenfold, and to raise the level of exports, but to retain 100 percent ownership. On the third occasion, with the enhanced offer and the promise of more technology and the establishment of secondary and tertiary enterprises, the Mexican government found itself much less able to resist the clear balance-of-payments and employment benefits to be produced by the project, and agreement was reached.

The final agreement called for IBM to invest a total of U.S. $91 million dollars. This money was distributed among expansion of the Guadalajara plant ($7 million), investment in local research and development ($35 million), development of local suppliers ($20 million), expansion of its purchasing and distribution network ($13 million), contribution to a government-sponsored semiconductor technology center ($12 million), and the remainder to begin local university partnerships and other linkages to local computer-related activities. Also, IBM agreed to achieve 82 percent local content by the fourth year of operation and to export 92 percent of the PCs produced in Mexico. The firm retains 100 percent ownership of the plant.

In our model of government/TNC relations (Figure 8.1.), this agreement falls somewhere around point M on the back surface of the cube, where the government's stakes are higher than the firm's, the firm has medium bargaining power because of reasonably acceptable alternative suppliers of PCs, and the interests of both parties are very similar (i.e., both want to see production of a large quantity of PCs with export to the rest of Latin America and elsewhere).

KEY ISSUES

Key issues addressed by the mixed policies are those surrounding constraints on ownership and the competition with SOEs. Other issues are also raised, such as the mere fact of negotiation required with the government for various approvals and the potential problem of obtaining permission from one government only to find a different attitude held by a succeeding government, which might seek to renegotiate the arrangement. Governments are also concerned to maintain their power base, which is not usually built on TNCs.

Competition from State-owned Enterprises

The mere fact that an SOE exists introduces some hesitation on the part of private TNCs to enter a host country in the same sector of activity. An advantage can be held by the SOE in obtaining governmental support or subsidies. This advantage is enhanced if the SOE is also used as a "national champion," making it the "point man" for new directions desired by the government, which may have a purpose of discouraging foreign entrants.

Fortunately for private TNCs, there are limits to the support that governments can afford to give SOEs. If the SOE is not efficient in market terms, it can become quite expensive in the national budget. This was found to be the case in one country after another in the 1980s, but each has moved differentially in returning the SOEs to the private sector. At the end of the 1980s, it appeared that the trend to "privatization" was an accelerating one, making opportunities for TNCs worldwide more attractive in that the private sector is given a larger role in the economy.[8]

Joint Ownership

A major distinguishing factor between the open and mixed countries is the restriction on ownership introduced in the latter. There are concerns that local firms not be acquired by foreigners, that local capital or entrepreneurs not be squeezed out of new opportunities by foreigners, and that existing companies not have to face overwhelming competition when they are able to supply needed products satisfactorily (even if not with market efficiency).

To remedy all of these concerns, governments have placed restrictions on ownership—usually reserving to local capital the majority—from 51 to 60 percent. The foreigner then holds a minority position, but still sufficiently large that he will pay careful attention to his contribution—especially technology and management—and the success of the venture. (It has been found that TNCs usually consider a stake of less than 25 percent as a "portfolio" investment, and will therefore not involve themselves significantly in the management or development of such ventures.)

As with virtually all other governmental interventions, the purpose of restrictions on ownership is to shift the benefits to the host country—at least the *perceived* benefits. The concerns that are mitigated may be more imagined than real, more political than economic, and more public relations than substantive. But, for whatever reason, since the constraints are imposed the TNC must respond—either by rejection of the opportunity abroad, acceptance, or negotiation of other considerations, which make the minority position acceptable.

The predominant TNC response is to negotiate. The negotiation then addresses virtually *every* aspect of the future operation, beginning with selection of the joint-venture partner, the contributions of each, rights in decision making, proprietary rights, imports of components or kits, obligation to export, prices (if under control), production limits, profit remittances, local borrowing, establishment of R&D labs, and so on. Any one of these can be "improved" so as to make the joint venture more attractive *or* to permit the TNC to hold more than a minority position. For example, a third party (such as a lawyer or banker) may be brought into a joint venture to balance interests and prevent control by the local partner.

In some cases—as with IBM in Mexico—a higher export guarantee was accepted by the government as adequate "compensation" for permitting 100 percent ownership by the TNC. In other instances, the transfer of highly desired technology will trigger the same permission. Or, greater ease in imports, local borrowing, or relaxation of price controls will ease the "pain" of TNCs in having to accept a minority position.

One of the most difficult aspects of such negotiations, however, is the selection of the joint-venture partner from among various local candidates. In Mexico, the Nacional Financiera is frequently a candidate, either because of the government's desire to be on the board or informed regularly of the company's progress from inside, or because of desire to profit from what appear to be financially rewarding ventures. But, the government can—as it has in Kenya, Spain, China and others—suggest an appropriate (read "acceptable") candidate. Such an intervention raises potentially serious problems if the government changes hands, and its supporters are not those accepted into the joint venture.

The resolution of differences depends on the relative strengths (balance of power) of the parties; no one pattern is "best." One of the dangers that governments must consider is that the TNC will make adjustments in its strategies to equalize benefits as *it* sees the project, without the government realizing that these trade-offs have been made. For example, the TNC can simply reduce the flow of technology to the joint venture, for fear of the local partner dispersing it into other companies. Thus, what the government sought is not gained; and no TNC is likely to raise such an intended trade-off in the negotiations.

The entire set of issues around ownership and control produce a series of myths, which must be matched against economic and political realities in determining the negotiation positions of TNCs governments. This assessment is provided in Chapter 15.

NOTES TO CHAPTER 8

1. See, for example, M. Y. Yoshino, and Thomas B. Lifson, *The Invisible Link* (Cambridge, MA: MIT Press, 1986).

2. For more details, see Chalmers Johnson, *Japan's Public Policy Companies* (Washington, DC: American Enterprise Institute, 1978).

3. Mary Shirley, *Managing State-Owned Enterprises*, p. 95.

4. This commentary is based largely on Business International Corporation, "Digital's French Investment Puts Satisfaction First," *Business Europe* (May 25, 1985), pp. 161–162.

5. Jean-Jacques, Servan-Schreiber, *Le Defi Americain*, (Paris: Editions Denoel, 1967).

6. This description is based largely on Business International Corporation, "Why Novo of Denmark Emphasizes Japan, Expects Improvements," *Business Asia* (Feb. 17, 1986), pp. 50–51.

7. This section is taken largely from Stephen Weiss, "The Long Path to the IBM-Mexico Agreement: An Analysis of the Micro-Computer Investment Negotiations, 1983–86," Working Paper no. 3, NYU School of Business, Oct. 1989.

8. See Raymond Vernon (ed.), *The Promise of Privatization* (New York: Council on Foreign Relations, 1988).

CHAPTER 9

Restrictive Policies

The major restrictive countries have been members of
the Soviet bloc, other socialist nations such as Yugoslavia
and China, along with India which is only marginally in this
group. These nations have chosen to severely limit the presence of foreign firms in their economies. Bargains struck
between these governments and TNCs have been long delayed in negotiation and implementation and frequently less
profitable than anticipated. The ultimate result of these conditions is that the amount of TNC activities in the restrictive group is small relative to that in the rest of the world.

Until the late 1980s, the Soviet bloc was almost entirely
closed to incoming FDI. Trade was controlled through state
agencies who purchased or sold abroad. By the end of the
1980s, however, all but Albania were relaxing or intending to
relax their restrictions, but the turbulence of late 1989 prevented any actual change in regulations. The new moves
were a reflection of the recognition that without a major
policy shift they would lag further behind in economic
progress. The stagnation in both agriculture and industry
in most of these countries had become unacceptable.

Efforts were begun to attract technology and joint venture capital, and to learn foreign management techniques.
Export drives were mounted by some. But in each case, the
stagnation of bureaucratic governmental systems, the lack
of entrepreneurial experience, and the backwardness of the
agricultural sectors posed apparently insurmountable problems in creating quickly the necessary infrastructure and
in offering appropriate resource bases. The conflict between
the necessity to open and the desire to remain restrictive
will continue to be a difficult issue—both economically and
politically.

The policies used by Communist and socialist nations
not only limit the share ownership of foreign companies,

but also restrict their activities in other ways. In the Communist countries, limits on access to foreign exchange make business very difficult to pursue, since imports are often required and profit remittance is constrained. Most of the Communist nations have implemented "zero-balance" rules on foreign exchange; these require foreign-owned affiliates to generate at least as much foreign exchange through exports as they use for importing components and equipment and remitting funds. Beyond the limits on ownership and financial transfers, a variety of other rules are selectively used by different countries to constrain the activities of the TNCs, each having different impacts on and eliciting different responses from TNCs. In early 1990, it was still not possible to know whether and how these restrictions might be relaxed, though a few initiatives had been taken in specific negotiations.

COUNTRY POLICIES

A number of developing countries, both socialist and nonsocialist, have employed restrictive policies toward FDI—Albania, Algeria, Burma, Thailand, Nigeria, Madagascar, Ghana, Ivory Coast, Paraguay, and Sri Lanka. But these are much less significant in FDI potential than China and the Soviet bloc (USSR and Eastern Europe). In addition to the Communist countries, India has followed a socialist ideology and applied restrictive policies toward foreign firms. India's policies since 1973 have been "populist," inward-looking, and socialist, but not derived from central planning. Foreign firms interested in the Indian market are largely limited to export/import contracts, "collaborative agreements" (mostly licenses for technology and know-how), and minority joint ventures with Indian investors. The restrictive countries discussed here—some of which have adopted more relaxed policies, but not yet implemented them significantly—include China, East Germany, Hungary, India, the U.S.S.R., and Yugoslavia.

China (PRC)

In 1978, the People's Republic of China announced a 10-year plan for economic modernization that has led the country to relax its former prohibitions on most foreign business activities. Since 1949, when the Communist party won its civil war with the Kuomingtang (Nationalist) government, China has followed a Marxist economic policy, with virtually all industry, agriculture, and services owned and operated by the state. Although there were some periods of greater willingness to permit foreign firms to do limited business in China, overall the country was essentially closed to foreign TNCs, except for export/import transactions through agencies of the central, state, or city governments. After the debacle of the Cultural Revolution, the government recognized that the country was far behind the West and that autarchy was no longer feasible if China were to keep up with worldwide progress. The National People's Congress adopted a new constitution in 1975, which began the process of opening the economy; and the 10-year plan of 1978 put into practice the principle of drawing upon outside sources of goods and technology.

From the passage of the Law on Joint Ventures in 1979 through 1987, it has been estimated that China contracted for over U.S. $20 billion of foreign direct investment in over 6,000 projects.[1] These include mostly (the loosely controlled) contractual joint ventures (essentially manufacturing contracts), followed by (more closely regulated) equity joint ventures with majority ownership held by the Chinese partner, then majority foreign-owned ventures and some 120 wholly foreign-owned ventures. The rules for undertaking these kinds of ventures are still being developed, since some 100 laws have been passed and require the promulgation of implementing regulations. Actual implementation of these laws is becoming better understood through the continuing dialogue with foreign companies, government officials, and legal experts. A further complication is that both provincial and some city governments are empowered to apply their own regulations on foreign enterprises, requiring negotiations at three governmental levels.

In the late 1980s the Chinese government made some moves to free state enterprise managers from central control, however, private property was not permitted to Chinese save in family-scale enterprises. (After the events of Tiananmen Square in mid-1989, the government sought to reassert central control, so the picture became more murky.) Private foreign firms found their partners restricted to government enterprises, with managers who were essentially government officials.

As in most LDCs, most TNC business *with* China is done through direct trade, not by FDI. With total international trade at about U.S. $60 billion per year, China has become an inviting trading partner. Because of its large-scale purchases, China tends to appeal to the large Western TNCs that can afford the time and manpower to pursue protracted negotiations of sales or purchases with the Ministry of Foreign Economic Relations and Trade (MOFERT) and other appropriate agencies. Consequently, China's foreign trade with the West is dominated by large TNCs to a greater extent than is trade between industrial countries, where many smaller firms are able to enter and operate relatively freely with local counterparts in a wide variety of market segments. The exceptions are some small enterprises in Hong Kong, Singapore, and even Taiwan that are owned by ethnic Chinese and are trading with and investing in the PRC effectively.

Doing business *in* China is a more recent phenomenon, responding to China's "open policy" to TNCs begun in 1978. But, again, the familiarity of Hong Kong, Macao, and Singapore with customers' needs and opportunities in the PRC has meant that these countries are the source of the large majority (by *number*) of FDI arrangements with the PRC over the decade of the 1980s, though the major projects (by *value*) have been with Japan and Western countries.

Since most of the economy is managed through SOEs or government agencies, foreign entry requires bargaining with both; negotiations are protracted also by the fact that the government agencies often consider that they have more bargaining strength than the opportunities warrant. The TNCs have alternatives in other countries not adequately recognized by Chinese officials. China seeks high technology, employment with higher wages, and export opportunities; but TNCs are mostly interested in serving the domestic market, which the government opens only reluctantly. The rules permitting joint ventures and wholly foreign-owned firms to operate in China are clear in terms of their statutory requirements, but interpretation of the rules by the Chinese government is, of course, subject to significant change.

Joint ventures may be created either as "equity" or "contractual" ventures; the latter are less precise as to the sharing of responsibilities and the former are under closer government regulation. The majority of joint ventures have been "contractual," because the partners choose to maintain the flexibility to specify each other's obligations as the projects develop. In either form, every joint venture must establish a fade-out date (usually 10 to 30 years) at which total ownership of the venture reverts to China; however, extension of the original arrangement is permitted subject to agreement by the parties involved.

Within this general framework, Special Investment Zones were created both to contain the large number of joint ventures expected and to be the locus for these autonomous regions to compete with each other. They were seen as laboratories of economic incentives—"experiment stations"—to determine which package would most benefit both the venture and the country. Most of the joint ventures established in China have been located in the Special Investment Zones, due to the attractiveness of the tax incentives, subsidized borrowing, local labor, transport, and other benefits available.

Since the rules in China have been developing and changing rapidly over the 1980s, this overview must remain general, but the key is the extent and duration of the relaxation of restrictions. However, the basic economic reality suggests that foreign business in China will continue to grow *if* the government continues its opening of the economy. China's location in the most rapidly growing region of the world portends business development within that Asian context. Governmental incentives offered to investors of Chinese ancestry from anywhere in the world can be expected to draw a continuing flow of FDI. The creation of the Special Economic Zones, along with very low wage costs, will continue to attract "foreign-sourcing" investment. And finally, the fact that China is the most populous country in the world will continue to create interest among TNCs in doing business there, though obstacles can become insurmountable.

German Democratic Republic[2]

In 1989, the German Democratic Republic (or East Germany) was the only major East European nation that did not allow joint ventures with Western equity partners. But the opening of the economy and destruction of the Berlin Wall late that year added it to those seeking foreign investment. Arguably the most technologically advanced of these nations, the GDR *sells* as well as buys technology licenses and has entered into a number of nonequity industrial cooperation agreements with Western firms. Most often these contracts are with companies in West Germany, by far the GDR's largest trading partner in the West.

The continued close relationship between the two Germanys is reflected in substantial West German exports of manufactured goods, technology, energy, and financing, and East German exports of low-tech manufactured goods and some raw materials. Some West German exports were exchanged for political considerations by East Germany, such as the extension of human rights and emigration permissions to dissidents. By far the largest amount of business between any two East-West countries is that between East and West Germany. Thus, socialist policies of isolation are relaxed by heritage. The degree of relaxation was accelerated by the events of 1989, even resulting in the call for reunification of the two Germanys. The reunification that is planned in 1990 will make the current section of our analysis an interesting historical note; a united Germany is expected to follow the existing policies of the Federal Republic, as far as TNCs are concerned.

Licensing agreements with the GDR are fairly numerous in both directions. That is, the GDR licenses many foreign projects to use its industrial technology, often in developing countries that are seeking intermediate ("more appropriate") alternatives to expensive high-tech machinery or processes available from the West. Also, East Germany selectively purchases technology licenses to pursue its economic objectives.

Production cooperation agreements generally enable Western firms to coproduce goods in East Germany, with compensation to them from exports of the same goods or other (countertrade) products. These 'permission contracts' allow the Western brand names to be used, which is desirable since West German broadcast advertisements spill over into the East German airwaves and create customer awareness.

One example of a coproduction agreement is Volkswagen's contract with the GDR to sell a ten-year-old engine production line with licenses to upgrade the motors. This project enabled the GDR to improve the efficiency of its auto production and maintain ties to new developments at Volkswagen. The Western firm demanded payment in diesel engines, since new emission control standards did not permit the use of the gasoline engines manufactured by the old plant. Events have overshadowed this agreement, with both Daimler-Benz and BMW signing joint-venture agreements to manufacture in East Germany upon reunification.

The processes of a negotiation are fairly bureaucratic, with approvals needed from the foreign trade organization of the particular industry, plus the relevant ministry, the Central Office for International License Trade, and the Foreign Trade Ministry. New restrictions can be imposed by any of these, including prohibition. The GDR's external debt to Western banks, at U.S. $7 billion, is high enough to pressure the government to keep imports low through restrictive decisions and to push for greater exports to the West.

Hungary

With the introduction of the policies under the New Economic Mechanism in 1968, the Hungarian government put into motion many economic reforms that foreshadowed the more recent Soviet *perestroika*. Local factory managers were given more control over production enterprises, and their decisions were based more on market signals. They were permitted to set their own export prices and to choose their own suppliers for any regularly needed imported inputs that supported those exports. This opening to Western firms also led to hundreds of licensing and coproduction agreements during the 1970s.

Hungary also created Eastern Europe's first joint-venture law in 1972, but it took five years to complete the rules. Since 1977, only about 100 joint ventures have been established with Western firms, most of which have come from West Germany and Austria. Majority as well as minority partnerships are allowed to Western firms in these joint ventures, and restrictions apply most importantly to financial transfers such as profit remittance and other use of foreign exchange. All such cooperation is subject to interdiction if the government so decides.

Unlike the situation in the U.S.S.R., Hungarian SOEs are not guaranteed the raw materials that they need for production. Most economic planning takes place at the ministerial level, and factories have autonomous responsibility for sourcing their domestic inputs from suppliers and at prices only loosely prescribed by the government. This limited competition can make a Western partner very valuable in a joint venture. Not only does the Western firm bring access to export markets, technology, and management expertise to the venture, but it also provides emergency access to foreign production factors when local Hungarian sources are (temporarily) inadequate.

Joint ventures are more restricted when they target the domestic market, because the government wants TNCs to provide foreign exchange. Such joint ventures enter Hungary's wholesale distribution channels with little end-user or end-seller contact. Hungarian retail prices are also strictly controlled; when its currency (the forint) devalues against free currencies, the cost of imported inputs rises and cannot readily be passed through to customers.

Through a series of bilateral investment protection treaties, joint ventures can often qualify for Western government guarantees (such as those offered by the U.S. Overseas Private Investment Corporation). Hungarian banks are willing to extend risk capital for particularly attractive projects, and they allow the Western partners to buy back the capital shares once the venture becomes successful. The World Bank's International Finance Corporation capitalizes one such bank, which also leases imported capital equipment to Hungarian and joint-venture firms and finances these operations against projected exports. In all, the support system available for joint ventures in Hungary has developed into a range of services wider than in other socialist countries.

Once in place, the most significant restrictions on joint ventures stem from the balance of payments. To prevent FDI from worsening the payments situation, Hungary imposed a requirement for joint ventures (such as Poland, and the Soviet Union now use) to balance imports with exports or achieve an export surplus. This constraint does not appear likely to be relaxed in the near future, given Hungary's U.S. $18 billion foreign debt, which uses about half of gross export earnings for servicing alone. Profit remittances are not tied into the zero-balance requirement, but they are constrained in amount by other means and their transfer is often delayed because of the unavailability of foreign exchange at the central bank.

India[3]

India is the least restrictive of this group and is on the borderline between it and the mixed category. Since independence from Britain in the 1950s, India has been cautious in permitting the participation of foreign firms in the economy. Despite a relatively low ratio of government expenditures to GDP, India may be classified as a quasi-socialist country. Though Rajiv Gandhi began to open the economy in the mid-1980s, FDI decisions are more ad hoc than guided by clear policy. Public opinion has also followed government policy in prescribing a large role for the state in owning and controlling industry.

The goal of Prime Minister Indira Gandhi to attain self-reliance for India was partly incorporated in the 1973 Foreign Exchange Regulation Act, which not only imposed more stringent controls on foreign exchange but also placed foreign TNCs under the regulation of the Reserve Bank of India. Foreign ownership was restricted so that 100 percent ownership could be retained only for those exporting all production or using high technology; some other high-tech companies (in computers and optical fibers) could own up to 75 percent; others could own up to 51 percent if other desired technologies were used (such as in switch-gears, turbines) and also exported a prescribed portion of production; all others had to accept 40 percent or less, making them essentially Indian companies.

Since 1973, the Foreign Exchange Regulation Act (FERA) has essentially limited foreign equity investment to a maximum of 49 percent of the capital in any Indian company. While exceptions are sometimes negotiable, this limit is usually maintained, and firms that had invested before 1973 have been required to adjust to the FERA rules. According to one recent estimate, there are fewer than 150 foreign firms with more than 49 percent ownership of Indian affiliates, and none of those have Indian equity of less than 26 percent. Compared with any of the other mixed countries, this barrier to FDI entry is more extreme; it is, however, less stringent than overall requirements in China and the U.S.S.R.

In response, TNCs adopted one of three strategies: to leave, to continue majority control under constraints, or to become an Indian company. Coca-Cola and IBM took the first route; Siemens the second, and Colgate the third. Under the more receptive policies of Rajiv Gandhi, in the late 1980s, IBM and Coca-Cola entertained proposals to return.[4]

A total ban is imposed on FDI in sectors reserved to the state or to the local private sector. The industries that are set aside for SOEs include: iron and steel, oil, most mining and production of mining equipment, arms and ammunition, heavy electrical equipment, aircraft, shipbuilding, all utilities, and others. Beyond this, FDI is generally precluded when the desired technology and products in a sector are available locally. In fact, FDI is permitted only in those industries designated as "core sectors" in which technology or exports are also desired; investment is limited to locally owned firms in all other sectors.

For the industries that are open to FDI, the process of obtaining approvals is difficult; one fundamental license and at least three more key approvals must be obtained. First, the firm must receive an industrial license under the Industries Act of 1951. For a very small foreign firm, or one that intends to export a large part of its Indian production, this license is not difficult to obtain. For most other firms, the process is typically complicated and slow. The second key permission is an endorsement by the Foreign Investment Board concerning the terms of the FDI and especially the arrangements with the Indian partner. Third, consent under the 1947 Capital Issues Act must be given to issue new capital stock. And fourth, a license must be obtained to import capital equipment related to the project. The time required to comply with all of these requirements is at least four months, and usually it takes close to two years.[5]

From a bargaining perspective, India's government took the position (until the mid-1980s) that its domestic market is highly attractive and that foreign firms had to accept onerous terms in order to gain access to it. On the other hand, exceptions to the rules were generally made for firms that possessed two bargaining advantages: key proprietary technology and/or access to foreign markets for exports. Some such firms were permitted up to 74 percent equity ownership in their affiliates.

Along with local ownership rules, the Indian government seeks to maximize local content in production. Import licenses are usually issued only for products that cannot be made locally. The presumption is that production inputs are available from Indian suppliers, unless the firm can demonstrate otherwise.

Consistent with the foregoing, access to foreign exchange is also highly restricted. Permission from the central bank (Reserve Bank of India) is required to purchase foreign currency for any purpose. To date, the central bank has made foreign exchange available to firms for remitting profits, royalties, interest payments, etc., though sometimes with a significant delay.

Import restrictions take the forms of mandatory licenses for all imports and very high tariffs on all products. The rules are so numerous and complex that one advisory service notes that, "The import controls that India imposes are so extensive and product-specific that interested companies should verify the exact status of the particular product they have in mind."[6] Tariff rates range from 30 percent to 100 percent of the value of the shipment. In all, India's import policy is consistent with its overall restrictiveness toward foreign business. These trade restrictions both induce licensing and investment projects and make them less profitable to foreigners. Bargaining power on projects is thereby shifted toward the Indian government, with the TNC having the major choice of "Go" or "No Go." With India's gradual progress, some 15 percent of its 800 million people have living standards above the average in Spain. This is a market of 120 million (equal to Japan) with a substantial buying power concentrated in the large cities.

Soviet Union

Throughout its history, the Soviet Union has permitted very little foreign business presence within its borders. The exceptions have been primarily import and export purchases and sales, which have offered little direct access to Soviet enterprises for foreign trading partners, and technology transfer agreements with Western firms. It has over 400 collaborations of various types with foreign firms, but only a few were highly significant.

Technology agreements have followed two general forms. First, technology licenses have been negotiated by ministries responsible for the production of specific groups of goods (e.g., automobiles, chemicals, electronic instruments) through their own foreign trade organizations. Under the typical agreement one or more of the ministry's factory units would make the goods under license and pay the licensing fee either in hard currency or, increasingly, in kind. Payment in kind usually involves a share of the goods produced under the license that are then made available for sale in the West (though other goods have sometimes been substituted, subject to their availability and acceptability by the Western licensor). These goods are then sold (usually at a discount) for what they will bring; thus, the licensor does not know what he will receive in return from the license, even if the licensee is successful. The second form of technology licenses are production cooperation agreements, under which Western companies provide production inputs such as machinery and skilled manpower, and the Soviet ministry provides local facilities and labor, plus a market for the goods produced. Payment under these agreements also is often made through export of the product to the West, since hard currency is scarce.

The latest shift in Soviet economic policy toward foreign firms took place in 1987, when the first legislation authorizing joint ventures with Western partners was adopted by the Soviet Council of Ministers. By March of 1988, 36 jointventures had been registered—many of which were extensions of previous licensing and production cooperation agreements. All of these joint ventures are between SOEs and large, well-established Western partners that have been active in the Soviet Union for years.[7] The contracts include the modernization of one of the largest steel plants in the U.S.S.R., upgrading the country's medical equipment, building a large agro-industrial complex, and programs by West Germany to train thousands of young Soviet managers.

To help finance these deals, European banks (British, French, German, and Italian) are extending some $6 billion in new credit lines to the Soviets. These initiatives are a signal to Gorbachev that his policies are welcomed and supported, and they are well in advance of any concrete response by U.S. business or banks. A deal announced in February 1989 between six U.S. TNCs and more than thirty Soviet trade and economic organizations required nine months of negotiation and will open the way for two dozen joint ventures; it also sets the rules on future joint ventures related to taxation, foreign exchange, labor, accounting, insurance, arbitration, and other aspects.[8] Of particular significance is the arrangement that foreign exchange must be earned (over a period) to permit repatriation of earnings; any excess earned by a joint venture will be sold to another joint venture to permit it to repatriate earnings. The opportunities for smaller (Western) firms will likely remain scarce, since the Soviets generally "think big," and bureaucratic negotiations are too time-consuming for smaller companies to endure, though the new "rules" may make subsequent negotiations easier.

Soviet sectors open in the late 1980s to joint-venture participation include the upgrading of transport; storage and processing of agricultural products, including improved veterinary products and facilities for livestock; computerization and better quality control in industry; improved tourist facilities to earn hard currency; and production of consumer goods for the domestic market. Western partners in all such ventures must receive their profits through export sales or countertrade. (For example, Coca-Cola will be sold for rubles in the U.S.S.R. with the company to receive Soviet-made Lada automobiles in exchange for the soda concentrate and equipment; then the cars will be sold through established British dealerships for pounds sterling, thus generating hard currency for the Coca-Cola company.) The Soviet Union was, therefore, accepting FDI inflows for both import substitution and export promotion in the late 1980s.

Financial controls on the foreign ventures are severe. At present, joint ventures are permitted to repatriate hard-currency profits only from any *surplus* of hard-currency export earnings over hard-currency import costs. Any profits earned beyond that limit must be retained in the joint venture or remitted in the form of products rather than money. Of course, if a joint venture sells its products/services in hard currency, there are likely to be funds readily available for repatriation. Ventures in the tourism industry are especially well placed in this regard. The Savoy Hotel in Moscow is being renovated in conjunction with Finnair; the hotel will bill guests in dollars when it is finished, so obtaining hard currency for repatriation will be relatively easy. Similarly, McDonalds has planned to sell its fast food for dollars in tourist locations and for rubles in others.

Under *perestroika* the foreign trade agencies and channels of the U.S.S.R. have been dismantled or decentralized. Individual factory enterprises are being given more authority to trade with and sell to foreign companies directly. The significance of these changes for FDI is not yet clear, although more Western firms are seeking access to Soviet customers and suppliers through joint-venture arrangements and are negotiating directly with the enterprises.

Yugoslavia

Yugoslavia is not a member of the Soviet bloc and has taken many independent initiatives. Yugoslavia legalized joint ventures with Western partners at about the same time as Hungary in the early 1970s, but it had much more success in attracting such business because it immediately implemented its statutes while Hungary delayed. More importantly, Yugoslavia's semiautonomous political status was accompanied by a more tolerant government attitude toward FDI and more encouragement by Western governments to TNCs to respond.

Similar to the Hungarian case, Yugoslavia's central planning extended down to the ministerial level, with individual enterprises responsible for securing production materials, assessing market needs, organizing production, exporting, and showing a profit.[9] The introduction of Western technology licenses and production cooperation agreements was motivated more by a desire to stay up-to-date and competitive in the Yugoslav sector. But progress was set back by the economic and political problems in the late 1970s and 1980s. Burgeoning foreign debt (U.S. $20 billion in 1986) has caused the government to place limitations on access to foreign exchange; the government forced Yugoslav exporters to convert most of their export earnings to dinars. Government budget needs led to an imposition of surtaxes for energy costs, national defense, and other specific uses. Rapid inflation beginning in 1984 resulted in a severe devaluation of the dinar continuing through the decade. Wage and price freezes have been imposed and relaxed repeatedly, leading to bursts of cost and price inflation.

Because of its foreign exchange problem, Yugoslavia's government has repeatedly imposed restrictions on imports and funds outflows during the 1980s. Since late 1986, imports of production inputs are required to generate 1.3-to-1 ratios of exports to imports. At the same time, lists of permissible imports were drawn up, further limiting access to foreign inputs. The crisis nature of the problem seems most likely to remain until the overwhelming burden of the foreign debt can be restructured.

In the late 1980s, the absence of strong and effective leadership in the central government led to friction among the several different ethnic nationalities of Yugoslavia—Serbs, Croatians, Slavs, Moldavians, Albanians, and others. Overall, these difficulties caused the inflow of joint venture capital to halt, while the foreign firms waited for an improved environment. Yugoslavia's restrictive classification is less a result of socialist ideology than an inability to provide a favorable climate for FDI.

Policy Review

Across the board, limitations on TNC activities are much stricter in restrictive countries than in the other two categories. Chart 9.1 (pp. 192–93) compares the six selected countries in this category.

In the restrictive countries, FDI entry is permitted only under highly regulated conditions, and even then with minority TNC ownership usually required. Imports are highly restricted, with some products not permitted and others requiring licenses and other government approvals. In many cases, imports are permitted only when counterpart exports are offered by the firm. Financial flows are greatly limited, since all of the currencies are inconvertible except the Indian rupee. Price controls are extensive throughout the group.

Despite the many differences in treatment of foreign TNCs among India and the Communist countries, ranging from Hungary to Yugoslavia, all of these countries seek to keep control of their business activities in local hands. This policy is clearly more interventionist than in the mixed or open countries.

TNC RESPONSES

In each of these countries, the experience of TNCs in both trade and investment has been that of sporadic success in negotiation and operations. In the absence of policies specifying what *can* be done, the generalized prohibitions and restrictions permit exceptions in each case, with the bargaining aimed at getting around projected restrictions. Some TNCs have found personal payments or favors expected by government officials. As a consequence, the operations are seldom as expected by either the TNC or the host government, since each tries to redress inadequacies or inequities in the bargain. These results have not encouraged others to try new arrangements until the recent "openings." Some examples illustrate the difficulties.

Sadolin (Finland) in the Soviet Union[10]

Since the Soviet law permitting FDI (via minority joint ventures) was instituted only in 1986, not much experience has been garnered about the bargaining strategies of foreign firms and the Soviet government. Of the 85 ventures that were approved by May 1988, all involved large Western firms, and most called for export of at least some of the output of the joint venture's production. The first venture to be contracted was a plant to produce paints, sealing compounds,

Chart 9.1: Summary of Policies

RESTRICTIONS	China	East Germany	Hungary	Soviet Union	Yugoslavia	India
1. FDI entry and exit	Mostly contractual JVs. Still highly bureaucratized; Special Economic Zones for FDI	No JVs with West partners, only nonequity industrial cooperation (licensing) agreements, mainly with W. Germany.	Mainly through JVs, most of which come from West Germany and Austria. Incentives for high-tech & export-oriented firms.	Trading, technology licenses, production cooperation agreements & recently JVs with Western partners. Large-scale projects.	Technology licenses, production cooperation agreements & industry FDI by Western firms. Western equity share remains 25%.	Most firms limited to 40% of foreign equity. Exceptions in case of high-tech and export-oriented firms. FDI only in core sectors.
2. Import limitations	Firms required twice a year to submit list of imports. Duty incentives for export oriented & high-tech contracts.	Not applicable.	Zero balance required for JVs: exports $\geq$ imports. Devaluations not easily compensated with higher pricing, limiting imports.	"Zero balance" regulation prevents JVs from being a net user constraining imports.	Imports required to generate 1.3 times exports. Priorized system of imports. Continuous foreign currency shortage.	Mandatory licenses & high tariffs on all imports. Allowances on machinery & industrial raw materials not available in India.
3. Financial flows	Access to FX for repatriation of profits, dividends & royalties if enough earned by exports.	Western firms required to take almost all payments in East German goods, technology, and service.	Profit remittances not tied to "zero balance" requirements but delayed due to FX constraints encouraging countertrade.	Repatriation is easier if JV deals only in hard currency. Otherwise, the zero balance rule applies: ruble income-ruble profit.	No legal constraints, but unavailability of foreign currency encourages repatriation of profits in kind.	FX transactions require permission from Reserve Bank. Approved FDI financial flows never blocked but frequently delayed.

4. Intellectual property	Increasing recognition of IP rights of IP-holders; limited by term contracts.	Highly developed since FDI is replaced by purchases of technology licenses.	When created by JV, becomes property of the partners shared according to equity.	Accept world standards on compensation for licenses & royalties but no clear rules about ownership of JV's R&D or engineering.	Recognized, but substitution may occur either to remain internationally competitive or increase FX earnings.	Royalties and fees paid to foreign licensors subject to close scrutiny & kept as low as possible. Piracy is not a problem.
5. Local-content requirements	Broad, with policy of increasing "localization".	Not applicable.	Encouraged, not imposed, by the lower trade cost of Hungarian goods for which hard-currency can be charged.	In the administration & support services of JV by assigning state insurers, banks, shippers & export customers.	Foreign exchange earnings have priority over local-content requirements.	Decided at the time of investment approval. Governments seeks maximum use of local equipment, components & raw materials.
6. Taxation	No taxes on repatriated profits & 40% rebate if reinvested. Incentives in SEZs and for export & high-tech firms.	Not applicable.	Profits: 20% 1st 5 years, 30% after that. Material value-added: 25%. Incentives in priority sectors and for reinvestments.	2-year tax holiday after JV first makes a profit. After that, 30% of profits. If repatriated 20% additional tax.	Western partners in JVs: profits: 10% royalties, patent earnings & technology transfer: 20%.	Corporate taxes are high (50%–60%) although incentives are several which makes the normal range 30% to 50%.

FX = Foreign exchange; JV = Joint venture.

Note: East German summary will be altered by ties with West Germany especially.

Source: *Business Eastern Europe, China & India.* New York: Business International Corp., 1988.

and other wood-finishing products for the construction industry to substitute for imports.

The Western partner in this venture, Sadolin (the Finnish subsidiary of a Danish firm), had worked for the previous three years in the construction of a production cooperation project with an Estonian enterprise. With the advent of the new law, this plant was expanded into a joint venture.

The Finnish firm had already found the Soviet (Estonian) plant to be satisfactory in the production of wood-impregnating agents. In addition, the size of the Soviet market was sufficiently attractive to entice the firm to accept the forced minority ownership and the severe restrictions on profit remittance and other uses of foreign exchange in return for access to that market. Although its main market was the Soviet Union, Sadolin could receive dividends in hard currency only if generated by exports of the products to Western markets.

The Soviet government agreed to accept this particular venture, apparently because the firm had already demonstrated its capability to run a local manufacturing plant under the production cooperation agreement. Also since its output replaces imports, it directly helps the balance of payments. Further, any profits can be remitted only if foreign exchange is earned.

Given the large size of the Soviet market and the relatively smaller size of the firm involved, it appears that the government was able to force the bargain in its favor. Sadolin offers management skills, access to foreign markets, and possibly some proprietary production technology. These factors evidently did not outweigh the government's bargaining strengths enough to achieve a more favorable outcome in terms of profit and foreign exchange remittances. This bargaining outcome lies at about point S in Figure 9.1.

Parker-Hannifin in China[11]

One of the earliest joint ventures in China's decade of opening to Western TNCs was an industrial seal manufacturing plant in Wuhan, Hubei. This U.S. $1 million plant is 49 percent owned by the U.S. firm, Parker-Hannifin and 51 percent owned by the Hubei Automotive Industrial Corpora-

Figure 9.1: The Bargaining Relationship Between TNC and Host Government

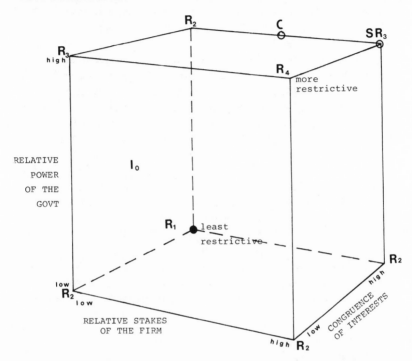

Relative levels			Points	Regulation level (X+Y+Z)
	low	high		
Firm Stake (X)	0	1	R_1 (M)	0
Govt Power (Y)	0	1	R_2	1
Congruence (Z)	1	0	R_3	2
			R_4 (G)	3

tion in China. The project was originally proposed in 1980, after a commercial mission by the governor of Hubei province to Ohio had stimulated (Cleveland-based) Parker-Hannifin's interest in China. The joint venture began operating in 1983, producing O-ring seals for industrial tools and other applications.

Bargaining advantage in the projected venture would appear to have been in China's favor, given the small size of

the operation, the attractiveness of the market, and the potential availability of seals from other TNC manufacturers.
Parker-Hannifin sought access to the huge Chinese market
for industrial seals through the venture, offering in return
some industrial technology and also access to Western export markets. The Chinese government offered a desirable
market, low-cost labor, and protection against competing
imported products. It insisted on exports to gain foreign exchange for itself and for remittance of dividends. This situation would appear near point C in Figure 9.1, showing a
rough equation of interests, with the resources of government being greater.

The project operated its first 5 years, on the terms noted
above, with modest success. Most of the production is sold
in the domestic market, though the Chinese partner has
constantly pushed for greater exports. Because of weak
world demand for the seals, Parker-Hannifin has not at-
tained the levels of export growth expected, and difficult negotiations continue. The Chinese market clearly has proven
attractive, so it appears that the firm will try to meet China's export requests in order to maintain its local presence
and sales.

Coca-Cola in India[12]

The Coca-Cola Corporation had a physical presence in
India beginning with its branch office established in 1958.
By the mid-1970s, the Indian affiliate had sales of about 50
million rupees (U.S. $5 million). As in the United States,
Coke operated production facilities for making the soda
concentrate from its proprietary ingredients, but sold the
concentrate to various independent Indian bottlers who in
turn sold the soda at the retail level. During this period, the
Indian operations (other than bottling) were wholly owned
by Coca-Cola Corporation.

In the early 1970s, when anti-TNC fervor was at its peak
in developing countries, India passed legislation that required majority (at least 51 percent) Indian ownership of
"low-priority" businesses (e.g., low-tech, consumer products, and services); this included Coca-Cola. Also, the new
legislation required that foreign parent firms divulge rele-

vant technical know-how to their Indian partners for making the products. This would have required Coca-Cola to disclose the secret formula for flavoring its soda. Both of these new rules were extremely onerous to Coke, and the results of renegotiations reflected the strengths of the two parties.

The firm possessed a product made with proprietary technology. Sales in India accounted for far less than 1 percent of Coke's worldwide revenues at the time. Coke had very little physical capital invested in India that could be held "hostage." India, on the other hand, had no particular resources that attracted Coke to undertake local production. The government, however, apparently believed that the large domestic market would be incentive enough to persuade Coke to reach a bargain under the restrictive rules. Also, the product was not a necessary good, so India's government was not handcuffed into reaching an agreement with Coca-Cola.

The result of these conditions was that India in 1977 demanded at least 60 percent local ownership and divulgence of the secret formula from Coca-Cola. The firm was able to avoid negotiating with the government from the time of the initiation of the restrictive legislation in 1973 until elections put a new party in power in 1977. At that time the two demands became binding, and after several months of negotiations Coca-Cola chose to close down its Indian operations rather than meet the government's demands. Neither party gained the concessions that it had sought, but neither lost much in benefits, given the small volume of Coke operations in India. The bargaining situation represented here would lie at about point I in Figure 9.1, showing that neither side felt that its stakes were high, their interests were divergent, and their relative bargaining strengths were roughly equal.

NOTES TO CHAPTER 9

1. Price Waterhouse, *Guide to Doing Business in China* (New York: Price Waterhouse, 1988), p. 1.

2. The sections on Soviet bloc countries were initially drafted by Kevin Kendall, to whom a debt of gratitude is due. Mr. Kendall is currently developing an exchange program for U.S. MBA graduates to take short-term assignments as technical advisors in Soviet businesses.

3. This section is largely based on information provided from India by Ajit Dayal, former MBA student at the University of North Carolina, and presently with Birla (Bombay).

4. However, even in 1990 India remains very restrictive, as evidenced by its rejection of the Coca-Cola proposal and several anti-foreign pronouncements by the Singh government. See "Firms Find India's Welcome Mat Frayed," *Wall Street Journal* 10 April 1990, p. A20.

5. Business International Corporation, *Investing, Licensing, and Trading Conditions* (1987), p. 6 (India Section).

6. *Ibid.* p. 30.

7. The new joint ventures are described in Business International Corporation, *Business Eastern Europe* (Apr. 25, 1988), p. 131; (May 2, 1988), p. 141; (Aug. 15, 1988), p. 259.

8. *Business Week* (Feb. 27, 1989), p. 54.

9. An account of foreign operations of SOEs of Yugoslavia and other socialist countries is given in *United Nations CTC Reporter* (Autumn 1987), p. 17ff.

10. This example is largely drawn from *Business Eastern Europe* (June 29, 1987), pp. 201–202.

11. Business International Corporation, *Business China*, (May 16, 1988), pp. 65–66; (May 30, 1988), pp. 73–74.

12. This section is largely based on information provided from India by Ajit Dayal, former MBA student at the University of North Carolina, and presently with Birla (Bombay).

CHAPTER 10

Strategic Responses

The strategic responses of TNCs to the different policies of governments have been illustrated in each of the three preceding chapters. These strategies are seen in decisions as to affiliate location and operation and in responses to specific governmental interventions. When a business moves abroad it inevitably meets governmental requirements that differ from those in its home country. They respond in strategies *toward* governments: in institutionalized government relations, in country-risk analysis, in divestment options, and in negotiation procedures.

In addition, each TNC will, after a negotiation is completed, change its operations (imports, exports, components, pricing, technology) to reduce the adverse impacts of governmental restrictions. These trade-offs are frequently not observable by governments, which only makes them more concerned to narrow TNC choices. But the interactive process can lead to lower payoffs for each, as each tries to "protect" its share or interest rather then expand total benefits. In a highly dynamic world economy, which requires considerable flexibility on the part of both TNCs and host economies, such protection is likely to shrink productivity through higher costs, lower revenues, lower scale, or slower growth. The difference between *anticipated* implementation and results and *actual* operations and returns should be a part of the considerations each party brings to the negotiations on entry and later adjustments.

INTEGRATION, COLLABORATION, AND SEGMENTATION

Virtually any TNC prefers to achieve efficient production and distribution for the markets served through rationalizing the production process—thereby increasing productivity and profitability. This is done by obtaining the least-cost

inputs of resources and capital, the most efficient processes, the most efficient distribution system, effective market research, plus appropriate product development and
adaptation. For a TNC operating in many countries, it is
highly advantageous to have freedom in making these
choices. The TNC can then decide how much to "localize"
its operations and how much to "internationalize" (integrate) them. Even the market-seeker TNC, at times, finds it
advantageous to import components or materials in order
to be more competitive in the host-country market. And,
both the labor- and natural-resource seekers integrate their
operations into world markets with the latter importing
equipment and the former importing components and materials. The efficiency seekers are, of course, those most interested in *integrating* their worldwide operations, though
they are frequently prevented from doing so by the policies
of governments, as reviewed in the previous three chapters.

Therefore, the primary response of TNCs to government
policies is to seek ways of achieving the highest *feasible*
levels of efficiency of their worldwide activities, given market characteristics and governmental constraints. (Obviously, even with market differentiation and governmental
protection, market seekers look for efficiency *within each*
market, so as to be most efficient worldwide.) In order to
achieve this, almost every firm has a strong preference for
100 percent ownership and, therefore, undisputed control.
This degree of ownership and control is needed for the purposes of appropriating the gains ("rents"), of selecting
the most appropriate suppliers, maintaining quality in production, eliminating disputes over product design or production processes, protecting proprietary information and
technology, and forming an integrated distribution network
(where feasible). Even market seekers *prefer* wholly owned
affiliates. Only where there are mandatory governmental requirements or significant economic or commercial advantages (such as acquiring a needed technology or access to
a distribution network) will a foreign investor seek a partner in the host country or from a third country leading to
a network strategy. But since these conditions exist virtually around the world, such "strategic alliances" are increasingly common. (It is too soon to tell whether this

response is "faddish" and will result in many difficulties and divorces.)

Some sectors—particularly chemicals, electronics, aircraft, and aerospace—use technologies so complex and rapidly changing that no one company can expect to stay on the forefront in all product lines of the industry. Consequently, it has become necessary for companies to establish joint research projects, even to form joint R&D labs. A consortium of European computer companies (ICL, Bull, Siemens, and others) was formed for research in semiconductors and computer applications. Begun in 1984 and called ESPRIT, it has already generated several technological advances that are increasing the members' abilities to compete against IBM, NEC, and other major TNCS.

The specific obstacles to success through 100 percent owned ventures have led to three types of collaboration short of a full joint venture: cooperative marketing arrangements for a specific line of products, joint production, and joint development. These are sometimes set up "permanently" and sometimes on a project-by-project basis. As with ESPRIT, joint R&D activities are sometimes set up, with the final products developed separately and sold under different names and networks. Or joint production occurs out of different R&D activities, with the products marketed competitively. Also different products are marketed through a common distribution system to reduce costs.

Some such cooperation exists without government pressure, simply because of the commercial advantages to each of the parties. Given the high degree of specialization that is arising among TNCs in components and in high differentiation of products, there is a large arena for collaboration. TNCs are developing similar new products and new processes, so that marginal improvements are readily made by competitors. But even marginal contributions can be important in view of the severe competition and low profit margins, making alliances attractive and specialization profitable.

When a government mandates collaboration, the TNC has no choice but to comply or to stay out of that national market, at least in terms of production. It then settles for whatever sales it can achieve through exports into that market, which it may consider the best route given the difficulties of operating through a joint venture. On the other hand, it will accept a joint venture when it assesses that the costs of doing so are more than offset by the market returns it can anticipate.

While the problems of working through joint ventures are many, establishing a joint venture *only* for a host-country market is relatively simple compared to integrating joint ventures into worldwide operations. Joint-venture partners not only have different interests than the TNC in terms of its worldwide strategy, but the partner shares in a network he did not help to set up. In fact, full-fledged integration of a joint venture into worldwide operations of a TNC probably has not occurred; beyond the strategic problem of being in a joint venture with a competitor, the U.S. TNC could have some antitrust problems in doing so. Joint ventures are limited, contractually and otherwise, to certain kinds of activities and opportunities, by each parent company. Again, this occurs so that the sharing of assets, costs, and benefits is deemed fair by both parties. The major trade-off that a host government must accept when it insists on joint ventures is a limited opportunity for the joint venture in pursuing markets worldwide.[1]

The host government, of course, wishes the venture to export and to do so with high-tech inputs from the partners—particularly the TNC—so as to be competitive internationally. To limit the marketing area, some TNCs are separating their worldwide activities into regional operations (Americas, Europe-Africa, and Asia), letting joint ventures serve the regional but not the worldwide market. This reduces the difficulties of meshing numerous joint ventures into a single system. A TNC's joint venture in Asia would not be meshed (or in competition) with its joint venture in Europe unless the second is a joint venture *of* the first joint venture with a third party—as Rank-Xerox had in Fuji-Xerox. Gains would be divided only two ways in each area, rather than three ways. The results may or may not be less efficient than if there were an open worldwide market, depending on the economies of scale that are reached and the contributions that the joint-venture partners make to the total operation. But, whatever the cost, many host governments have concluded that joint ventures are in their interest.

Where the TNC is able to do so, requirements of joint ventures or local content will cause it to segment markets, either regionally or nationally. This segmentation prevents the joint-venture partner from benefiting from the international or regional distribution network previously established by the TNC. The joint venture is limited to its home market also because it is often unable (or the government unwilling) to remunerate the TNC adequately for sales opportunities opened to the joint venture abroad. Segmentation also occurs simply to isolate or contain the impact any one government can have on total TNC operations; unless this is done, a single government can hold an entire TNC "hostage" by interfering at critical times or in critical phases of an integrated operation.

A further operational shift taken by the TNC is through the flow of technology. Government requirements may include the compulsory licensing of TNC technology to independent companies or to joint ventures, with or without royalties. In this event, the TNC is likely to restrict the flow of technology it permits to the joint-venture partner or licensee so that the potential losses are minimized. This restriction also leads to a limitation of growth of the joint venture and therefore a further segmentation of economic activity, not necessarily anticipated by the government when it set its rules. Typically, the TNC transfers technology that it has already developed and tested through several years of marketing, having established its competitive position fairly securely. It is highly unlikely to transfer results of research projects that have not yet been innovated, or even that which it is currently innovating but has not yet fully commercialized in the more profitable markets. Thus, government requirements slow the development of joint ventures compared to what would occur if the affiliate were wholly owned or fully supported by worldwide operations.

These internal TNC trade-offs, arising from government regulations on ownership, have caused many governments to perceive that ownership is not the critical issue; rather, *performance* is! Therefore, they have turned more towards "performance requirements," including the introduction of certain product lines, exports of given amounts or percentages of outputs, price limitations, local purchases of inputs, establishment of local R&D labs, and so on. The host country's objective is to get a larger benefit from the more efficient expansion of the affiliate through an internationally integrated network. Again, the more extensive the government interventions, the more complex the TNC responses—both organizationally and operationally—to lessen the impact of government policies on productivity and competitiveness.

The precise consequences of the intervention/response sequence are unknown both to governments and TNCs, but comparative results are visible qualitatively if not quantitatively. Efforts on the part of a government to achieve a more acceptable distribution of benefits lead to repeated negotiations or at least a flow of information between the company and the government. The necessity to continue a dialogue on these questions gives rise to the need on the part of the TNC to maintain an effective "government relations" activity. For many managing directors abroad, these activities consume well over half of managerial time but provide considerable returns in reducing surprises and conflicts.

GOVERNMENT RELATIONS

The government relations function of a company (sometimes called external relations) seeks to improve the environment for TNC activities in each country by gathering the necessary information (involving large expenditures of time and some funds for entertainment and favors), feeding it to decision makers, and using it in negotiations with governments. This information usually also goes to top management, and often to the board of directors, so that they are kept aware and can set basic policies, even if not directly involved.

The objectives are to make politicians and government officials aware of the contributions made by the TNC, prevent adverse legislation, and make the regulatory environment more flexible. The process is a dialogue with the elites in a society, which include not only the governmental leaders but intellectuals, media, professionals, and sometimes university students. This activity is much wider than mere public relations, however, because TNC and government decision makers become involved. Intelligence gathering as well as information dissemination is required. Particular elites or audiences are pinpointed. Companies are active in initiating long-run personal and institutional relationships, since they are seen as a necessary means of improving the firm's position in the host country. The improvement of the external environment results from the foreign affiliate being gradually legitimized by acceptance in the host country by leading groups. This acceptance indicates that the power and decision making of the TNC are seen as being used broadly for mutual objectives; without acceptance, additional constraints can be expected to attempt to move it in the direction desired by the host country.

Government relations are a concern of all levels of management, both in the home and host countries. In fact, the CEOs of major TNCs become involved in government relations merely by visiting an affiliate in another country. For these contacts to be successful, the local managing director must have already developed sufficient interaction with appropriate officials so that the CEO's dialogues are on target. This interaction seeks not only to modify prior agreements in favorable ways but also to set the stage for future negotiations. They must also be conducted in ways appropriate to the culture of the country, so the managing director must brief a visiting CEO on proper behavior.

To set the stage for these negotiations officials at appropriate levels or ranks in the company and the government must meet sufficiently frequently to establish a rapport and to understand the guidelines within which each is negotiating. Since lower-level managers cannot commit the company to or in *serious* negotiations, this function has to emanate from the top levels in the corporation, matching the official, executive and legislative levels in the host country.

The degree of top management involvement is related partly to the type of company—resource seeker, market seeker, or efficiency seeker. The natural-resource seekers are exploiting a "national heritage" of the host country, so that this type is normally more involved in continuing governmental relations than other companies. The labor-resource seeker can generally obtain an agreement with the government and anticipate that it will be implemented very much as agreed upon—simply because the TNC has the ability to move completely out of the country and eliminate jobs fairly readily. For the reason that they are close to the host country's "life blood," it is very difficult for the extractive companies to obtain legitimacy in the host country; whereas the mobile companies are more readily accepted as legitimate. The market seekers are also more readily accepted because their orientation is almost wholly to the host country; in this case, local management can more readily handle government relations. Finally, the efficiency-seeker affiliate, for whom policies are most often determined by the parent, often faces more difficulty in dealing with the host government than the market seeker, but has an easier time than the natural-resource seeker. Under the extreme TNC centralization of the efficiency seeker, government relations are handled by top management through visits to the host country. But such centralization is ineffective for ongoing operations, for use of top managers is "overkill," and they cannot keep up with the details.

The most excruciating negotiations for a company are those on termination or expropriation. These almost always draw in top management from headquarters, though seldom is the board of directors involved unless one of its members has substantial influence in the host country. (Some TNCs have "advisory boards," consisting of elites from within a major region, to keep them informed and to help in the event of serious conflicts with one or more governments.) A negotiation on expropriation not only involves the highest levels of management and directors, but also generally draws in intermediaries in government-relations activities—lawyers, economists, consultants, and even home-government officials. These intermediaries are used to strengthen the case of the TNC, both in direct negotiations and before any courts. The reliance on home-government officials, usually through the embassy in the host country, raises serious questions of interference, but the U.S. government has stood willing to represent the interests of a U.S. TNC if international law on expropriation is not applied appropriately (see Chapter 11).

The ability of embassies around the world to provide assistance in government relations varies widely from country to country, both from the standpoint of the country represented and the country in which the embassy is located. Thus, the instructions to U.S. embassies as to the extent and intensity of support for the positions of U.S. affiliates abroad are different from instructions given by the French, German, Japanese, Dutch, and British governments to their embassies.[2] In fact, the instructions given by each of these governments is likely to differ from some others in significant ways. The U.S. government, for example, is wary of making representations on behalf of a single company in terms of bids for projects overseas, although it represents the interest of all U.S. companies simultaneously if they are bidding on a project.

The U.S. government enters into the relations between a U.S. TNC and a foreign government only where interests critical to the United States are involved—either in security or economic areas or where precedent is being broken under international law (see Chapter 11). If for any of these reasons the interests of the United States are being adversely affected, the government will decide to represent the company case through the embassy abroad or through the State Department to the foreign embassy in Washington. The extent to which the U.S. government supports TNC positions depends also on the willingness of particular ambassadors or officers in the U.S. embassies to make such representation. Some are uncomfortable in this role; others find it much easier to carry out. Specific guidelines are too rigid to deal with the many nuances in each case. But the U.S. State Department has on occasion sent out instructions that its embassies should be more supportive of the positions of U.S. affiliates in foreign countries—helping companies locate, negotiate, and improve relations with the host country. A large number of economic and commercial reports are sent in from these embassy posts to help U.S. companies in their operations overseas. These reports go through the State Department and the Commerce Department, with the latter sending them to Field Offices or directly to companies which have so requested.

The corporate structure for handling government relations differs significantly among TNCs, principally according to the organization of the company itself. A company organized along product divisions often has all international operations divided among these units, with each of them necessarily having their own government relations unit. A corporate group sometimes oversees all of these activities; if so, it is frequently closely tied into the corporate planning staff, since both are concerned with intelligence gathering. In the host country, the managing director himself is usually very much involved in government relations, supplemented by some intermediaries or partners, which may include banks, private individuals, or other companies. If the foreign affiliate is a joint venture, the local partner frequently has an extensive set of contacts with the government, which the foreign TNC can tap more or less readily. However, sometimes the strength of the foreign TNC is greater than that of a local company in dealing with the host government; in this case, new lines of contact have to be developed, or the foreign company may decide simply to use the local network. (Japanese companies have spent millions of dollars hiring U.S. lawyers to lobby for their interests before the U.S. Congress). One problem is that the interests of the host-country partner may not be the same as that of the foreign TNC or the joint-venture affiliate, depending on the market orientation of the joint venture.

In the local affiliate, intelligence gathering is frequently carried out by nationals who are managers or consultants. These individuals are used particularly for scanning intelligence sources, monitoring the activities of particular individuals or government units, and forecasting the events that will affect the company in its operations. The success of government relations depends upon the analysis of this information and its dissemination throughout the organization so that it is used by appropriate officials in their decision making. This is a difficult task, since such information is not seen as directly related to "the bottom line" by most line managers. This flow of information is sometimes bottled up or not effectively used. Companies that handle this function well involve top management in the continuing process, which signals others down the line that they should do the same. And the network of information-gatherers will extend from the CEO out to the farthest affiliate abroad and over all sources in between, including intergovernmental agencies.

The sources of intelligence include not only the media in the host country and government embassies but also a number of business associations with which the foreign affiliate has membership, the American Chamber of Commerce in the host country, various nonprofit organizations operating in the country, intermediaries and consultants with whom the company deals on a regular basis (lawyers, engineers, bankers), and a variety of personal contacts that the managers develop in the normal course of living in the host country.

Sources within the home country include not only the ministry of foreign affairs, through which embassy-generated intelligence flows, or the ministry of industry and trade (the State Department and the Commerce Department in the United States), but also the network of company representatives located in the capital to report on activities of the executive and legislative branches (e.g., Washington reps). In addition, each industry association has intelligence-gathering functions and disseminates the results to its members; consultants are available to ferret out information in specific situations; foreign embassies in the home-country capital also provide information on request; finally, a variety of personal contacts make up the network of information both on home government policies and regulations as well as its policies toward investment and trade with other countries.

If done effectively, all of this information and dialogue will enhance negotiation success through a continuing analysis of the climate in the host country or what is known as a "country-risk" analysis.

COUNTRY-RISK ANALYSIS[3]

For the purposes of improving dialogues on problems of foreign direct investment and of making negotiation with governments more effective, an analysis of the events that are likely to change the climate for such investment is critical. Although country risk has sometimes been treated as a direct result of political instability, they are not always linked. Political instabilities can exist and cause substantial political shifts in a country with no change in the attitudes or policies toward FDI. What is significant to a TNC are events that change legislation, regulations, or attitudes in the TNCs negotiations with the government. These may occur with or without political instability. In fact, they may change as a result of events in third countries that impinge on the balance of payments or the growth prospects of the host country. Alternatively, a particularly untoward event with a TNC in a third country may cause the host country to alter its attitudes—as with the reactions throughout Latin America to ITT's involvement with the CIA in opposition to the Allende regime in Chile.

Subjects of Analysis

The subjects of country-risk analysis are not the financial or commercial risks inherent in operating abroad but adverse changes in the orientations of the government toward the particular foreign investment—whether a project is being initially negotiated or is in the operational or terminal phases. It does not matter whether a given event is foreseen, the question is the ability to analyze its impacts (risks) on the investment itself. Even shifts in the climate of overall investment that are foreseen may not have a serious effect on a particular investment—the general climate may deteriorate while the particular investment remains favored because of its contribution to exports, technology inflow, employment, or some other results highly desired by the government.

The risks to analyze are those likely to affect the profitability of the enterprise through its pricing, its costs, the ability to repatriate earnings, the access to foreign exchange, access to local borrowing, entry and exit of technicians or managers, cost allocations among the affiliates and headquarters companies, and so on. Virtually any aspect of operations can be interfered with in some way by the government, meaning these operations are all "at risk" from changes in the investment climate.

Changes in any one of these aspects can be introduced simply by a shift in the individual occupying a ministerial post, or a change in leadership in a province where the specific investment is located. Almost any change in the sociopolitical/socioeconomic environment can lead to changes in policies toward foreign investment.

Changes in the investment climate in a host country can also be stimulated by shifts in the governmental policies or practices in the home country.[4] For example, penalties imposed on the foreign direct investor by the home country (such as export controls, technology controls, funds controls, capital outflow limits, and so on) can have repercussions in the host country in the effort to offset the unfavorable impacts of home-country controls. When the U.S. government imposed voluntary (then mandatory) restraints on direct investment outflows in the 1960s, some host countries retaliated by restricting access to local funding so as to prevent a diversion of demand for capital from the home country to the host economy. Similarly, pressures from public interest groups in a home country can lead to adverse reactions in the host country to the foreign investor—such as efforts to alter policies of apartheid in South Africa through pressure on the TNCs to withdraw. Such threats did not enhance the investment climate in South Africa.[5]

The complexity of events that can affect the climate for foreign investment is seen in the following list of factors evaluated in one firm's assessment:

- the constitutional environment of the country—whether it is a country under a "rule of laws" or "rule of men," charismatic leaders or institutionalized parties
- the composition of political parties—a one-party or multiparty system, or a long-lived dominant party
- the quality of government—the efficiency of the bureaucracy
- governmental crisis—party strength and stability
- shifts in foreign policy
- the economic system—the extent of private enterprise
- social structures—inequities, inequalities, discrimination, etc.
- demographic structure—dependency on industrialization or rural development
- ethnic and religious structures—conflict among religious sects

- labor relations—governmental intervention in negotiations
- regulations on foreign investments—the extent or frequency of change
- social turmoil—student riots, ethnic conflict, etc.
- civil strife
- coups and revolutions
- corruption
- intervention by third countries—embargoes, discrimination, threats of violence[6]

Even with an accurate assessment of these factors, a large step remains in determining their *impact* on TNC activities.

Availability of Information

A most difficult problem in dealing with country-risk analysis is obtaining relevant information. There is frequently a surfeit of information, but it is difficult to determine what is relevant and important.[7] For example, student riots may appear to be innocuous initially, but their rapid acceleration and the destabilization of a government can lead to adverse impacts on FDI—especially if the students are opposed to "foreign exploitation" or "imperialism." It is exceedingly difficult to get good information on student attitudes or intentions, much less on the likely extension and acceleration of their acts into violence that would harm foreign investors.

Similarly, the potential impact of an event in a third country on the host country is difficult to predict, especially since no country-risk analysis is likely to look at the whole world as the cause of specific national events. However, disturbances in the Middle East, and therefore in the supply of oil can have serious effects on the balance of payments in host countries, leading to constraints on foreign exchange and the repatriation of earnings, forcing a reinvestment of capital in the host country, thereby raising the overall risk exposure and requiring new negotiations with the government as to the proper use of these funds.

Nor is it necessarily useful to rely on analyses of international events coming out of official agencies, such as the UN, embassies, and foreign affairs ministries. Although these are clearly sources of information, neither the reliability nor the currency of such information is sufficient to permit it to be the basis of TNC decisions in government relations. One part of the assessment of aggregate risk is the ranking of countries according to credit risks by entities such as the World Bank, the International Monetary Fund, Foreign Credit Insurance Association, private international banks, and the Institute for International Finance (Washington), the last of which was formed by commercial banks to assist members in obtaining relevant data on a country's likely performance in international borrowing.

Process of Analysis

Once the data are gathered, the problems of analysis begin. One company sought to make this analysis more rigorous by developing a large computer model of the countries with which it was dealing, assessing the various impacts of different events by giving them a probability index, and weighting them according to the likely adverse results on their investment. The company gathered information and ran the program for several years at substantial expense, only to find that the results were hardly better than the "seat of the pants" (intuitive) reactions of informed individual managers. The danger of such models is that they are believed without a careful assessment of the ways in which they are generated. In the case mentioned, one of the major events—the return of Juan Peron to power in Argentina in the 1960s and the resulting adverse policies toward foreign investment—was not even picked up in the model. It is difficult to introduce "wild cards" into a model and to provide them with appropriate weights as to their potential impacts; yet, such events are often the most important ones because they are unprepared for. Further, the sources of information are frequently highly personal in the sense that individuals feel more comfortable with information gained from others on the scene. The major problem with this, however, is that the managers of particular companies in host countries tend to circulate among their peers (even their own nationality), thereby reinforcing their biases and any misinformation.

Complicating the analysis on the part of companies is the fact that political or economic events elsewhere in the world can be so serious that the investment climate in the host country is changed even without the volition of the host government. That is, the host government may still be quite favorable to foreign investment, but the conditions of successful operation are so adversely affected that these have to be calculated in the country risk. The significance of such events may be much greater for some countries than others—as with those countries that were dependent on oil imports when the embargo on oil hit and the price was run up significantly, or the pressure on TNCs in South Africa related to its policy of apartheid.

The indefinite nature of such events and the uncertainty of the effects make corporate officials wary of country-risk analysis, seeing it as too "soft" and not providing "hard" information on which to base "go or no-go" decisions. Another difficulty is that few TNCs are willing to establish a worldwide information network to provide continuous, relevant data. The objective is not only an adequate response to change but also anticipating and shaping the change itself. The cost is substantial, and gathering information seems less relevant when the climate is favorable. But, when the climate turns adverse, it may be too late to gather appropriate information. (The problem of intelligence-gathering is complicated by the ethical issues raised by industrial espionage and corporate secrecy.) Another complication is that adequate analysis requires assessments by individuals with widely diverse expertise—economists, political scientists, management analysts, lawyers, sociologists, cultural anthropologists, and so on. The techniques for analyzing the situation are not held wholly in any one discipline or methodology. Some broad-based assessments are required, and the abilities to do so are not normally held within the TNC, they have to be carefully acquired.

Further complicating the process is the problem that one of the causes of political risk in a host country can be the actions of the TNCs themselves. A significant affiliate of a single TNC or several acting collectively can operate in ways that raise public, elite, or political opinion against them. A large industrial disaster, a serious problem of waste disposal, a revelation of attempts to corrupt government officials, or any untoward act can alter the perception of the legitimacy of a foreign-owned affiliate. Given the propensity of corporate managers to seek a way to do what they want, rather than assessing critical impacts of doing so, this source of political risk is likely to be overlooked.

Finally, a major criticism of country-risk analysis is that it usually attempts to squeeze into a formal or rational structure events that are seen as irrational by the parent company. What appears to be illogical from the standpoint of the TNC is usually based on an interpretation from within the managers' own culture, rather than observing the foreign culture as it *is*. Understanding of cross-cultural effects on comparative management styles is not a strong suit of TNC top management anywhere. This myopia is particularly curious given that the mere presence of a TNC changes the culture in the host country to some extent. Some changes made by TNCs—such as the introduction of the automobile for mass use, the introduction of fast foods, or the introduction of herbicides and pesticides—so significantly alter the culture of the host country that they affect the TNC's legitimacy. Thus, TNCs themselves change the environment that they are trying to assess, yet few adequately assess the impact of their own operations in the host country. This is a myopia of most managers, who have not been encouraged to observe much more than market and economic phenomena. But a wider observation and analysis is necessary.

Another curious aspect of country-risk analysis is the greater environmental *certainty* in countries that are less democratic or participatory in their political institutions. Those countries that have a more centralized decision-making system are more able to *form* the climate for the foreign investor (whether favorable or unfavorable) and make certain that it is continued—as in Romania and even in South Korea. The TNC has fewer groups to deal with in assessing risks, since a high degree of stability is provided by the government. The major concern becomes that of finding a cooperative or collaborative relation with the government, so that it provides a favorable climate. If a country such as Romania in the 1980s seeks a certain foreign investment, it

can and will provide quite specific support—even to guaranteed wages for a five-year period. Still, when such a government does change its policies (as with Castro in Cuba,
China's opening, and Poland's turn to more democratic politics), the effects on TNCs tend to be more traumatic than
when they occur in a more open political system, which can
make minor changes more readily. Similarly, as analyzed in
previous chapters concerning the open or restrictive nature
of host-country policies, the more closed the economy the
more certainty provided to the foreign investor, though the
scope of the opportunity is less.

Adequacy of TNC Effort

Because of the complexity of this analysis, the wide
range of information required, and the absence of any formal model for gathering, assessing, and disseminating appropriate information, few TNCs adequately examine
country (or political) risk. They consider the financial/com-
mercial analysis complex enough and more important. An
example of the depth of analysis of political shifts is seen in
the conclusion by a vice president of a U.S. TNC, in assessing an opportunity abroad, that "the opportunity for investment in Iran appears to be highly favorable, unless
something happens to the Shah, and I can see nothing
which would upset his continuation in power." This was
written less than a year before the overthrow of the Shah.

A number of TNCs have set up a formal procedure for
political-risk analysis; others do a more informal, usually
subjective, assessment which becomes a "threshold analysis" that simply rejects some countries out-of-hand as being too unstable or unfamiliar and not warranting further
examination. Yet, even those countries that are seen as relatively stable and receptive are subject to significant shifts
in policies towards foreign direct investment and can become adverse to all investors or to specific activities—such
as extraction, manufacturing in a defense-related sector, or
even the service sector. Cuba was seen by most companies
as a safe haven in the 1930s, 1940s and into the 1950s; but
it expropriated all foreign investment under Castro; Brazil
welcomed foreign direct investment save in a few sectors,
yet in the early 1980s virtually threw out many foreign in-

vestors in the electronics sector. The service sector has been selected for differential restraints in many countries, and local-content requirements in manufacturing continue to be increased in others. Failing to assess the probability of such events is to remain unprepared for prompt and effective negotiation with host governments when these events occur. Many of the issues for which negotiation is required are in the legal field or in the sociopolitical arena—as discussed in succeeding chapters—often outside the scope of managerial attention or abilities. The risk of expropriation has diminished greatly since the 1970s; it caused considerable tensions, and host governments found other means of constraint. In the 1980s, nations became more welcoming.

TNC Defense Against Risks

There are a number of ways in which the corporation can reduce its exposure to "political risk" in a host country. They can develop alternative sources of supply of the items produced in the host country, in the case of resource or efficiency seekers. Or, they can increase some contributions to the host country so as to reduce potential penalties imposed, move funds among affiliates so as to reduce exposure in one country, or reduce the amount of investment in fixed assets so as to enhance mobility. Finally, they can purchase "political risk" insurance, which is available to protect against war, riot and revolution, and expropriation, but not against changes in regulations that may constitute a form of "creeping expropriation."

Creeping expropriation is an attempt on the part of the host country to shift the benefits of development to itself and away from the foreign investor. This is another attempt to redistribute the benefits, using bargaining power to alter the results. The ultimate power of the foreign investor is the threat to withdraw (divestment), but that threat must be credible; it is less so the larger the investment in fixed assets. Large investment in fixed assets, means less flexibility among TNC affiliates, and greater reliance on the market in the host country for overall profitability of the TNC, or on stability of production to support profitability in other affiliates. It also increases the difficulty of relocating the particular production facilities to other countries. All of these reduce the bargaining strength of the TNC because withdrawal is more costly.

The bargaining power of the foreign investor is also weakened by the existence of strong local competitors, who may be pressing the host government to put restraints on the foreigner. Finally, the bargaining power of the foreign investor is further weakened if the technology that has been brought into the country has become mature or even somewhat obsolete, making it easy for local companies to take up the slack if the foreign affiliate is withdrawn. All of these are related to the concept of the "obsolescing bargain," discussed previously.

Therefore, one defense against interference by the host country as a result of political or economic shifts is to sequence the investment so that there is always some potential expansion that is seen as desirable by the host government, thereby reducing the host government's willingness to intervene. Similarly, the integration of the activity in one country with operations of affiliates in other countries of a region can bring pressure to bear from the other countries so that operations in each are not affected adversely by the policies of the others. Another defense, of course, is the acceptance of a joint-venture partner who is seen as concerned with the interest of the host country; in some cases, the mere existence of a joint-venture partner is a protection against further constraints because the enterprise is *seen* as having a local presence, and that is sufficient to legitimize its activities.

DIVESTMENT

The ultimate response of any TNC to pressure from the host government is withdrawal. This is not an easy task nor an easy decision. TNCs invest in countries principally to stay there. Only a few have a policy of entry and quick exit, and they are easily recognized by the type of arrangement which they make when entering the host country. These are generally contractual ventures that lead to cross-border plants, or manufacturing contracts that can be readily terminated.

All other foreign affiliates and even most licensing arrangements (unless stipulated that they are for a limited duration) are seen by the foreign investor/licensor as continuing arrangements and expected to be rather permanent. It does not pay for a TNC to make a multimillion dollar investment for only a four or five-year duration. In addition, few potential buyers are likely to exist unless the economy changed in the interim. Local companies were not strong enough to preclude foreign entry to begin with and other TNCs will be looking at the same problems facing the affiliate. (Of course, if the problem has arisen because of poor government relations, either a local or foreign company with better ties could find a purchase attractive.) In the advanced countries, a local company looking to buy a foreign-owned affiliate may be put-off if the parent company found the market difficult to penetrate. However, the increase in multifaceted networks opens opportunities for a "fit" with a differently oriented network so that the buying and selling of affiliates is likely to increase. Also, a potential buyer can see an opportunity differently from the foreign parent or have a stronger position with the government so as to make the project profitable. In the developing countries, it is usually few local enterprises with sufficient capital to buy a wholly owned affiliate of a foreign company, since it is not likely to be small scale. The most likely buyer is another TNC from an advanced country looking for entry into the host country. However, if the reason for divestment is governmental pressure, the second TNC is not likely to be interested either.

Apart from the difficulties of finding an appropriate buyer, the decision to terminate is still traumatic for the parent company, because it demonstrates failure on the part of the managers who proposed or operated the venture, and it signals a withdrawal from a market and a potential reduction of market share worldwide. TNCs tend to try every avenue open to them to keep an affiliate alive and moving towards profitability. The problem is that of taking a large known loss or a smaller probable loss over an unknown number of years. In one instance a major TNC decided to try to turn around an operation losing $25 million a year, rather than walk away from its $250 million in fixed assets. After 10 years and a cumulative loss of $250 million, it still faced the same decision. There is always a reluctance on the part of some managers (usually those who participated in the decisions or were responsible for the start-up) to close down an operation; there are often personal ties to earlier decisions, and optimism about the future usually prevails.

Such sell-outs do occur, but it is very difficult for TNCs to accept large lump-sum losses, with no way of making them up. Obviously, the rest of the company might be made more profitable by diverting resources in another direction, but this is not certain and it is not tied to the operations in the divested enterprise.

Finally, there is no accepted theory of divestment comparable to the theory of investment in a new or acquired enterprise.[8] One cannot use marginal analysis in assessing the use of fixed plant and equipment, the value of continued presence in a foreign market (which may yet take off, and which may be difficult to reenter once divestment has taken place), and the value of goodwill with the government. The TNC entered with a commitment, and it is difficult to assess the impact of the elimination of that commitment on the host country (and other countries seeing the action) or on TNC managers who are tied to that commitment.

Divestment, therefore, generally occurs under very strong pressure—from the host government (as with Coca-Cola in India, noted in Chapter 9), from the home government (as in South Africa, noted in Chapter 14), or from unexpected or long-term economic reversals. The TNC tends to think that it can "work things out," since problems will yield to competent assessment and negotiation. This is what TNC management prides itself in doing, and it tends to stay in the game as long as it is at all feasible. Consequently, the host government acquires a strong bargaining position and is able to push the TNC affiliate into making concessions. The TNC affiliate responds more to these negative pressures than to any positive inducements, and therefore bends quite a bit before it breaks off and withdraws.

NEGOTIATION PROCEDURES AND CHANNELS

Entry through foreign investment or technology transfers, into any country with few exceptions, requires a negotiation with the national government and possibly with the state or local government as well. These negotiations set the basic relationships between business and governments. Both TNC and government need to know a great deal about the other in order to negotiate successfully.[9] This requires a substantial investigation, which should be part of a continuing assessment of the other player (via country-risk analysis for the firm), so that there is ample time to pull specific data out of extensive background information.

The negotiating positions of each of the parties depends on the opportunities available to the firms in the host country and elsewhere, the objectives of the TNCs seeking to enter and the urgency (to the government or the TNC) of their entering, the number of companies seeking to take advantage of a given opportunity, the pressure of unemployment, the need for tax revenue, the ideological orientation of the government, the attitude of national companies, and so on. (Refer to the bargaining model in Chapter 1.) Each negotiation has its unique aspects, and these need to be recognized early by each party.

Once adequate background information is available, the negotiators on each side need to understand the positions, backgrounds, and interests of each individual on the other's team. They should identify the precedents that the others are likely to draw on. This initial phase of the negotiations offers the freest movement to both sides, and new arrangements are feasible, depending on the negotiating strength of each. In this initial phase, the negotiating strength of the TNC is greater, relative to the government, than it is in later stages, i.e., when the company is already in operations, when it is seeking to expand the operations, or when it is facing termination or withdrawal.

The government's negotiating strength is greater when the company is doing well and seeking to expand operations but requires government approval to do so. The TNC's strength in the phases of winding down, withdrawal or termination depend on how eager it is to leave and its timeframe for doing so. Since it is already in a process of disposing of assets, it is not negotiating *whether* to depart— only how and at what cost. Obviously, it seeks to minimize losses, but the government gains an advantage over time. The "obsolescing bargain" weakens the TNC's strength, but the eagerness of the government to take advantage of or to redirect the TNC's behavior probably also declines as the TNC becomes more "legitimate." The host government becomes more familiar with TNC operations and is able to establish long-term relationships, and the company learns how to fit its culture into that of the host country. In addition, bargaining strength shifts with the political atmosphere, with one political party being more strident in its criticism and harsh in its constraints on TNCs than another.

The nature, extent, and intensity of negotiations is altered also according to the type of company that is seeking to enter. As discussed earlier, companies seeking resources, markets, or efficiency offer different contributions to the host country. In turn, the host country provides different opportunities to each. There are different precedents for each type of arrangement both in the host country and within other countries, so that different patterns of negotiation can be drawn upon for guidelines.

Negotiations also differ according to the subjects of negotiation—investment, joint ventures, or technology transfers. They become more complicated when several aspects are combined. For example, a joint venture typically involves both investment and technology transfer with local and foreign enterprises and often government officials involved, making it the most complex of negotiations.[10] In addition, a joint-venture negotiation first requires bargaining with several potential partners to determine which would be the most compatible, then a more detailed negotiation of the roles of each party and their contributions. When both private companies and the host government are involved there is an opportunity for each to use the strength of the other to increase its benefits.

There are a number of issues that arise for negotiation, depending on the nature of the arrangement. There are at least 25 different provisions that are likely to be the subject of negotiation under an investment, with some 12 or 15 more added, into a joint-venture negotiation and another 10 specific to a technology agreement. If these are negotiated in combination, the numbers are additive. A partial list of the issues to be negotiated in an investment project includes the following:

A. Financing
- Capital to be invested
- Foreign exchange availabilities
- Stock issues
- Availability of local capital

B. Trade
- Import of capital goods
- Imports of components
- Exports anticipated

D. Labor
- Training of employees
- Labor law and strike settlement

E. Regulations
- Licensing of imports
- Capital repatriation
- Dividends
- Local ownership
- Location site (depressed region)
- Pricing and price controls
- Hiring and promotion of locals
- Payment of head-office expenses
- R&D charges
- Addition of R&D laboratory
- Protection of proprietary information
- Patent rights
- Compulsory licensing

F. Law
- Arbitration
- Court jurisdiction

G. Incentives
- Provision of infrastructure
- Tax and other incentives

If a joint venture is involved, the list would also include:

- Voting rights of each partner
- Capital contributions

- Management arrangements
- Product lines
- Technology contributions
- Protection of proprietary rights
- The use of patents and trademarks
- Marketing areas
- Development of design center

Negotiation of technology transfers (either in combination with, or independent of investment) introduces the following provisions:

- Royalty payments—amounts, type, frequency
- Specific technology transferred
- Visits of technicians
- Trouble-shooting
- Market areas for licensee
- Cross-licensing
- Return of improvements
- Rights to sublicense
- Purchase of components or materials from licensor
- Purchase of product by licensor
- Rights of licensor to inspect the books of licensee

Each of the provisions in the various arrangements is potentially tradable against other provisions, so that the negotiation becomes complex in timing and subject matter. In both the joint venture and the licensing arrangements, two different companies are being brought together in a new relationship, which is quite similar to a marriage in that the various situations that will need to be worked out between the parties cannot be foreseen. Yet, to make the arrangement highly legalistic is to fail to recognize the dedication and commitment that is necessary to be able to respond to new events in a flexible and mutually agreeable manner.

As shown in the prior bargaining comparisons, the interest of each of the parties to the negotiation differs on the issues, and their ability to affect the outcome depends on

Figure 10.1: Structure of Negotiations

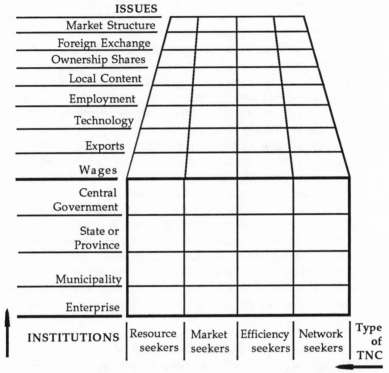

the specific position of each of the negotiating entities. But in many situations the TNC faces several levels of government, and they in turn face TNCs of different types. When these aspects are added, a three-dimensional matrix results showing the issues, the types of TNCs, and the government levels. A fourth dimension would show the phases of the project at which the negotiation is taking place—initiation, operation, or termination. Each box within the matrix indicates the relative interest and strength of the company or government relative to the issues, as in Figure 10.1 and in the various cubic figures in prior chapters; adding the fourth dimension would inject information relating to the stage of the project from initiation to termination.

Not all of the issues involve conflicts between the parties, but those that are of mutual interest still require negotiation to make certain that they are moving in the same direction and to the same extent as desired by the other. Thus, a foreign investor will use local suppliers to some extent, but it may not be in the same way or for the components that the government would like to see developed locally. The company will certainly bring capital into the host economy, but again not necessarily in the amounts desired; it will bring technology, but not necessarily as desired by the government; and so on. Negotiation is, therefore, not wholly adversarial; but differing views on virtually every issue are likely to arise.

To prevent any of the issues from turning sour in the period of operation or implementation of the arrangement, a heavy responsibility rests on the managing director to maintain close contacts with the governmental agencies responsible so as to anticipate problems and reduce the necessity to renegotiate the arrangement on a formal basis. Such a renegotiation can only upset headquarters and potentially raise issues that otherwise were quiescent. Negotiation, therefore, is a continuing process whether on a formal or informal basis and melds into the government relations function of the affiliate in an almost imperceptible way.

NOTES TO CHAPTER 10

1. P. Beamish, and J. C. Banks, "Equity Joint Ventures and the Theory of Multinational Enterprise," *Journal of International Business Studies,* Summer, (1987), pp. 1–16.

2. J. N. Behrman, J. J. Boddewyn, and A. Kapoor, *International Business - Government Communication* (Lexington, MA: Lexington Books, 1976).

3. See also, S. Prakash Sethi and K. A. N. Luther, "Political Risk Analysis and Direct Foreign Investment: Some Problems in Definition and Measurement," *California Management Review* (Winter 1986), pp. 57–68. For an assessment of international political risk and TNC strategies to offset it, see Theodore Moran, *Multinational Corporations* (Lexington, MA: Lexington Books, 1985), chap. 5. A short but classic assessment is given by Stephen J. Kobrin, "Political Risk: A Review and Reconsideration," *Journal of International Business Studies* (Spring/Summer 1979), pp. 67–70 and reprinted in Dymsza and Vambrey, *International Business Knowledge.* See also S. J. Kobrin, "Political Assessment by International Firms: Models or Methodologies?" *Journal of Policy Modeling,* vol. 3, no. 2 (1981), pp. 251–271.

4. A reverse assessment of home-country influences on direct investment outflows is given by Stephen B. Tallman, "Home Country Political Risk and Foreign Direct Investment in the United States," *Journal of International Business Studies* (Summer 1988), pp. 219–234.

5. "Leaving South Africa, IBM, Others Sell Units to Employee Trusts," *Wall Street Journal* (Aug. 24, 1987), p. 1, "Divestment Proves Costly and Hard," *Wall Street Journal* (Feb. 22, 1989), sec. C, p. 1.

6. Thomas E. Krayenbuehl, *Country Risk: Assessment and Monitoring* (Lexington, MA: Lexington Books, 1985), pp. 24–29.

7. In support of the developing countries who have inadequate information on activities of TNCs, the UN Centre on Transnational Corporations publishes a series of industry studies, a series on contractual relations between TNCs and governments, and studies on how to strengthen governmental bargaining positions; for example, *Measures Strengthening the Negotiating Capacity of Governments in their Relations with Transnational Corporations. Joint Ventures in Latin America: A Technical Paper* (New York: United Nations, 1983). (A catalog of UNCTC sales publications is available for 1973–1987 from the Centre.)

8. Jean Boddewyn has begun such an assessment; see "Foreign and Domestic Divestment and Investment Decisions," *Journal of International Business Studies* (Winter 1983), pp. 23–35.

9. An extensive examination of various aspects of international negotiations is found in Frances Mautner-Markhof, *Processes of International Negotiations* (Boulder, CO: Westview, 1989). An assessment of Japanese practices is provided by John L. Graham and Y. Sano, *Smart Bargaining: Doing Business with the Japanese* (Cambridge, MA: Ballinger, 1984); another is provided by Boye de Mente, *How to Do Business in Japan* (Los Angeles: Pepperdine University, Center for International Business, 1972). On other countries, see Ashok Kapoor, *International Business in the Middle East* (Boulder, CO: Westview, 1979); and John Fayerweather and A. Kapoor, *Strategy and Negotiation for the International Corporation* (Cambridge, MA: Ballinger, 1976).

10. See the account of Xerox's negotiations of a joint venture with Shanghai (PRC) in James E. Shapiro, Jack N. Behrman, William A. Fischer, and Simon G. Powell, *Investing in China* (Shanghai: Shanghai Translation and Publishing Co., —forthcoming 1990).

TNCs, International Law, and Intergovernmental Institutions

The relations of TNCs with governments are made more complex by the number of intergovernmental agencies attempting to harmonize national policies toward international business. These institutions focus on particular problems or particular geographic areas. A number of nations are members of each, but not even the United Nations encompasses all nations of the world. The subject of international law relates to operations of these entities, but it also covers conflicts of national laws. Chapter 11 addresses the application of national and international law to TNC activities.

Efforts to include FDI in formal international law began as early as 1946, with the signing of the Charter for an International Trade Organization. It contained provisions for the treatment of private investors, aimed at providing a favorable climate, and included means of handling expropriations. This charter was negotiated by U.S. State Department officials and signed by the President, but it died for lack of ratification by the U.S. Senate. A subsequent effort was made in the OECD "Code on the Liberalization of Capital Movements" signed in 1961 (discussed in Chapter 12), but which never fulfilled its promise. Again, in the mid-1960s, the OECD drafted a "Convention on Protection of Foreign Property" to promote and protect FDI, but the principles were not implemented by members.

In order to reduce the acrimony over government disputes concerning TNC activities, particularly expropriation,[1] the World Bank formed an Internaional Centre for the Settlement of Investment Disputes (ICSID) in 1965, where settlements would be arbitrated. The desire to promote FDI led to the signing of some 200 bilateral investment treaties, principally between advanced and developing countries; these provide for compensation and settlement of disputes, especially in cases of expropriation. Some 50 percent of these treaties use the ICSID.

After a searching study of the role of TNCs in developing countries by selected officials from around the world, known as the Group of Eminent Persons, the UN Economic and Social Council (ECOSOC) established in 1975 a Commission on Transnational Corporations and a Centre on TNCs, as its secretariat. It provides research and technical advice, information, and training to member governments. The Centre has had the major responsibility in attempting to formulate codes on TNCs.

To indicate the ways in which such a code should be formulated, the advanced countries, through the OECD, set forth a "Declaration on International Investment and MNEs" in 1976; it provided guidelines for TNC behavior and encouraged the extension by members of "national treatment" to foreign investors.

To assist LDCs as they shifted from restrictive to more open policies, the International Finance Corporation of the World Bank established a Foreign Investment Advisory Service, which provides information on the ways to attract and regulate TNCs so LDCs might gain the most benefits for domestic development. In 1989, the Bank established the Multilateral Investment Guarantee Agency (MIGA) to help insure TNCs against commercial risks; this followed some 25 years of bilateral treaties and national guarantee agencies and continuing pressure on the Bank to provide a multilateral facility. Movement in the intergovernmental realm is measured and slow, but nonetheless important, and TNCs have not been as fully involved in the formulation of these policies or institutions as is warranted, given their potential impacts and precedents for future cooperation.

Chapter 12 examines the ways and extent to which TNCs are involved in the deliberations and policy implementation of various regional associations as well as the impacts of these associations on the TNCs. Not all of these groups have formal ties with TNC associations, but they have received representations by TNCs or association officials on specific issues. Likely expansion of regionalism through new groups or new members in existing groups will increase the dialogues between TNCs and officials of such associations.

At the intergovernmental level, the United Nations Organization has a number of subunits or affiliates that are concerned with various activities of transnationals around the world—both functionally and regionally. Chapter 13 discusses the scope of UN activities and the channels of communication between these and TNCs. It also addresses the efforts in the UN to formulate codes of behavior for TNCs around the world and weighs the future of intergovernmental regulation.

It is not possible in this volume to assess each of the policy approaches or experiences in the field of intergovernmental relations affecting the TNCs. This section addresses the communication between TNCs and the intergovernmental agencies and examines briefly some of the issues so as to indicate the reasons for the differences of views on TNC practices and to present some of the resolutions accepted.

Although it is likely that the primary thrust in the near future will be toward regional harmonization and sectoral agreements, activities at the UN will continue to engage the attention of at least some of the TNCs and private international associations. The absence of pervasive attempts to regulate TNCs further through intergovernmental agreement is testimony to the effectiveness of TNCs and some host governments in helping to relieve this pressure through continuous dialogue over the past decade. Since new areas of concern arise and new institutions are formed—as with the United Nations Center on Science and Technology for Development, created in the early 1980s—TNCs can expect to be drawn into further dialogues on a variety of subjects.

NOTE to Part IV Introduction

1. The expropriations in the post-World War II period that raised concerns in the U.S. government are examined in Robert G. Hawkins, Norman Mintz, and M. Provissiero, "Government Takeovers of U.S. Foreign Affiliates," in Dymsza and Vambrey, *International Business Knowledge*, pp. 58–71.

CHAPTER 11

Legal Issues and International Law

Legal issues are a frequent subject of dialogue between TNCs and national governments. Where laws of different nations conflict, a TNC may be caught between them and have a difficult time reconciling its behavior in one or both countries. Where multiple national laws conflict, uncertainty increases and indecision becomes more intense. TNCs are subject, around the world, to national laws; there is no international institution or tribunal prescribing or judging the behavior of TNCs. Where national laws are the same or quite similar, the TNC has no significant difficulty in determining what its behavior should be—whether or not it decides to accede. Where applicable national laws are similar, but one is more stringent than others, the resolution is easy enough in that the TNC merely has to follow the more stringent requirement. Of course, it may be reluctant to do so, since this may result in higher cost and lower profits, but at least the TNC knows what the trade-offs and potential penalties are.

The United States, particularly, but also some of the other advanced countries, has sought to assert the application of international law—overriding the sovereignty of any single government—in matters affecting FDI. The assertion is that this law has been established by precedent under a number of agreements and treaties, showing the way that governments are to behave in certain situations. Whether such a thing as "international law" covering governments even exists is a matter of debate, but U.S. State Department officials insist that the world cannot be permitted to act *as though* there is no such thing as international law—otherwise, it would simply be one government's position against another's. But most of the world, including the socialist countries and the third and fourth worlds (the NICs and LDCs) claim that they were not party to the formation of such law, being colonial subjects at the time. In addition, there is no court with obligatory jurisdiction over such law. The World Court (International Court of Justice at The Hague) can take jurisdiction only if national governments wish to bring a case before it. And there is no supranational government that can implement decisions under it.

Much of the dialogue between the North and the South over the legal issues and the regulatory codes under the United Nations reflect the South's objective of formulating new international law. But the North does not see the desirability of any new law that alters significantly the historical patterns and precedents. The advanced countries wish to have agreements that do not necessarily form new international law, whereas the LDCs (and some NICs) seek to substitute the new agreements for prior law, because they see the existing laws as favoring the interests advanced countries.[1]

When the subject of dispute involves FDI, the TNCs are caught in the middle; sometimes they wish not to be seen as a foreign company; sometimes they wish to have the protection of the home government as asserted through international law, but are wary of asserting such rights in a host country. The issues that are subject to legal treatment include some related to taxation, antitrust, information disclosure and transfer, the application of the national laws of one country in a foreign jurisdiction, export and technology controls, investment treaties, expropriation, proprietary rights, investment guarantees, and procedures for settlement of disputes. The positions of TNCs from different nations and industry sectors differ on each of these issues.

EXTRATERRITORIALITY

The extraterritorial extension of one country's laws into another country remains a sore point in diplomatic relations. In several instances, the TNC is caught in this process and finds it difficult to work its way out without offending one or the other government. The U.S. Monroe Doctrine originated in 1823 in order to prevent European countries (later any others) from extending jurisdictions (later "interfering") in Latin America in ways that threatened U.S. interests; it was later to protect U.S. business interests in those countries. This protection was resented by the Latin American nations, who responded with the Calvo Doctrine. It asserted essentially that national law was to apply with reference to any activities undertaken within the countries of Latin America, and no intervention by the U.S. government in defense of U.S. companies would be accepted.[2] The U.S. government has never recognized the Calvo Doctrine, continuing to assert that international law takes precedence, and that it has a *right* to extend national laws over the behavior of U.S. companies anywhere in the world, including the right to protect them against unjust treatment abroad. (There have been, however, differences of view among the Executive Branch, the Supreme Court, and the Congress on whether such intervention *should* be undertaken in a number of instances.) Other countries have also rejected at times the extension of U.S. law into their domains through the activities of the TNCs. And even some states in the United States have extended their laws in ways having impacts on operations abroad.[3]

Antitrust

The U.S. government has sought to extend its antitrust laws into the operations of U.S. companies abroad to prohibit actions harming U.S. commerce. The antitrust legislation stipulates that anticompetitive behavior abroad of U.S. companies is illegal if it damages U.S. commerce or the competitive position of other U.S. companies abroad. (It does not reach to the behavior of foreign-owned companies—unless they have an affiliate in the United States.) The U.S. government has been able to assert this right through ownership by U.S. TNCs of foreign affiliates and through licensing arrangements. It does so through its ability to "punish" the parent for its decisions, permissions, or acquiescence to prohibited acts.

Under this legislation, the U.S. government is able to prevent affiliates of U.S. TNCs from joining cartels in foreign countries, from entering into trade restraints, or making pricing agreements with other companies. It is also able to prevent U.S. licensors from restricting the activities of licensees in terms of sources of supply of components or services, from setting prices, or limiting marketing territories.

In the main, foreign governments are not particularly averse to the application of antitrust laws to American-owned affiliates, but they sometimes oppose their application to joint ventures with local companies. The U.S. government considers that it has the ability (and therefore authority) to intervene in a foreign joint venture that is more than 50 percent owned by a U.S. TNC. Since the mere existence of a joint venture makes it *possible* for the U.S. TNC to conspire with the foreign partner to restrict U.S. commerce, all joint ventures are suspect. The U.S. government takes a flexible attitude, however, unless violations are flagrant. Some governments have considered that this extension of U.S. law is harmful to the local joint-venture partner, and diplomatic exchanges have resulted. The U.S. Justice Department has, in practice, cut back on the number of its own complaints about TNC behavior abroad. Further, as other countries—particularly European—have strengthened their own antitrust legislation, the U.S. government has felt less necessity to act. Yet, the problem can still arise to confront unwary management.

Information Disclosure

One problem in applying the antitrust laws is finding information that demonstrates the validity of the case brought by the U.S. government. The U.S. Justice Department has jurisdiction over all information held by a company that is needed in prosecution of an antitrust case. In pursuit of violations abroad, the government has, on occasion, sought to acquire information held by a foreign affiliate of a U.S. TNC. Several European countries have passed legislation requiring such affiliates within their jurisdiction to obtain permission for releasing information to the U.S. government. In this way, they hope to prevent critical commercial/economic or strategic information from leaving the country unless they approve its transfer. In any event, they are concerned to assert their own control over information within the country and its transfer to foreign jurisdictions. It is difficult, in practice, to apply these restrictions, but governments still wish to assert their *right* to do so. Again, the U.S. TNC acts under two different laws, and reconciliation may have to come at the diplomatic level.

Technology and Export Controls

A similar double-bind exists in the controls exercised by the U.S. Department of Commerce over the export of sensitive technology and commodities. These controls extend to items that are declared in "short supply" and any that adversely affect U.S. security or national interests. A list of prohibited commodities and prohibited destinations is drawn up by the Office of Export Control in the Department of Commerce. For these items, specific licenses must be obtained in order to permit the transfer or export to controlled destinations; all other items can be exported under a "general" license. Other countries also have export controls, and major Western countries formed a Coordinating Committee (COCOM), under which a list of goods and destinations requiring licenses is agreed upon, so that an "enemy" cannot play one supplier off against another. But U.S. prohibitions are more extensive than those of other members, and the U.S. government has, on occasion, unilaterally prohibited technology transfers *from* affiliates abroad or licensees of the U.S. companies to "prohibited destinations," plus sales of goods made under such technology. For example, a French licensee of a U.S. company bid in 1982 on part of the construction of a Soviet gas pipeline; but the U.S. government, through its controls over the licensor, denied the French licensee a right to ship its product to the U.S.S.R.[4]

The application of U.S. law to the foreign affiliates is done only if the affiliate is owned more than 50 percent by the U.S. parent *or* if there is a licensing agreement under which the licensor controls the flow of technology. Where the licensor has such control, the U.S. government considers that its control over the U.S. licensor extends to the licensee and his exports. The prohibitions can cover exports into friendly countries, especially if it is considered the *ultimate* recipient is in a prohibited destination—as in the Toshiba case mentioned earlier. The prohibited destinations have principally been countries in the Soviet bloc plus China, but a number of companies in friendly countries have been blacklisted for violating the rules against transshipment into prohibited destinations.

Given the fact that other countries have less stringent controls, they are more willing for their companies and joint ventures to export to countries that the U.S. government seeks to deny similar products or technology. Disputes over the similarity of goods and technology arise within the COCOM, frequently after shipments or transfers have already been made. When the company involved is a joint venture with a U.S. TNC, or when a wholly owned U.S. affiliate has been ordered by a foreign government to fulfill a given transaction, the U.S. company is caught in the middle. This was the case when Ford's affiliate in Argentina received orders from the Cuban government for trucks. The Argentine government wished to fulfill the order for employment and foreign-exchange purposes, however, the affiliate was constrained by the parent, who recognized the application of U.S. export controls. Nevertheless, the Argentine government forced the export, despite U.S. government objections, and the latter exacted no recompense—in fact, its hands were tied by the "Act of State Doctrine," which states that a sovereign government cannot be brought into foreign courts by private parties for acts taken wholly within its national jurisdiction.

At the extreme, there is no way that the U.S. government can prohibit a foreign affiliate from violating U.S. export controls *if* the host government insists on the completion of a given transaction. Punishing the headquarters company would not prevent such an occurrence in the future. Even so, the situation is an uncomfortable one for the headquarters company in the United States and leads to considerable negotiation in both countries—as with the case of Fruehauf in France, when the U.S. parent's vice president faced indictment in courts of both countries.[5]

Foreign Corrupt Practices

Still another area in which U.S. law extends overseas is the existence of corrupt practices of U.S. companies or their affiliates or agents in transactions with foreign governments. The U.S. Foreign Corrupt Practices Act (FCPA) was passed in 1977 to prevent bribing of foreign government officials or payments of rebates or excessive fees to intermediaries (with the implication that they are used for such bribes) on the grounds that this is not the way in which business should be done in a free-market economy and that it can harm both the national interest of the foreign country and its diplomatic relations with the United States. Host governments do not object to this extension of U.S. law, but TNCs and their affiliates do, simply because they believe that they are losing business since foreign competitors do not have to comply with such constraints.[6] This law avoids the problem of information disclosure by requiring that the headquarters company keep adequate records of transactions so that it knows whether or not corrupt practices have occurred. It also requires disclosure of any violation to the Securities and Exchange Commission (SEC). (This issue is discussed further in Chapter 14.)

The issue of extraterritoriality appears to be unique to U.S. TNCs and their relations abroad. No other countries have a practice of such extension of their laws into other countries, partly because they do not attempt to control the activities of their TNCs so strictly, nor are they as concerned as is the U.S. government with frustration of national law by the activities of affiliates abroad. It is anathema to the U.S. Congress that it can pass a law constraining U.S. parents in dealings abroad and then find that the prohibited transactions are being carried out by foreign *affiliates* of the same companies. Therefore, it has approved the efforts to extend the jurisdiction of U.S. law. Most European governments have a history of treating commercial activities in their colonies (or foreign countries) differently from the commercial activities of national companies in their home market. They are, therefore, less concerned with acts abroad by their TNCs, which appear to the U.S. government as violations by U.S. TNCs of its national law. (For example, the United States is the only nation prohibiting bribery *abroad*.) Given their orientation in other countries, European governments are frequently upset by the attempt of the U.S. government to extend its jurisdiction into their countries.

Where there are constraints of a similar nature in the host country, but U.S. law is simply more stringent, the TNC can fairly readily comply with U.S. law without endangering its position abroad. It is only when the two are in conflict that it finds itself in a quandary and must negotiate its way to a settlement. There are no institutional mechanisms for assisting in this negotiation. The company is virtually on its own facing the two governments, who may or may not be willing to work toward an agreement.

TAX TREATIES

One legal area in which the TNCs have historically found themselves clearly in the middle is that of taxation. The host country would tax operations within their jurisdiction, and when earnings were repatriated, they would be taxed again. In order to avoid double taxation, tax treaties have been signed, providing for the deduction or crediting of foreign taxes on a mutual basis between the signatory countries. Over the years, the U.S. government has taken the initiative to negotiate 46 such treaties with foreign countries, easing the tax burden on returns to FDI.

Disagreements do arise as to the coverage of the treaties, the exclusions, the types of taxes to be considered, and tax waivers. For example, the tax treaties cover only income taxes and not sales taxes or taxes on value added (TVA or VAT), despite the fact that they are imposed on the same companies. The treaties do cover taxes imposed "in lieu of" income taxes, but the legislation of the host country must clearly state that this substitution is intended. What constitutes "in lieu of" is frequently a matter of discussion between TNCs and the U.S. government—for example, are taxes on the *retention* of earnings taxes on *income?* Tax sparing, as discussed earlier, is also a matter of contention.

INVESTMENT TREATIES AND GUARANTEES

The U.S. government in the 1950s and 1960s, and European governments in the 1960s and 1970s, sought to assist developing countries through the promotion of FDI. The major obstacle was the existence of what were considered "unfavorable climates" in host countries (particularly LDCs). The unfavorable characteristics included expropriation, unstable exchange rates, currency inconvertibility, and threats of war, revolution, or riots; these risks are not covered by insurance on the usual commercial risks.

In an effort to help improve this climate, a number of countries have entered into investment treaties with LDCs and provide investment guarantees to FDI by their TNCs. The early post-World War II agreements were called Treaties of Friendship, Commerce, and Navigation (FCN), (the traditional name for treaties guiding the opening or expansion of commercial relations between two countries). After the 1950s, they were called Treaties of Friendship, Commerce, and Investment, and more recently, simply Investment Treaties.[7] Provisions are included in which the signatory countries agree to abide by international law, and the host country agrees to provide "prompt, adequate, and effective compensation," in the event that it expropriates foreign-owned property. The reason for the "prompt" qualification is that the process of settlement of an expropriation usually takes years; it can be so drawn out that compensation in local currency could be withered away by inflation in the host country. "Adequate" compensation relates to the valuation of the expropriated assets, which is often difficult to determine and is usually judged to be lower by the host country than by the TNCs. "Effective" means that the payment must be in assets that can be effectively transferred; governments had a practice of paying in government bonds that quickly became worthless either through the inability to sell or through inflationary reduction in their value. (Of course, no TNC considers that an expropriation of its assets abroad is *ever* fair.)

The U.S. government has never opposed expropriation, since it adheres to the Act of State Doctrine. The State Department has only insisted that the process follow international law and be subject to the qualifications just mentioned. The role of TNCs in the negotiation of such treaties is simply to make certain that the agreements provide as much protection to TNC interests as is possible.

The investment treaties are linked to unilateral investment guarantees by home countries, which provide compensation against loss of assets through war, riot, revolution, and expropriation. U.S. guarantees are not offered for any country that does not have an investment treaty, and it requires further that the foreign country accept the subrogation of rights, in the case of expropriation, to the U.S. government. That is, if the settlement is not "prompt, adequate, and effective" and the U.S. government has to make good its guarantee, the U.S. government then will become the claimant in the courts of the host country. The investment guarantees are available only for countries that have accepted the responsibilities laid down in the agreements, and all investments have to be "approved" for a guarantee to be extended. Licensing arrangements can be covered. These guarantees are now offered by the U.S. Overseas Private Investment Corporation(OPIC), which is an independent agency spun out of the Agency for International Development (AID), so as to remove support of private FDI from the negotiations concerning foreign aid.

The settlement of insurance claims by OPIC is not automatic, though 90 percent have been honored and only 7 of the total 227 claims have gone to arbitration in order to obtain restitution. No claims under guarantees have ever been denied, and since OPIC's inception, it has paid out over $123 million, recovering "significant" amounts through continued collection efforts.[8]

In the 1960s, efforts were made to set up a Multilateral Investment Guarantee Association (MIGA) to substitute for the various national programs. It opened its doors in 1989, after 25 years of negotiation. The establishment of MIGA is an attempt to bring the *host* countries into the guarantee process along with the investing countries, thereby putting pressure on any country that expropriates to make an adequate settlement. Some LDC governments have not joined, however, and presumably would not like to pay for potential losses from acts of appropriation by others. (Members of MIGA have subscribed to its capital, and these subscriptions will be called on a pro rata basis if MIGA has to pay a claim against it.) In addition, many of the receiving countries can accept membership without the appearance of dependence on any specific advanced country, which they thought the bilateral agreements created. TNCs were generally in favor in this new institution.

EXPROPRIATIONS

Most of expropriations that have occurred were not under investment guarantees at the time, so a number of disputes arose over the application of domestic or international law and the form and amount of compensation. The

"Act of State Doctrine" prevents governments from objecting—except, of course, in the case of treaties or international agreements covering such acts. Even then, enforcement is only possible through retaliation, publicity, sanctions, or war. The U.S. government has made representation to many countries about the undesirability of expropriation, but generally to no avail.

The largest portion of expropriations have been in and by the developing countries, and the most extensive occurred when *all* foreign investment was taken in a single sweep—as in Cuba and China (1949). The majority by far have been in the extractive field—nearly 40 percent of expropriations of U.S. affiliates abroad,[9] notably in the Arab counties—followed by manufacturing affiliates plus some banking and insurance companies. Acts of expropriation peaked in the 1960s and 1970s, tailing off substantially in the 1980s partly because most of the sensitive sectors (notably the extractive) had already been taken and partly because other techniques of acquisition or control (e.g. joint ventures) were applied by host countries. Instead of expropriation a number of constraints have been imposed upon the affiliates—known as "performance requirements" (illustrated in Chapters 7–9), which have been seen by TNCs as "creeping expropriation." The profitability of affiliates to TNCs has been reduced, and more benefits were retained by the host country, without the formal act of expropriation. Further, the loss of foreign technology and management after expropriation caused many such companies to become inefficient.

The threat of expropriation raises government/business relations to the highest level within the TNC. In this event, the president and chairman of the board become directly involved. There are few other government relations in which this is the case, except possibly the entry negotiations. Negotiation on expropriation is taken as a matter of life or death, with death hardly being recompensed in any effective way, for a TNC does not invest abroad *just* to get its money back. In addition, expropriation sets a precedent for other countries to take similar action. It is for this reason that TNCs have argued so vociferously against expropriation in any country and have fought so hard in foreign courts, and through the U.S. government, to gain adequate remuneration when it does occur.

For fear of such acts, one American copper company in Chile sought to protect itself against what it saw as an impending expropriation by making loan arrangements with European banks that eventually permitted the taking of copper ore exported by the Chilean government after the expropriation when it was landed in European ports.[10] Foreign courts upheld this taking, and the company was more adequately remunerated. The more difficult and complex negotiations occurred under expropriation when the U.S. government attempted to assist the parent company in representations to the host government.

In the mid-1960s, the U.S. Congress was so exercised over expropriations that it passed two amendments to Foreign Aid bills: the Hickenlooper Amendment requiring termination of aid to a country expropriating U.S. assets without adequate, prompt, and effective compensation; and the Gonzalez Amendment requiring the administration to oppose any loan being considered by any international organization to such a country.

PROTECTION OF PROPRIETARY RIGHTS[11]

Protection of intellectual property rights in patents, trademarks, copyrights, and know-how is of critical concern to TNCs. These rights stem from successful research, invention, and innovation, and they provide the return of profits necessary to continue R&D. All countries protect such rights, but the degree and nature of protection varies widely—particularly in the treatment of foreign-owned rights. The more advanced countries have had long experience in the extension of industrialization. But many of the developing countries have viewed such rights as establishing monopoly positions for the advanced countries—or at least the TNCs therein—and have sought to eliminate or modify them so as to give local companies a stronger competitive position. Some countries, such as Taiwan, have not recognized copyrights and have pirated the publication of large numbers of books and materials. This problem is exacerbated by the inclusion of audio and video cassettes under copyright protection, and by the ease of duplicating printed materials made possible by highly automated copiers. Protection of copyrights has become difficult, but is still quite important to TNCs.

Protection of trademarks is important for the purpose of maintaining product differentiation and protection against product-liability suits. In some cases autos have been imported into the United States without the changes mandated by U.S. regulations, since the price of, say a Mercedes in Germany is much less than in the United States. The importer must then modify the product to meet U.S. standards, but the customer is not protected in case of malfunction since Mercedes itself did not make the changes, and the auto is no longer a "Mercedes." Piracy of trademarks has become frequent around the world, with products made by a second company under inadequate quality controls yet sold under the trademark of a more famous company in a foreign country.[12] For example, in the 1970s, one could buy a Gucci bag or a Cardin tie in South Korea for one-sixth the price in Europe; the copies were virtually precise, even having the trademark, though the quality of materials was lower. Protection of the trademark is a continuous battle for many TNCs, requiring the engagement of investigators and lawyers.

The same fight is necessary to protect patents, since it is profitable on the part of competitors to copy or design around a patent and produce a similar product. At times, patent claims are disputed, even by a licensee. It is even more difficult to protect know-how, though the courts of most advanced countries will do so where there is clear evidence of an intent to keep the technology secret. Licensing agreements are written so as to protect proprietary rights in know-how, but they are easily violated if the licensee wishes to do so.

Over 30 international conventions have been signed since the Paris (1883) and Berne (1886) agreements relating to the filing and protection of patents, trademarks, and copyrights. In order to harmonize policies in this area, a World Intellectual Property Organization (WIPO) was agreed to in 1967 and established in 1970, consolidating over 20 conventions. In 1974, it became an affiliate of the UN. The WIPO has over 90 members, 51 of which are LDCs.

Under the Paris Convention, the principle of national treatment has been guaranteed to members, giving foreigners the same access to national courts as local companies in the case of infringements. Given the spread of TNCs around the world and diverse national laws, mere national treatment is not adequate in the eyes of advanced-country governments and pressure has arisen to revise the WIPO jurisdiction and harmonize (or unify) the protection provisions.

Given the variety of national treatments, there is no standard of protection around the world. Provisions include the ability of a member state to compel a patent holder, who does not actually produce under or use the patent, to grant a license to some local company (know as a "compulsory license"). There is little protection for so-called "process patents" because of the alleged difficulty of doing so. The biogenetic revolution has raised new issues of protection. TNCs are also concerned about the uncertainty as to future modifications of the Paris Convention, which has already been modified five or six times since it came into being in 1883.

TNCs remain quite concerned over proprietary rights in intellectual property since the expenses for R&D have increased greatly. It has also become easier and cheaper for competitors to reproduce protected products, to modify them with little liability, and to discover secrets by reverse engineering. In addition, many developing countries do not have the capacity to enforce adequate industrial standards or proprietary rights, and infringers even in advanced countries frequently go without punishment.

In the 1970s, an initiative was taken to shift responsibility for proprietary rights to the General Agreement on Tariffs and Trade (GATT). Some years later, U.S. TNCs launched a second initiative to obtain a comprehensive code under the GATT, which would cover all types of proprietary rights, plus provide for dispute settlement and sanctions against offenders. TNCs in Europe and Japan did not join in this initiative, considering that the WIPO was adequate as a mechanism and merely needed guidance. To complicate the issues, those businesses concerned mostly with copyrights have separated themselves from those concerned with trademarks, and both have distanced themselves from those concerned with patents. This split in the support for new initiatives has limited the resolve of the U.S. government to proceed in the GATT, especially since there are differences of view among other countries. The developing countries wish to retain the WIPO jurisdiction, since they are not in control of GATT and fear that it might approve more stringent provisions protecting intellectual property.

The TNCs oppose any attack on proprietary rights, and such attacks have been frequent at the hands of the members of the United Nations Conference on Trade and Development (UNCTAD), which has sought to obtain or provide access by companies in the developing countries to the technology in advanced countries as readily and as cheaply as possible. TNCs seek to protect these rights by provisions against disclosure of technology as a result even of project negotiations or negotiations on potential investment or licensing agreements. Again, it is difficult to do so if the host countries are opposed to such protection.

Considerable disagreement remains as to the appropriate role of such rights, and their extension into foreign countries. Therefore, proprietary rights are a subject of continuing dialogue between companies and governments, and among the governments themselves, as in the United Nations Conference on Science and Technology in Development (Vienna, 1979).

LEGAL JURISDICTION AND DISPUTE SETTLEMENT

In anticipation of potential disputes over the workings of a licensing arrangement, it has been the practice of licensors to attempt to set the locus of legal jurisdiction within their own country. However, when an infraction of the agreement takes place in the country of the licensee, it is difficult to obtain a transfer of the proceedings into the home country of the licensor. Provisions have, therefore, been written in some license agreements asserting that although the dispute is processed in the host country "the laws of New York" or of some other locale will apply. This is not an adequate resolution either, since it becomes difficult to explain in a foreign court the application of the laws of a state of the United States, particularly when translated into a foreign language, and the foreign court may not accept U.S. (or state) laws at all.

Consequently, alternate mechanisms are offered for settlement of disputes. One is the provision of arbitration through a group in the host country, through the International Chamber of Commerce, or through the various associations of arbitrators, such as the American Arbitration Association (AAA). Given the spotty and uncertain procedures for accomplishing arbitration, governments of concerned countries established the ICSID in the World Bank, but many of the developing countries have refused to join, as discussed in Chapter 13. They see it as an application of present international law, which they do not accept. Many of them are continuing to insist upon the application of domestic law through their own national courts, fearful of any encroachment on their national sovereignty. TNCs are not themselves able to shift the jurisdiction out of host countries (which they see as often biased), so the locus of jurisdiction remains a subject of negotiation, primarily resolved by the host-country courts.

TRADE LAW

TNCs are subject, as are all companies involved in international trade, to the national laws and intergovernmental agreements surrounding the export and import of goods and services. Trade law can be used to facilitate the movement of goods or to make it more difficult, thereby becoming a means of protection, and raising a potential conflict of laws. Many more companies are concerned with trade law than just TNCs. Still, the TNCs are large traders, accounting in the United States for nearly half the international trade in manufactures. They also account for a large percentage of the trade in extractive products as well as in processed agricultural goods. Japanese TNCs, through their trading companies (Sogo Shosha) account for over 80 percent of the country's imports. Trade law covers a number of aspects of the trading process, including customs procedures, negotiations on tariffs, quotas, subsidies, retaliation on unfair trading practices, imposition of voluntary export restraints, assistance to labor adversely affected by imports, liability and insurance of foreign credits.

Customs Procedures

The passage of goods through customs requires a process of determination of the duty, if any, which sometimes requires the determination of the country of origin (when products from different countries face different tariffs entering a given country); determination of the classification or type of goods imported; determination of their value or volume (to help determine whether they are underpriced or overinvoiced); and the possibility of holding them in bond pending the final determination of appropriate duties. The procedures of each country have varied according to the methods of classification of goods, the evaluations procedures, and even the determination of country of origin (e.g., made difficult when goods have passed through one or more countries, with processing occurring in stages to add value to the final product).

Tariff schedules are either single column or multiple column. The single-column tariff means that all nations face the same duties on entering the importing country; a multi-column tariff schedule provides differential duties for different countries. Most countries have sought to move towards the more simple and nondiscriminatory, single-column schedule; but not even the U.S. has done so completely, since it does not extend the same duties to the socialist countries as it does to the rest of the world. For almost all countries, U.S. law provides "most-favored-nation" *treatment*, which means that it extends to all member countries the lowest duty negotiated with any country—so that all are equal. Such treatment was not extended to the U.S.S.R., most of Eastern Europe, North Korea, and Cuba; but events in late 1989 paved the way for extension of most-favored-nation treatment to the U.S.S.R. and Eastern Europe, at least. Members of the General Agreements on Tariffs and Trade (GATT) provide "most-favored-nation" treatment to each other, but do not always do so to nonmembers. Since a company can avoid a higher duty by moving its product through a country that has most-favored-nation treatment and declaring it as the place of origin, "marks of origin" are required to be placed on products; valuation procedures are applied to determine where the majority of the value was added in production. The use of "marks of origin" can become a protectionist tactic by raising costs (e.g., each piece of lumber having to be marked "made in Canada," rather than the entire pallet being so marked).

The classification of products is exceedingly difficult, simply because the language itself is indefinite, and names of products do not necessarily identify their purposes nor make adequate distinctions. Classification may be used by a country to protect items of a given type within its own economy by making complex distinctions. One can make numerous distinctions under surgical instruments, clocks and watches, tires, toys, autos and trucks, and so on. The items under tariff classifications run into thousands, with some of the classifications merely ending up as "n.e.c." —meaning "not elsewhere classified." These catch-all classifications frequently cover as many items as are classified in a given category, and are often given a higher duty to shut out unexpected competition. The classification process was historically used as a means of limiting entry of foreign products, pushing the competing products into high-duty categories, and the noncompeting items into a low-duty category.

Valuations of the imported products can be on cost-plus, on invoice price, on cost plus insurance and freight (c.i.f.) or free-on-board (f.o.b.), meaning the insurance freight and other charges are paid by the importer. These different evaluation procedures may alter the duty paid, so disputes arise.

Disputes over custom procedures are handled in custom courts, which are in the country of importation, and there is no effective appeal from their decisions. Importers do not like to become involved in such disputes, because goods then are held in bond in customs, pending the settlement of duty, and storage charges are assessed. In addition, inventories are tied up, sales are lost, and retail outlets become discouraged. However, the duty applied is often so important in terms of final cost and competitiveness, that test shipments are made in order to establish the proper classification and valuation. Then a decision may be made as to whether or not it is feasible to export into the country. These matters are of concern to TNCs planning to expand interaffiliate trade to reduce costs. The negotiation of drawbacks of duties is important in reducing double or triple duties on products as they pass through several stages of production and assembly in different countries.

Since World War II, a number of attempts have been made to simplify customs procedures, and broad agreement was achieved among many countries on the adoption of a classification system called the Brussels Nomenclature. Members adopted the same system of classification in order to reduce the number of disputes over what types of products were being imported, permitting comparison of duty levels. Valuation procedures were also harmonized. The United States initially refused to accept this system because it considered the changes too great for its customs agents to handle, given the volumes of trade that were passing through U.S. ports.

But by the early 1970s the United States joined with the Brussels group and several other countries in forming a Customs Cooperation Council (CCC) working to simplify and harmonize all member-country tariff schedules. Representatives of government and industry worked for more than 12 years on the system and will remain in a review capacity on its implementation by members. Adoption by the United States of the new Harmonized Coding System was provided in the Trade and Competitiveness Act of 1988. The new system replaces all former systems of member countries, so that the same code numbers will exist for the same items; it went into effect on January 1, 1989. Such harmonization facilitates the monitoring of trade agreements and any concessions under them eases disputes over custom treatment; it also facilitates collection of trade data.

Negotiations on Trade Barriers

Nations have negotiated the level of trade barriers or duties among themselves for over 400 years—since the nation-state was formed and fees were charged for movement of goods across borders. The process of reducing duties in one country in exchange for the reduction of duties in another resulted in bilateral agreements. When many bilateral agreements were negotiated, each country was concerned not to face higher duties than competitors, so each bargained for the same (or better) duty reductions. When a country offered the same duty reductions as offered to the "most-favored-nation" *but* on condition of an offsetting duty reduction by the second country, the arrangement was called "conditional most-favored-nation" treatment. Thus, tit-for-tat bargaining was conducted for reduced duties. A number of bilateral agreements were made under this process, but they broke down during the 1930s when protectionism was at its peak.

In 1930, the U.S. Congress passed the infamous Smoot-Hawley Tariff Act, raising the barriers to their highest levels ever. This protectionism accelerated the Depression, as trade volumes declined and other countries sought to protect their markets. Stability was further disturbed by progressive currency devaluations, in an attempt to regain exports. To reverse the decline in world trade, the Congress passed the Reciprocal Trade Agreements Act of 1933 to authorize bilateral negotiations to reduce tariffs. It set the stage for the introduction of "unconditional most-favored-nation" treatment and opened the way to multilateral bargaining after World War II. In order to expand this process after World War II, the United States proposed the formation of an International Trade Organization (ITO), which would have had the authority to negotiate reductions of barriers among all member nations simultaneously—each offering "most-favored-nation" treatment unconditionally to all negotiating countries. Although the ITO was never established, out of it came the General Agreement on Tariffs and Trade (GATT), under which the signatory countries have bargained multi-bilaterally. These negotiations have continued intermittently in several long but relatively successful sessions. Several LDCs have refused to join the organization; only in 1988, after long opposition, did Mexico agree to join.

The GATT covers not only reductions of duties but also prohibits the imposition of direct controls over trade, meaning principally the imposition of quotas and licenses, which restrict the *volume* of trade, regardless of the value or the duties that might be imposed. These direct controls void any competitive advantage from lower prices, since the foreign exporter simply cannot sell if the quota is already fulfilled. Also the GATT prohibits export subsidies by governments, on the ground that this gives an unacceptable competitive advantage to exporters, in violation of free-market concepts. Members of the GATT have been much more willing to bargain for the reduction of duties than they have for the elimination of nontariff barriers, which have arisen to replace duties. Many countries have found it necessary to obtain exemptions from the prohibition of quotas and subsidies—the United States subsidizes tobacco and wheat, for example.

The negotiations under the GATT are conducted simultaneously among the more than 100 member countries, with teams of several dozen individuals sent by each member to Geneva for months at a time to negotiate the "multi-bilateral" discussions. A single complete negotiation or "round" takes several years. Each country negotiates bilaterally with each other *major* trading partner before the multilateral agreement is signed. Promulagation is still done by each national government. The developing countries have been given preferential duties by the advanced countries, and have been relieved from the same timetable for reduction of duties, which gives them a longer time to make their industries competitive.

In this process of negotiation, representatives of a number of industries are selected as advisors to the official delegations, and they remain through that portion of the negotiation that covers the products in which they are interested. The representatives have been drawn not only from TNCs but also from industrial and commercial associations in each country.

The GATT has been successful in reducing duties across the board, and trade has become much freer from nontariff barriers (NTBs), of which there are many, and which have arisen as a means of restricting trade without the imposition of duties. NTBs include not only quotas and subsidies but also tax rebates or waivers, R&D grants, tax deferrals, low-cost loans, export incentives, safety and health regulations, and so on.

In the Uruguay Round in the late 1980s, greater attention was turned to the nontariff barriers and to the restrictions imposed on trade in services, which became much more important and had not been previously covered in ne-

gotiations. The increase of NTBs was a reflection of continued attempts to redistribute gains from trade to the country
imposing the barriers. The more tariffs were removed the
more other barriers were imposed. This development points
out the importance of the issue of the distribution of benefits and the absence of an acceptable solution.

Escape Clauses

Given the extensive reductions of duties under the
GATT negotiations, a provision was made that any member
could restore the *former* duty levels on an item if the increased imports resulting from the reduced duties injured
its industry. To be justified in applying the clause, there
must be proof of damage to domestic industry from increased imports, and proof that the damage resulted from
the reduction of the duty. Both of these are difficult to
prove, so each country has established procedures for their
determination. If a case is found for applying the escape
clause, the damaged country declares that it will at least
partially restore the duty to the higher (prenegotiation)
level. Countries that have "paid-for" this reduction with
their own duty reductions are permitted to select some
items on which they will raise duties in compensation. Either country has a right to complain to the GATT about the
other's action, and a GATT committee will, if necessary, decide what constitutes "reciprocity."

Requests for the application of escape clauses usually
come from the *injured* companies or industries, but the
damage claimed may be from their own ineptness, from general economic conditions, or from imports from countries
other than those who had bargained the duties down in the
first place. The importing country imposes the escape
clause through its own administration procedures (in the
United States, the International Trade Commission). Repeated use of the escape clause through duty restoration
and retaliation seriously damages the atmosphere of agreement, so it has not been used often.

Antidumping and Countervailing Duties

In order to make certain that trade among countries is
"fair"—that is, countries abide by the rules agreed upon—
prohibitions exist against dumping of products from one

market into another or of subsidizing the exports of a product from one country to another. "Dumping" is the selling of a product in a foreign market at a price lower than the cost of production and transport of the product. (Dumping does *not* arise when a country sells a product abroad at a price lower than it offers at home; this is simply discriminatory pricing, often made successful by barriers against imports of a similar product. But this is not prohibited even if considered unfair. An offended government may bring diplomatic pressure to bear, but this is difficult if the exports are sold at *world* prices.)

The determination of whether a country is dumping products is difficult because it is hard to discern the cost of production abroad. There are procedures for making at least rough determinations as to the existence of dumping; if it is found, the remedy is to impose a duty on the imported product sufficient to make the imported price "reasonable"—which usually means equal to the domestic price. Disputes over dumping are not frequent (compared to the volume of trade), but they are highly emotional when alleged, and the cases have to be proven by argument. (Cases in the United States related to Japanese steel and electronics and to Brazilian shoes.) The "offending" country often redresses the situation in order to avoid penalties, though there have been some hard-fought cases. An importer can sell the goods before the case is settled, but he is then subject to paying whatever duty *is* imposed, and this may make his sales highly unprofitable. The mere threat of an antidumping procedure is enough to cause a foreign exporter to reassess his pricing.

Countervailing duties are imposed to offset the use of subsidies by the exporting country. (A subsidy actually transfers wealth from the exporting to the importing country, but it is opposed in the latter for reasons of competition and employment.) Even the GATT has not been able to prohibit subsidies, but it provides a means to offset them by the importing country imposing a duty of equal amount. Problems of proof arise again, but the decision is within the importing country, and it is generally up to the injured industry or companies to demonstrate the existence of such subsidies. Sometimes evidence is requested by the government of the importing country from its counterpart in the exporting country. Whether cooperation in information disclosure is forthcoming is a matter of diplomatic relations. There is no court at the international level to resolve these issues, so the companies hurt by trade are the prime actors in initiating complaints.

Voluntary Export Restrictions

The U.S. government has been the forerunner in the application of voluntary export restrictions (VERs) to foreign countries, requiring them to restrain their exporters by imposing "voluntary" export quotas, on goods coming into the United States. The United States is, historically and in principle, opposed to the application of direct controls and especially to the use of import quotas, since they are a direct, quantitative intervention in the market. It prefers *price* interventions through tariffs, permitting buyers to determine quantities bought. It has also been the leader in the reduction of tariffs, so that it opposes, in principle, two of the major restrictions against imports—duties and quotas.

However, when it found in the 1960s that textile imports were increasing rapidly and at levels that threatened the existence of a large number of U.S. companies, the government negotiated a multilateral agreement on textiles and fibers (Multi-Fiber Agreement [MFA]) with exporting countries under which signatory countries restricted their sales into the United States to agreed amounts. U.S. Customs monitored the trade, signaling whether or not the agreement was being followed, and the Department of Commerce was made responsible for implementation and modification of the MFA, as needed.

In many cases it was not followed, or the exporters shifted from products under quotas to textile items that were not, continuing to expand exports to the United States. Subsequent negotiations expanded the list and attempted to tighten the levels of quotas, but dissatisfaction remains within the U.S. textile industry and among the foreign suppliers in this highly mobile industry. The MFA has been successful in permitting the more gradual adaptation of U.S. industry to the growth of foreign suppliers.

Although there are some TNCs in this industry, most U.S. companies concerned with the MFA are oriented toward the U.S. domestic market plus some exports. The TNCs in the industry use mostly "cut-and-sew" branch plants in countries such as Mexico, and Hong Kong, and on several of the Caribbean Islands.

The U.S. auto industry also came under significant pressure from imports, particularly from Japan in the 1970s and 1980s. The U.S. government, again refusing to apply import quotas since they would violate the GATT, insisted that the Japanese government encourage those companies to agree among themselves to limit their exports to the United States and allocate the limitation among themselves in whatever manner they wished. (Such an arrangement among U.S. companies would be considered in violation of antitrust laws, but since this was done by Japanese companies with their government's guidance, no legal objection was made.) The U.S. government did not set the level of the quotas; but, with guidance, the Japanese found an acceptable level and have gradually raised it over the years to 2.3 million cars per year in 1988—each increase causing more negotiations (informal if not formal).

The application of auto quotas has given the Japanese manufacturers a level of profits they could not otherwise have achieved, simply because the total supply of Japanese cars is thereby limited, and they are able to raise their prices. Had duties been imposed, the added revenue would have gone to the U.S. government rather than the Japanese companies. However, raising the duties would have violated agreements under the GATT. Using the escape clause would have permitted the Japanese to retaliate with duty increases of their own—at a time when the United States was seeking export markets. Therefore, the export quotas were "voluntarily imposed" by the Japanese.

Another result of these quotas has been that the Japanese have gradually moved to higher value cars (at the luxury end of the range), increasing their profits and their market penetration in the United States. U.S. TNCs have eventually established joint ventures with Japanese companies, and the Japanese companies on their part have entered the U.S. market through FDI, some of which is in joint ventures with American companies. The result of the voluntary quotas, therefore, and the threat of further restrictions against the Japanese has been to establish a "network" of ties among U.S. and Japanese companies in the auto and auto parts sectors and to permit the Japanese to gain a larger portion of the U.S. market—through production in the United States.

Trade Adjustment Assistance

One of the more difficult aspects of the expansion of trade through reduction of duties is the impact on labor in import-competing companies.[13] In many instances, the company itself can make some adjustments through shifting to a different product line, but labor may not be trained on these new lines or it may not be needed at the same level as before. Unemployment frequently results, and labor unions (historically in favor of freer trade) have more recently opposed any expansion of trade that damages their members. In order to reduce the objection of labor groups to the reduction of trade barriers, the U.S. Congress provided, in the Trade Expansion Act of 1962, for trade adjustment assistance to workers laid-off because of greater imports resulting from the reduction of barriers. Here again, a complex test of suitability for assistance became necessary to prove that unemployment was a result of higher imports and that imports had increased as a result of duty reductions. These facts were difficult to prove, and for some time the adjustment assistance offered was much less than labor thought appropriate for the damage that was occurring. Congress appropriated larger sums and the tests were loosened somewhat, but labor remained unsatisfied.

European countries have been much more successful in providing such assistance to labor and removing their objections to the higher level of imports because of a greater willingness to use government intervention. In some cases, such as the British textile industry, the government simply bought out plants that were redundant, removing the objection of both capital and labor, then provided assistance to labor and the community in finding alternative employment.

The representatives of industry in the United States have generally opposed trade adjustment assistance for fear that it will become a subsidy to inefficient companies or industries and for fear that costs might escalate, damaging the profitability of the more efficient companies and the competitiveness of the country. However, it was recognized that such assistance was necessary to buy off the objections of labor, so the assistance has been offered in a case-by-case basis. It has been kept at such low levels that labor has continued to complain of inadequate support for adjustment.

Transactions Law

In the process of importing and exporting, a number of issues arise that require adjudication. These have to do with breakage, nondelivery, late delivery, inadequate quality, spoilage, returns of products, consignments, agency contracts, losses at sea, and product liability. In many of these complaints, the question of where a transaction took place has to be resolved in order to determine the jurisdiction of the courts. In some situations, multiple jurisdictions are applicable, and a dispute arises as to which is the appropriate locus.

These matters constitute what is known as *transactions law*, for which again there is no international tribunal. Every company engaged in international trade must have legal counsel familiar with this law and its application to their products. Contracts can stipulate that disputes will be taken to arbitration rather than to court and there are a number of sources of arbitration around the world that can be drawn upon.

Foreign Credit Insurance

Because of the disturbed conditions in international trade in the 1950s, it became clear that uncertainty as to transfer of funds from one currency into another would seriously dampen the volume of trade needed to help countries develop after World War II. Given the inability of almost any exporting company and of most banks to determine the soundness of an importer abroad, several countries—principally the United States, Canada and major European countries—formed foreign credit insurance groups to insure or guarantee the exchange and commercial risks in the payment of an import bill, if the importer defaulted. In the United States, the Foreign Credit Insurance Agency (FCIA) was formed by a group of insurance companies with the support and encouragement of the U.S. government. It divides the countries of the world into four risk categories, charging variable premiums for each category. The classifications of countries into these categories change as the risks increase or decrease. Costs are relatively low, and the insurance is amply used.

TNC Roles

The TNCs (either as separate entities or a collective body) are not necessarily at the forefront in the formation and application of trade law. They are heavily involved at times, but generally with reference to their own company (or industry) interests—as with the auto and textile quotas. In all other aspects of trade law, companies that are predominantly domestic or import-oriented have taken the lead in discussions with the governments. TNCs, being both importers and exporters in host and home countries, have generally been supportive of the removal of all *barriers* to trade and investment but not necessarily of all incentives. Still, TNCs are affected by the results and are, therefore, involved directly or indirectly in this aspect of control over international business.

DILEMMAS FOR TNCs

TNCs would like a more stable world, one ruled by international law containing provisions suitable to their worldwide operations. They would also like to have means of settling disputes outside of national jurisdictions, thus avoiding the political or social pressures that arise in that setting. But, there are few opportunities for the establishment of international law that would be supranational in effect. No country is yet willing to have international law override its own law. The nearest move in that direction is treaty law, under which each party accepts the provisions as binding and superseding national legislation or regulation.

Since the developing countries were not involved in the formation of international law, and object to its application, any *new* international law to which they would agree will be less favorable to TNCs and their operations than the present situation. Therefore, despite their desire for more stability and a greater "rule by law," TNCs are reluctant to support the formation of *new* international law in any intergovernmental forum (see Chapter 12). They see such pressures by the developing countries as formulating a set of rules that would shift the distribution of benefits to the developing countries or at least constrain the operations of TNCs in favor of domestic companies in the host countries. Their fears are supported by acts such as those of Brazil in ejecting the foreign companies in the informatics industry and in imposing severe "performance requirements" on the auto industry (see Chapter 8).

The TNCs, therefore, find themselves arguing on both sides of the issue—for greater law and stability and for no *new* law for fear of the loss of favorable positions at present. This fence-straddling posture leads to a continuing dialogue between the TNCs and governments, including negotiations in intergovernmental bodies.

NOTES TO CHAPTER 11

1. Differences of views among U.S., European and LCD legal experts are shown in the proceedings of a conference held in Vienna on "Foreign Investment," edited by Detlev Chr. Dicke, *Foreign Investment in the Present and a New International Economic Order,* (Boulder, CO: Westview, 1988).

2. See C. Sepulveda, A. M. Baez, and A. G. Robles, "Carlos Calvo: tres Ensaos Mejicanos," *Colleccion del Archivo Historico Diplomatico Mexicano* (Tlatelolco, Mex: Secretaria de Relaciones Exteriores, 1974).

3. California employs a franchise tax based on a "unitary business" theory under which corporate income of both headquarters and affiliate companies are taxed according to the *portion* of the enterprise's worldwide payroll, property, and sales that arises in California. Thus, income is attributed to the California entity even if it did not arise there. This system was challenged by U.S. TNCs because of potential double taxation; the case went to the U.S. Supreme Court, where California won. Because of continued efforts by the companies, some of which threatened to leave California, and pressure from the State Department in Washington, arising from complaints by foreign governments, California adopted an alternative procedure, effective January 1, 1988. Under it, the company can use a "water's edge" apportionment system, basing the taxation only on activities within the state's boundaries; however, a fee for such an election is charged ranging from .01 to .03 percent of the payroll, property, and sales within California. Banks are treated a bit differently. Ernst & Whinney, *1989 Guide to State Corporate and Individual Taxes in the United States* (Washington, DC, 1989), pp. 5–6.

4. See Gary K. Bertsch, *East-West Strategic Trade* (Totowa, NJ: Allanheld), 1983; and for broader discussion his edited papers on *Controlling East-West Trade and Technology Transfers* (Durham, NC: Duke U. Press, 1988).

5. See J. N. Behrman, *National Interests and Multinational Enterprise* (Englewood Cliffs, NJ: Prentice-Hall, 1970), pp. 110–111.

6. John L. Graham produced evidence that U.S. firms have not lost significant sales due to the Act, see "Foreign Corrupt Practices. A Manager's Guide," *Columbia Journal of World Business* (Fall 1983).

7. See UN Centre on Transnational Corporations, *A Study of Bilateral Investment Treaties* (New York: United Nations, 1988).

8. See OPIC, *1988 Annual Report* (Washington, DC), pp. 10–11.

9. S. Korbin, "Expropriation as an Attempt to Control Foreign Firms in LDCs. Trends from 1960–70," *International Studies Quarterly* (Sept. 1984), pp. 329–348.

10. Theodore Morgan, "Transnational Strategies of Protection and Defense by Multinational Enterprises," *International Organization* (Spring 1973), pp. 273–287.

11. See Helena Stalson, *Intellectual Property Right and U.S. Competitiveness in Trade* (Washington, DC, NPA: 1987); an assessment of international issues and controversies over protecting intellectual property rights is given by Robert P. Benko *Protecting Intellectual Property Rights* (Washington, DC: American Enterprise Institute, 1987); and by R. M. Gadbaw and T. J. Richards, *Intellectual Property Rights: Global Consensus, Global Conflict?* (Boulder, CO: Westview, 1988).

12. See Ebba Dohlman "International Piracy and Intellectual Property," *The OECD Observer* (Oct./Nov. 1988), pp. 33–37.

13. See Steve Charnovitz, "Worker Adjustment: The Missing Ingredient in Trade Policy," *California Management Review* (Winter 1986), pp. 156–173) also *American Trade Adjustment: The Global Impact* (Washington, DC: Institute for International Economics, 1989).

CHAPTER 12

TNC Relations with Regional Associations

Most of the relations between TNCs and government institutions occur at the national level, but a number of intergovernmental entities have been formed—the European Community, the Latin American Integration Association, and the Association of Southeast Asian Nations, for example—which have adopted policies toward TNCs. In some instances, the regional rules and orientations have been quite significant in altering TNC decision making. In others, the regional orientations have been supportive of TNCs strategies. Regional groups attempt to harmonize national policies of the member countries, particularly incentives to TNCs.

Regional organizations exist among advanced countries, NICs, LDCs, and the Communist nations. Since the three organizations that cover the advanced countries contain most of the world's TNCs, each has host and home countries that guide and protect TNC activities. The NIC and LDC associations have historically been formed among countries that are hosts to TNCs, though a few are also home to some TNCs (e.g. Brazil, India, and South Korea). Their regional policies have sought to alter TNC behavior in favor of the host countries and to reduce competition among members for FDI inflows. The major communist countries opened their economies only in the late 1980s, so the amount of FDI is still relatively small, and they have not developed a unified policy towards FDI from the West. The socialist regional association has led mainly to intra-regional cooperative ventures and guidance of trade among the members.

The main regional organizations among the advanced countries are:

Organization for Economic Cooperation and Development (OECD)

European Community (EC)

U.S.-Canada Free Trade Agreement

Those including NICs:

Latin America Integration Association (ALADI or LAIA)

Association of Southeast Asian Nations (ASEAN)

Those among LDCs include:

Central American Common Market (CACM)

Caribbean Free Trade Association (CARIFTA)

Andean Pact

The organization formed by the U.S.S.R. and Eastern Europe:

Committee for Mutual Economic Assistance (CMEA or COMECON).

Some of the key characteristics of each regional group are shown in Chart 12.1. As yet, within these regional groupings, there is no supranational entity to which the member governments are subservient. National governments have in every case retained their sovereignty. Most resolutions or decisions of regional associations must come before national governments for approval; implementation of some decisions is left to the regional secretariats, but many are carried out only through the national institu-

Chart 12.1: *Types of Economic Integration*

Type	Associations	Member Nations
1. Free-trade area: no tariffs among members; each maintains own tariffs toward nonmembers	European Free Trade Area (EFTA)	Austria, Norway, Sweden, Switzerland
	Latin American Integration Association (ALADI)	Argentina, Bolivia, Brazil, Chile, Colombia, Costa Rica, Ecuador, El Salvador, Guatemala, Honduras, Mexico, Panama, Paraguay, Peru, Uruguay, Venezuela.
	Association of Southeast Asian Nations (ASEAN)	Indonesia, Malaysia, Philippines, Singapore, Thailand.

Chart 12.1: (cont.)

Type	Associations	Member Nations
2. Customs union: no internal tariffs; common external tariff	Andean Pact	Bolivia, Colombia, Ecuador, Peru, Venezuela
	Caribbean Common Market (CARICOM)	Antigua and Barbuda, Bahamas, Barbados, Belize, Dominica, Grenada, Guyana, Jamaica, Montserrat, St. Kitts-Nevis, St. Lucia, St. Vincent, Trinidad and Tobago
3. Common market: customs union plus free movement of capital and labor, goods, and services.	European Community	Belgium, Denmark, France, Greece, Ireland, Italy, Luxembourg, Netherlands, Portugal, Spain, United Kingdom, West Germany
4. Economic union: common market plus common or harmonized fiscal and monetary policies.	Belgium-Luxembourg Economic Union (BLEU)	Belgium, Luxembourg
5. Political union: economic union plus a central government	Soviet Union	Russia, Ukraine, Latvia, Lithuania, Estonia, and the Republics
	United Kingdom (The United States, Switzerland, and some other nations were formed out of sovereign states or cantons—not nations.)	England, Wales, Scotland (and Northern Ireland)

tions. Although TNCs have formal or informal representation in each of the regional associations (except the COME-CON), the associations do not have direct jurisdiction over the TNCs; final jurisdiction rests with the national governments.

EUROPEAN COMMUNITY

The European Community has come strongly into the forefront of international business discussions with the decision in the mid-1980s to form a complete common market by 1992. Some three hundred barriers to business (trade, investment, services, workers) were identified and slated for removal by 1992 so that goods, resources, people, and funds could move rapidly across the borders of member countries. If this initiative succeeds, it will have taken 35 years from the inception of the European Economic Community (EEC or Common Market) in 1957 to achieve the original objective.

The EEC itself was a outgrowth of previous efforts at European integration through the European Coal and Steel Community (ECSC) formed in 1951 and the abortive Western European Union, aimed at cooperation in defense. After the EEC, the European Atomic Energy Community (Euratom) was established. This, plus the ECSC and EEC, were combined to form the European Community (EC). The EC became the largest regional association in the world and has continued to add members to the original six Continental countries—West Germany, France, Italy, Belgium, Netherlands, and Luxembourg.

The Scandinavian countries and Britain formed a European Free Trade Association (EFTA), including Switzerland, to achieve some of the advantages of integration without the larger effort to form a common market sought by the Continental countries. In addition, Denmark, Greece, Ireland, Portugal and Spain have joined; Turkey holds associate status, some others have asked for a similar affiliation but have not yet been granted it. After the success of the EEC, Britain gave up membership in EFTA and joined the Continental countries.

Members of the EC have remained protective of their national sovereignty. They are, therefore, unlikely to give up authority over fiscal or monetary policies through the formation of unified taxes or a single currency system. Although the EC governments have used a common currency standard (the ECU) for several types of transactions, and the ECU standard is used in some commercial and financial dealings, it is not yet a circulating currency. The ECU is composed of differing percentages of the major currencies in the EC. The EC is attempting to achieve exchange-rate stability through agreements to maintain rates within an agreed range, so as to prevent wide swings among the members' currencies. Similarly, the EC countries are attempting to harmonize value-added taxes and other fiscal measures such as unemployment insurance, social security, and agricultural subsidies. These may not be accomplished by 1992, but if major strides have been made on the three hundred barriers, the acceleration of growth in the member countries will undoubtedly be a strong attraction to foreign TNCs. Many were already moving into Europe with mergers or acquisitions in 1988 and 1989.

Policies Toward TNCs

The EC members have remained relatively open to cross-national investment among the members, though there have been objections particularly to acquisitions or mergers across national boundaries—noticeably between France and Italy in the automotive and tire sectors. A merger of British Dunlop and Italy's Pirelli in the 1970s came apart from continuing disagreements. In the late 1980s, a number of cross-national mergers and acquisitions within Europe took place, anticipating the 1992 integration and thereby accelerating it.

In fact, European integration in the 1960s and 1970s took place substantially through the FDI of U.S. TNCs, who saw the reductions of barriers within the EEC as raising the *relative* barriers against U.S. exports and thereby necessitating a manufacturing presence within the Common Market. This investment not only accelerated growth inside of Europe but also enhanced moves toward integration across borders simply because the U.S. companies sought to serve the entire market through one or two manufacturing locations within the region. Although France attempted to control the inflow of FDI, the existence of a relatively open regional market made it easy for TNCs simply to locate elsewhere in Europe and yet serve the French buyers. Thus, French reticence in accepting the U.S. TNCs was undercut, and more open FDI policies were adopted.

The moves in the late 1980s to achieve a more complete Common Market by 1992 sparked new interest in investment by foreign TNCs into the region. No new efforts at gov-

ernment intervention have arisen. The most important obstacles to operations of foreign TNCs are tariff and nontariff
barriers to trade. Of secondary importance are the rules on
anticompetitive behavior, which may be used to guide or
limit mergers with companies outside of the EC.

Once an investment has taken place, the TNC affiliates
are subject to all of the national and regional regulations
concerning corporate behavior. Thus, they are subject in
Germany to the codetermination laws, which have been
largely extended throughout the EC in principle, though not
yet in practice. These laws provide for participation by labor
in a Supervisory Board that selects management and has
authority over personnel decisions. They are also subject to
the laws on plant closings, social welfare, fringe benefits,
and so forth.

Responses of TNCs

The responses of TNCs to European integration—
whether the EC or the EFTA—demonstrate that the strongest inducement to FDI is the actual or potential loss of an
opportunity or a penalty imposed on operations. The idea
that FDI is stimulated *solely* by market access is not supported by any of the experiences since 1950. On the contrary, if a foreign market can be well-served by exports, it
will be. And as trade barriers have dropped, exports and imports have been increasing at rates faster than GNP growth
in most major countries. Given open trade, the growth of
markets initially stimulates only the growth of exports and
imports—not FDI. No company in any country prefers direct
investment over exports simply to serve a market. Quite the
contrary, the Swiss companies have long built their competitiveness on large-scale production in Switzerland, exporting over 90 percent of total production. The Japanese built
their competitiveness on exports, as did West Germany.

It is the actual or potential *loss* of a market served
through exports or the inability to be cost competitive in
exports that cause direct investment. The export opportunity is closed off either by government barriers, by increased competition by local companies, or by the existence
of more efficient production factors in the host country.

These elicit the shift of manufacturing facilities. Alterna
tively, customers may have a *preference* for local supply
(or national suppliers), effectively discriminating against
imports. It is necessity, not opportunity, that moves investment overseas. Once trade is precluded, the best opportunities of entry are sought. Adam Smith was quite right when
he said that factors of production *tend* to be immobile in a
free-trade world. The absence of free trade or the existence
of an oligopoly facing substantial cost differentials abroad
induces the movement of factors.[1]

U.S. TNCs responded immediately to the *potential*
closing-off of markets by the EEC and EFTA. Neither group
had to raise duties on U.S. exports; the mere reduction of
barriers among the members of the two regional associations sufficed. The potential result is known as trade-
diversion, meaning that trade previously with nonmembers
of the group shifts to member countries through the reduction of barriers among the latter, leaving barriers *relatively*
high to outsiders. Although the market in the newly integrated region increases and therefore creates some new
trade, there is likely to be a restructuring and rechanneling
of trade so that nonmembers who previously were exporting
can no longer do so at the same level or in the same
products.[2]

Historically, U.S. corporations became modern TNCs by
investing in facilities in the EEC or the EFTA, with careful
attention given as to which was the preferable manufacturing location. Many U.S. TNCs sought entry into the United
Kingdom because of familiarity with the language and culture and because of the projected likelihood of a later entry
by the United Kingdom into the Continental group. Others
saw the opposite probability and entered the Continent,
with the hope that they would be prepared to compete if the
United Kingdom did join; but, if not, they would still be
serving the larger market. The strategies, therefore, were
dependent on anticipation as to the existence or removal of
barriers. It is the trade barriers, therefore, that caused the
formation of TNCs, who were building on their former export positions. The TNCs did not move significantly into
Europe until they were threatened with the loss of export
markets. Obviously, if the market had not been significant,

it would not have warranted the investment. Still, U.S. TNCs would have preferred to serve Europe through exports.

There are other barriers that cause companies to invest abroad besides those imposed by governments. Obstacles to exporting also arise in the form of customers' *preference* for local supply (or even for *national* companies as suppliers), for shorter delivery times, closer communication, prompter service, and so on. Some of these factors relate to efficiency, others to tradition and preferences. In addition, some resources can be obtained only through collaborating with a domestic firm for research, technology, marketing abilities and contacts, as well as managerial or labor skills. These factors are, however, not customer and market oriented; they are productivity and supply oriented. FDI, therefore, occurs when it is feasible to reduce costs by investing or to gain access, which is otherwise precluded. (Joint marketing can be done when only a local company knows how to analyze the market, satisfy local tastes, and negotiate the local distribution system—as in Japan—but such teamwork does not require FDI.)

The formation of the two European associations provided both types of stimuli. The closing of markets to non-members and the expansion of the regional market to members would have begun to restrict access of U.S. companies. The improvement of resource availabilities added to customer preferences for local supply. The TNCs were able, therefore, to seek lower-cost locations within the region to serve the member countries. In addition, regions in some of the members—notably Ireland, Scotland, Southern Italy, and Southern France provided incentives through various subsidies, tax relief, low-cost plants, etc., to attract the FDI into depressed areas. In most instances, the TNCs decided that the incentives did not compensate for the costs, and did not respond. Many who did found that the incentives did not compensate for the problems in the particular areas. Both Ireland and Scotland have continued to have difficulties attracting major TNCs, and Southern Italy remains far behind Northern Italy and Europe as a whole. The TNCs, again, responded less to incentives than to prohibitions or restrictions.

In terms of bargaining strength, the TNCs have greater power when incentives are offered, because others who wish to attract FDI must also offer incentives, and the TNCs are then able to bargain between them *for* the best deal. The host locality is, in effect, bidding not only for the TNC but also *against* other localities. Where the attraction of a market or resources is already strong, the bargaining power of the host government (national, state, or local) is enhanced by the imposition of conditions, interventions, or restrictions on a TNC if it is eager to enter. Except in a few countries (notably Canada, Switzerland, and China—where provinces, cantons, and cities have substantial independence in negotiating with TNCs), only the national government is able to impose FDI restrictions. This is because, if one state or province imposes restrictions, the TNC simply moves to one that does not do so. And, given the free movement of trade within the region, it can still serve any national market. TNCs are vitally interested in all countries freeing trade, which permits optimum strategies in location, manufacturing, products, and marketing. If not all do so, TNCs will seek protection from home and host governments. Thus, in the absence of free trade, TNCs must deal directly with governments, raising the issues surrounding TNCs to international levels.

ORGANIZATION FOR ECONOMIC COOPERATION AND DEVELOPMENT

The OECD is not an association such as the EC, since its mission is *not* economic integration, but cooperation. It is an intergovernmental organization, which encompasses the major noncommunist advanced countries of the world: Australia, Austria, Belgium, Canada, Denmark, Finland, France, West Germany, Greece, Iceland, Ireland, Italy, Japan, Luxembourg, the Netherlands, New Zealand, Norway, Portugal, Spain, Sweden, Switzerland, Turkey, the United Kingdom, and the United States. (Yugoslavia participates as an observer.) It has been called the "rich countries club" since it has none of the countries recognized as "developing" (LDCs) or "newly industrializing" (NICs). The member countries account for less than 20 percent of the world population, but over 60 percent of the world's industrial output and over 75 percent of its trade. The OECD began in 1960 as an association among the countries of North America and Western Europe, gradually adding others as they were able to comply with the underlying principles and the specific duties of membership.

The OECD seeks to promote joint efforts by its members to raise the level of worldwide economic development and to expand and liberalize world trade and investment. It undertakes studies and sponsors conferences aimed at determining the best ways of achieving its objectives, and it regularly publishes macro information about the member countries, some industry and country studies, and a large number of papers on a variety of topics related to economic policies. The committees of the OECD that are relevant for the activities of the TNCs include the Economic Policy Committee, the Trade Committee, and the Committee for Scientific and Technological Policy, the Industries Committee, and the Committee on International Investment and Multi-national Enterprises.

In developing its policies toward TNCs the OECD has relied substantially on two outside advisory committees—one from the TNCs themselves called the Business and Industry Advisory Committee (BIAC), and the other from organized labor among the member countries called the Trade Union Advisory Committee (TUAC). The BIAC is composed of elected officials from national groups representing major industrial associations in each country. In the United States, the member organizations of the BIAC are the U.S. Chamber of Commerce, the U.S. Council of the International Chamber of Commerce, and the National Association of Manufacturers. The secretary of the group is the U.S. Council, but members of all three associations attend the meetings of the BIAC. The BIAC itself assesses OECD policies and activities related to trade, FDI, taxation, economic growth, energy, and the environment.

In the TUAC, U.S. members come from the AFL-CIO matched by the Trade Union Council (TUC) in the United Kingdom, the Confederation Generale du Travail (CGT) in France, and so on. The TUAC is mostly concerned with industrial and labor relations, but also it will make its voice heard on other issues affecting employment and labor conditions. These advisory committees play important roles in the formation of issues and the generation of national government policy recommendations related to OECD deliberations.

The earliest position taken by the OECD on foreign investment was its "Code of Liberalization of Capital Movements," agreed to in the early 1960s. It encouraged members to free the movement of capital, particularly through FDI and by providing national treatment to foreign companies setting up affiliates in host countries. The code was approved in principle but seldom implemented. Companies found it inopportune to complain to the OECD about restrictive treatment, simply because they did not want to agitate a national government when they had other business to do with it—such as selling to the government or exporting into the country, or setting up additional investment activities in other parts of the country. Given the multiple interests of TNCs in any given country, it is not always easy to bargain strongly on one particular project or activity, unless the total position of the company in the host country is quite strong. Also, given the number of TNCs that can make similar contributions, it is difficult for one TNC to command a strong bargaining position with any given advanced country.

In an attempt to demonstrate a "proper" policy on TNCs to the developing (host) countries, which were pressing in the early 1970s for a stringent and mandatory code on TNC behavior, the OECD countries adopted in the mid-1970s several measures relating to multinational business. The documents included a *Declaration on International Investment and Multinational Enterprises*, that included specific "Guidelines for Multinational Enterprises," and three decisions related to (a) intergovernmental confrontation procedures on the Guidelines, (b) national treatment of foreign investors, and (c) international investment incentives and disincentives.

The OECD agreed to make the Guidelines voluntary, since the OECD governments wished to signal the LDCs in the UN (UNCTAD) that restraints on the TNCs should not be made mandatory. In fact, the entire package was an attempt to signal LDC host countries *how* the home countries wanted TNCs to be treated worldwide.

The Declaration explicitly recognized that TNCs made positive contributions to the economic and social progress of host countries and that they should be encouraged in this pursuit. (This position was contrary to the view of many LDCs at the time; LDCs considered that the TNCs also had adverse impacts on host countries and should be constrained rather than encouraged.) The consultation procedures agreed upon were to provide for surveillance but not for penalties. The Committee on International Investment and Multinational Enterprise (CIIME) was instructed to hold periodic meetings to review the experience under the Guidelines, to hear from the BIAC and TUAC as to how the guidelines were been fulfilled, and to hear from any TNCs concerning its activities or any problems that had arisen under the Guidelines. There is, therefore, a continuous examination of a proper agreement on FDI flows.[3]

The provision on national treatment required that member governments communicate to the OECD any conditions that each considered warranted its withholding "national treatment" from "foreign-controlled enterprises." Otherwise, each member agreed to provide national treatment to TNCs of all other members. The decision on international investment incentives and disincentives was an attempt to harmonize and reduce them so as to remove competitive bidding among members for FDI inflows. Again, the members were to supply the CIIME with full information as to the incentives and disincentives related to TNCs, so as to permit collective assessment of their impact among the members.

OECD Guidelines[4]

The OECD Guidelines took a positive approach to TNCs by encouraging cooperation among countries to enhance TNC contributions to economic and social development. They encourage member states and others to cooperate in gathering and exchanging information on TNC activities, which assists in creating effective dialogue among governments and with TNCs on issues arising.

The Guidelines themselves encouraged TNCs to take into account the policy objectives of host countries, particularly with regard to economic and social development, industrial development, protection of the environment, employment, and the development and transfer of technology. TNCs are also admonished not to be involved in bribing public officials and to abstain from improper involvement in political activities in host countries.

TNCs were further expected to provide voluntary information on a number of their activities around the world, permitting the OECD to assess their continuing contributions. In addition, the Guidelines encouraged TNCs to comply with rules on competition and antimonopoly regulations in host countries. They were also asked to ensure that their foreign activities fit within the science and technology policies of host countries and to encourage the diffusion of technology as rapidly as feasible under reasonable terms and conditions.

The most activity under the Guidelines, however, occurred in the fields of employment and industrial relations. These provisions urged a positive response by TNCs to the formation of labor unions and the practice of collective bargaining. Management also is to provide information as to its operations and intended activities (so as to permit labor unions to bargain effectively for their members), including a reasonable notice of intention to close a plant or to lay off or to dismiss a significant number of workers. TNCs were also admonished not to engage in foreign investment that "constituted runaway plants" (a "runaway" arises when a home-country plant is closed and a similar operation initiated abroad). This reduces the bargaining power of labor in the home country by shifting employment to a host country where labor is less organized.

The Guidelines were couched in language broad enough to constitute policy recommendations, rather than mandatory provisions. This was the clear intent of the member governments, which was applauded by the TNCs. The TNCs were fearful of detailed provisions which would tend to constrain their operations and make them unprofitable. Governments were trying to demonstrate that voluntary guidelines could be effective and hoped that the TNCs would respond adequately. The nature of the provisions and the expectations, however, raised a serious question of whether the Guidelines were, in fact, voluntary.

If certain behavior was expected, and it did not occur, would the OECD Guidelines become mandatory? The TNCs had a strong interest in making the OECD Guidelines successful; so, in the main, they complied in most respects. TNC support of OECD policy stemmed in part from the fact that OECD members are *home* countries for TNCs and also the major *host* countries; thus, there was a mutuality of interests.

TNC Responses

The TNCs were encouraged in the United States by the three Secretaries of State, Treasury, and Commerce to comply voluntarily with the OECD Guidelines and to demonstrate publicly that they were doing so. The USA-BIAC Committee on International Investment and Multinational Enterprises published *A Review of the OECD Guidelines for Multinational Enterprises: Disclosure of Information* encouraging a favorable response by members; in April 1978, it issued a report to the CIIME on responses showing voluntary cooperation—*U.S. Corporate Response to OECD Guidelines: Examples of Voluntary Cooperation,* plus a report on the provisions on competition and one on employment and industrial relations. Each of these pamphlets provided an assessment of behavior as well as historical positions of TNCs and the U.S. government, which show their views on the usefulness of such guidelines.

The industrial relations section of the Guidelines generated more controversy and assessment by the CIIME than the others since some problems in this area arose immediately. In March 1977, 10 cases involving labor relations problems were presented by the TUAC to the CIIME, illustrating the problems in implementation of the Guidelines. Immediately the question arose as to whether or not the CIIME should issue an "interpretation" of the Guidelines in specific cases. But the U.S. government strongly objected to any move toward a mandatory code, and a majority of countries agreed that such a judicial interpretation was not expected or desired. The issues were, therefore, remanded back to the local or host countries for resolution under local law and practice. The CIIME did take note of the problems for purposes of the scheduled review at the end of three years.

Some countries wanted to make the Guidelines stronger and to provide for more judicial procedures, with the TUAC wanting to bring specific charges against TNCs and to obtain "judgments" as to improper behavior. (Even with no penalties, the TUAC considered that such a "judgment" would apply moral suasion.) But the BIAC opposed such change, and the Guidelines remained "voluntary." The labor unions, however, have used the Guidelines as a reason for continuing to present information on the practices of TNCs so as to enhance the acceptance of labor-management bargaining across countries on a multinational basis. They wish to bring affiliates of a single TNC under similar regulations and employment practices for each of the unions involved.

The diversity of industrial relations among affiliates of the same TNC has stimulated unions to seek ways of harmonizing or unifying employment relations practices, but TNCs have opposed such moves adamantly. The OECD has continuously refused to take a position on this matter, seeking rather to maintain an exchange of information. This exchange should lead, in its view, to a closer accommodation of national laws and practice, rather than harmonization being promulgated through the OECD itself. Again, therefore, the bargaining relationship is between TNCs and national governments.

The difficulties facing the OECD in the industrial relations arena are exhibited by the first case that was brought before it—the Badger case in Belgium.[5] Badger, a wholly owned subsidiary of the Raytheon Corporation, closed its Belgian operations and claimed bankruptcy; consequently, it had no funds to pay its employees the usual compensation for separation from the company. The OECD code was interpreted by the TUAC to imply that the parent firm should back its subsidiaries financially in situations where obligations of affiliates exceeded their own abilities to provide appropriate or required compensation. Complaints were lodged by a Belgian trade union, supported by the

TUAC. Raytheon, the parent, refused to supply the necessary funds, despite the fact that it was profitable worldwide, and in the United States, and funds were available at headquarters. The matter was forced to adjudication under Belgian law. Finally, the parent company agreed to offer compensation to the laid-off Belgian workers, according to Belgian law on worker dismissals. All other cases have been remanded to local authorities for final disposition, with the OECD Guidelines being essentially signals as to the views of government, business, and labor officials.

In sum, company responses to the OECD Guidelines have been supportive of the principles in the document, but there has been little evidence of significant change in TNC behavior. As expected, the changes that have taken place can be traced primarily through requirements imposed by national governments, which in turn embodied some of the OECD Guidelines in their own legislation. Again, national governments are the bargaining partners, and the bargaining strength depends upon the interest of the governments in attracting foreign investment. In the case of OECD countries, this desire has remained strong for most of the postwar period.

U.S.-CANADA FREE-TRADE AGREEMENT[6]

Americans have found investments in Canada attractive for nearly a hundred years. U.S. FDI into Canada increased steadily from some U.S.$15 billion in the mid-1960s to some U.S.$57 billion in the late 1980s. U.S. ownership in Canada has been a political issue for the past two decades with many questioning whether the Canadian economy is not too dependent on the United States. As noted in Chapter 7, efforts were made during the late 1970s and early 1980s to review and even to restrict or guide that inflow.

During the early 1960s, the Canadian government became disturbed over the substantial trade deficit in automobiles and auto parts with the United States as a result of the investment in Canada by U.S. auto companies and the resulting pattern of intracompany trade. It offered rebates to the companies if they would reverse the pattern, producing more in Canada and exporting to the United States. The U.S. government responded with a threat of countervailing duties to offset these export subsidies. This raised the negotiation to the intergovernmental level, taking it out of the hands of the companies. Previously, the negotiation had been between Canada and the auto manufacturers, which were willing to increase their investments in Canada. U.S. government officials saw this as a "distortion" of business decisions in an attempt to create a "comparative advantage" on the part of Canada. The negotiations between the two governments resulted in a U.S./Canada Auto Agreement under which the two countries opened up a free-trade corridor in autos and automotive parts, *provided* that U.S. companies would increase their investments in Canada and shift the pattern of trade so as to achieve a closer balance of trade in that sector.

The agreement has worked relatively well, with minor negotiations from time-to-time in order to redress significant imbalances that have arisen. The American companies found that they could readily increase investments in Canada—principally in Windsor, Ontario, which is just south of Detroit. Plants were also established elsewhere in Canada, responding to economic factors and provincial incentives.

During the 1980s, FDI from Canada into the United States exceeded that flowing from the United States to Canada. Canadian investment in the United States rose from $10 billion to over $30 billion from 1978 thru 1984 and rose further in the late 1980s so that it aggregated over half the total of U.S. investment in Canada. The two economies have become closely integrated through cross-investment and large volumes of trade, which have made each country the largest single trading partner of the other. As a result of this progressive integration, the governments considered that it would be to the advantage of each to establish a free trade area between them. The combined national incomes of the two countries in the late 1980s was over $5 trillion.

The complete opening of the markets would hasten the rationalization of industry, making it more efficient and competitive with the rest of the world. In 1986, the two-way trade between the countries totaled over $125 billion in merchandise alone. In that year, Canada purchased twice as much from the United States as Japan did, and more than the combined imports of Mexico, West Germany, and the United Kingdom from the United States. Canada is the fastest growing export market for the United States and is also the major importer of U.S. services. In the same year, nearly 70 percent of Canada's imports were from the United States. A U.S. deficit on merchandise trade is nearly matched by a surplus on nonmerchandise exports, giving a current account balance of less than $3 billion in favor of Canada in 1986.

U.S. investment in Canada was over seventy-five percent of total FDI in that country, while Canadian FDI in the United States was fourth behind the United Kingdom, the Netherlands, and Japan. By far the major merchandise imports into Canada are of autos and auto parts—comprising sixty-five percent of the top ten exports from the United States into Canada, with the rest representing high-tech goods, essentially in the electronic, aircraft, and equipment sectors. Conversely, of the top ten imports from Canada into the United States, autos, parts and trucks comprise just under sixty percent, with the rest being materials and natural resources. Thus, there is substantial complementarity in the trade between the two countries, with the most significant integration in a single sector being that in autos.

The United States and Canada had signed a free-trade agreement as early as 1854, even before Canada became a nation. This agreement was abrogated by the United States in 1866 as a result of the hostilities during the Civil War, and efforts to revive the agreement over several decades were frustrated by shifting positions in one government or the other. In 1911, a new agreement was concluded, but with the fall of the Canadian party in power, it was never put into place, with the result that protectionism grew between the two countries during the 1920s and 1930s. In 1935, a "most favored-nation" agreement was signed under the U.S. Reciprocal Trade Agreements Program, and a new series of efforts were made to relax restrictions on trade between the two countries. From the late 1940s to the 1980s, the two countries significantly reduced barriers and smoothed trade regulations through the GATT negotiations. In 1965, the Auto Pact integrated that sector to the extent that the automotive industry became the mainstay of the economy in the province of Ontario, employing over 130,000 Canadians and exporting 90 percent of its production.

In March 1985, the two governments began a cooperative effort to conclude a new free-trade agreement, which was eventually signed in October 1987 and ratified by the two legislative bodies in 1988, going into effect January 1, 1989. It is primarily focused on trade in merchandise, although national treatment is provided for trade in goods, most services, and some investment activities. Barriers to trade in goods and services between the two countries are to be eliminated over phased periods; cross-border investment is to be liberalized; a joint administration of the agreement and joint resolution of disputes is provided for; and further steps are envisioned to expand the benefits of the agreement bilaterally and to third countries who might wish to join. Safeguards are included to prevent third countries from using either country to gain free access to the other's markets.

Immediate concerns on both sides of the border were raised by those who saw the agreement as necessitating significant adjustments in agriculture and industry. U.S. auto and rubber workers feared investments moving into Canada, where wages and benefits remained somewhat lower. The high-tech companies seemed likely to scale their operations down in Canada and expand in the United States. At the same time, the likely shifts in the pattern of exports and imports caused rumblings among those who considered their markets well-established. In the late 1980s, many companies sought to secure market and investment positions in anticipation of the Agreement's effective date of January 1, 1989, despite the fact that ratification had not occurred. By 1988, TNCs on both sides of the border were looking at acquisitions and sell-offs to establish a stronger competitive position. U.S. TNCs controlled some 17 percent of corporate assets in Canada and were seeking to consolidate their position, while Canadian companies were expanding their stakes in the United States—such as Seagram (liquor), Campeau (retail), Dominion (textiles), and John Labatt (foods). If the immediate trends continue, by the early 1990s, Canadian companies could own as much in the United States as U.S. companies in Canada.

The opening of the border will cause a restructuring and rationalization of manufacturing and distribution. It will gradually shift the sources and types of advertising and public relations as restrictions on the media and service sectors are lifted. The financial sectors also will be tied more closely together, giving some Canadian institutions pause over their reduced independence.

The Agreement provides that the benefits of free trade accrue only to companies that are more than 50 percent U.S. or Canadian owned—thus it will not be possible for a South Korean or Japanese majority-owned affiliate in either country to enjoy free movement of goods between them. For this reason, the Japanese government took an initiative in 1988 to begin discussions on its participation in at least the auto agreement, since it had made substantial investments in the automotive sector in the United States. South Korea has made investments in the same sector in Canada, and would likely also be interested if the Japanese worked out a reasonable accommodation. The U.S. government responded by asking for consideration of a wider free-trade arrangement between the United States and Japan, which was not enthusiastically received in Japan, though it reportedly continued to consider the U.S. initiative. This pattern of discussion, focusing on sectoral agreements within regional associations, appears a harbinger of greater sector-by-sector cooperation in trade and investment.

The United States and Mexico have discussed some sectoral agreements but have not seriously pursued a North American free-trade agreement. The U.S. government has been opposed in principle to regional blocs ever since its initiative after World War II to create a "one-world economy." Mexico has long opposed any closer dependence on the United States, seeking rather to gain assistance for independent development. By joining the Latin American Free Trade Association in the 1960s it put a damper on any consideration of a North American grouping. However, in the late 1980s it signed a "Framework Agreement" with the United States covering economic issues. This agreement encourages subsequent sectoral agreements on manufacturing and service activities, direct investments, trade, and protection of intellectual property. Several bilateral accords are anticipated.

LATIN AMERICAN INTEGRATION ASSOCIATION

The Latin American Integration Association (ALADI) replaced the Latin American Free Trade Association (LAFTA) in 1980. The initial organization, established in 1960, sought to achieve a free-trade area among the whole of Latin America from the Rio Grande to Tierra del Fuego. But only the South American countries joined, plus Mexico. Tariffs were to be reduced progressively to zero; they were negotiated on a multi-bilateral basis (similar to the GATT), but opposition was so strong that the largest reductions aggregated over the years to only 50 percent of existing duties. The easier reductions were made fairly readily, but the remaining reductions were opposed by both domestic business and various government agencies. Even this opening of the Latin American economy was attractive to foreign investors, and FDI began to flow into the major countries— Mexico, Brazil, and Argentina. As a consequence, the other countries saw the major benefits accrue to the most advanced countries. Consequently, the countries along the Andes decided to form their own regional association, as discussed in the following section.

The LAFTA continued to try to reduce barriers, and they were able to do so through some company-complementation agreements under which individual companies offered to establish operations in two or three countries under the conditions of free trade among them for their own components and products. These agreements were ad hoc and did not cover all the members of LAFTA. The progress of LAFTA virtually halted in the latter part of the 1970s. In order to take new initiatives, the ALADI (LAIA) was formed by all the countries of Latin America, except the Guyanas, Nicaragua, and the Caribbean.

The Central American countries formerly had their own Common Market (CACM) which was virtually abandoned due to the hostility between some of the countries (Honduras and El Salvador) and the political disturbances within Nicaragua and El Salvador. Panama was not a member of this five-nation group. A major economic difficulty in achieving a common market in the region was an attempt to balance the benefits of foreign direct investment among the members. This is the same problem that broke the LAFTA and has confronted all regional associations. The CACM sought to resolve this difficulty by allocating to each of the five members a significant industrial sector, such as rubber products or chemicals, but they could not find five sectors in which foreign investors were interested. The governments of the five countries wanted simultaneous investment in each selected sector, so that they could be assured of an equitable balance of benefits.

ALADI, to avoid the obstacle in the reduction of duties faced under the LAFTA, side stepped the objective of creating a single free-trade area by permitting multicountry trade accords that lowered barriers to exports and imports among the agreeing members, excluding those members that did not want to participate. This goal implied a more limited strategy of bilateral or trilateral accords (or wider) that were more likely to be implemented than full eleven-country agreements. The implementation would be more easily achieved because the balances of benefits could be readily discerned, and disagreement over impacts would not be as frequent or serious. Thus, within the region, foreign investors still face a wide range of tariff and nontariff barriers on their shipments into and between ALADI members, rather than there being a uniform external tariff or even uniform barriers within the group.

ALADI has continued to offer company complementation agreements, and some 25 arrangements are in place covering industries such as chemicals, pharmaceuticals, electrical appliances, and telecommunications.[7] These agreements offer reduced duties on the trade of a given company among the countries where it has production facilities and in which the host governments see the integration of the facilities as desirable. These agreements have not been sufficiently widely approved to be a factor in attracting significant FDI to the member countries. The TNCs in Latin America remain mostly interested in serving the domestic market in the host country. Helping to establish the regional Latin American market is not a high priority among foreign TNCs—though it should be, because the TNCs are an important mechanism for achieving cross-national integration, as shown by their activities in Europe.

A singular problem with the company-complementation agreements, however, is the favoritism it implies over domestic companies not having multiplant locations among the members. Thus, there has not been strong support from the private sector for such agreements in favor of foreign TNCs. Nor is there much evidence that these programs have altered TNC strategies in locating their production facilities. In addition, various country restrictions on FDI inflows and the remaining high transportation costs and differential duties restrict TNC interest in cross-national integration. TNCs that are already in existence in the Latin American countries do have advantages because of some tariff concessions under ALADI, and competitive situations are changed thereby, but the overall attraction has not been significant in the past decade.

Because of the absence of a harmonized approach by ALADI members toward FDI, and the relative significance of duty reductions within the group, there is not a strong negotiation process between the TNCs and the ALADI organization. The more extensive negotiations still take place between the TNCs and individual country governments, reflecting the weakness of the regional organization. Neither Latin America as a whole or the subregions of Central America, the Caribbean, and the Andean countries have been as serious in their pursuit of the proposed goal of economic integration as their words and agreements would appear. The power of words compared to deeds remains strong in the Latin culture. The goal of integration has been espoused since before the time of Bolivar and his attempt to form the Gran Colombia, so that the goal of an integrated Latin America remains a dream, but one that is repeatedly stated and acclaimed. There remains a heavy overburden of a concern for reciprocity and equity and an insufficient basis for a community of interest to achieve it. The need for efficiency and competitiveness, therefore, remains unattended, despite the fact that TNC activities *could*, accelerate equitable regional integration.[8] Such a result requires concerted policies on the part of TNCs and governments, as discussed in Chapter 17.

THE ANDEAN PACT

The Andean Pact, established in 1969, is composed of Bolivia, Colombia, Ecuador, Peru, and Venezuela. (Chile was a member until 1976; Venezuela joined in 1973.) These nations found themselves bypassed in the development accelerated by the LAFTA among the three major countries; they sought to separate themselves somewhat at the same time to increase the size of their national markets by regional integration. They hoped to achieve economies of scale in industrial production through the larger market and to attract both domestic and foreign investments, potentially diverting some investment from the major countries of Latin America. But the role of TNCs in Andean development was frustrated by two attitudes within the region. One was a general acceptance of the idea that the TNCs behavior should be greatly restricted because of the potential adverse affects on host-country development. The second was an attempt to reserve the regional Andean market for domestic companies. The restrictive policies were put into effect in 1971 in "Decision 24," which TNCs considered a serious obstacle to investment in the region. Its application was never uniform among the member countries, leading to negotiations between TNCs and national governments that were more significant than those between TNCs and the Junta of the Andean Pact.

Rules on TNCs

Two sets of regulations under the Andean Pact were addressed specifically to TNCs—Decision 24 and the sectoral programs for regional industrial development (complementation agreements). In the latter, 14 industrial sectors were structured, in principle to be regionally organized—with manufacturing locations distributed around the member countries. Actually, agreements were achieved only on the auto, pharmaceutical, metalworking, and telecommunication sectors, but none of these have been implemented. The effect of the programs was, in fact, to prevent integrated operation of FDI affiliates in several countries of the region in these targeted sectors, since free trade in these sectors was permitted only to regional-based (Andean) multinationals, that is, firms with at least 51 percent local ownership. The program involved the assignment (after extensive negotiation) of specific products in a sector to each of the pact members, thus encouraging investment in facilities in each of the assigned countries for the specified products. By participating, a company obtained tariff-free entry into the other members of the groups. While production was not *precluded* in the other members by foreigners for any specific component or product, free trade was limited to companies following the complementation assignments. This incentive system tried to distribute production of key products more equitably among the group to achieve reciprocity in the benefits of integration among the members.

The sectoral programs failed; five factors were important:

- the programs were not open to FDI except through minority joint ventures
- the incentives were not strong enough to entice Andean firms to set up production outside of their national markets
- transport difficulties made cross-national trade costly within the region
- member governments remained in disagreement over precise implementation of the program
- the entry of Venezuela and the departure of Chile required reassignment of specific products among the countries, opening the negotiations to further disagreement

The existence of Decision 24 also affected the attitude of foreigners to the entire integration movement within the pact countries. This decision, also called the "Andean foreign investment code," was in effect from 1971 until 1987, when it was replaced by a set of rules aimed to *attract* greater TNC investment rather than to restrict it. This latter change (Decision 220) of the pact reflected the significance of the foreign debt crisis that overshadowed Latin American development, and the member countries' needs for greater private capital inflows during the late 1980s to stimulate employment, production, and exports to service the debt.

Decision 24 required foreign firms to sell at least 51 percent of the ownership of their affiliates in the Andean countries to local investors over a period of 15 years, leaving themselves in a minority position. Operations established before 1971 were not required to fade out their ownership, unless they wanted to take advantage of the regional tariff preferences or the complementation agreements. Thus, companies exporting to nonmembers could retain 100 percent ownership or they could export to members under previous tariff rates. In addition, profit remittances were limited initially to 14 percent of the firm's registered capital base—later raised to 20 percent. Royalties from subsidiaries to their foreign parents were prohibited, and some activities, such as domestic marketing, were precluded as the sole purpose for foreign investment. The whole package of restrictions was the most onerous in Latin America and among the most burdensome in the noncommunist world.[9]

By 1987, governments were disaffected by years of uneven enforcement of Decision 24 and widespread exceptions to rules. When member governments found it desirable to attract FDI to ease payments pressures and increase employment, they formally replaced the restrictions with a new code that opened most activities to foreign firms and promoted more similar treatment for TNCs as that given by government to private sectors in their own countries—that is, national treatment.

TNC Responses

The TNCs argue that the sectoral programs for industrial development (complementation agreements) were an initiative to which they could have responded, but only if they were permitted to retain 100 percent ownership—that is, not sell a majority ownership to local parties. They had the ability to allocate production of components among member countries according to the agreement and would have done so with a few incentives to move into the less desirable locations. With 100 percent ownership they would be able to balance the benefits of production in the more economic countries with the potential losses in the less suitable locations. But the governments were determined "not to integrate their economies for the benefit of multinational enterprises." Thus, they rejected the only available means for achieving the reciprocity that they sought among their members.

Decision 24 initially led to a significant drop in the inflows of FDI and technology. However, after the first four or five years, member governments began making significant exceptions. Subsequently, the code itself appeared to have no differentially restrictive impact on the inflows of FDI, which became a matter of national negotiation. Still, TNCs found that in many cases the conditions were not that attractive, even though ownership percentages were raised by the national governments. In others, they found that a joint venture was *not* wholly destructive to the success of the enterprise. Acceptance of joint ventures in these cases reflected the orientation of TNCs to servicing the local market or to seeking resources—that is, they remained market seekers or resource seekers, as described in Chapter 2.

The integrative effects of the efficiency seeker were not made available because of the restrictive code in the region. The TNCs remained in the countries where they were located, serving the national market and taking no advantage of the reduction of some barriers, simply because of the other obstacles to doing so. Under Decision 24, the TNCs were restricted even in entry into regional markets among the pact countries—unless they sold a majority of equity to locals. The national markets of some countries alone were unattractive, slowing FDI; though Venezuela remained sufficiently attractive, even with restrictions, to bring in some FDI. Negotiations on each project arrived at modifications acceptable to the government and TNCs, bypassing the Andean Junta.

When the Latin American debt crisis arose in the 1980s, all the Andean countries were viewed as risky locations for TNCs, and much of the bargaining power of national governments was lost. When severe doubt existed on a country's ability to obtain sufficient dollars to pay foreign debts and to permit private firms to import needed products or remit their profits, the host countries became hard pressed to attract foreign investment at all. Even the offer of competitive incentives was not highly successful. The situation led to a virtual reversal toward more open policies throughout Latin America, similar to other countries. This was an attempt not to lose ground in economic development, but these moves are too recent to be able to assess results.

ASSOCIATION OF SOUTHEAST ASIAN NATIONS

The ASEAN group was formed by Indonesia, Malaysia, the Philippines, Singapore, and Thailand in 1967 to promote economic development in the region and was later joined by Brunei. In comparison to the "Four Tigers" (Hong Kong, South Korea, Singapore, and Taiwan), the ASEAN group has grown less rapidly and achieved a lower level of per capita income during the 1970s and the 1980s. Yet, these countries have achieved levels of per capita income similar to those in more prosperous Latin American countries, as a result of growth rates during the 1980s that far exceeded those in Latin America. The ASEAN nations also are more open to international trade and investment (as shown in Chapters 7 and 8) than their Latin American counterparts. International trade typically accounts for over half of the GDP in the ASEAN region, far above the average of the world or Latin America. In sum, ASEAN presented a much more positive economic picture at the end of the 1980s than did Latin America.

As a regional organization, ASEAN imposed few restrictive policies towards TNCs, both within the individual member countries and through the regional association. The regional agreement also provided for industrial complementation agreements and avoided the (Andean) error of excluding the TNCs from participation. In fact, some agreements have been proposed by TNCs themselves in order to achieve greater efficiency and broaden the market regionally. These proposals were similar to the company-complementation agreements within the LAFTA, but they were also intended to extend to the industry as a whole rather than be restricted to just one company.

The governments in the ASEAN group committed a different error, however, deciding to let the existing private companies in each country in a given sector determine the new pattern of production and trade—rather than doing it through government negotiation as under the Andean Pact. As occurred in the auto industry proposals, conflicts among existing suppliers in and among the member countries prevented a formal agreement. There was no entity capable of bringing about the necessary trade-offs, so long as governments remained on the sidelines in negotiations. There were simply too many vested interests in small auto parts providers and in existing investments in auto assembly to permit anyone to give up their position. Given this situation, a bargaining relationship between TNCs and the ASEAN administration was never formally established. There were continuous discussions but few formal negotiations on these agreements.

The ASEAN association has been successful in reducing some barriers to trade but has not achieved an integrative pattern of FDI within the region.

COUNCIL FOR MUTUAL ECONOMIC ASSISTANCE

The communist grouping for economic integration (COMECON or CMEA) was formed in the 1950s as a response to European integration efforts, with the Eastern European countries tied closely to the U.S.S.R. Through it, the patterns of trade and investment among the Eastern European countries (Poland, Czechoslovakia, Hungary, East Germany, and Romania) and with the U.S.S.R. were arranged by negotiation—mostly through the Soviets laying out plans for the entire region. No multinational companies evolved within the region to assist in economic integration, and foreign TNCs were precluded from participating. Conflicts arose repeatedly over the equitable allocation of production and trade within the group.

COMECON as a group has no policies toward FDI, but members have been closed to foreign business except for imports and exports, contracts for technology transfer, and some few joint ventures—notably in Hungary. In the 1980s, most of the communist countries established rules permitting foreign joint ventures and other contractual forms so as to permit some foreign business. The attraction of serving a regional market, however, was shut off for TNCs through the decision that exports of foreign enterprises from one member country to another had to be paid for in hard currency (*valuta*). Since TNCs could as easily export to any Eastern European country from a location *outside* of the region, the advantage to investing in a COMECON country was to serve the host market itself or to export to the West out of a low-cost production facility. Thus, the investment in these areas by TNCs has been of the market-seeker or resource-seeker type, and mostly for low-cost labor. The major impact of the group on foreign TNCs has been not as a regional market but simply at the national level, as discussed in Chapter 9.

However, the events of 1989, in which Eastern Europe severed its communist ties, led to prompt requests to COMECON to abandon its planning of trade among its members and to support free-market arrangements. Presumably such an opening would permit more freedom for foreign investors to sell across countries within the region and throughout Europe. All Eastern Europe began to seek foreign investors, but the rules were uncertain.

In conclusion, the TNCs have not been effectively used in achieving the objective of industrial integration among countries, save among the advanced countries and then not as a matter of conscious policy. That the TNCs are an effective means of achieving such integration is seen from the experience in Europe and between the United States and Canada in the auto sector. The rest of the world has not yet learned the lessons, essentially because there has not been a sufficient community of interest to permit the making of acceptable trade-offs to achieve reciprocity.[10]

NOTES TO CHAPTER 12

1. See Stephen E. Hymer, *The International Operations of National Firms: A Study of Direct Investment* (Cambridge, MA: MIT Press, 1976).

2. The classical study of the impacts on trade of regional groupings is by Jacob Viner, *The Custom Union Issue* (New York: The Carnegie Endowment for International Peace, 1950).

3. See the proposals by Donald L. Guertin and John M. Kline, *Building an International Investment Accord* (Washington, DC: The Atlantic Council, July 1989).

4. Two studies published some seven years later provide not only the original documents but a commentary on the effect of the guidelines and the responses of TNCs and labor unions. See Philip Coolage, George C. Spina, and Don Wallace Jr. (eds.), *The OECD Guidelines for Multi-national Enterprises: a Business Appraisal* (Washington, DC:

Georgetown University, Institute for International and Foreign Trade Law, 1977); also Duncan C. Campbell and Richard L. Rowan, *Multinational Enterprises and the OECD Industrial Relations Guidelines* (Philadelphia: University of Pennsylvania, Industrial Relations Unit, 1983).

5. See R. Blanplain, *The Badger Case* (Deventer, Netherlands: Kluwer, 1977).

6. *The Canada-U.S. Free Trade Agreement: Synopsis* (Ottawa: Department of External Affairs, 1988); an analysis of the effects on TNCs was prepared by Donald G. McFetridge, *Trade Liberalization and the Multinationals* (Ottawa: Economic Council of Canada, 1989). An assessment of the U.S.-Canada Trade Pact was given by U.S. Treasury Secretary James A. Baker, "Implications of the U.S.-Canada Trade Pact," *The International Economy* (Jan./Feb., 1988), pp. 34–41.

7. Specific examples are given in Jorge Rabella and Evelyn Samore, *Gaining a Competitive Advantage in Latin America through LAIA* (New York: Business International Corporation, 1988).

8. J. N. Behrman, *The Role of International Companies in Latin American Integration* (Lexington, MA: Lexington Books, 1972).

9. See, for example, Robert Grosse, "The Andean Foreign Investment Code's Impact on Multi-National Enterprises," *Journal of International Business Studies* (Winter 1983), pp. 121–133.

10. The argument is more fully developed in J. N. Behrman, *Industrial Policies: International Restructuring and Transnationals* (Lexington, MA: Lexington Books, 1984).

CHAPTER 13

TNC Relations with United Nations Organizations

The United Nations Organization (UN) took over many of the economic, social, and legal aspects of international relations from the League of Nations after World War II. The League contained a number of international economic and social agencies, but only the International Labour Organization (ILO) survived to become affiliated with the UN. The UN created a number of subunits under its Economic and Social Council (ECOSOC), and later brought into affiliated status some of the other post-war institutions that had been created about the same time as the UN—notably the World Bank and the International Monetary Fund (IMF); see Chart 13.1. Diverse channels of communication exist between these entities and TNCs. In addition, many of these agencies are requested by member governments to supply information on the activities of TNCs. These requests appear to the TNCs to be excessive, so a dialogue ensues on the flow of information itself.

Many of the developing countries have sought sufficient information to learn how to form their own regulations concerning TNCs and to negotiate more effectively with them. LDCs have also frequently pressed the UN agencies to form codes of behavior for TNCs, which would be enforced by the home countries and serve as a model for host-country regulations. Only one such code has been agreed upon; others are still in negotiation after more than a decade of dialogue. The roles of TNCs in the debates over these codes have varied from country-to-country, with many TNCs feeling a level of frustration in dealing with both the issues and the UN delegations. The UN has also, in various forums, and over several years, passed resolutions urging TNCs to pull out of South Africa in protest against the practice of apartheid and illegally occupied Namibia.

Chart 13.1: United Nations Economic and Social Council

UN Agencies (Subunits)	Specialized Agencies and Affiliates
Economic Commission for Europe (ECE)	World Bank
	International Finance Corporation
Economic Commission for Latin America and the Caribbean (ECLAC)	International Development Association (IDA)
Economic Commission for Africa and the Far East (ECAFE)	International Centre for Settlement of Investment Disputes (ICSID)
Commission on Transnational Corporations	Multinational Investment Guarantee Authority (MIGA)
Centre on Transnational Corporations (UNCTC)	International Monetary Fund (IMF)
Development Program (UNDP)	Food and Agriculture Organization (FAO)
Environment Program (UNEP)	World Health Organization (WHO)
Centre on Science and Technology for Development (UNCSTD)	International Civil Aviation Organization (ICAO)
	International Labour Organization (ILO)
	World Intellectual Property Organization (WIPO)

SCOPE OF ACTIVITIES OF UN AGENCIES

The major international organizations that are *affiliated* with the UN include the International Bank for Reconstruction and Development (IBRD, World Bank, or Bank), the International Monetary Fund (IMF or Fund), the International Finance Corporation (IFC), and the International Development Agency (IDA)—the last two are affiliated with the World Bank directly and through it with the UN. The International Civil Aviation Organization (ICAO), the World Health Organization (WHO), the Food and Agricultural Organization (FAO), the International Labour Organization (ILO), and the World Intellectual Property Organization (WIPO) are also UN affiliated agencies. All such organizations are funded by member governments through subscriptions or annual contributions to an approved budget.

World Bank and IMF

The Bretton Woods Agreements formed the World Bank and the International Monetary Fund, and subsequently the IFC and IDA were added (as well as the ICSID and the MIGA, discussed in Chapter 11). The World Bank was formed to stimulate the flow of capital from advanced countries to those needing reconstruction after World War II and to countries that were emerging from colonialism. The loans coming from it were supposed to be provided at low interest rates—lower than would have been the case commercially or even bilaterally from governments. In addition, it was to provide guarantees for private investment from the advanced to the developing countries, in order to stimulate the growth of private enterprise in the latter. Both direct loans and guarantees were to help build the base for private enterprise, including FDI.

The experience of the Bank quickly showed that there were a number of projects needing financing, which the developing countries could not pay for themselves nor sustain debt service even at low interest rates, simply because the projects would not directly generate foreign exchange. Consequently, the IDA was formed to provide even lower-cost loans on still longer terms, helping to build the necessary infrastructure. The IFC was created to provide equity funds and promote private investment through melding some public funds with those of TNCs in more enterprise-oriented activities. It has, thereby, reduced the risks to the private investor both by adding capital and making its own analysis of profitability. Once the project is successful, the IFC usually sells the stock to the TNC or to local investors. Among international economic organizations it has an enviable record of success. The Bank never really promoted its loan guarantee provision, which would have permitted it to stand behind the investor or lender in event of default. The Bank did not use the guarantee authority because member governments offered guarantees and insurance, FDI volumes were slow to rise, and the Bank preferred to borrow in capital markets for its own lending.[1]

The IMF provides short-term loans to member countries who are in balance-of-payments difficulties. The Fund provides foreign exchange to help maintain stability in foreign exchange rates. The Bretton Woods Agreement provided that the value of currencies was to be fixed in terms of U.S. dollars, backed by gold (in 1945, at $35 per ounce). The Fund's borrowing facilities were not as readily available to those countries that had not fixed the dollar-value of their currencies or that retained multiple exchange rates or fluctuating rates.

Advice and pressure from the Fund plus its short-term lending gradually brought more and more countries to stabilize their exchange rates, and the system worked relatively well until 1971. At that time, the United States untied the dollar from gold, and it began to float against other currencies. Many countries maintained a relatively fixed relationship to the dollar so that their currencies fluctuated as the dollar did against other major currencies.

The dollar depreciated in the early 1970s, strengthened in the late 1970s and early 1980s to become overvalued in international markets, only to sink again in the late 1980s to levels nearly half its high value in terms of major currencies (e.g., Deutschmark and yen). Since that time, the Fund has largely been giving advice and has been reluctant to make loans without attaching stringent conditions on governments to assure repayment. Since exchange rates are permitted to move to adjust the balance of payments, there is less need for exchange reserves in each country. The country that has needed the borrowing capacity of the Fund more than any other in the past several years has been the United States itself, but instead it has turned to the international financial markets, where it has absorbed billions of dollars of capital, essentially to finance its twin deficits— the government budget and balance of trade. Even so, the dollar has sunk to quite low levels, and the instability of the dollar has significantly altered the role of the Fund as well as the operations of TNCs.

The names of these two institutions are probably inappropriate, as Lord Keynes himself asserted during the early negotiations. The Bank is really a *fund* of capital that is available on noncommercial terms, whereas the Fund is really a *bank* that lends to governments on short-term at relatively commercial rates. The shifting nature of these organizations has been hammered out in annual international monetary conferences at which officials of governments, banks, and TNCs from around the world meet to discuss current problems and the operations of the Bank and Fund and their affiliated entities. TNCs, therefore, have an impact as indirect users of their financial resources; multinational banks are particularly involved.* TNCs are not directly asked by these two institutions for advice, however, key TNC officials use the annual international conference of the Fund and Bank to get acquainted with top government officials and express their views.

ICAO

The International Civil Aviation Organization was formed immediately after World War II to help in the reconstruction of the airlines around the world, particularly the international network. The agency has promulgated a number of rules for cooperative behavior, routes, and safety; however, the primary responsibility for routes rests with national governments. Hence, even regarding international routes, airlines deal more with home and host governments than with the ICAO.

WHO

The World Health Organization promotes health programs of its members around the world and has advised LDCs on the minimum list of 100 pharmaceuticals that they should have available. Since the WHO perceived the TNCs as acting against the interests of LDC governments in pro-

---

*The multinational banks are especially involved with the IMF in dealing with the LDC debt crisis of the 1980s. The banks have demanded that debtor governments follow IMF advice as a condition of receiving new commercial bank loans, and the IMF has been urging these banks to make new loans to these countries.

motion of pharmaceuticals that were "unnecessary" for poorer countries, it was slow in developing adequate relations with the pharmaceutical and health-care companies around the world. Pharmaceutical TNCs have sought to expand the list or obtain its removal.

However, as it has become clearer that the objectives of the WHO could be better served by private industry in many respects than by government institutions, a closer relationship has developed between the WHO and TNCs. A number of corporate advisory committees now exist, both permanent and ad hoc. Though companies were earlier jaundiced by the attitudes they found among WHO delegates, they have become more satisfied with the cooperative attitudes emanating from the organization during the latter part of the 1980s. Some of the issues relative to pharmaceuticals are discussed in Chapter 14.

FAO

The Food and Agriculture Organization early established bilateral relations with TNCs in agro-industry around the world because it was basing the success of agriculture on the "Green Revolution," i.e., the application of new technologies to farming. These technologies came in part from major corporations, through the provision of fertilizers, the exchange of techniques on storage and distribution of food and feeds, and the processing of foods for further distribution. Since the role of private industry was critical, an advisory group of agro-industry companies has deliberated with the FAO rather continuously.

ILO

The International Labour Organization, the longest-lived intergovernmental economic organization, was formed in 1919 to help eradicate poverty and unemployment in the world and to strive for better working conditions and industrial relations. Its tripartite membership—representatives of governments, labor unions, and business—is unique. Almost all countries are members. Three delegates are selected by the foreign ministry of each member country, with the advice and consent of appropriate governmental, labor, and business organizations. Each delegate has a vote, and those from the same country do not necessarily vote alike.

The ILO has a number of divisions or departments, which are related to different aspects of industrial development—by sectors, by regions, and by functions—so that it promotes not only improved labor conditions but also employment, benefits, and training in many countries of the world. It also has helped in the formation of free labor unions, without entering the field of labor adjudication or conciliation. The delegates pass resolutions, which, to be effective, require adoption and implementation by member governments, as they wish. The United States has one of the poorest records of promulgation of the resolutions, mainly because it considers its labor legislation better than the ILO guidelines. Many governments "adopt" the resolutions but do not actually comply. The ILO has no adequate means of surveillance, and no enforcement mechanism; compliance is wholly voluntary.

In the 1960s it began a series of studies on the role of the TNCs in employment and social welfare. By 1977, its members reached consensus as to the companies' appropriate roles. A *Tripartite Declaration of Principles Concerning Multi-national Enterprises and Social Policy* was issued,[2] covering industrial relations, information for workers, improvement of working conditions, collective bargaining, and more. It had the support of both TNC and labor representatives, but its implementation has frequently left labor unions dissatisfied.

Many other ILO documents and studies relating to TNC activities have been and are undertaken, covering country studies of women workers, health and safety, plant closing, employment shifts, training, technology transfers, personnel policies, and decision-making structures, as well as industry studies and wide surveys.

UN Subunits

There are a number of UN agencies that are subunits of the organization, rather than affiliates. Some were formed early, such as the regional economic commissions of the Economic and Social Council (ECOSOC)—the Economic Commission for Europe (ECE), the Economic Commission for Africa and the Far East (ECAFE), the Economic Commission for Latin America and the Caribbean (ECLAC)—each of which examines the cross-national problems that arise within the region and seeks to help resolve them. The ECE has members from both Western and Eastern Europe. (There is no counterpart for North America since Mexico is in the ECLAC, and the United States and Canada maintain close communication anyway.) On occasion, the meetings of these commissions are open to invited guests from industry and labor, so that their viewpoints can be given directly. The ECOSOC is the overall economic subunit of the UN to which all others are related at least in a reporting fashion. It covers all commercial, financial, technological, and social aspects of economic development. Here, also, industry and labor representatives are invited on occasions.

Later subunits of ECOSOC were created to deal directly with matters affecting international business. One is the UN Commission on Transnational Corporations, which was established after a series of hearings in the early 1970s before The *Group of Eminent Persons*, selected from around the world. This was a time of considerable concern over the expansion of TNCs, particularly in the developing world, and over the impacts they would have on industrial development. Socialist governments were especially concerned to demonstrate that the TNCs were damaging their future growth. The hearings did not prove that argument, but demands for information on TNCs arose, particularly concerning their operations and impacts and the means to control them.

It was the conclusion of ECOSOC that a specialized unit should be formed under the auspices of the UN. It would monitor and guide policies on TNCs. These policies would be enunciated and implemented by member governments, but they would have the guidance of deliberations within the Commission on Transnational Corporations; a permanent secretariat was created as the UN Centre on Transnational Corporations (UNCTC). The UNCTC itself has three major divisions: one to gather information on the TNCs, a second to study individual industry sectors to determine their impacts on host countries, and a third to train government officials in legal matters and other areas so as to improve negotiation skills in the host countries. Its first assignment was to define (characterize) a TNC, which it has not been able to do after more than a decade of debate; a major disagreement over inclusion of state-owned enterprises was a stumbling block.

This organization became a major interface of TNCs with the UN, though three others are also important—the UNDP, the UNEP, and the UNCSTD. The UNDP (UN Development Program) is aimed at assisting developing countries in the better formation and implementation of their programs for economic growth. It provides some grants and low-cost loans for projects that are tied into overall development programs—in contrast to the pure project loans financed by the World Bank or its affiliate the IDA. Although there is not a direct connection between UNDP and TNCs, the success of the UNDP is critical to foreign investors in developing countries, and the head of the UNDP has on many occasions kept a dialogue going with TNC officials.

The UNEP (UN Environmental Program) was established after an international conference sponsored by the UN on environmental problems. The inability to resolve the problems at the conference led to the formation of this subunit, and out of that came the formation of an industry advisory group, which meets annually with secretariat officials in Nairobi. Subcommittees of this advisory group attend on specific aspects of protection of the environment and depollution. A number of TNCs have environmental programs of their own guided by vice presidents who are responsible for corporate environmental policies worldwide. These officials provide ready TNC representation at UNEP meetings.[3]

The UNCSTD (UN Centre on Science and Technology for Development) was formed out of an international conference, held in Vienna in the late 1970s. TNC representatives were included in the U.S. and U.K. delegations.[4] For most of the countries, however, industry representatives were not included—even in the formation of the positions of the government members. In the case of the United States, an extensive program of gathering views of industry and the public was carried out under the guidance of the State Department. In turn, it sought business inputs through several major groups, including the National Academy of

Science and the National Academy of Engineering. These and several others polled their membership on issues, held seminars and small conferences, and developed position papers out of some extensive studies. The Fund for Multinational Management Education (New York) produced a three-volume study on the role and issues of technology in international development, as supplied by and seen through the eyes of TNCs; the study was based on extensive interviews with TNC officials and numerous case studies written by them.[5] These several contributions helped form the U.S. position before the conference, which turned early to the role of the TNCs in the transfer of technology and the development of R&D in both the advanced and developing countries.

At the conference, one of the major demands of the developing countries was the formation of a Centre which would be a channel for contacts with sources of technology and guidance on the negotiation of technology agreements. A Centre for Science and Technology in Development (UNC-STD) was set-up, but the LDC request that it develop a technology data bank was not agreed to by the advanced countries, since they considered this to be an excessively expensive way of sourcing technology. A major question was that of whether the potential users would even know the kinds of questions to ask in order to access the data. It was resolved to provide merely information on information— that is, the sources of technology information, so that the potential users would be able to ask specific entities about different types of technology. These concerns signal the particular importance of information to the developing countries, a subject addressed next. The conference also was faced early with demands regarding an international code on technology transfer which was already under negotiation through the UNCTC, also discussed below. The Centre has had a difficult time determining the scope and direction of an effective program. And TNCs have not seen it as particularly useful in supplementing their own activities.

DEMANDS FOR INFORMATION

Adequate and relevant information is a necessity for the success of all economies. Economics has generally assumed that information is both freely available and widely disseminated. But it has become amply clear, especially to the developing countries, that information is a necessary basis for entry into and success in the game. Information is power, but it is also costly; yet one cannot play the game effectively without it. Consequently, the United Nations has become the organization through which developing countries have demanded more and more information on and from TNCs.

There are four basic aspects of the issues: the provision of information, its transmission or dispersion, its understandability, and its appropriate use. The fear of improper use of the information supplied to international agencies by governments receiving it from the UN was a major factor in the lack of eagerness of TNCs to cooperate in UNCTC studies. The inability to understand data provided to the UN agencies, for example, caused the ECOSOC to seek the international standardization of accounting. After many meetings directed at achieving some harmonization of standards and reporting, an agreement remains decades away.

An Intergovernmental Working Group of Experts on International Standards of Accounting and Reporting (ISAR) was established in 1982. The group studied national accounting standards and TNC practices. The issues involve not only the comprehensive information system of the UNCTC but also reporting requirements under projected UN codes on TNCs.[6] It is sometimes difficult enough to translate the accounts of one division of a company to that of another or to consolidate the accounts of a large conglomerate; it is much more difficult to consolidate the accounts of foreign affiliates or even to understand them— particularly when they are composed of joint ventures under which foreign accounting standards are applied. When there is an attempt to compare the activities of General Motors with those of Volkswagen, the problems of different accounting methods come quickly to the fore. The UN is still struggling with the issues, and meetings continue to be held to achieve some kind of agreement, but progress is exceedingly slow.[7]

A more fundamental issue is the disclosure of information by those who hold it. The holders of information relative to business are the corporations themselves and the government agencies that have required reporting on various kinds of activities or results. Any government can demand whatever information it wants from any entity that was incorporated in its jurisdiction. The demands of the U.S. government must be met when mandatory questionnaires are sent to U.S. companies, but the government must handle the information in such a way as not to disclose the operations of any single company through its dissemination of the information received. That is, it must maintain confidentiality. Many foreign governments, however, want company information so that they can compare operations or determine whether the TNC is operating appropriately within their own borders, given its worldwide activities. That is, is it transferring revenue from one country to another? Is it hiding funds? Is it engaged in excessive use of transfer pricing? What are its R&D expenditures? and so on. Information from merely one location may not sufficiently answer these questions. In order to negotiate effectively with TNCs, host governments desire information as to the *patterns* of behavior and the types of agreements that TNCs have concluded with other countries.

Consequently, TNCs faced a heightened demand for information during the 1970s and 1980s. Although the intensity of the demands seemed to wane in the late 1980s with more welcoming policies of governments, there are still pleas for more information and for exchanges of information among governments. Governments, of course, have the final say as to the flow of information outside of national boundaries. This has been the reason for the attempts to establish agreement on "transborder data flows," again under the aegis of the UN. Governments have put controls on the flow of data across national boundaries to reduce the ability of corporations to transfer sensitive information from one country to another; governments see such transfers as potential violations of laws on proprietary information and an invasion of national privacy. In these negotiations, the TNCs were intimately involved—not only those transferring the information but the computer and communication companies who provided the channels and mechanisms for doing so.[8]

The demand for information comes largely from national governments who are seeking to establish policies on technology flows and both the inflow and outflow of investment so as to protect their exchange rates. Their demand is still unmet, even by the "Comprehensive Information Program" of the UNCTC; LDCs continue to ask for more and for greater cooperation from TNCs in providing information to the UNCTC—so as to make their negotiations with TNCs more effective. In the absence of information from the UNCTC, LDC governments have sought UN assistance in setting up their own (mandatory) information systems. They would then at least have better information on TNC operations in their own countries. With adoption of national industrial policies, information on specific companies will be critical.

The U.S. government itself has joined the developing countries in seeking information on the inflow of foreign capital, particularly since much of the direct investment into the United States is (especially in real estate) through intermediaries, which can hide the ultimate owner. A significant increase in foreign capital takeovers of U.S. industry will lead to calls for more information as to what is happening sector-by-sector and geographically.

The U.S. government has the most extensive data-gathering network of any country of the world, but given its support of "national treatment," it does not *require* data on entry of direct investors. It does require disclosure of information on various activities, through mandatory census requirements and a variety of reports to the SEC, FTC, ITC, FAA, FCC, plus customs and bank regulations, and so on. Governments of other host countries (West Germany, Canada, France, Switzerland, and some of the NICs) are reluctant to pass disclosure laws similar to those in the United States, but their demands are increasing. In addition to the national governments, the regional commissions or associations (discussed in Chapter 12) also seek a substantial amount of information. Even Caribbean countries have sought information on foreign investment in their area, looking towards the best means of guiding and controlling that investment toward the objectives of development in those countries. In the main, regional associations obtain their information on corporate activities through the national governments, but some seek information directly from companies with whom they have dialogues.

The most eager consumers of corporate information besides national governments are the international and intergovernmental organizations—all of those mentioned in the previous section plus a number of others. Competitors or other private organizations, including private voluntary organizations (PVOs), are not permitted to ask the UN for its information, but they can get it *through* their national governments, if the latter cooperate.

The pressure to obtain information for UN members was the basic reason why the Group of Eminent Persons recommended in the early 1970s that a Centre for Transnational Corporations should be formed. Through this and other organizations, three different types of information have been demanded from TNCs by governments: statistical data, information on company practices, and information on the impacts of foreign investment on host countries (See Chart 13.2).

No TNC has all such information; much would have to be collected and processed so it could be understood. The costs of doing so would run to tens of millions of dollars each year for a single TNC with 25 or 30 foreign affiliates.

Information on the different topics has quite different purposes and would lead to diverse uses, depending on whether it was aggregated for all affiliates, whether both foreign and domestic companies had to report the same information, whether it was made available to all governments or only the host government and with references to only the affiliate located in that country, and whether it was to be consolidated in some way and reconciled among different accounting systems so that it could be readily compared.

The United Nations' demand for information through the UNCTC and other agencies has been essentially short-circuited by the unwillingness of any government to force its TNCs to provide such information. The UNCTC has, therefore, gone to public sources and has sought information directly from the TNCs themselves, who have been willing to provide mainly information that is already public or which is not sensitive. They are especially concerned about

Chart 13.2: Information Demanded by Government
from TNCs

Statistical Data	Company Practices	Impacts
Balance of payments	Nature of operations	Political
Sources and uses of	The organization	interference
funds	structure	Social responsibility
Purchases and sales	Location of	Cultural identity
Profits	activities	Employment
Wages and	Product lines	—skills
employment	Ownership and	—level
Exports by	shareholdings	Environmental
destination	Control channels	protection
Imports by source	—management	Participation in
Remittances by type	contract	industry
—dividends	—licenses	associations
—royalties	Transfer pricing	Communication
—fees	Taxes paid	with government
—loans	—where	Location and
R&D expenditures	—how much	control of
	Labor relations	technology
	Capital movements	and R&D
	—long-term	Acquisitions,
	—short-term	mergers, and
	Restrictive business	takeovers
	practices	Pursuit of
	Market concen-	host-country
	tration	economic and
	Financial operations	social objectives
	Collective	Obedience to local
	bargaining	laws and
	Returns by type of	regulations
	operation	Interference by
	Accounting	home government
	practices and	Preferential
	reconciliation	treatment of TNCs
		—incentives
		—subsidies

how the information is used. The UNCTC has, consequently, been an information gatherer and analyst for LDCs.

Given the lack of consistency in information provided, the variation in information available from different countries, and the differential willingness of companies to provide information to anyone other than national agencies requiring information for government use, it is difficult to find a common pool of information on TNCs around the world. Consequently, a number of studies have been made of the activities of the TNCs with different results, depending on the companies studied and the information available. Several privately-financed and government-financed institutes have done studies of the TNCs seeking to gather information that would help in the better formation of government policies.[9] In addition, "corporate responsibility" groups have included the TNCs in their scope of inquiry for the purpose of advising governments as to the means of regulating the TNCs. Such studies frequently conclude by recommending the collection of more information concerning the operations of TNCs, reinforcing the interest of governments in TNC activities.

As all inquiring agencies and institutions have become more familiar with TNC operations, the demand for new information has waned, but there is one sector in which high interest remains and information is constantly requested— that of science and technology. Governments especially seek information that would help in the determination of appropriate technology and the appropriate terms of technology transfers or exchanges, as well as the proper role of R&D activities. They are particularly concerned to inquire into the R&D activities of parents and the dissemination of results abroad, the location of technical laboratories, the decision to innovate technology in different countries, the methods of such transfers of technology, the fees paid to the parent, and so on.

Since the mobility of TNCs has an impact on labor and employment in both host and home countries, a demand has arisen for more information on hiring and firing, closing of plants, movement of plants, investment in foreign sourcing, and appropriate methods of maintaining employment while investment shifts. Increasingly, information will be demanded on what is being done to achieve "fair labor standards" across national boundaries.

As more concern is raised over the social responsibilities of TNCs, there will be requests for a so-called "social audit," looking at community giving, support of educational activities, environmental protection, maintenance of the quality of life, maintenance of labor safety and good working conditions, and protection of the local culture. These and other requests imply that there will be a continued pressure for information from TNCs. The requests are justified on the ground that virtually anything the TNC does affects a significant part of the lives of those involved. Finally, the mere size of TNCs invokes inquiry and even attack, and the cross-national mergers and acquisitions of the late 1980s will exacerbate these inquiries.

For the TNC itself, serious questions arise as to Who should gather the information from the companies? How is it to be done? Who will bear the cost? Who is to receive it? and How will it be used? When governments mandate the supply of information, the company itself must bear the cost, which is one reason governments are reluctant to mandate a large amount of information. Of critical concern to TNCs is whether or not the government will pass the information on to people or institutions inimical to the TNCs. The governments generally aggregate information coming from companies so as to make it impossible for others to disaggregate it and find out what a particular company is doing. Yet, disaggregation is necessary in many studies in order to be able to find out the impact of a particular investment. Statistical data may be aggregated, but company practices and impacts need to be disaggregated. But, of course, disaggregated information raises the question of comparability and consolidation of information from widely different sources. If further raises the question of the need for harmonization of requests from different agencies to the same companies so that duplication of information gathering does not occur and nuances among the questions do not produce answers that are not readily interpreted.

Without such harmonization, companies are likely to supply data of the same type to different agencies, though the questions may have been phrased to obtain different information. Yet, harmonization of reporting is some years away, as seen in the problems of accounting standardization.

Of considerable concern to the TNCs themselves is who will use the information and for what purpose. If the user is the host government, and the questionnaire is mandatory, TNCs will usually reply even if they do not understand the

full use of the information. However, TNCs can have re-
course through the administrative process by appealing for
relief from the demand for disclosure because of the cost
and difficulty of gathering information. In some LDCs, they
may simply not reply, knowing they can get away with doing
so. In the United States, there is a Statistical Users Conference made up of government and private parties, which attempts to determine appropriate uses of data and whether
or not more data are needed for particular institutions or
entities. This provides something of a check against over-
requests for information, and it also is a way of achieving
some harmonization among requests. There needs to be
some check on the gathering of information to make certain that the purposes are significant enough to justify the
cost of gathering, processing, and analyzing it.

One of the dangers to TNCs of supplying information is
that it may get into the hands of competitors. This is certainly a possibility under the U.S. Freedom of Information
Act, which permits anyone to request information supplied
to the government, including contract bids—unless the procedure was secret. Since little government negotiation with
companies is secret, it is possible to obtain information
that helps to determine the size of a competitor's market,
its market share, its pricing policies, and sourcing of materials. TNCs operating in other countries are particularly
concerned that the host government will use industrial information for the purpose of controlling the economy and
specific segments within it—through national industrial
policies—or for giving national companies an advantage.
Where the policies are themselves supported by the industry sector involved, the provision of information is
more open and ready. Where government policies are objected to by the industry, there is an attempt to withhold
information.

If information given to the government reaches the public, it is not likely to be presented in the same way that the
TNC would choose, if it were trying to reach the same audi-
ence. The provision of information to the public is usually a
function of the "public relations" division of the company,
and it prefers to place the information supplied in the appropriate setting and supply its own interpretation and nu-

ances, all of which is likely to be lost in a governmental transmission.

One of the basic reasons that companies are reluctant to disclose more information is that the TNCs themselves have provided information to the public in ways that raise criticism. They continue to stress that their single objective is that of profit maximization in service to their shareholders, when that singular goal is not accepted by either the community or the company itself. Companies do not, in fact, operate for that simple objective, and to stress that they do is a disservice to themselves as well as to the community. No institution operates in such a singular fashion, but TNCs continue to talk as though they do in order to simplify the evaluation of performance within the company and among companies. Secondly, when companies do tell their story, they seem to focus on the more favorable aspects of their operations, being unwilling to let the public assess the balance of the good and the bad or the pluses and minuses. Consequently, the public questions the information offered and whether undisclosed minuses might not outweigh the pluses claimed. But they are not given the chance to make that judgment from the information provided, and in many cases it is too sparse or so mishandled by the media as to be inadequate for making judgments. Finally, companies sometimes give information under duress—that is, after they have been charged with some untoward practice. Information given under such circumstances is often seen as questionable.

TNCs cannot continue to supply less information than the public demands. Such a stance is likely to incur new disclosure regulations through the governments, as TNCs are too large and important to "keep a low profile" or "stay away from the government." TNCs cannot afford to be seen as dragging their feet or as unwilling to provide government decision makers with the information necessary to make good policies. There is a real danger, therefore, that reluctance on the part of TNCs will lead to new laws forcing information disclosure.

However, TNCs should have little to hide and should be able to explain themselves adequately enough to prevent attacks by opponents from being successful. If the TNCs can defend practices that the public questions, then the defense should be brought forward. If they cannot be defended, the company should examine carefully whether it should continue such practices.

TNCs are well advised to take government requests for information more seriously than they have in the past so as to avoid further regulation. This is done by achieving a higher level of legitimacy in home and host countries and that, in turn, is accomplished by the familiarity that comes with adequate information.

INTERGOVERNMENTAL CODES FOR TNCs[10]

International codes are seen by proponents as a major means of redistributing the benefits of FDI more toward host countries. They, therefore, warrant careful consideration as a prime means of reducing TNC/government conflict. Codes have been proposed for TNCs partly as a means of regulating their behavior and partly as a means of obtaining more information from them.[11]

Beginning in the mid-1970s, with a discussion of the Mexican proposal for a "New International Economic Order," four UN codes for TNCs were also requested: one on foreign direct investment, one on technology transfers, another on restrictive business practices, and one to prevent illicit payments or corrupt practices. These had the objective of eliminating the negative effects of TNC activities perceived by host countries. Only the one on restrictive business practices has been agreed upon and signed (in 1980).[12] Those on TNC behavior and technology transfer remain in negotiation, with that on corrupt practices set aside despite strong advocacy by the U.S. government. (The absence of an intergovernmental agreement on corrupt practices was a principal reason for the United States going ahead with its own national law on Foreign Corrupt Practices, discussed in Chapters 11 and 14.) The lack of agreement on the TNC and technology codes is a reflection of the different positions of home and host countries and of the disagreement on remaining issues.

The provisions still in dispute include those relating to reliance on "customary international law" and "international obligations" of governments to uphold it, to noninterference by TNCs and home governments in internal political affairs of host governments, to jurisdiction and settlement of disputes, to nationalization and appropriate compensation, and to national treatment of TNCs. The provisions are opposed by many of the LDC delegations, but the positions of many advanced and developing countries are not solidified.[13] The differences are "fundamental" and "ideological," but the U.S. government and TNCs consider that the longer-run need of LDCs for inflows of capital will bring a shift in views toward welcoming TNCs and, therefore, toward a voluntary code. The different interests of host governments in seeking or controlling FDI inflows in the 1980s did cause a relaxation of strong LDC positions on the codes.

The U.S. government has remained skeptical of the usefulness of UN codes, partly because of the general ineffectiveness of UN commissions, centers, or programs in obtaining agreements and getting them implemented; partly because of the voting power of socialist-leaning countries; partly because of the continued questioning by some members of "customary international laws"; and partly because of the high costs attached to the programs and their administration. In addition, having been rejected on a code on illicit payments, it has not been eager to accede to codes restricting behavior of TNCs to suit host countries. Its continued participation in negotiations has, however, been beneficial in educating *all* parties—governments and TNCs—to the real concerns of each.

The negotiating countries formed into three groups: the advanced countries, the socialist countries, and LDCs. The last is composed of over 120 countries—members of the UN Conference on Trade and Development (UNCTAD, or "The Group of 77," which was its original membership); it has taken the most interventionist positions. The socialist group generally supports the LDCs and seeks to keep state-owned enterprises out of coverage by the codes. The advanced countries are led by the United States, though Japan and Switzerland have "held firm" with the United States. The Europeans are more blasé, believing that the codes are not likely to be implemented in a serious fashion, therefore, it will not hurt TNCs if stiffer rules are accepted in a formal accord. The United States stands firm against yielding on "principles," whereas the Europeans are more concerned with practice.

TNCs or their representatives were directly involved in the negotiation of each of these proposed codes—both in the delegations at the intergovernmental conferences discussing the codes and at the advisory level in national governments, helping to form the national policies vis-à-vis the codes. TNCs and governments have cooperated extensively also in this activity.

Since three of the proposed codes have not been agreed upon, rather than going through the specific provisions and the country positions, this section focuses on arguments surrounding the value of codes and the role of TNCs in different approaches to codes.[14] The basic issue of whether there should be any code stems from the question of who should control the activities of TNCs and for what purposes. An intergovernmental code tends to shift the center of authority to intergovernmental institutions, but real control stays with national governments. Governments already can control those elements of the TNCs that are within their borders; although they may need advice on doing so, but an international code gets guidelines that may be inappropriate for any given country. The first questions, therefore, are whether there is need for international codes and, if so, what limitations are there on their use? What should be the scope of codes and what should be the purposes or specific objectives sought?[15] With these questions in mind, one can then assess the different roles that might be played by the TNCs in negotiating and implementing codes.

Needs for Codes

One of the basic needs for an intergovernmental code lies in the inability or unwillingness of national governments to impose appropriate national controls on TNC behavior, but there are other reasons as well, including the attempt to standardize rules on TNC behavior worldwide.[16]

National Treatment. A large part of the activities of any TNC falls entirely within the boundaries of a single nation and is, therefore, readily subject to governmental control—

without any encouragement from an intergovernmental code. But, to impose controls nationally usually implies that they will be imposed on all companies, regardless of origin. To impose a set of national controls only on foreign investors raises the issue of discrimination, and puts the matter into dialogue between governments. This is the question of "national treatment," which is a critical element in all intergovernmental negotiations on foreign investment—as under the treaties of friendship, commerce, and investment discussed in Chapter 10. Obviously the answer is to impose the same regulations on all companies, both domestic and foreign-owned, but many governments do not wish to impose such stringent controls on domestic enterprises. For example, Canada has much weaker information requirements on its domestic companies than it wishes to impose on U.S. and other foreign-owned affiliates. It generally is able to obtain information from Canadian companies on an ad hoc basis, and does not wish to pass such legislation. There are few, if any, of the provisions of the codes proposed that could not be handled by national legislation, but many governments are unable to pass this legislation by themselves and need an intergovernmental agency to put pressure on their legislatures and to guide them in the formulation of the appropriate rules.

Harmonization. The possibility of substantial differences among national controls encourages formation of intergovernmental codes. Such differences do exist and TNCs appear able to "walk between regulations" skirting the basic purpose of the controls. Harmonization or even unification of the rules imposed by national governments would lead to greater compliance on the part of the TNCs, and many would welcome greater certainty in the rules if it did not bring greater intervention. In addition, no country wishes to be "left out" by imposing controls so much more stringent than those in other countries that it loses desired FDI (this is particularly true of LDCs).

Enforcement. An intergovernmental code would also presumably encourage national governments to enforce existing national legislation and regulations, under the presumption that other governments were doing so as a result of intergovernmental agreement. Some acts in which TNCs engage are already declared illegal or prohibited—such as bribery—but the prohibitions are not enforced.

TNC Compliance. Codes have also been sought to obtain the accession and persuasion of *home* governments in encouraging TNC compliance. If the home countries agreed to the international codes, they would then seek to encourage their TNCs to comply, seeing their implementation in the host country as valid and reasonable. Under national controls, the home-country government often sees host-country regulations as unreasonable, interfering, or discriminatory and, therefore, does not support TNC compliance. An intergovernmental code would reduce the ability of the home-country government to complain about what a host country does, so long as the regulations are consistent with the code. The code then legitimizes the national controls of the host country and reduces friction between the home and host countries when both sign it.

Law. A code is seen by some supporters as a step toward international law. Since what is known as international law today was formed by the advanced countries, such codes are urged by LDCs as a new substitute. The U.S. government has considerable difficulty with this view, in that it considers present international law as appropriate and seeks to have it accepted by all countries. Any new "law" would supplant the past precedents. Therefore, the U.S. position has been that of making any code voluntary, rather than mandatory, as to compliance by governments or TNCs. Only if a government passed a national statute giving effect to the code (or selected provisions) would it become mandatory for a TNC operating in that country.

The United States is willing for the codes to be fairly precise, so long as they are voluntary; it sees a mandatory code as unacceptable if the provisions are precise, since that leads to a great deal of litigation and argument. Mandatory codes would, therefore, have to be rather vague, which would make them difficult to apply as law and therefore unsatisfactory to many LDCs. Further, compliance is easy to

claim and difficult to prove. There is also considerable difficulty in agreeing to precise provisions, given the number of
different views among the countries negotiating the codes.

Certainty. Some TNCs have seen a potential gain of
greater certainty in the climate for direct investment in host
countries as a result of an international code. To the extent
that nations adopted the same types of regulations or lim-
ied the stringency of those regulations because of a code,
TNCs would find the environment more stable. This would
not mean that they would necessarily expand investments
in every country, because certainty must also be coupled
with an attractive climate, both economically and socially.
Also, TNC resistance to mandatory controls would decrease
FDI flows.

Information. As discussed earlier, codes should regu-
larize the requests for information on TNC operations and
behavior. Similarly, TNCs would be more readily encouraged
to provide information if the same information would be acceptable to all agencies involved—both national and international—and credible controls on dissemination could be
devised.

Consistency. Some of the activities of TNCs cut across
national jurisdictions, making it impossible to control
these effectively from a single country. Activities such as
those influencing the balance of payments affect more than
one country, and meeting the regulations of one may reduce
the ability to meet the demands of another. Some accommodation among countries is required, and this would be made
easier with an agreed code. Such a code would also limit
the misuse of the freedom of power of a TNC in moving between national regulations. To do so would require some
cooperation among governments in the surveillance of activities, with governments swapping information in prior to
the imposition of any penalties. Or, alternatively, an international agency would have to be established to provide
surveillance and impose any penalties. Without cooperative
procedures either nationally or internationally, mere agreement on a code would be ineffective in guiding TNC activities in approved directions.

TNC Contributions. An international code could be the setting for a worldwide recognition of the special contributions of TNCs to the more effective use of the world resources, to the growth of host and home countries, and to the integration of the world economy. It would give some legitimacy to the TNCs and reduce contingent charges against them of misdirection of activities and misuse of power.

Limitations of Codes

An intergovernmental code is not a panacea, and will not of itself prevent many of the undesirable acts of TNCs. It can guide some into more appropriate behavior, for TNCs seek some certainty and stability in the rules. Any code requires implementation—either through voluntary compliance or through surveillance and penalties. But, in the international realm, an additional problem exists: not all TNCs are alike either in ways of operation or in their effects, and any one code provision is likely to be inappropriate for one or more of the types of TNCs. Finally, a code may alter the orientations and activities of TNCs, minimizing the favorable contributions to national or world economic growth. Codes cannot be discriminatory without having adverse impacts.

Implementation. Any international code presently requires implementation through national agencies, since no international agency has authority to reach into or through a national government. But potential differences in implementation by national governments immediately raise the possibility of undercutting of the code provisions, for each will interpret them in their own ways. It is this desire to protect the national interest that prevents political control by international technocrats, and governments are wary of creating an international policing agency. But even within the national regulations that implement a code, exceptions will likely be granted to one project or another. These exceptions—creating differences among countries or even within them on different projects—raise the problem of one government's granting approval to acts that are seen as "undesirable" in the code and thereby legitimizing what was supposedly illegitimate. Thus, no code can fully legitimatize

acts of either governments or TNCs without an international enforcement agency.

Voluntary Implementation. If an international code is
to be implemented voluntarily, it faces additional limitations, which multiply if the TNCs are left free to determine
how they will comply. If it is up to the governments to determine how to apply the code, the results will vary considerably, as they are today in the application of the resolutions
under the ILO or the investment guidelines of the OECD.
Countries will apply the provisions to the extent that there
is a domestic need to do so or because some overwhelming
external pressure arises—such as a need to ease balance-
of-payments deficits through investment inflows.

Voluntary implementation will make agreement on an
international code easier, for the disputes over specific provisions are not quite so lengthy or detailed. It is then easier
for any member to implement the code as it wishes.

But voluntary implementation by each government or
TNC means that there is considerable reduction in the potential harmonization of rules in the world economy, since
each will be protecting its own interests. The absence of an
agreed foreign-investment code among the Central American countries was one of the major reasons for their lack of
significant progress toward industrial integration. The two
more attractive countries received the major inflows of industrial investment and the three less attractive were left
out in the distribution of benefits, as they saw it. Similarly,
on the world scene, if TNC activity continues to flow to the
more advanced countries or the NICs, the desired growth of
the LDCs and greater integration with the more advanced
countries will not take place readily enough.

If the implementation of the code is left to the TNCs
themselves—as under the OECD code—different and even
more severe limitations exist for its effectiveness. First, the
only pressure on the TNCs is moral suasion or public opinion, which will seek to elicit the primary response of more
published information. When the information itself is not
forthcoming—as labor unions have complained—some additional pressure will have to be brought to bear. In order to
prevent substantial competitive inequities from arising

among TNCs, as some are more forthcoming than others in supplying information, some surveillance will be required merely to keep account of which companies are doing what and why others are not following the guidelines.

If such surveillance is instituted, the question arises as to who will do so and under what criteria. If companies are not found to comply, and a review procedure is established to question the nonresponse, what is the implied penalty?—and is compliance any longer voluntary?

In a sense, the OECD code provides the worst of both worlds—a set of regulations that are expected to be met but for which there are no penalties. It is one thing for a specific group to adopt its own code of conduct voluntarily, in expectation of compliance; it is another for a code to be imposed from outside without penalties for noncompliance. Substantial inequities arise among those who seek (at considerable cost) to comply and those that decide not to do so. Each acts without knowledge of either rewards or penalties—hardly a proper way for rules to be set for any game.

Company Differences. A third limitation on the applicability of codes is the fact that TNCs differ in orientation, structure, operations, and effects—as detailed in Chapter 2. Not only do companies operate differently in different sectors, but TNCs within the same sector operate differently, seeking different objectives. And, in some situations a single company operates as a resource seeker, a market seeker, and an efficiency seeker in the same or different countries, depending on its product line and its degree of integration among affiliates. It will then respond to a single provision in a code in three or more ways. A single code provision will, therefore, produce different reactions from different companies and even from the same company in different settings or at different times.

Surveillance and penalties are difficult to apply since proof of "wrong doing" is not easy. For example, is it appropriate to expect a market seeker to comply with the proposed provision that "all companies will add to the favorable balance of payments of the host country"? Or, is it reasonable to expect all extractive or human-resource seekers to add significantly to the technological capabilities of the host country? Because of their varying contributions, each type of company has a different capability in negotiating its way through the provisions of the codes, as explained in Chapter 4 relative to negotiation.

Rejection by TNCs. A final limitation on any code is that the TNCs have the option not playing the game at all. Thus, if constraints on technology transfer are too severe, TNCs may simply not offer their technology to foreigners or even to their own foreign affiliates. If restrictions on operations are too severe, domestic opportunities will appear much more attractive. Given the demand for capital in the advanced countries and the potential discrimination between local companies and TNCs involved in codes, one can anticipate a shift in the relative attractiveness of foreign opportunities—as has been evidenced in the greater attractiveness of opportunities in Southeast Asia, where the regulations are less stringent compared to other developing countries.

Excessive constraints on TNCs in terms of their direct investment are likely to change the way in which international business is conducted, moving it in favor of turnkey projects, independent, or debundled operations. But such activities as these are suitable only to countries that can provide the capital, trained manpower, and a technological base needed to continue the growth of the new industry. Under such constraints, the more advanced countries within the developing regions would be favored, moving closer to the industrialized countries—as the NICs have, increasing the gaps between them and the LDCs. NICs have, in fact, stopped pressing for codes.

Scope of a Code

The proposed codes on FDI and on technology transfer have overlapping provisions with the code on restrictive business practices (RBP) and with the proposed code on corrupt practices. The four codes constitute an all-encompassing policy on TNCs; yet they have been negotiated separately, and only the RBP code is signed. The scope of the codes is itself an issue, relating not only to their specific provisions but also to the types of companies to be covered.

Institutions Covered. Although it is generally accepted that the codes are addressed principally to TNCs, the U.S. government has insisted that they also be addressed to governments *and* to domestic companies so as to assure "national treatment." Including domestic companies would mean that "national treatment" would become "international treatment" under a rule of harmonization. The objective of the U.S. government is to put a limitation on the ability of governments to restrict operations of TNCs differentially.

A second difficulty has been the determination of what is to be designated as a TNC. For example, are state-owned companies that operate abroad to be included? Are intergovernmental companies (those chartered by treaty) to be included? How are joint ventures to be included? Are relations between parents and wholly owned affiliates included? And, if the code is not to be discriminatory, is it to apply to domestically owned companies in each signatory country? For example, would a TNC be required to abstain from bribery when local competitors were not? Or, should TNCs provide information to trade unions or the public, when locally owned companies were not required to do so? Should TNCs be prevented from engaging in particular restrictive business practices, while local competitors were not? To include domestic companies raises again the problem of national treatment—are the domestic companies to be treated similarly to the TNCs? Or, are the TNCs to be extended "national treatment"? Which takes precedence, the code or national law?

Further, if the codes are to fulfill the objectives of facilitating harmonization of government regulations, encouraging the use of TNC capabilities, and legitimizing government controls, what responsibilities should governments assume? Should governments harmonize incentives to foreign direct investments? Should they harmonize performance requirements? Should they agree on measures to be taken in the event of an expropriation? Should they agree on the means of settlement of disputes? Should they agree on the limits to extraterritorial interferences, and should they agree on limits to renegotiation of contracts? These have been the subject of continuing negotiation, pre-

venting agreement on the extent to which governmental behavior is to be included in the codes.

Provisions. Two types of provisions tend to be mixed
within the two codes on TNCs and technology transfer: one
having to do with specific company policies and practices
and the other with broader orientations, loyalties, and behavior.

There is an understandable desire to prevent activities
that are considered undesirable by host countries, as exemplified by the agreement on provisions in the code on restrictive business practices. But such specificity gives rise
to avoidance behavior on the part of individual TNCs; if investment is desired by the government, it will negotiate co-
vert exceptions to entice the TNC. In time, they are likely to
become embarrassing to both government and TNC when
they are revealed. Such privileges tend to legitimize acts
that are otherwise seen as undesirable. And, if the company
accepts this dispensation, it may be criticized later or even
punished by a subsequent government for damaging the national interest.

The broader provisions, such as those requiring "a net
contribution to the balance of payments" tend to be un-
specified as to how to do so or how much is required. Still
broader ones requiring "support of the national economic
and social goals" or "the giving of allegiance to the host
rather than the home government" are of a different order.
They can be readily accepted by the TNCs and most governments without there being a clear understanding of their
application or the specific acts required. Ready acceptance
does not mean that all will be happy with the implementation, because what is done is likely to be interpreted in
many different ways, leading to later disputes.

Within provisions on TNC behavior, one finds stipula-
tions that "corrupt practices will be avoided" meaning the
offering or receipt of bribes. This is a quite specific provision, but it applies to every activity of the companies in
their purchasing or sales and apparently extends to dealings with private companies as well as government purchasers. As discussed earlier, such an activity does not need to
be prohibited by an international code, for it can be taken

care of quite readily through a national regulation, law, or penalty. A code is needed only to highlight the need to restrain or prohibit such acts, to encourage imposition of adequate penalties, and, most importantly, to form the basis for cooperation among governments in gathering evidence and in prosecution of offenders.

Objectives of Codes. Three rather distinct objectives are served by an international code, if properly drawn: one, to improve the efficiency of the market as a decision-making mechanism, letting the market distribute benefits; two, to change the distribution of benefits among countries or groups from that which would occur under market decisions (equity); and three, to expand the contributions of TNCs to economic growth by providing greater certainty in the rules. Conflicts between the first and second objectives force a continuation of the dialogues.

Since many of the TNCs operate within oligopolistic markets, one of the prime objectives of codes is to strengthen competitive forces and remove the special advantages of the foreign companies. It is, however, not at all clear that the host governments are seeking the establishment of "free markets," rather, they appear to wish to shift oligopoly power from the foreigner to local companies. This objective, therefore, shades into that of the redistribution of benefits.

Governmental expropriations in the extractive sector have demonstrated the extent to which governments will go to redress what they consider to be an inequitable distribution of benefits from TNC activities. The intent of codes is to move TNC activities toward the greater benefit of the host country. Home governments will accept such moves only if there is no alternative or if the longer-run benefits in terms of a more stable, expanding, and integrated international economy are also evident. Some of the proposed provisions seek to redistribute benefits among groups within the host countries—for example, in favor of labor. Such redistribution affects not only labor in the host country but also capital and labor in the home country.

Since almost all governments recognize that TNCs do make some contributions to national economic and social welfare, a singular objective of the code must be to make certain that these contributions remain, despite the curtailing of undesirable activities. This can be done through the use of a code to provide greater certainty in the rules of the game, to assure the continuation of opportunities for equitable earnings, and to assure equitable treatment in the event that the rules must be changed. But the major contribution that TNCs can make toward integrating the world economy must also be kept in the minds of the negotiating governments, and this has not been the case in the proposed codes. On the contrary, the only one that has been agreed upon—the restrictive business practices code—has been mainly aimed at competition in the domestic economy and could have as easily been accomplished by national antitrust or antimonopoly laws or regulations. For this reason, it was not given strong support by the U.S. government.

In sum, the effective objectives of codes are not achieved, or even pursued, by the proposed UN agreements. Continued dialogue to achieve more useful purposes will be necessary, though the issues will simply fade away if competition for FDI inflows become more intense.

FUTURE OF INTERGOVERNMENTAL REGULATION AND TNC RESPONSES

The representatives of TNCs helping to negotiate the UN codes have generally been opposed to any codes whatsoever, arguing that national regulations were sufficient to meet the requirements of governments. Their fear, of course, has been the generalization of more stringent controls under the persuasion of the more active and opposing governments. They have, however, been willing to support voluntary codes, considering that TNC behavior in specific situations would then be under continuing dialogue with governments; this approach has been accepted for all three codes. But critics consider that the RBP code is ineffective as a result. Most TNCs have been reluctant to increase the amount of information provided; they have simply distributed more efficiently what they were already publishing. However, as a result of the code negotiations, many TNCs have become somewhat more forthcoming in disclosing information and in presenting their policy viewpoints.

A major response of TNCs has been to increase their dialogues with host countries on a number of the issues raised in the codes, and these dialogues have made the host countries realize that companies are quite different in their orientations and impacts and that their own national interests are not necessarily served by harmonization of national controls or performance requirements under an intergovernmental code. Consequently, the pressure from a number of LDCs has diminished.

It is likely that the three unsigned codes will remain in negotiation for some time, despite continued efforts in the UN. The only situation that might bring agreement is if they are sufficiently modified toward the positions of the advanced countries, particularly that of the United States. Or, the behavior of TNCs could become so unacceptable, through some untoward events—such as a number of Bhopal-type accidents, massive relocation of industry, plant closings through worldwide depression, or whatever—as to call forth an agreement as to what should be done with TNCs in the pursuit of new governmental objectives. Alternatively, the intergovernmental arrangements on TNCs could shift out of the orientation of codes of restraint toward agreements to promote or guide the activities of TNCs into greater international integration—either regionally or sectorally. Such guides would also apply to the behavior of TNCs, but not in the specific ways included in the codes under negotiation. Once again, TNCs face continuing dialogue, if for no other purpose than to prevent undesirable regulation.

NOTES TO CHAPTER 13

1. Two assessments of the role of the World Bank, by Barber Conable and Louis Schirano, are found in *The International Economy* (Oct./Nov. 1987), pp. 28–39.

2. Geneva: ILO, 1977; 5th impression, 1985.

3. See *Problems of International Business Cooperation in Environmental Protection*, prepared for the U.S. Environmental Protection Agency by J. N. Behrman and William G. Carter, published by the Fund for Multinational Management Education, New York, Nov. 1975.

4. See J. N. Behrman, "A Post-Mortem on the UNCSTD," *Technology and Society*, Vol. 1, (1979), pp. 339–51.

5. Fund for Multinational Management Education, et al., *Public Policy and Technology Transfer: Viewpoints of U.S. Business*, vols. 1–4, (New York: FMME, Mar. 1978).

6. See *CTC Reporter*, no. 24 (Autumn 1987), p. 14ff.

7. See various issues of *The CTC Reporter* (e.g., Pieter A. Wessel, "Standards of Accounting and Reporting by TNCs," *The CTC Reporter* (Autumn 1987), pp. 14ff.); and UNCTC, *International Standards of Accounting and Reporting: Report of the Ad Hoc Intergovernmental Working Group of Experts on International Standards of Accounting and Reporting* (New York: United Nations, 1984).

8. For a brief analysis leading to the conclusion that U.S.-based TNCs do not consider regulations on transborder data flows of the late 1980s as being an obstacle, see M. J. Kane and D. A. Ricks, "Is International Data Flow Regulation a Problem?" *Journal of International Business Studies* (Fall 1988), pp. 477–482.

9. Private groups include Centers at the Harvard Graduate School of Business and Reading University (England); the American Enterprise Institute, the Brookings Institution, the Fund for Multinational Management Education, the Conference Board (New York), the Twentieth Century Fund, the National Planning Association, the International Economic Policy Association, the Americas Society, the International Chamber of Commerce and many others.

   Government agencies and institutes include the Department of Commerce and the Treasury, the Government Accounting Office (GAO), and the National Science Foundation, plus the Government-sponsored National Academy of Science and the National Academy of Engineering.

10. See CTC, *Transnational Corporations: Issues Involved in the Formation of a Code of Conduct* (New York: United Nations, 1976).

11. See R. Grosse, "Codes of Conduct for Multinational Enterprises," *Journal of World Trade Law* (Sept./Oct., 1982), pp. 414–433.

12. Philippe Brusick, "The restrictive business practices set of principles and rules," *CTC Reporter* (Autumn 1987), pp. 41–43.

13. For a proposal that LDCs should "go it alone" and agree on a regional code among themselves, see Kwamena Acquaah, *International Regulation of Transnational Corporations: The New Reality* (New York: Praeger, 1986).

14. For a proposal that TNCs should take the whole matter into their own hands, setting up their own corporate and internationally agreed codes, see John Kline, *International Codes and Multinational Business* (Westport, CT: Quoram Books, 1985), esp. chaps. 7 and 8.

15. On some of these issues, see Pedro Roffe, "Code of conduct on the transfer of technology," *CTC Reporter* (Autumn 1987), pp. 39–40.

16. The continuing debates and resolutions are recorded annually in the *Official Records* of the U.N. Economic and Social Council, Commission on Transnational Corporations; for example, *Report on the Thirteenth Session* (April 7–16, 1987), suppl. no. 9, and *Report on the Fourteenth Session* (April 6–15, 1988), suppl. no. 7.

PART V

Prospects

The future of TNC/government relations depends on the ability to resolve issues that are the collective responsibility of business and government. There are essentially two types of issues that must be faced cooperatively, instead of adversarily: social/ethical/political issues for which governments have the primary responsibility but which are significantly affected by the behavior and operations of TNCs; and economic issues, of which the macro realm is principally the responsibility of governments while the micro issues arises principally out of the activities of TNCs. Although TNCs have responsibilities in both areas, none are eager to accept them unless all do, jointly and severally. And, except in almost unique instances, governments must provide the stimulus for each joint action. Without it, one TNC will consider that a "socially responsible" action that diminishes profits will damage its survival. Thus, TNCs are reluctant to take initiatives in these areas. If governments are also reluctant, the issues remain unresolved.

The social/ethical/political issues, discussed in Chapter 14, relate to subjects such as consumer protection, environmental safety, discrimination (by race or sex), corruption, and exploration of the seabed. A major question is how to develop mutual responsibility for resolution of these problems among TNCs and governments.

The unresolved *economic* issues are quite fundamental, e.g., where should economic activity be located around the world, not only production and services but also research and development. Nations have not agreed as to the appropriate criteria for decisions on these issues and on who should be empowered to make such decisions. The fundamental question of the distribution of benefits is a major hurdle, which can be surmounted only with a new set of rules for international economic affairs. Since we cannot now achieve worldwide rules, we will be able to progress only through bilateral or regional associations to gain a halfway house on the way to a wider resolution.

In resolving the economic issues, assessed in Chapter 15, there is still no agreement on the extent to which nation states wish to be independent, self-reliant, or interdependent. The world is moving toward greater interdependence through integration industrially, technically, commercially, financially, militarily, and even culturally, yet we are not ready psychologically or politically for this development—at least not worldwide and across all issues. We have to take some partial steps cooperatively first, which lead into more successful development of an agreed and acceptable interdependence. This is best done on regional and sectoral bases in which clear priorities can be surfaced. In achieving any such resolution, the appropriate roles of government, business, and labor as well as the public are yet to be defined. In the meantime, governments and TNCs are proceeding to resolve some of the problems in fairly narrow ways, including bilateral approaches of counter-trade, coproduction, buy-backs, counter-purchasing, and clearing agreements—discussed in Chapter 16.

Once again, the issues arise about who is responsible for resolution of the issues and under what criteria of acceptability.

Since a major question of all of these issues is who will come forward to accept responsibility and proceed in a manner acceptable to others, the fundamental issue is one of leadership—toward a wider concept of community. But, from what quarters will leadership come? Where do we see it arising around the world—regionally, governmentally, corporate-wise, or individually? What are the requisites for such leadership to arise and be accepted? And what are the prospects for it occurring successfully? These are the fundamental questions that remain in TNC/government relations, as the world economy becomes increasingly integrated; they are addressed in the final chapter.

CHAPTER 14

Social, Ethical, and Political Issues

A number of unresolved social/ethical/political issues in the international arena are subjects of dialogue and negotiation between TNCs and governments. The TNCs are major actors in each area, and governments are concerned because of the peoples they represent and the environment in which all live. Only a few TNCs have adopted international strategies on these issues; and governments, for the most part, approach them from a national viewpoint though they clearly have important international (even global) dimensions.

The greater interdependence of the world—resulting from technological change, increased economic, social, cultural, and political contacts, crowding from increased population, migrations of peoples for political and other reasons, and the worldwide effects of environmental degradation—all have raised concerns about our management of the "international commons." The concept of a commons is that of an area or resource to which everyone has access but which is finite and is wasted if *anyone* uses it to excess, for it is soon denied to all. However, the absence of property rights and control induces all to use such a resource wastefully, in order to "get their share." Thus, all are harmed eventually, even those using the resource extravagantly. The international commons is both the entire world and its specific elements—such as forests, the ocean, beaches, the seabed, rivers, air, water, and even outer space.

The issue of the commons arises in the *management* of ocean resources, the development of natural resources, the utilization of land, and the penetration of outer space, which lead to the necessity for rules to prevent damaging the "common heritage of mankind," which is the earth itself. The earth is a single entity of closely related peoples and resources. The use of these resources must be man-

331

aged "in common" to achieve an equitable distribution of benefits and to provide for future generations. The recognition of the international commons raises questions of responsibility for their management and the establishment of new institutional mechanisms—some regionally oriented and some functionally oriented.

Other problems have to do with mistreatment of one's fellow man through an attempt to profit at the expense of others. These actions also indicate a rejection of the value of individual dignity for others and a lack of individual responsibility for one's own actions. Further, there is an absence of accepted rules and even a lack of common understanding of the way in which the members of humanity are related to each other, economically, socially, and politically. These concepts are highly culture-bound.

Another source of these problems is that here is differential access to technology around the world. Some can exploit this asset more readily than others. And technology sometimes leads to products that are harmful to others, leading to exploitation of others and to an expropriation of wealth in ways society deems ethically unacceptable. The significance of the TNC to these issues is that it is both a transmitter of some of the damage and a controller of some of the benefits. Therefore, it is intimately involved and is, in significant ways, responsible.

It is not the purpose of this chapter to attempt to resolve these issues or even to lay out *all* of the arguments on either side. Rather, it is to discuss them sufficiently to show the extent to which the TNC is involved along with governments, so that it will be understood why and how such issues enter into TNC/government relations.

Since one of the major problems confronting the TNCs internationally is the legitimacy of their activities and influence in foreign countries, TNCs will find greater acceptability abroad if they show reasonable concern for the social/ethical/political objectives of the host country. Neither U.S. nor European TNCs have been observed as evidencing serious concern for *worldwide* problems in the noneconomic realms. They have not shown a concern with *all* of the major problems faced, nor should they be expected to do so. But their views are still considered myopic by most governments.

The TNCs themselves are more likely to assert that they are principally (and appropriately) concerned with only one of the many problems facing the world economy—that of achieving higher rates of industrial growth by meeting worldwide market demands through efficient operations. But of serious concern to all governments is *how* these market demands are met and whether there are noneconomic costs that are too great to bear. TNCs bear many of these costs directly or indirectly, but it is argued further that they should also accept some responsibilities for the preservation and enhancement of the world community. The TNCs are not merely economic actors; they affect ecology through the use of nonrenewable resources; they affect conditions in the workplace by management decisions, and they affect life-styles by income-generation and distribution and by product changes—all of which are affected by changes in technology.

CONSUMER PROTECTION

A major justification for free enterprise is its purpose of *serving* the consumer, but not all TNCs have developed such an orientation. Rather, a viewpoint has developed that the market economy was made for the producer and *not* for the consumer; once again, the caution has arisen to "let the buyer beware." It is for this reason that almost every country has laws on product sanitation, harmfulness of products, and product liability—to constrain the desire of some companies to sell products without taking adequate care to protect the consumer. In the international realm, the dialogues between TNCs and governments on products have focused on five major concerns—related to pesticides, pharmaceuticals, foods and feeds, banned manufactured goods, and genetic research.

Pesticides

There are two concerns over pesticides: the export and use abroad of pesticides banned in the home country, and the improper use of approved pesticides. Both problems may arise out of ignorance on the part of those in the host country, which, it is alleged, could be eliminated by more active and energetic efforts of the TNC itself. A further issue is the fact that a pesticide—such as DDT, that is banned for *use* in the United States—can be produced and exported and then be imported on agricultural goods from abroad. For example, cheese imported from France was found to be contaminated upon inspection in the United States, and the French authorities agreed; it was contaminated when cows fed in acreage on which imported DDT had been used. Similarly, DDT is used in the control of weeds around coffee plants and is reimported into the United States on the beans.

Obviously the responsibility for determining appropriate (foreign) manufacture and sale of such products rests on the host government, and if the government is an advanced one (such as France) one can assume that it is fully aware of all dangers and has made determinations that are appropriate to that society. However, in many LDCs, there is insufficient personnel with expertise to test all products, and there may be considerable pressure locally to continue the manufacture or sale of potentially harmful items. In such a case, the TNC that proceeds with both manufacture and sale may find that the government later deems such activities irresponsible and moves to prohibit them and even punish the firm. At the very least, the host governments have asserted individually and through the United Nations that the TNCs should provide them with adequate information to make appropriate decisions. But using such information appropriately requires education as to what it means and how to apply it in different circumstances.

The misuse of approved chemicals is even more difficult to handle, since the TNC may have put all explanations that are appropriate on the package or in a folder contained therein, but the product will be used by individuals who cannot read or do not do so, even if they can. Many users of such products in the field do not understand the importance of care and may over apply the pesticide, let it fall in undesirable areas, get it on their clothing, and even reuse containers for purposes of storing foods, water, or for cooking, thereby slowly poisoning themselves. Complaints are then filed against the TNC, though it has no effective way of preventing these abuses. Some TNCs have changed the packaging to make reuse of the container difficult, but even this does not mean that it will be appropriately destroyed.

Sending instructors into the field educates the distributors, and maybe major buyers, but does not reach all users, particularly uneducated and illiterate peasants.

Thus, whether acting responsibly or irresponsibly, TNCs continue to face dialogues on the use of agricultural chemicals and become involved in intergovernmental discussions on regulations.

Pharmaceuticals

Some pharmaceuticals are also banned from use domestically or from export. Again, the mere banning of use in the United States does not prevent their manufacture and export, raising similar problems as pesticides, except that drugs are not normally used in ways that they would be reimported back into the United States (though hormones or other drugs given to animals might be reimported in meat). In pharmaceuticals, however, there is a further issue of the manufacture or export into poorer countries of products deemed unnecessary or too costly for the consumers of that country. In order to protect LDCs against the sales pressure and the enticement of sophisticated pharmaceuticals to the medical profession, the World Health Organization (as discussed in Chapter 13) issued a list of a hundred "acceptable and necessary drugs," which it deems appropriate for developing countries. It is presumed that restrictions against imports of non-listed items would cut the cost of health care in poor countries without damaging the level of care. International pharmaceutical companies, of course, disagree with any such limitation and argue that the selection of the items on the list is inadequate for many of the people in LDCs, particularly those who can afford a level of protection or care/cure that low-income individuals cannot.

There are two issues here—one related to potential harm (such as the Dalkon shield) and the other related to costs and efficacy (such as some drugs for stress or heart attack). The pharmaceutical companies have been involved not only in extensive negotiations with individual host countries but also with various committees of the World Health Organization on both of these issues and on a third issue relating to claims that the TNCs are not doing enough for the special problems of developing countries, especially in the area of tropical diseases.[1] Tropical diseases are not usually found in any of the advanced countries; despite wide incidence of these diseases in LDCs, their poverty means that there is little market demand for the drugs. The inducement to the headquarters company to work on them is therefore weak. However, these diseases are serious and extensive enough to have called forth considerable research by a few of the pharmaceutical TNCs, but the results have not yet been sufficient to eradicate or adequately control any of the tropical diseases besides malaria. Some relief has been found for diseases such as leprosy and schistoso-miasis. Still, the WHO has argued that more should be done to provide protection at less cost, particularly through efforts to achieve immunity rather than wait to cure. It has given grants for research and sponsored field studies. Many of these diseases are systemic, meaning that they are related to the whole life-style of the communities in which they arise, and eradication will require systemic efforts—unless it is possible to provide immunity, which is exceedingly difficult when parasites or worms are involved rather than viruses.

The pharmaceutical TNCs have also faced long dialogues on patent protection and licensing. They have had a rather unique position in government relations and will continue to do so because of governmental involvement as consumer (via national health ministries and public health services); this means that even pricing is a subject of business/government negotiation and regulation.

Foods and Feeds

The problems with foods and feeds are those of contamination and misuse. Some foods that are declared unfit for human use are exported, frequently marked "not for human use" but are, in fact, sold for that purpose after repackaging in the importing country. Worse, some feeds are exported with unacceptable levels of trash, rat droppings, and moisture content, which means that they are potentially dangerous or will spoil. Serious violations usually become the subject of intergovernmental discussions, with the perpetrator subject to punishment.

One of the most celebrated cases in the 1970s and 1980s was the infant milk formula controversy stemming from Nestlé's promotion of a formula for babies in African countries where the necessary facilities for its sanitary use were not available. The milk would often spoil or become contaminated and would then be refused by the baby. As a result, babies died of malnutrition, causing a furor and giving rise to an indictment in the Swiss courts. Boycotts in the United States and other countries were aimed at Nestlé products. The company faced negotiations not only with governments but also with the UN (which passed a resolution condemning such sales) and with the public which had been aroused. Other companies were drawn in through their own sales of milk formula, and some immediately ceased doing so. Nestlé eventually formed a commission of public individuals to oversee its distribution of the product in order to regain sound governmental and public relations.[2]

Manufactures

There are a variety of manufactured goods that have been exported or manufactured abroad that have been prohibited in the home country—such as pajamas for children treated with tris (a fire retardant chemical developed at government urging to prevent crib deaths but later found to induce cancer). Garments treated with tris, when prohibited from sale in the United States, found their way to foreign markets. Such sales were not necessarily the direct activity of the manufacturers, who had already sold the garments to wholesalers, but they did know that the garments were to be distributed for final sale somewhere.

Toys that are considered too dangerous in one market find their way to others, and guns and ammunition prohibited from ownership in one country are exported to others. Products for which advertising claims are regulated in one country are sold under less constrained claims in others.

Auto emissions became an international issue when the United States imposed stringent regulations. These led to the development of the catalytic converter to remove toxic elements from exhaust fumes. These national regulations and those adopted by some other countries were first opposed by auto manufacturers but eventually acceded to. Differential requirements led, for a time, to different equipment in autos produced in different countries; and cars from Europe still have to be fitted to meet American regulations. The Japanese TNCs jumped ahead with equipment surpassing U.S. requirements.

Once again, it would appear that the responsibility for protection of the consumer lies in the host country, but information is not always there as to the dangers involved. Efforts to set up a network of information exchange have not been wholly successful, even through the UN. But multilateral agreements on such issues would be beneficial in encouraging the sharing of information and the standardization of regulations, reducing an obstacle to trade.

Genetic Engineering

Finally, despite the constraints imposed by some countries on genetic research and production of biogenetic products, not all countries have imposed the same restrictions. Efforts to achieve harmonization have not been successful, leaving the TNC exposed to a tightening of regulations in the future and claims for damages from activities later considered inappropriate.

How should the TNC respond to these issues?—the answer cannot be to seek removal of all regulation. Rather the issue is one of what source and level of regulation the TNC can accept compared to the wishes of society. When such problems arise and the public or government is sufficiently aroused to require change in behavior, the TNC can either regulate itself, anticipating the problems and adjusting its activities appropriately, or it can wait for guidance from the home or host governments through national legislation or regulation. With or without national regulations, if the issue is important in many countries, the TNC will face intergovernmental regulation probably through the UN. The initial responsibility of the TNC is to provide all relevant information to the home and host governments so that they can determine the significance of the problem and the best means of handling it. If the TNCs in a particular sector understand the seriousness and can agree on appropriate alternatives, they can propose actions prior to government regulation. Such collaboration requires a new attitude on the part of TNCs (as is recognized by some CEOs) and probably a shift in the attitude of the U. S. government to permit discussions *among* the companies on agreed patterns of behavior without triggering antitrust complaints.

ENVIRONMENTAL PROTECTION

The protection of the environment has become a concern of all nations as demonstrated by the formation of the UN Environmental Program (UNEP). This worldwide concern reflects the facts that the environment extends beyond any national borders and that, as oceanographers have repeatedly emphasized, all pollution eventually reaches the oceans. Since corporate activities affect the environment in the use of various materials and the products made, environmental issues should be a concern to all TNCs. To date, neither efforts by national governments, international agencies, nor TNCs have significantly reduced the threats to the environment.

Given the differential treatment of environmental issues in countries around the world, there has been a concern over the creation or use of "pollution havens" into which companies can move without serious constraints on their production processes or the materials used. Japan has become quite strict on pollution levels in its own country, making sites in less strict foreign countries more attractive. Some of the Southeast Asian nations have welcomed the transfer of polluting industry, but higher standards are likely later. Others (such as Singapore) can absorb relatively few such industries without being seriously affected.

Activities of TNCs that involve pollution or pollution control arise through their bids for construction in foreign countries, their own investment projects, and their development of production processes that might reduce pollution or pollution-control devices.

In tendering bids for construction projects, TNCs usually are required to include specifications on the level of pollution control of production processes. Some of their specifications are so complex, however, that the purchaser abroad is not quite certain what the results will be in pro-

tecting the environment. This is especially the case of LDCs
where experience with pollution control is not extensive. In
the latter case, it is appropriate for the TNC to make information on environmental protection available to the purchaser and even to appropriate governmental agencies. At
least the trade-offs should be made known to them. On a
more cooperative basis, TNCs might agree among themselves not to compete for projects on the basis of offering
low levels of environmental protection, or to provide cost
estimates on several levels of protection.[3]

In setting up TNC operations overseas, there are four aspects related to environmental protection: the inputs of water, air and energy; the manufacturing processes employed;
control over emissions into the air or water; and waste disposal. Some industry sectors have more problems with pollution than others—such as producers of nonferrous
metals, iron and steel, chemicals, petrochemicals, paper
and pulp, rubber, and petroleum.

In the erection or expansion of industrial plants overseas, the TNCs have the capacity to design them so as to
use process and control systems protecting the environment. Not being requiring to do so (in "pollution havens") is
seen by some critics as a strong attraction to TNCs. There
is some doubt that this avoidance is a significant magnet,
simply because the cost reductions are probably not large
enough to induce a company to bear the disadvantages of
location in a distant country or one where the other factors
attracting the investment are not favorable.[4] It has been estimated that the cost of even the most modern of control
systems raises the total production cost less than five
percent.[5] While this is a substantial addition, it may well be
lower than the costs imposed by a host government in
meeting more stringent regulations later and retrofitting
pollution control devices or completely changing the manufacturing processes. At the extreme, some federal and local
authorities have closed plants down when the pollution was
found to be more than acceptable. It is a sign of mature citizenship by TNCs to anticipate these requirements in building new plants or expansion of existing ones. And it is a
sign of an economically mature country to require strict
pollution controls.

Further, TNCs are capable of developing production processes that are less polluting than at present, and many of them are paying special attention to this problem within their home countries. Again, it would be a sign of social responsibility to make alternative processes known to the host country during the negotiation of entry or expansion of facilities abroad. Control devices are also produced by TNCs, which they sell, export, or license, and some also develop measurement devices to determine the levels of pollution in air and water. Some companies have been induced to enter the field through pressure of governmental regulations. The development of measurement devices increases the problem of constraints in that the more precise the measurement, the higher the standards that are imposed by regulations. Some officials appear to seek "zero polluting effluents," and are seeking measurement devices to achieve that level. However, the processes of production do not permit a continuous reduction of pollutants, and the cost of reaching zero may be prohibitive. This disagreement over appropriate levels of pollution raises the question of whether or not there can be closer cooperation among TNCs, and between TNCs and governments, in the determination of appropriate levels of measurement and pollution control, as well as in the development of devices for both control and measurement. The relationship in the United States has been highly adversarial but the more cooperative systems in Europe and Japan have not produced significant environmental programs either.[6]

Strong and continuing efforts were made during the 1970s and 1980s, at national and international levels to increase the protection of the environment. The OECD and the UNEP have sought harmonization of pollution regulations and the establishment of protective programs. Without harmonization, high levels of pollution in one country will spread to others eventually, reducing the effectiveness of the others' controls and creating tensions among governments—as with the acid rain emanating from the United States and falling on Canada. Acid rain results when the emissions of coal-burning public utility plants in one region get caught up in rain clouds and deposited elsewhere. Acid rain eats away at buildings and has made many lakes

uninhabitable for fish. At the extreme, the lakes become bi-
ologically dead; even the cessation of acid rain will not
bring them back to life in the near future, though it is a first
step. Some lakes relieved of pollution some years ago are
now showing renewed signs of life.

To assist in this area, TNCs helped form (with governments) the Nairobi Center for cooperation in protecting the
environment. Although it has not been able to harmonize
national regulations, it has kept the issue in the forefront of
TNC considerations, raising the attention given to the problems. It would appear that this issue would be more appropriate for treatment by a UN code than the ones discussed
in Chapter 13.

The problem of harmonization of regulations is made
more difficult by the fact that within some countries the local and federal authorities are in disagreement as to the levels of pollution allowed. The prefectures in Japan frequently
have more stringent regulations than are required by the
central government, because average levels of protection for
the country of Japan may be inadequate for some crowded,
industrial localities.

Another problem affecting large areas is the clearcutting
of lands to open them for agricultural and industrial development. Vast forests in Brazil have been cleared, causing
the rain patterns to change and the runoffs to shift, virtually drying up principal rivers as well as the large lagoons
that have been the source of life for the fishing industry.
The changing climate in the Amazon is predicted to result
in a desertification of the area, as has occurred in the Sahel
(the semi-arid, southern fringe of the Sahara Desert) eventually affecting the climate of the whole world adversely.
Such cutting has resulted in the worldwide elimination of
rain forests equal to the size of Cuba each year for the past
several years.[7] Of course, the responsibility is not wholly
that of the companies involved, since governments have
promoted and facilitated much of this activity. In the late
1980s, it was proposed that the swaps of external debt be
used to buy this forest area so it could be put in a nature
conservancy. Brazil saw this as a ploy to hold back its
growth and to maintain U.S. dominance. It is reluctant to
place "its national heritage" in foreign hands or to slow its
agricultural growth.

In the late 1980s, accounts surfaced of TNCs contracting with poor but spacious countries in Africa to dispose of large volumes of toxic waste in land fills. The sums involved ran into hundreds millions of dollars and opened an opportunity for official corruption that did not take national interests into account. Though it was asserted that sites were chosen carefully to avoid aquifers (underground water flows), it is doubtful that sufficient information exists to provide assurances that future populations will not suffer damage. Since some governments have stepped in to prohibit such practices, they could also prohibit production of the waste. TNCs are faced with a difficult decision to cease using processes that produce toxic wastes but which are profitable if the cost of waste disposal is passed to society.

Nor is waste disposal a concern only of TNCs, since governments themselves have a great deal of difficulty finding appropriate places for waste. (In 1987, a barge full of garbage from Philadelphia was pulled up and down the Atlantic and Caribbean for months, seeking a dump site to no avail.) Oil spills also are not the singular responsibility of companies, since governments have sought the revenue that results from exploration in the ocean. However, the production of fluorocarbons for use in industry and consumer products is largely a result of TNC activities (spray cans and refrigerators, especially), and the seriousness of the emissions of fluorocarbons into the air has become a worldwide concern. It has taken well over a decade of continued research and persuasion to get major countries of the world to recognize that further emissions of this sort are likely to deplete the ozone layer. Reduction in the ozone would permit much higher levels of ultraviolet rays from the sun to penetrate into the earth's atmosphere, seriously increasing the incidence of skin cancer and other damage to the human body.

A warming trend reportedly has already arisen from the "greenhouse effect" of chemical changes that prevent the sun's rays from escaping back into space. Speculative results include droughts and large-scale shifts in the location of agriculture and populations. The earth's atmosphere and its ecology are in a precarious balance, and any substantial shift can have harmful effects on mankind. This is true not only for sunlight but also for the level of oxygen around the world; conceivably, a rise in the percentage of oxygen by a few points would produce worldwide conflagration from any fire, and a fall would leave us gasping.[8]

Given the pervasiveness of the problems of pollution and environmental protection, the TNCs are not likely to be relieved from continuing negotiation with governments on these issues. The fact that governments themselves are not able to come to an agreement to harmonize their regulations means that the dialogues will likely be more pointedly directed to the TNCs. This would seem to be one area in which the TNCs should take an initiative toward international cooperation, preferably with the understanding and support of the governments involved, but at least to form agreements within major industrial sectors around the world on the existing effects and what can and should be done. Presently, many central governments are working with industry sectors to determine the best ways of achieving protection of the environment (United States, Europe, and Japan.) Yet, not enough has been done to obtain agreement even on the development of measurement and control devices. This is partly the result of the desire of companies and governments to achieve competitive breakthroughs, making it difficult to establish standards, and partly a history of antitrust legislation that discourages collaboration. But there is much duplication in R&D in pursuing different standards and techniques of measurement, and cooperative efforts would appear highly desirable.

What is needed is an institutionalized and continuing cooperative effort within industry sectors and between business and government in the formation of measurements and control standards, providing a better milieu in which to achieve the goals of environmental protection. Such cooperation flies in the face of traditional adversarial relations between business and government in the United States, but it fits quite well with the more cooperative orientations in countries such as Sweden and Japan. A solid base of national cooperation would be the foundation for cross-national cooperation among R&D institutes and TNCs as well well as ministries seeking means to protect the environment.

As a means of developing more cooperative arrangements among TNCs themselves, industrial associations should establish exchanges of information on control processes and devices, costs, and results. They should encourage licensing of the best techniques and the cooperative development of control and measurement devices. Several industry sectors (petroleum, nonferrous metals, paper and pulp, chemicals, and iron and steel) do have international collaboration among their national industrial associations on these issues. Nevertheless, these ties are not effective in much more than the exchange of data, falling short of what is needed if harmonization is to be achieved. A significant step would be the establishment of cooperative R&D institutes to determine appropriate environmental standards and how to meet them.

However, achieving cooperation among TNCs will require some change in the present rules to permit formation of new cooperative arrangements and to rescind the application of antitrust regulations on such activities. Since the elimination of antitrust regulations might raise serious questions about cooperation among the TNCs in prohibited activities, it is desirable to have governments associated with cooperative endeavors within an industrial sector. The U.S. government has been more reluctant than others to permit this kind of collaboration. To encourage it to shift its position, greater pressure will be required from the TNCs through the development of information that would show how successful and appropriate international collaboration could be in protecting the environment. Once again, appropriate initiatives can be taken by TNCs, demonstrating both "enlightened citizenship" and leadership.

DISCRIMINATION

One of the most excruciating and difficult concerns has been that over racial discrimination, especially concerning South Africa's policy of apartheid. A second is that of sexual discrimination—which the expanding women's movement will bring increasingly to the fore in many countries—in the forms of both employment discrimination and sexual harassment. Discrimination arises from deep cultural orientations, evident around the world, and will require struggles of a magnitude not yet faced by TNCs. Although many countries claim that they are without racial discrimination, it remains everywhere, including in the United States. And while American business is progressing in its elimination of sexual discrimination, cultural attitudes have been hard to change in the workplace. Denmark, Sweden, and China are ahead of the United States in this regard, and Japan, further behind. Much is to be done worldwide before this problem is significantly ameliorated, much less resolved.

Since discrimination is a cultural issue, embedded in social ethics and mores, any attempt on the part of one country to force a change in another, particularly through the activities and behavior of TNCs, is seen by the second country as "unwanted and unwarranted interference." Such interference is a form of "ethical imperialism" and raises delicate and difficult issues of diplomacy and business/government relations. Although the most celebrated case of discrimination is that in South Africa, we find discrimination against the ethnic Chinese in many countries of Southeast Asia, and against ethnic Indians and Asians in Africa and Southeast Asia. In the United States, discrimination exists against blacks, Hispanics, and other minorities. In Africa, discrimination exists among various tribes within the same country. In Europe, discrimination occurs against Turkish, Italian, Spanish, and North African workers who are considered "guest workers," not having the full rights of nationals. One could find in almost every country some discrimination based on race, color, or creed—the last is the basis of the conflict between Catholics and Protestants in Northern Ireland, between Indians and Pakistani, and between Israelis and Arabs.

TNCs generally attempt to "fade into the background" in following the cultural norms of the host country. This is relatively easy when the norms are similar in the home and the host countries. When these norms are not in accord, serious problems arise. This is the case between South Africa and the United States. TNCs from other countries do not face the same problems in South Africa, since their governments are less concerned.

The pressures in the United States rose in the late 1980s to the point of persuading a number of companies to sell their operations in South Africa and leave, but neither the purchasing companies nor their home-company elites

(South African or other) were as concerned to remove discrimination as the American pressure groups. The results have not necessarily been favorable for the blacks, and the South African government has not felt it necessary to alter its policies significantly, though it has removed some restraints. For example, whites and blacks have been permitted to intermarry, but they are still not permitted to live in the same house.

The conservative Afrikaaner government was reelected in the late 1980s despite threats of and actual divestment by U.S. companies. Such challenges frequently strengthen the very group that is being threatened through a coalescence against the foreigner—as was the case with General Noriega in Panama, and as would be the case in the United States if a group of foreign-owned affiliates insisted on certain policy changes unwanted by Americans.

The pressures to force the United States pullout from South Africa arose from black leaders in the United States, as well as others sympathetic to their cause, who were effectively able to urge the disinvestment by churches, universities, and others holding large portfolio investments in companies remaining in South Africa. These threats were raised in the United States, in an attempt to reinforce critics in Africa.

The result has been a disengagement, contrary to the "constructive engagement" sponsored by the Reagan Administration. Congress itself felt sufficient pressure to reject the Administration position and force the imposition of some sanctions by the U.S. government on South Africa. These sanctions—consisting of prohibitions against loans to the South African government—were hardly significant and were easily circumvented by borrowing from others or relying on the substantial reserves of gold in that country.

Where such pressures are employed, those using them must be willing to take some responsibility for the results. The actual results are not necessarily those desired. The history of embargoes in general is one of little success. There are too many ways to get around them, and they signal to the subject country what it needs to fill the gaps. In the case of South Africa, the *kraal* mentality (derived from the pioneers circling the wagons against attacking natives) was merely strengthened by the threats from outside, and the position of the blacks can be considered worse. Even if the techniques had succeeded, and the government had given in to demands of the blacks and coloreds (mixed blacks and whites), the history of such relaxations under pressure is that they generate even higher demands from those affected, escalating the conflict to new levels and heightening the tensions. Even if the white government had acceded to a coalition with the blacks, historical evidence suggests that the blacks will fight among themselves for power. This does not mean that change should not be sought. It merely means that those instigating it from abroad should be aware of the potential results and be ready to assume some responsibility for them. It is not satisfactory to cause bloodshed and then to wash one's hands; nor is it acceptable to witness genocide and do nothing. The situation in South Africa demonstrates that TNCs are often in difficult circumstances that require continuous analysis as to techniques of resolution and feasible results.

Sexual discrimination also exists virtually around the world, but with more or less political or social awareness of the problem and pressure to change the situation. The woman is subservient still in many societies. In Japan, young women are hired as "office wives" to be the feminine "go-fers" for the male managers. Women are also hired into companies, not on the "lifetime employment" basis of the men, but on a part-time or temporary basis, with the full intention that they will no longer be employed when they are married. It is the responsibility of the Japanese wife to manage the home, raise the children, and keep the husband happy and able to contribute effectively in his company. In Saudi Arabia and India, women remain in the shadow of men. And it is still exceptional to find female managers in Europe, Japan, Latin America, or on Wall Street.

All of this will change; but how and how rapidly will depend partly on the orientations and behavior of TNCs themselves. This is a problem for which they should become prepared, but for which there is little evidence that they are doing so. The extent to which this will become a subject of dialogue with governments will depend on whether or not the TNCs anticipate the regulations that are likely to be forthcoming and stay ahead of them. If they do not, they will face a set of regulations in this area as they have in many others. It is one area, however, in which they could happily and profitably take the initiative without any serious complaints from within many of the countries in which they operate abroad. There are, of course, some countries in which such breaks in the customs would be traumatic, and these cultures must be carefully prepared. However, even in these, the long-term trends are in the direction of sexual equality reflecting the emulation of Western cultural concepts, as illustrated in the Japanese comment that "In Japan, the only things that have gotten stronger are nylon stockings and women."

ILLICIT PAYMENTS

The question of corrupt or illicit payments (bribes) has largely become a matter between the TNCs and the U.S. government, for other governments see the matter differently. Although the Organization of American States (OAS) and the United Nations both sought to pass resolutions on this matter, the efforts came to nought. A considerable amount of dialogue occurred among TNCs, international organizations, and the U.S. government. But the major event was the passage of the Foreign Corrupt Practices Act (FCPA) by the U.S. Congress in 1977, to prohibit the bribing of foreign government officials in purchases of products or services by U.S. companies—at home or abroad. The FCPA covers all payments to government officials or intermediaries involved in a government purchase and applies to any U.S. company dealing with a foreign government.

No such legislation has been passed by any other government, each continues to rely on prior legislation prohibiting bribery in their countries. All countries of the world have such prohibitions, but they have not prevented widespread practices of asking for, giving, and taking of bribes. There is much less concern over such payments made between private companies for commercial activities; the concern is almost wholly with government purchases and bribing of government officials, or their asking for rebates as a condition for purchases.

The company dialogues with the U.S. government have now turned to the provisions of the act, their implementation, and (hopefully) their relaxation. The provisions are quite stringent, requiring the company not to pay any bribes, to disclose their payment if in fact they are made, to control the flow of funds sufficiently to know when such payments have been made or to be able to prevent them. As stipulated by the act, the responsibility for such controls rests with the top executive officers and it is a criminal act not to have sufficient controls to prevent such payments and not to disclose such payments if they do slip through the controls. U.S. companies have argued that they have lost considerable business, being unable to offer the same inducements that foreign companies do, and they assert that this is damaging the U.S. balance of payments through reducing the volume of exports. There is considerable disagreement as to what the volume of such an impact is, and still further disagreement as to whether any calculation of money losses is appropriate at all.[9]

The basic argument against such bribery is that companies are supposed to make profit through competitive strength in free markets, and when side payments are made to secure business, the profitability of the business is falsified. Since the Securities and Exchange Commission (SEC) and the Internal Revenue Service (IRS) are supposed to have full information as to the cost of doing business, the nonreporting of such payments hides the true activities of the companies. Yet, to disclose such payments would be highly embarrassing in foreign countries; and, therefore, a requirement of disclosure effectively prohibits such payments. If made, U.S. company officials are endangering themselves or are endangered by acts of their subordinates. This is a very uncomfortable position to be in, and officials of U.S. companies have sought relief from the U.S. Congress through modifications of the provisions of the Act, the last effort being in the Omnibus Trade Bill of 1988 (vetoed by President Reagan for other reasons, but later enacted).

However, to propose modifications that would move in the direction of permitting some (if not all) bribing of foreign officials would be political suicide for a Congressman. To reduce the stringency of the controls or the recording requirements would make it easier to violate the act; the appearance of permitting bribes would still exist, even if the companies did not make illicit payments. U.S. companies, therefore, are stuck with the FCPA and can do little but live with it. It was brought down on their heads through their unwillingness to follow the rules of the free-market game and their acceptance of the illicit behavior of others.

Not all companies are engaged in such payments, but between 350 and 400 of the top 500 U.S. corporations were found by the SEC to have made them during the 1970s.[10] The SEC also found that in each case at least one top company official was aware of what was going on. Thus, there arose a considerable skepticism about the willingness of U.S. companies to abide by ethical constraints in their dealings abroad. These questions arose at the same time that U.S. companies were found donating substantial sums to the Committee for the Reelection of the President (CREEP) set up for the second campaign of President Nixon; these payments were clearly illegal and raised doubts in the minds of many about the ability to trust companies to use funds in legal and ethical ways. Claims by TNCs now that they would abide by the law even if control requirements were relaxed do no fall on sympathetic ears.

The major lesson from this experience is that the absence of self-regulation will bring governmental regulation—if not intergovernmental regulation.

EXPLOITATION OF THE SEABED

U.S. TNCs have missed another opportunity to demonstrate a collaborative approach in resolving problems in the world economy and community. The development of resources from the seabed has been under negotiation for a number of years, with most countries seeking to achieve a cooperative arrangement that would permit the sharing of developmental opportunities and benefits from the exploitation of minerals on the seabed. The seabed is clearly an international commons; to prevent its destruction or misuse, international cooperation is necessary.

The U.S. government position, supported by the major U.S. companies that would benefit, was that seabed development should occur at the hands of unfettered private enterprises, staking out their claims where they could and developing the mineral resources under market criteria. The benefits would then go to the companies making the substantial investments (up to $20 billion per company, by estimate). This did not satisfy other governments, which saw these resources as part of the "heritage of mankind" and not appropriately accruing to any one country or company.

In any event, an agreement was made among a number of countries for the establishment of an intergovernmental enterprise that would license the rights to development, taking royalties that would then be distributed among the signatory countries. The U.S. government refused to sign, preferring an "open bidding" procedure and finally insisting on the right of U.S. companies to develop the seabed as they saw fit.

To recognize the favorable results of collaboration, the TNCs should have come forward with proposals for consortia to develop the seabed under the guidance of an international authority, which would then make certain that the revenues went to all of the countries of the world, including the least developed. Such a move would have been seen as a high degree of social responsibility and a recognition of the desirability of redressing the imbalances in national wealth around the world.

The pressure on TNCs was relaxed by the fact that the demand for the minerals that would come from the seabed—copper, manganese, magnesium—fell sharply, reducing the pressure to develop the resources. There is time for the U.S. companies to reassess their position and help to develop collaborative approaches. Such a new position will have to be hammered out in dialogues with the U.S. government and then between it and the other countries that are already signatories to the agreement.

NEW ISSUES

Looking ahead, there are new issues that are likely to arise and become the subject of dialogues between TNCs and governments. For example, one of the major concerns of host countries is the loss of their culture through incursions from influential foreign countries. The culture of Japan is shifting toward the West, as is the culture of parts of China. One of the reasons for rise to prominence of the fundamentalist groups in Arab countries is a revulsion against Westernization, and one can see the same phenomenon in some of the South Asian countries.

Efforts to protect national cultures have centered on the maintenance of national languages (despite the fact that in many countries the establishment of a national language is not yet complete) and the continuation of national dress. Both the English language and Western dress have dominated the world of business. It is conceivable (though unlikely) that the antipathy to English as the international business language could begin a move to the creation of a business language itself, which would become a lingua franca for the commercial and financial world. In many languages it is difficult to translate many of the commercial and financial terms found in English. A separate common language would increase efficiency without placing one national language over others. As to dress, it is also conceivable that fashions will change into more comfortable and functional styles simultaneously around the world so that no one cultural influence will dominate.

More proximately, the present effort to establish international accounting standards has stalled, but there will continue to be pressure in this direction. A common standard or at least a harmonization of existing standards would be a substantial step toward providing more realistic information on the operations of companies and is therefore desired by governments as well as by headquarters companies. This development will engage the time of TNCs both at national and international levels.

The commercial use of outer space will become a critical issue for TNC/government relations as more and more satellites are launched and used for commercial purposes and especially for R&D activities. The use of research results will continue to be a question of politics as well a economics, engaging governments in the determination of proprietary rights. Also, space orbits are already becoming crowded, since there is only "limited space in space" for stationary satellites; higher orbits are unstable and lower ones cause the satellite to reenter the atmosphere too soon.

Thus, agreement among governments and companies will be required to ration space.

The ability to reclaim vast areas of the world's resources (the Sahel, polluted rivers, and dead lakes) and to develop economically regions that cross national boundaries (the Indus Valley, the Mekong Delta, the Euphrates River, the Fertile Crescent, the Amazonian lands, and the Mongolian-Manchurian-Siberian region) will require consortia of companies, calling for intergovernmental guidelines and decision making with TNCs. Similar large-scale cooperative efforts will require extensive dialogues in the conceptualization, formation, implementation, evaluation, and development of the Arctic and Antarctic resources, plus the final distribution of benefits.

New technologies in communication, transportation, manufacturing processes, distribution, and financial instruments and mechanisms will call for greater collaboration between TNCs and governments in ways not yet foreseen. TNCs should consider ways to prepare for these events through the formation of appropriate units within the TNCs and the development of appropriate ties with governments on existing and emerging issues. The multiple facets of "development," which require attention to social, ethical, and political evolution, should not be ignored by TNCs. TNCs affect all of them, requiring a cooperative orientation on the part of both TNCs and governments so as to buttress successful negotiations for effective solutions. The criteria for decision making are more complex than "market efficiency," which is only one objective that both TNCs and governments seek to achieve.

NOTES TO CHAPTER 14

1. See J. N. Behrman, *Tropical Diseases: Responses of Pharmaceutical Companies* (Washington, DC: American Enterprise Institute, 1980).

2. J. F. Baker, "The Infant Formula Controversy: A Dilemma in Corporate Social Responsibility," *Journal of Business Ethics*, no. 4 (1985), pp. 181–190.

3. See J. N. Behrman and W. G. Carter, *Problems of International Business Cooperation in Environmental Protection* (New York: Fund for Multinational Management Education, Nov. 1975).

4. On TNC responses to environmental regulations, see Thomas A. Gladwin and Ingo Walter, "Multinational Enterprise, Social Responsive-

ness, and Pollution Control," in Dymsza & Vambrey, *International Business Knowledge*, pp. 405–422.

5. Behrman and Carter, *Problems of International Business.*

6. See S. Prakash Sethi, Nobuaki Namiki, and Carl L. Swanson, *The False Promise of the Japanese Miracle* (Marshall, MA: Pitman, 1984).

7. See Lester R. Brown, *State of the World 1988* (New York: W. W. Norton, 1988).

8. See James A. Lovelock, *GAIA* (New York: Oxford University Press, 1979). His concept of the earth as a "living, intelligent system" includes the possibility that mankind might be replaced by other life forms.

9. John Graham, "Foreign Corrupt Practices: A Manager's Guide" *Columbia Journal of World Business* (Fall 1983), pp. 89–94.

10. Neil H. Jacoby, Peter Nehemkis, and Richard Eells, *Bribery and Extortion in World Business* (New York: Macmillan, 1977), p. xv.

CHAPTER 15

Continuing Economic Issues

Most of the economic issues between governments and TNCs in the 1950s and 1960s remained unresolved in the late 1980s. The concerns are the same, but their intensity and resolution have varied with world and national economic conditions. Concerns still remain with TNC effects on employment, generation of income, financial and product flows between countries, technology transfers, R&D activities, exchange rates, ownership and control, industrial relations, and so on.

Only with familiarity through long association between TNCs and governments do these concerns attenuate. In the entry negotiation and early stages of operation, these issues are seen as complex, requiring difficult trade-offs on both sides. They are attenuated only by experience in "living together" so the TNCs affiliates are seen as "our companies" by host countries.

As reviewed in Chapter 12, resolution of these issues has not been gained through intergovernmental agreements. Rather, in the decade of the 1980s, governments pursued nationalistic (and protective) policies leading to a neomercantilist world economy.[1] The emerging modes of resolution of the issues are the practice of industrial policies, coproduction, and countertrade, plus a variety of cooperative ventures induced by governments directly in negotiations or through regulations. These approaches appear likely to continue, altering or redressing the balance of benefits and burdens among nations, and between governments and TNCs, circumventing market-determinations.

Potential disagreements between TNCs and governments exist in every situation where the distribution of benefits of a TNC activity is open for negotiation. In such cases the government involved seeks to enhance the benefits accruing to it and the economy, while the TNC seeks to keep what it can appropriate from its worldwide operations.

The problem of the distribution of benefits is solvable only through negotiation—unless governments are willing to abide by decisions of TNCs, as was recommended in the 1970s by George Ball, former U.S. Under Secretary of State.[2] Host-country laws or regulations *may* unilaterally change the benefits for some TNCs in the country, but there will still be responses that rebalance benefits. And other TNCs will reassess their plans to enter that country. The two main categories of economic issues that create tensions between governments and TNCs are: (1) efficiency concerns such as the degree of economic integration and dependence, and (2) equity concerns such as the distribution of benefits of company activities. These are reflected in negotiations over

- the location of production
- employment: levels, worker skills, and compensation
- access to desired technology
- the location and focus of R&D
- international trade: substitution for imports and stimulation of exports
- international capital flows: restriction of outflows and encouragement of inflows
- ownership and control
- remittance of dividends

Each of these issues arises in the continuing relationships between governments and TNCs.

In the absence of agreement between governments, and also between governments and companies, each actor *tries* to resolve these issues unilaterally. National governments have sometimes implemented general policies that treat all TNCs alike—whether favorably or not. And TNCs often do "broken-field running" between the obstacles and incentives in order to increase their sales and profits.

During the 1980s, both industrial and less-developed countries have inclined more toward open policies in dealing with the TNCs. This shift is largely due to the slowdown in worldwide growth, the volatility of the international economy, and the recognition by most governments that the purported benefits of international debt in fixing the level of repayments (as compared to variable and presumed higher returns to FDI) were overblown.[3] During the 1980s the stakes of host governments in these negotiations have shifted toward seeking the contributions of TNCs, giving the TNCs a better bargaining position. With so many choices of location for production and investment, along with continued reduction in costs of transportation and communication, the TNCs negotiated or received more favorable governmental reception in the 1980s than in the 1970s. Governments seeking to boost their own national incomes were competing to bring in capital investment; at the same time many have increased the role of market decisions. Both of these tendencies result in more opportunities for the TNCs—though they are often constrained by various "performance requirements" and ownership restrictions imposed by governments.[4]

The TNCs, in the absence of coordinated policy from home and host governments, tend to put their activities in locations that offer the best competitive position, namely in large markets and low-cost locations that are politically stable. Neither governments nor TNCs appear to be paying much attention to the progressive integration of the world economy and what it will mean for policies toward TNCs. Rather, each seems to consider the economic issues individually, or on an ad hoc basis, from their own provincial viewpoint. Yet both efficiency and equity are issues that require *systemic* solutions—both among governments and between them and TNCs.

PRODUCTION LOCATION

Under the 1945 Bretton Woods Agreements, the location of economic activity around the world was supposed to be decided according to market signals. All signatories to the agreements accepted *in principle* the U.S. government position that economic activity should be based on comparative advantages, leading to market efficiency and, therefore, the most rapid economic progress for the world. As a result of such progress, the entire world *could* be better off with countries receiving the benefits of growth according to their proportionate production in world output. The idea that production would be located according to wishes of governments or through planning guidelines was rejected in favor of relying on the "natural" factor endowments of countries.

However, this principle was applied selectively, even in advanced countries. Most of the rest of the world has remained committed in policy and practice to government intervention, mercantilist orientations, and *national* economic growth as distinct from worldwide progress. Nations have continued to be more concerned with their own relative wealth and power than that of the world as a whole. Therefore, efforts have continued to enhance *national* comparative advantage through subsidizing or generating required factors of production or inducing industry to locate within the country so as to gain comparative advantages and increase international competitiveness.

To leave such decisions wholly to the officers of TNCs, who were making decisions for the benefit of the company and its shareholders, was seen as unacceptable by most host countries, and this attitude remains prevalent throughout the world (including the United States). Only when there is a wider community of interest among nations will company decisions as to the location of production be left largely unfettered. Even within nations, there is a constant effort to shift the location of production from the more crowded or advanced regions to those more open or depressed.

Thus, there is a constant push and pull over the location of economic activity both within and among nations. The fact that the TNC makes the final decision as to whether it will locate in a given area, under guidelines set by governments, means that there is a continuing negotiation on this issue. Economic growth itself causes the relative abundances of factors of production to change among countries, and every factor of production—land, labor, capital, technology, and management—is subject to being moved either physically or through changes in ownership from one country to another. These facts mean that comparative advantages are not static but dynamic; they change and can be changed especially by altering FDI decisions. These decisions themselves are dynamic and subject to stimuli from several directions. Consequently, the mere location of a TNC in a given country can shift its comparative advantages, and host countries seek the contributions that TNCs can make to improve national competitiveness.

Once national interest is injected into a TNC's location decisions, "economic" criteria are displaced or altered to elicit a different decision by the TNC. The ability of the TNC to design products so that components can be produce in many locations and assembled in several others with great precision and high quality means that differences in comparative advantage among countries are significantly narrowed, increasing the intensity of negotiations between TNCs and governments for the specific capabilities of efficiency seekers. It is feasible to put any of several production stages in one or more countries, so the pattern of comparative advantages can be set through TNC/government negotiations.

Governments are not able to dictate production locations to TNCs because of the availability of alternative locations. National economies are growing more similar in factor endowments (or availabilities) given the expansion of trade in resources, components, capital goods, and transfers of labor and technology. Consequently, minimum-efficient-scale production is viable in many countries. As a result, more countries are competing for the same industry sectors. As more firms become multinational, they offer additional access to foreign markets that interests host governments seeking exports, thereby further strengthening the bargaining position of the TNCs. The winners will tend to be countries with larger economies because TNCs are more be attracted by market size. These countries can subject TNCs to greater enticements to enter, to support local suppliers, and to accept other performance requirements. In addition, as more firms become multinational and compete in more national markets, the competition itself will increase the ability of governments to shift terms in their favor. If one firm can be persuaded to follow the government's request to locate a facility within that country's borders, another is attracted as a defensive measure. As technology becomes more widely diffused, and as product life cycles shrink over time, governments have more firms to choose from to obtain proprietary knowledge.

These features of international business lead to an expectation that, because of increasing supply and demand, the wider opportunities will lead to greater need for information and negotiating skills. Competition among governments will be acute. Only if nations develop closer regional economic integration will they likely agree on principles of location for TNCs, including support for production in less advanced countries or regions.

EMPLOYMENT

Since production requires human resources, the discussion above applies also to the goal of greater employment. Whether an elected democracy, a military dictatorship, or a communist system, the government is concerned with jobs, quality of work life, compensation, and other employment-related issues. Since TNCs provide significant and typically diverse opportunities, their entry has favorable results for this government objective.

However, the technology employed by TNCs permits *some* degree of substitution of labor for capital, so TNCs can somewhat alter their employment levels depending on costs, risks, and government policies. Governments frequently argue that firms favor capital-intensive operations at the expense of additional employment of people, and this divergence of interests is an important part of ongoing TNC/government relations. Changing technologies will shift location more to advanced countries as low-cost labor declines in importance raising new problems of TNC/government relations.

Government policymakers are concerned not only about the level of employment, but also about the skill levels of that employment. All governments seek higher skill levels for their labor forces, in both managerial and blue-collar categories. TNCs do offer training to their workers and managers in affiliates around the world, but the skills used even in similar situations are not necessarily the same. Therefore, governments press firms to train workers to higher skill levels and to add local managers.

Similarly, governments are concerned that key decisions about local affiliates are sometimes made at the TNC's home office. In this instance, the governments want TNCs to place sufficiently high-ranking decision makers

(preferably locals) in local affiliates so that key decisions
will be made locally. But, it takes some years for headquarters to feel comfortable with a local making key decisions.
Once again, a divergence of interests exists between the two
parties.

Further, compensation of employees is a major concern
of both governments and TNCs. In most cases, TNCs tend to
offer higher compensation than their local counterparts in
similar activities.[5] This action is in line with governmental
objectives but is often opposed by local companies who fear
rising costs in their operations. Still, governments often
choose to push TNCs to employ more high-level, and more
highly paid, employees in their local affiliates. Also, since
compensation sometimes includes substantial nonsalary
benefits (often tax-exempt), disagreements also arise between host governments and TNCs regarding these benefits.
The compensation package for managers and employees is
a particularly difficult issue in negotiation. For example, the
Chinese government seeks "home-country" levels of remuneration for its enterprise managers; the government receives these payments and in turn pays the managers only
at local rates; this constitutes a considerable tax on joint
ventures there.

All of these issues are exacerbated by the reemergence
of a concern that first surfaced in the 1930s over "social
dumping"—the advantage of a country with low wages has
in exporting to high-wage countries—which forces wage
cuts directly in the same sector or indirectly through resulting unemployment in the importing country. Any intergovernmental action to adjust this situation (beyond the
existing resolutions of the ILO) seems far in the future.

At the bilateral or multilateral level, governments may
find that harmonization of employment policies leads to
fewer disagreements about incentives that pull TNCs from
one location to another, but policies that tend to equalize
wages will then fail to attract the very investment and employment that each (host or home) government wants in the
first place. This conundrum means that little joint action is
likely in the area of wages, salaries, or other compensation.

On the other hand, continued and expanded implementation of the ILO Code of Conduct on TNCs (1977) and the

industrial relations provisions of the OECD Guidelines
(1976) can be expected with respect to fair treatment of employees, layoff practices, safety standards in the workplace,
and other areas of employment policy that do not directly
affect relative costs among countries. Such action will result from continued publicity of TNC activities and a more
general insistence on "proper" behavior and recognition of
the dignity of every individual.

TECHNOLOGY AND PROPRIETARY RIGHTS

Rules on technology protection, payments for use of
proprietary technology, and technology transfer practices
vary widely between industrial and less-developed countries. The generation and use of technology in advanced
countries tends to be market based, with the government
playing the role of rulemaker, referee, and supporter. Patent
life is fairly consistent among these countries (in the range
of 15–20 years), as is the lack of limitations on intercountry
transfer of technology.

Despite the tendency of industrial-country governments
to allow market activity to determine technological advancement and diffusion, another factor needs to be considered. The government in each of the advanced countries
(except perhaps tiny Luxembourg) spends literally billions
of dollars annually on military and other government-
sponsored research. The U.S. government funds approximately 46 percent of R&D spending in the United States
(though industry carries out 74 percent of the actual research and development).[6] Viewed in this light, governments are clearly major players in the creation and
diffusion of technology. Their activities have significant impacts on TNC operations worldwide through the acceleration or redirection of technological advance.

The generation and transfer of technology by TNCs is
proportionately lower in LDCs than in industrial countries,
compared even to volumes of FDI in each. Many LDC's are
reluctant to offer protection of proprietary rights (patents,
trademarks, copyrights), since they consider that technology is the "heritage of mankind"—i.e., it should be freely
disseminated. They are also reluctant to grant such monopolies to foreigners. LDCs offer less patent protection, give

less protection against disclosure of information, and present greater demands for host-country participation in the process of technology creation and diffusion than TNCs consider appropriate. This should not be surprising, since these countries face a "technology gap" relative to the industrialized nations, and they see a need to catch up.[7] Chart 15.1 compares rules on technology use and transfer in selected countries.

Based on the intensive negotiations in the UN to create a code of conduct on technology transfer, pressure will continue for an intergovernmental agreement. But TNCs will remain opposed in principle, unless ideological differences among governments are resolved.

OWNERSHIP AND CONTROL

The issue of foreign versus local ownership and control is raised only in host countries. There was never a serious debate in the United States during the 1960s and 1970s of whether or not its ownership and control of foreign assets through TNCs was appropriate for itself, for others, or for the world economy as a whole. On the contrary, the view in the United States was that ownership by TNCs of foreign affiliates was perfectly appropriate as an extension of the rights of private property. Therefore, to the extent that the host countries extended property rights to individuals, they should accept private ownership by foreigners.

Conversely, as the United States became a net international debtor, and significant inflows of FDI occurred during the 1980s, considerable concern arose as to foreign ownership and control of banks, agricultural land, extensive residential developments, media, and manufacturing plants. The concerns were not only that the United States was being "sold" too cheaply but also that foreign ownership and control could be exercised to the detriment of U.S. interests. The presumption that private individuals would and *should* act in their own interests through market signals was not applied to foreigners, at least not by those who opposed such foreign ownership in the United States.

The concerns voiced in the United States, when it became a significant host country, were similar to those that have long been expressed in other host countries—begin-

Chart 15.1: Rules on Technology Use and Transfer

Selected Countries	Limits on Royalties	Unpatentable Items	Patent Duration (Years)	Trademark Duration* (Years)	Highest % Tax Bracket on Royalties
Canada	None	Chemicals for food and medicine	17	15	25
France	6% of sales	Nonindustrial items, animals, plants	20	10	33.3
Germany	10% of sales	Medical treatments	20	10	45
Italy	None	Theories	20	20	21
Japan	8% of sales	Nuclear transformations	15	10	20
United Kingdom	None	Scientific discovers artistic creations	20	7	20
United States	None	Noncommercial items	17	20	46
Argentina	None	Pharmaceuticals	5, 10, 15	10	n.a.
Brazil	1–5% of sales to unrelated firms only	Pharmaceuticals, food, chemicals	15	10	25
Egypt	None	Any substance, only production processes are patentable	15 (renewable)	10	40
India	8% of sales	Foods, drugs, chemicals	14	7	40
Korea	None	Food, drink, medicine, chemicals	15	10	25
Mexico	5%; many exceptions	Food, drugs, agricultural chemicals	10	5	42
Nigeria	1% of sales	Plants, animals, biological processes	20	7	45
Singapore	None	(NA)	Only UK patents are valid	UK registered only, 7 years	40

*All countries permit renewals.

Source: Business International Corp., *Investing, Licensing, and Trading Conditions*, New York: Business International Corp., 1985 et seq.

ning in the 1930s in Latin America, rising in pitch in the
1950s in Canada and in Europe in the 1960s, back again in
Latin America in the 1960s and 1970s, and into China in
the 1980s. Host countries have responded by insisting on
local ownership at least through joint ventures, by preventing acquisitions of existing companies by foreigners, and by
insisting on participation by local labor unions. For example, Peru in the 1970s passed a law creating "industrial
communities" in which labor was given increasingly large
percentages of the equity shares of companies until they
would own the companies; the government did not trust the
unions to exercise such control, however, and held the
shares for the benefit of the unions.

Ownership of foreign affiliates is probably the one concern on which governments have made the most successful
efforts in channeling TNC activities as the governments desire—but with the least real impact on the economic development of their countries. Many LDCs now require or
strongly encourage some degree of local ownership in ventures established by foreign TNCs, with the newest entrants
(U.S.S.R. & China) requiring majority local ownership in
most ventures. Industrial nations generally permit wholly
owned foreign affiliates, but even in these countries some
have established state-owned firms to operate as monopolies in key industries, keeping these activities under de
facto national control. In Latin America, though the Andean
Pact's Foreign Investment Code has been dismantled in an
effort to attract more foreign capital during the debt crisis,
this orientation is more likely a temporary shift in response
to pressing economic conditions than a philosophical
change. Until private enterprise itself is given a larger role,
foreign private enterprise will be held suspect.

In serving local markets, TNCs sometimes have decided
to take on local partners who know the market and other
environmental conditions better. Particularly in Japan,
Western European and U.S. firms frequently set up local operations jointly with some Japanese partner due to both local differences and government preference. Similarly, firms
in capital-intensive and research-intensive industries are
more often looking for partners to share investment costs,
agreeing as well to share the subsequent benefits generated
by the joint projects.

The ownership issue is cosmetic; the real issue is control. So control remains a contentious issue even when ownership has been divided more in line with the government's preference. But both TNCs and governments continue to perpetuate several myths that affect policies.[8]

LDC Myths

There are several myths surrounding the issue of ownership and control, and they should be separated from the real issues in order to reach a resolution of the concerns. The first myth is that ownership provides control and that control cannot be exercised without ownership. It has long been recognized in the economics literature that mere ownership of corporate property by the shareholders does not guarantee control. Though there may be local shareholders in a foreign-owned affiliate, even in those cases where local ownership exceeds 51 percent, control is not automatically guaranteed. Control lies within the management, and management can be determined through agreed techniques other than weighted voting by the board of directors or shareholders. The agreement can extend a management contract to the minority partner; a local official (lawyer, banker) can be given a 2 percent equity in the venture and agree (tacitly) always to vote with the foreign partner; bylaws can be written to give veto powers to the minority on key issues; or, key issues can be placed in the technology agreement, where the licensor (minority partner) has control. Thus, majority ownership does not provide decision-making authority. It *may* do so, but there are many ways to get around such control.

The second myth is that local control will mean that national interests are placed above private interests. It is more likely that *local* private interest will be placed above public interests at home and even above private interests abroad. If an enterprise is *wholly* owned by citizens of a country, that itself does not guarantee that national interests are pursued. Further, the record does not indicate that local capitalists and entrepreneurers are any better at following national interests than foreign investors. Rather, local entrepreneurs in some LDCs have a greater capacity to influence government in their own private interest and to disregard government interests when they wish; for example, they are more willing and able to circumvent exchange controls to get money out of their country.

A third myth is that governmental influence and control require that companies be locally owned or have local partners. Again, the record would indicate that local companies need the same regulation imposed on them that would be required for foreign-owned affiliates in order to induce the behavior desired by governments. And locals have a greater capacity to flout or avoid regulations than do foreigners. There is some evidence that local ownership would open opportunities to corruption of host-country government officials more readily than if the industry is owned by foreigners. Foreign investors are *more* likely to accede to host-government pressures, recognizing that they must be seen as "good corporate citizens" and can readily be pushed out. Governments have a variety of techniques they can use to influence corporate behavior, and they do not require one type of ownership or another to be successful.

These points do not lead to the conclusion that local ownership is not desirable. Since in many LDCs, there is a lack of managerial talent, the insistence on local ownership with foreign ventures is a means of accelerating the transfer of managerial skills into the domestic economy. If the company is a new start-up, entrepreneurial skills can be learned. Gradually, there is a social transformation of local management with a diffusion of skills and orientations through domestic businesses. However, many of these same skills can be transferred within a wholly owned company, if the parent wishes to do so. Once again, it is not ownership that is critical, it is attitude and behavior.

Real differences in the pattern of economic development and in the competitive structure of industry arise through foreign ownership of affiliates when the goals and orientations of the foreigner are brought into the host company. LDCs feel that the foreign company is more monopolistic and exploitative than locals would be. However, the history of capitalism in many LDCs shows local private enterprise to be highly exploitative and monopolistic. Local enterprises are frequently less innovative than are foreigners. Further, insistence on joint ventures when the local partner is small compared to the foreign partner would mean that the local party is likely to be unable to meet capital calls leaving him somewhat ineffective in guiding the company. And, if the local affiliate was intended to be part of an efficiency seeker, insisting on a joint venture would cause the parent to make trade-offs in technology flow and marketing that would reduce its contribution to the host country.

TNC Myths

The TNCs have perpetuated some of their own myths on ownership and control, with many of them insisting on 100 percent ownership. As shown in Chapter 2, the necessity of having wholly owned affiliates abroad depends on the type of company that is being established and its orientation to different markets. The recognition that there is no fixed rule on this relationship has led to a number of cooperative ventures in the past decade. Associations have been formed in which the minority partner is given control in particular situations; less formally, the larger company is often deferred to as the appropriate leader.

A second myth perpetuated by TNCs is that joint ventures become windows for technology transfer to leak out into the domestic economy and that this is virtually an automatic result. This has happened, but not always. A number of companies have found it possible to transfer high-level and recent technology without its dispersion or diffusion outside of the joint venture. The concern is real; the answer is found in sound negotiating to find the right partner. Also, because the cost of transferring the technology is often quite high, the dispersion may not occur.[9]

A third myth is that joint ownership with a state-owned enterprise (SOE) should be avoided. Yet, in many countries, especially China and the U.S.S.R. in the late 1980s (but even Egypt and Algeria), there are few private companies with which to join; and SOEs are the only alternative. Experiences in joint ventures with SOEs have not all been bad. TNCs have, therefore, become more willing to venture into the field. Contrarily, governments have found that SOEs are not necessarily more efficient than private companies; further, SOEs cannot respond to government interests differentially if in doing so they reduced competitiveness in the world market. Only if the companies are completely isolated can they serve national interests without concern for the competition. Moves to "privatize" SOEs have been made to enhance competitiveness, accompanied by links with TNCs.[10]

In sum, there is no fixed rule as to the desirability of local ownership or control, compared to foreign ownership and control. The matter depends on the type of operations desired and the cost that the host countries are willing to incur in order to have the semblance of ownership and control. The more open the world economy, the more pervasive will be the competitive forces, with governments intervening indirectly through subsidies or by providing infrastructure and support facilities. They cannot readily intervene in price and quality except to support higher quality and lower prices, which is in the direction competition would also move. These interests are the same ones held by TNCs.

LOCATION AND FOCUS OF R&D

Proprietary technology is arguably the single most important competitive advantage held by TNCs both locally and internationally. This technology must be created through R&D of the TNCs themselves, or be obtained from other TNCs or institutes that specialize in R&D. It is expensive to build R&D facilities that reach a "critical mass" of competence and diversity that will sustain worldwide competitiveness. Since technology is often the element that gives a TNC its bargaining advantage with host governments, firms understandably shy away from following government requests for making this knowledge more readily available or for dispersing R&D activities among many countries.

There are two basic trends that alternately assist and hinder government efforts to attract R&D by TNCs. The growth of *national* markets, which may be differentiated, makes TNCs more interested in entering additional countries and modifying their products, giving the governments greater ability to attract R&D facilities (though typically attracting more D than R). The shortening of product (or technology) life cycles pushes the firms to centralize R&D in a few locations, taking rapid advantage of innovations worldwide. The willingness of TNCs to extend R&D activities abroad depends also on the nature of company operations; that is, market seekers are more likely to place labs abroad than are efficiency seekers.[11]

Industrial R&D will remain primarily the province of the TNCs in the future, though governments do sponsor such research ventures either directly or through defense contracts given mostly to TNCs. Particularly in the area of patentable innovations, such as pharmaceuticals and other proprietary chemicals, the incentive for TNC support of R&D remains strong. The mere possibility of technological modifications or break throughs keeps TNCs (and other companies) spending for R&D.

TNCs for their part generally find that local R&D in LDCs is relatively inefficient (or not viable) because there are fewer skilled scientists, engineers, and R&D managers in such countries.[12] Therefore, TNCs tend to concentrate their basic research in developed nations and to carry out a minimum of product development (often merely adaptations to local conditions) in the LDCs that require it.

For *any* country to be left out of this creative process is to consign it to lagging industrially and competitively. Therefore, all governments seek *some* part of R&D activities to be located within their borders, be it within local firms or TNC affiliates. To achieve this objective, Canada in the 1970s offered subsidies up to 50 percent of costs of R&D laboratories, but few TNCs responded. They concluded that if R&D did not make sense at 100 percent of costs, no subsidy could make it cost effective. From an efficiency standpoint alone, dispersion of R&D is not necessarily the best policy for a TNC.

Government support of research in biotechnology, agriculture, electronics and various others sectors gives them some leverage over recipient firms in the direction of research and the innovation of results. Also, there are some private/public joint ventures in research and some cooperative government projects (such as ESPRIT in telecommunications/computers and Airbus Industrie in aircraft). Joint R&D efforts are difficult to negotiate, if close to the stages of innovation and commercialization. Pure research is easier to fund jointly and especially with governments because of uncertain success. Also projects such as alternate energy sources, medical research on critical diseases, or new forms of low-income housing, are less attractive to the private sector unless subsidized by governments. The high costs of such projects and relatively low probability of appropriating the benefits of the research will lead to joint efforts involving governments in TNC research projects and to the opening of other avenues for government participation in TNC activities.

BALANCE OF PAYMENTS

Maintaining an acceptable "balance" in international payments has historically been seen by TNCs as *the* major concern of host and home governments.[13] TNCs seek to operate so as to reduce potential criticism by governments, consequently, they seek to avoid major adverse impacts on payments balances. TNCs seek to minimize their foreign exchange risks by reducing the amount of (hard-currency) funds transferred into host countries and by borrowing locally. They cut costs by seeking least-cost locations and modes of production, and by trading among affiliates as necessary, but with an eye to effects on balances of payments.

Governments, on the other hand, want to see local production (and employment) for both import substitution and exports, since these lead to accumulation of foreign exchange reserves. Obviously, all countries cannot be net exporters. The resolution of this issue has historically been through protectionism or industrial policies (discussed below) rather than cooperative expansion of trade and payments. Even the United States, as its trade deficit continued to mount during the 1980s, erected barriers to imports in steel and autos and maintained or tightened others in textiles. In addition, it insisted that Japan (with which it had the largest trade deficit) invest in the United States to cut its exports to the surplus. Given the nature of trade and payments by TNCs, it was not evident that such investment *would* or *did* move the balance in the direction sought by the United States to reinforce its position. It passed a new Trade Act in 1988 seeking to achieve "reciprocity" in removal of barriers so as to gain a more acceptable balance.

In the absence of joint government action on a bilateral or regional basis the TNC will face continued constraint and guidance in trade and payments. The TNC can take the initiative, as some have, to assure governments that its operations in the country will have a balanced impact on the country's balance of payments annually. It then must arrange trade and financial flows to bring about this result. Most TNCs can do so if they merely include this goal among their planning criteria. Of greater efficiency, however, would be a balancing among several TNCs in a sector or among several sectors in a given country. This intercompany and intersector balancing is reportedly to be accomplished among the U.S. TNCs entering the U.S.S.R. under the 1989 agreements between the Soviet government and a number of U.S. companies.

From 1945 through 1971, governments of most of the noncommunist countries tried to deal with payments imbalances through assistance from the IMF. This joint effort began with a system of fixed exchange rates based on the U.S. dollar. Short-term loans were given by the Fund to replenish reserves of a member in temporary payments deficits. When the dollar was floated, in 1971, the need for loans from the Fund were expected to drop since the exchange rates adjusted to shifts in payments balances. This expectation was not met; rather, demand for IMF loans rose sharply because many LDCs found that devaluation did *not* solve their trade imbalances. The oil shocks had destabilized markets, and protectionism limited the gains from devaluation. Because the IMF operates only at the level of national governments, and not directly with TNCs, it is not a party to dialogues with TNCs. However, its involvement in the international debt problem has required detailed, drawn-out discussions with the multinational banks. Discussions of sovereign foreign debt restructuring require that the IMF and private commercial bank lenders reach understandings as to the terms of relief given to debtor governments—reductions of debt, reductions in interest costs, and stretch-out of payments, plus new loans. But since national treasuries or central banks are directly interested in and affected by defaults, write offs, or rescheduling of debts, the major discussions are between the private banks and national government agencies.

The issues focused on the balance of payments—trade balances, financial flows, funds borrowings, etc.—are exacerbated by the large overhang of international debt run up by LDCs *and*, in the late 1980s, by the United States itself. The world total is over $1 trillion, with the net United States debt expected to overtake *all* other countries' *net* debt by 1990. The impact on TNCs will arise as efforts are mounted to pay off these debts through exports or reduced imports on the part of debtors.

NOTES TO CHAPTER 15

1. For an assessment of TNC/government relations in the late 1960s and early 1970s, see Patrick M. Boarman and Hans Schollhammer (eds.), *Multinational Corporations and Governments* (New York: Praeger, 1975).

2. See former Under Secretary of State for Economic Affairs George Ball, "Nationalism—The Old and Growing Threat to the Multinational Corporation," Corporate Financing, (Jan./Feb. 1972), pp. 27–33.

3. For a debate on this issue—"won" by the proponents of debt but "lost" by the governments who followed the advice—see, A. O. Hirschman "How to Divest in Latin America and Why," *Essays in International Finance* (Princeton Univ., International Finance Section, Nov. 1969); and J. N. Behrman, "International Divestment: Panacea or Pitfall?" *Looking Ahead* (Washington, DC: National Planning Association, Nov./Dec. 1970), pp. 1–12; reprinted in A. Kapoor and P. Grub (eds.), *The Multinational Enterprise in Transition* (Princeton, NJ: Darwin Press, 1972), pp. 467–489.

4. See Stephen E. Guisinger, and Associates, *Investment Incentives and Performance Requirements* New York: Praeger, 1985).

5. See, for example, Robert Grosse, *Multinationals in Latin America* (London: Routledge, 1988), chap. 5; and Jerry Ingles and Loretta Fairchild, "Evaluating the Impact of Foreign Investment," *Latin American Research Review*, v. xii, no. 3, (1977) pp. 57–70, for data on Latin American affiliates of TNCs.

6. National Science Foundation, *National Patterns of Science and Technology Resources* (Washington, DC: NSF, 1984). p. 3.

7. For an assessment of the European gap in the 1960s, see Jean-Jacques Servan-Schreiber, *The American Challenge* (New York: Atheneum, 1968); also on the LDC gap, see R. Robinson, *The International Transfer of Technology* (Cambridge, MA: Ballinger, 1988).

8. The myths and realities are discussed more extensively in J. N. Behrman, "Foreign vs. Local Ownership," *World View* (Sept. 1974), pp. 39–46; also L. Franko, "Use of Minority and Fifty-Fifty Joint Ventures by U.S. Multinationals During the 1970s: The Interaction of Host Country

Policies and Corporate Strategies," *Journal of International Business Studies* (Spring 1989), pp. 19–40.

9. David Teece, *The Multinational Corporation and the Resource Costs of International Technology Transfer* (Cambridge, MA: Ballinger, 1976).

10. See Raymond Vernon (ed.), *The Promise of Privatization* New York: Council on Foreign Relations, 1988).

11. See J. N. Behrman and W. A. Fischer, *Overseas R&D Activities of Transnational Companies* (Boston, MA: Oelgeschlager, Gunn, & Hain, 1980).

12. See J. N. Behrman, *Industry Ties to Science and Technology Policies in Developing Countries* (Boston, MA: Oelgeschlager, Gunn & Hain, 1980).

13. J. N. Behrman, *National Interests and the Multinational Enterprise* (Englewood Cliffs, NJ: Prentice-Hall, 1970).

CHAPTER 16

Policy Shifts

Three major departures from free trade and free flows of investment have been tried by national governments during the 1980s. They seek to set new rules for FDI and trade to shift the location of economic activities and the distribution of benefits and burdens. They include industrial policies (sometimes called industrial strategies or industrial targeting), coproduction sponsored by the government, and countertrade under governmental guidance.

INDUSTRIAL POLICIES

Industrial policies are an attempt by the government to guide a specific industrial sector in international competitiveness, encouraging its expansion and increasing its productivity or easing its decline through protective measures. They were employed as early as the 1930s, but more extensively in the 1970s and 1980s, with some experimentation by France and Japan as early as the 1950s. The 1960s saw an increase in the frequency of such policies, with Britain, Germany, and even the United States and some LDCs selecting specific sectors for differential treatment.[1] Their objective is to restructure competitive advantages, making sure that the country does not lose out in the growth of a key sector—particularly the national security industries. Or, in the case of declining industries, it wishes to prevent a precipitous loss of employment that would disturb domestic economic stability.

The desired competitiveness can be aimed at import substitution, export generation, or the maintenance of domestic markets that would otherwise be lost to increasing import competition. These policies, therefore, are a substitute for tariff protection which may have been bargained away at GATT negotiations. A number of techniques are employed including R&D grants, tax relief, low cost loans, plant construction subsidies, land grants, subsidized labor (training cost, movement of workers, special benefits), support for mergers and rationalization of the industries, ease of credit, support of cartel arrangements, "voluntary" export restraint, quotas, and administrative measures (such as customs valuations, customs delays, inspections, etc.).

An industrial policy is to be distinguished from a policy of industrialization, which implies nothing more than broad-gauged support of industrial development, without a preference for any given industries. The preference is for industry over agriculture, in the sense that there is an encouragement of the movement of employment from the farm to industry. Industrial policies aim at quite specific targets, while a scatter shot is acceptable in the generalized policies of industrialization. Industrialization objectives can be distinguished from policies supporting economic growth in general, which do not discriminate between agriculture or industry necessarily, since any employment and production is acceptable as a contribution to growth.

National industrial policies are a move away from macro policies and from market determination of the patterns and rate of industrial growth. A particular balance in growth is sought through attention to heavy industry, light manufacturing, consumer products, and key service industries. In some instances, a key industry is seen as the central pole around which others will be developed, and priority attention is given to it—as with the machine tool sector in Japan in the 1950s and the auto industry in Brazil during the 1960s and 1970s and informatics in the 1980s.

France paid priority attention to the electronic and aircraft industries during the 1970s and 1980s. The concentration by the U.S. government has been on defense industries, out of which several commercially oriented industries (such as aircraft and electronics) have been supported. Japan built its post-World War II miracle out of a series of industrial policies setting priorities for basic industries first, the machine tool industries second, the lighter industries third and finally the consumer sector, including the auto industries, reaching further and further into the world market. At the same time, it eased some of the lower-technology sectors out of priority positions, letting them move into the

LDCs. This movement of industry sectors from predominantly in advance countries into the NICs and even into LDCs (particularly the low-wages countries) has produced the concept of *mobile industries* and raised the question of the appropriate movement of industries among the countries in different stages of development.[2]

The application of industrial policies elicits a continuing dialogue between government and TNCs, principally with their headquarters companies, though some of the major foreign subsidiaries are so significant in host countries that they also are included in the deliberations. These dialogues are usually conducted through the industrial associations with the governmental ministries of industry, economy, or trade, which have bureaus that maintain such contact. Major companies have the greatest influence on the direction of the policies, though "national champions" are sometimes selected to be the bellweather company. Sometimes the national champion is the state-owned enterprise in the sector, receiving the major support and guidance from the government itself.

In the case of the United States, despite the urging of a number of academics and others that strong consideration should be given to the creation of an industrial policy,[3] the private sector has predominantly argued against efforts to target industrial sectors for the process of the "reindustrialization of America." U.S. TNCs have argued further that the U.S. government should exercise its considerable weight in intergovernmental negotiations to get other countries to remove their industrial policies, leaving the location of economic activities to the market.[4] Prior to the latter part of the 1980s, U.S. companies considered that they would have a "fair" advantage in competition based on market signals.

Despite the views of U.S. TNCs, few host governments are willing to cede responsibility for industrial location to TNCs, believing that corporate strategies frequently conflict with national objectives. This perceived lack of agreement between the objectives of TNCs and governments has led to numerous interventions on the part of governments, which when collected together and focused on a specific sector gives rise to industrial (sectoral) policies. TNCs are then required to come within the governmental guidelines and are provided specific support if they do so.

The record of TNC/government relations shows that the TNCs respond more readily to penalties and constraints than they do to incentives and encouragements. The latter approach leaves the initiative to the TNCs, while the former puts it in the hands of governments. There has been no effort to harmonize industrial policies among nations, except through a recognition in Europe that the consummation of a complete common market in 1992 will require some such harmonization among the members.[5]

What is inadequately recognized is that industrial policies are essentially protectionist at a time when the world is moving toward closer international economic integration. Therefore, for these policies to support the underlying movements, new approaches are needed to address the problems of international industrial restructuring—or the mobility of industries among countries. Too little is known about the movement of industries and of companies within them and the corporate arrangements that are emerging. There is need for an international cooperative research program—whether it is institutionalized or merely emerges out of a network is less important than that the research be done. If there is to be a more coordinated set of policies among governments for the promotion and movement of industries, they should be formed out of information and not out of mere policy deliberations.

Whatever comes out of these deliberations, if they are to relieve the protectionist orientation of industrial policies, they will require substantial cooperation between TNCs and governments both in the exchange of information as to what is occurring and as to what each of the parties desires and is able to deliver. New initiatives will be required, as discussed in the final chapter.

INTERNATIONAL COPRODUCTION

Coproduction is the linking of production of independent companies in two or more countries so that a single product or system is produced by the two in cooperation. This is not necessarily a joint venture, for no new entity is formed and the arrangement may be limited to a single project. If several countries are involved, there may be several assembly locations drawing from several production sources, foreign and local. In some critical instances, such as NATO weapons production, the governments have *required* a single TNC to spread production of a system among its affiliates so that each may share in ways agreed among the governments. (If only the host government and local suppliers are involved, coproduction appears merely as a local-content requirement.) Coproduction, therefore, is a means of *sharing* the investment, technology, and production process among two or more participating countries under *non*market criteria. Related or unrelated companies may be involved. The marketing pattern is *not* necessarily a part of the arrangement, though in complex systems governments are often the customers.

Coproduction exists presently in a number of sectors— commercial aircraft, electronic systems, electrical generators, automobiles, military equipment, and several others. It arises in any situation in which a government requires production of specific components or assemblies within its national boundaries as a condition of permitting the final product to be sold in that country.

Local-content requirements are a less specific type of coproduction. These require the foreign investor to obtain a certain percentage of the final value of the product from local suppliers. The local content can vary from as little as 10 or 20 percent (as in Canada) to as much as 95 percent (as with autos in Brazil). Sometimes, the local-content requirements are relaxed on condition that some of the local production is exported by the foreign investor. This was accomplished in the auto sector by Mexican inducements to export into the United States in exchange for a relaxation of the constraints on imports of U.S. components. This resulted in a kind of counter-trade, in which the imports of components from the United States into Mexico by the TNC affiliate are matched by exports of Mexican components or final products to the U.S. TNC or its other affiliates.

Every country in the world has practiced, in one way or another, these local-content techniques for altering the location of production and thereby altering the distribution of the benefits. Even the United States threatened to pass local-content legislation unless Japan "voluntarily" located some of its automotive operations in the United States; the penalty would have been the prohibition of imports from Japan or a more severe quota limit.

Coproduction arrangements usually arise when the host government insists on local production of a specific component or assembly. (A company decision on local supply is simply market-based action involving no special costs.) It has sometimes proposed a specific local company—though it may let the TNC set up a local affiliate for the same purpose when there is insufficient capacity or competition. The host-government interest in requiring such participation is more intense in high-tech and national security industries. Complex coproduction arrangements arise when several countries are involved in production of components—as with military systems, aircraft, or communications networks—and the assembly takes place at one or more locations, with the final product sold to the participating countries or into third markets.

Given the interest in a national aircraft manufacturing capability, a number of nations have imposed coproduction arrangements as a condition of purchase of particular aircraft. Few nations are large enough economically or market-wise to sustain a full-scale commercial aircraft industry on their own, and few are able to serve completely the world market, even in concert with one or two other countries. Therefore, a type of specialization has arisen out of negotiation among governments and major aircraft producers both within Europe (in the production of the Airbus) and between European and American companies so that each has a role in production (learning the technology), assembly, and repair. The resulting pattern arises out of existing abilities and government preferences.

Still more complex arrangements have existed in the coproduction of military equipment or systems under NATO. This practice arose in the 1960s in order to develop common systems, standardizing or harmonizing the various equipment needs so that mutual support could be provided in the field, thereby reducing costs for NATO members. After several systems were produced cooperatively, the practice was terminated by the U.S. Department of Defense, partly because other countries insisted in participating in the R&D and design phases. Subsequent efforts failed to produce agreement on other coproduced systems; an agreement with Japan to codevelop and produce the FSX fighter plan ran into considerable difficulty during 1988/89. But the Department of Defense has called for a reexamination of the process to see if it should not be revived more widely.

Commercial arrangements for coproduction are much less complicated since much of the information required for decision making is based on prices and costs based on market signals. But there are some results from the military coproduction experience that are instructive for those trying to find ways of distributing the costs and benefits of industrial growth among nations.[6]

NATO's Experience

Beginning in the 1950s and continuing through the 1970s some 20 military projects were begun within NATO sponsorship, and most were brought to fruition. Those that were completed include the Hawk missile, the Atlantique aircraft, the Mark-44, the Sidewinder missile, the Star Fighter (F-104G), the SeaSparrow missile, the Bull Pup missile, the M-72 tank, the M1 rifle, the AWACs system, the F-16 fighter plane, the Mallard, and the NADGE early warning system. Although some of the projects could be considered successful from the cost standpoint—the F-104G was as good a performer as the U.S. model and cost less—most were more costly. However, they all met specifications, and all reduced foreign exchange needs significantly, providing more defense than would otherwise have been feasible given the unwillingness or inability to import final systems from the United States.

The NATO experience provides some lessons as to conditions likely to give rise to effective cooperation and some indication of the payouts. There are a number of cross-national projects that could benefit from an analysis of the NATO coproduction schemes. They include integrated transport systems, transport control systems, aerospace projects, communication systems, cross-national and oceanic resource development, energy projects, cooperative efforts in depollution or environmental protection, and regional development schemes that would harness rivers, develop cross-national valleys, or establish cross-national electrification systems. Even industrial projects (as with commercial aircraft), could be appropriately developed on a multicountry coproduction basis. Such coproduction projects would also be applicable in developing closer ties between Western economies and those in Eastern Europe, the U.S.S.R., and China, since each gives a high priority to large-scale, high-tech projects and local participation in them, including SOEs.

The major lesson to be learned from the NATO experience is that, despite differences in national interests, governments can and will cooperate in industrial/military projects when it is clearly to their benefit to do so. But they only do so if that benefit is commensurate with (not necessarily equal to) their contribution. The determination of the costs and benefits is therefore critical; even in this process, national bureaucracies and interests become sizable obstacles. In the 1960s, General Norstad, then Commander-in-Chief of the NATO forces, remarked that the "three unsurmountable obstacles to the joint production of armaments were first the United States, second the United Kingdom, and finally France." On a later occasion, he expanded the reasons to include Germany, Italy, and others.

Despite these obstacles, national governments *have* to become involved in such projects because they are too complex to be handled commercially (requiring inputs of many companies), they are fraught with national interest, and they require government financing and approval of the performance of equipment or the completed projects. They also require dovetailing with national programs of development and multicompany cooperation, including "foreign" TNCs, which arouse host-government fears of dominance.

The central problem of high-priority coproduction arrangements is the *political* one of dovetailing national interests with economic means and demands. The central problem of economics—the matching of economic ends and means—is altered by political objectives, and costs are generally raised as a consequence. That is, market signals have to be attenuated by criteria of political acceptability of the

project and its implementation. To make the meshing that
is required, governmental participation is necessary at the
national and international levels. The basic decisions as to
the objectives, the techniques of implementation, and the
means of resolving disputes—all involve political decisions.

The areas of agreement that must be negotiated among
the participating governments include: definition of the
problem to be met, the design of the systems to be produced, the countries that will participate, procedures for
bidding and procurement, financial commitments, impacts
on balances of payments, allocation of production and
sales, selection of companies to participate, pricing and
costing procedures, organization and management, transfer
of technology, taxes and duties imposed, plus the legal aspects (proprietary rights, termination, accession of new
members, arbitration of disputes, termination of the arrangement and liquidation of assets). Also, provisions may
be needed to dovetail this arrangement with other moves toward international or regional integration.

Throughout the decisions on each of the above elements, a fundamental conflict persists between the simultaneous desires of governments for *efficiency* (least-cost
solutions in a market sense) and *equity* (sharing the benefits). The participating governments seek an arrangement
that mitigates the undesirable effects of efficiency ("free-
market" or "private-enterprise") solutions. The intergovernmental arrangement automatically introduces some
constraints that are likely to reduce efficiency and raise
costs—this is the cost of "equity." Yet, no government will
bear *unlimited* additional costs just to achieve equity. Each
will seek not only to limit but also to disperse the costs of
achieving acceptable benefits.

To the extent that costs are higher than the "least-cost"
solution, an element of foreign aid arises in intergovernmental consortia, either explicitly or implicitly. The direction of aid flow is determined by the balance of
contributions and benefits. If the contributions of some nations are greater than their benefits, resources are transferred, even if aid is not explicitly extended. In several
instances, grants were necessary from the U.S. government
to other NATO members in order to get them to join in the

coproduction and in the use of a given system for mutual defense purposes.

In moving from the efficiency solution to the equity solution the issues requiring decision were magnified several fold. The relative simplicity of the efficiency solution in a single coproduction project is seen in that it contained only 12 decision elements influencing the project's structure and operation, compared to 132 cross-relationships which had to be worked out to achieve an acceptable (equity) solution among NATO governments.[7] These 132 cross-relationships had to be determined more or less simultaneously by the participating governments, with or without simultaneous negotiation with the private companies. The difficulties faced in achieving the equity solutions were evidenced further by the length of time it took to get decisions in each of the multinational consortia. The more complex the project the harder to determine total benefits for each member, but the easier to make marginal adjustments. Achieving the right (acceptable) equation takes time, especially since any agreement among negotiators requires approval by appropriate national ministries.

It was only through tenacious efforts that the many difficult issues were resolved. Yet, for these critical projects, there was no alternative to an equity solution. That is, the equipment simply would not have been bought from the United States by other members, nor would it have been economically feasible to have several bilateral coproduction arrangements between the United States and individual NATO members. The only solution was multinational coproduction, agreed upon in such a way that everyone felt they had an equitable share of the benefits and were paying no more than their "fair share" of the costs.

Fortunately, the equity solution did not have to be followed in the extreme, since some elements of the efficiency solution were acceptable also. Instead, a trade-off between equity and efficiency was made in each of the features of the project, producing an *effective* solution—that is, one that would permit reaching the desired goals. From examination of each of the NATO projects, there appears to be no single "best" coproduction arrangement. Each project led to a different set of trade-offs, partly because different countries were involved, partly because the size and makeup of each project was different, and partly because of the varying durations of each. For these reasons also, officials involved in each project did not communicate with others in similar projects; each started anew, as is frequently the case because of short "institutional memories" and the pervasive NIH syndrome ("if it's not invented here it can't be much good").

Although there were numerous relationships that required a decision as to the trade-off between efficiency and equity and the particular institutional arrangements that would be required, the fundamental problem facing each project was that of *who* should produce *what* and sell at *what price* to the other members. These problems were eased somewhat by asking TNCs for bids specifying their answers to these questions; this procedure injected some competitive efficiency into the projects. The joint projects were fundamentally production projects, affecting the present and future economic strength of each country. A wrong decision—in the sharing of production, in the configuration of the project, and in the location of production— would have potentially severe consequences on major companies (TNCs) within any one of the countries and their future competitiveness. Each government jealously sought opportunities for its own companies to participate and to learn advanced technology, and thereby become more competitive commercially in the future. Many of the arguments over the specification of equipment, the development of the system, procedures for contracting, the potential trade patterns, as well as the flow of technology were surrogate arguments, the hidden agenda was the determination of the allocation of production of specific components and the benefits each national economy would receive. That is, governments sought distributive justice, without which the governments would not be sufficiently motivated to participate, despite the urgency of providing for national security.

Implementation of Coproduction

The first issue in setting up a coproduction project is that of determining who will participate. The fewer countries, the easier it is to obtain an agreement, but with more countries it is easier to find a more efficient solution simply because there are more trade-offs available. Efficiency is easier to assess if comparative advantage is the criterion, while equity is more difficult to determine. In the case of local-content requirements, the host country is the major participant along with foreign enterprise, and the host government sets virtually all of the terms of reference.

In more complex arrangements, negotiations encompass the definition of the system to be coproduced, the companies to be involved, government financial commitments, distribution of production, the technologies to be used, the production locations, the assembly locations, the distribution and repair networks, and any third markets to be served. Each of these are balanced against the others to obtain an "equitable" distribution of responsibilities and benefits. National governments are also concerned about the effects TNC imports and exports of components and final products will have on the balance of payments within the system. The financial contributions and balance-of-payments considerations are linked, as illustrated in criteria set up to guide the management agency in its decisions. The management agency assumes responsibility for "dividing orders for equipment between the various industries and member States, so as to obtain maximum industrial specialization at the same time and insuring that over a given period the orders placed in each state are equal to the contribution of the State to the common budget."[8] The new "EC-1992" will face complex cooperative arrangements, probably altering their participation in NATO projects.

It is clear from the experiences of coproduction projects that governments consider it an inequitable burden if their international payments under the project are less than their receipts. It matters less to them that their total cost is more than it would be apart from such coproduction or that employment gained is less than in other members. Of singular importance is whether the balance of international payments is turned to deficit or surplus, and avoiding a deficit in the project is the overriding concern. That payments deficits might be returned through other channels is not considered.

A deficit implies that some other country is gaining more than it should. No nation wishes to bear the burden of contributing more to the advancement of other countries than it gains itself in the same process, unless it is consciously extending foreign aid—which West Germany did in the F-104G project. Once the criteria of equitable sharing is agreed upon, progress toward all of the other aspects of international coproduction is more readily made.

Criteria for determining the actual burden and benefits is not easy to set in an abstract way. They have to be worked out in each individual case. The items for consideration include impacts on such aspects as employment, industrial capacity, production runs, technical training, exports and imports, management skills, capital mobilization, relief of depressed areas, stability in exchange rates, government revenue, and others. Not every country weighs each element similarly; nor are the real-cost calculations of participation by each country the same even though money costs might be equal. In addition, each weighs differently the value of cooperation in defense, so that *both* costs and benefits are seen differently by governments. And, in making the balance of benefits, it is irrelevant to attempt to apply criteria of "efficiency" or "economy" arising out of other types of activities. Governments are willing to sacrifice efficiency if necessary to generate an acceptable participation and share of the benefits.

Results of Coproduction Projects

The NATO experience indicates that this type of cooperation was necessary in order to get equipment produced and available to NATO members at all. This was, of course, the primary result desired. But, most importantly, almost all of the conflicts over commercial rules and behavior fell away once the major agreement on equity issues was achieved. Once the balance-of-payments patterns were determined, along with the allocation of production, the selection of companies participating, the cost and pricing techniques, the organization and management structure, the technology transfers and so on, then the usual debates over taxes, duties, nontariff barriers, and exchange restrictions simply disappeared! All of these latter concerns are themselves evidence of a desire to redistribute benefits; once that distribution is considered equitable, efforts to impose restrictions that are inefficient and uneconomic simply evaporate. Equity then becomes a prerequisite to efficiency in such projects.

A major lesson from the NATO experience is that effective cooperation requires determination; it is built more readily on "resolution than resolutions; on will, rather than words." The techniques appropriate to the problems do exist, and the benefits are many. The problem is developing the will to proceed. That will itself is dependent on a (wide and intense) recognition of the seriousness of the problem so that government-officials overcome their reluctance to take cooperative initiatives with other countries. What helps overcome it is the recognition of the inability to "go it alone" in critical projects.

Where cross-national efforts are required, the stimulus is stronger. Even so, desirable projects that cannot be done without cooperation are still frequently avoided. Some observers, however, see the cost of noncooperation rising, especially in the electronics field. Industry analyst Arnold Kramish predicted nearly 20 years ago that it will be necessary to create rather close consortia of companies built around the production of microcircuits and to develop the microelectronics systems that would be needed by affiliates. He argued that the development of more and more complex systems will mean a smaller ability to farm out parts to nonaffiliated companies, because a "close dovetailing" of original equipment will be needed. He concluded that only if the European companies tie in with the U.S. companies would they be able to participate in advanced electronic production—especially defense systems.[9] This situation in the 1980s dictated the United States tying in with Japan.

How to get countries and companies together, however, leads to another lesson from NATO experience—that there must be a sufficient degree of mutuality of interests to overcome nationalistic reluctance. This is now occurring gradually through governmental requirements of participation through joint ventures or supply contracts, leading to networks and linkages among TNCs. In most cases, the interests of governments are not specific; rather, they insist on "a presence" in a key sector and even provision of a role for a specific company. The assessment of mutuality of interests is made complex by the fact that the "determination of benefits" is not amenable to quantitative analysis, such as "cost-benefit models." Equity is a result of perceptions, and these differ by individual and nation. Neither the benefits nor the burdens are readily calculable, for they are essentially not quantifiable; rather, both are subjective or political in nature. This indeterminacy adds to the difficulty of agreement, for each nation starts with a set of national interests distinct from that of others. It is, therefore, not acceptable to give each the *same* benefits or costs. Equality is not equity when positions and objectives differ. These differences complicate further the determination of precisely how to carry out the cooperative projects. At present, the more amorphous "strategic alliances" are acceptable, but they have not as yet been relied on for major coproduction projects.

Future of Coproduction

Although coproduction is not likely to become the major method of organizing production around the world, it is likely to become more important, since it does achieve efficiency of specialization while at the same time increasing participation, equity, and stability among nations. Governments are unwilling to permit specialization to the point where the nation is *dependent* on other nations and gains insufficient reciprocal benefits—especially in the military field. Buying whole military systems abroad means unacceptable dependence. Even at greater cost, they seek a portion of production (subsystems) in a desirable project, yielding *inter*dependence.

The benefits of coproduction depend on the structure of industry in each country and its capacity to participate profitably in several ways—financially, technologically, increased employment, and at least no drain on the balance of payments. The country with a number of small companies in the industry affected—none of which is technically capable of producing a piece of sophisticated equipment—is less interested in participating in coproduction, for it knows that it will likely get only the low-tech hardware to produce. At the same time, it would achieve a guaranteed (stable) market for some component and improve its balance of payments compared to importing the whole system. A first step for such countries in preparing to participate in coproduction would be to concentrate on specific components in the system, raising their technical capability and thereby their bargaining position.

The more difficult aspect of coproduction, not yet fully faced even in the military sector, is that of codevelopment of the projects leading to coproduction. Determining what the project is to be, and how it should be structured and divided is difficult enough. But to have to agree cooperatively on the design is even more difficult. Coordination of subsystems being developed by separate companies disassociated from each other is a major hurdle, for each subsystem must be developed in stages with corrections being made at each stage, requiring extensive collaboration among those designing the subsystems. Interfaces are critical, yet are sometimes forgotten in such multi-point design.

This fact of interdependence of subsystems introduces problems of the responsibilities for design and interfaces. Who is to make the pieces fit? Which one is more important? Which can accept a "second best" solution in order to fit with the others? A single design source, therefore, is more efficient, but at the same time this reduces the participation of countries in the early phases. Without that participation they do not feel that the system is necessarily what they want or that their production possibilities are being looked after adequately.

These considerations are less difficult when on is dealing with known products—such as cooperative extraction of resources from the seabed, or cooperative electrification projects, or cooperative design of a niche product for worldwide marketing by a "strategic alliance." They are much more important and more difficult for the high-tech, innovative, leading-edge activities sought by all advanced countries and some NICs.

Finally, the extent to which international investment is guided by such coproduction projects depends on the emphasis between equity and efficiency adopted in foreign economic policies. Developments in the 1980s indicate that the priority is on equity; sufficient levels of efficiency can be reached so that governments are willing to accept a smaller total pie if their relative piece is larger. Repeated experience in networking will make it easier to take the next steps toward coproduction in larger projects.

COUNTERTRADE

Countertrade is a process of linking the export of one commodity to the import of another, or vice versa. This trading technique arises when a company seeks to export to a foreign market but cannot do so under market criteria. Usually the customer is a foreign government, but this is not necessarily the case; the government may merely set the rules or bless the arrangement. The customer seeks to pay in commodities or services that it otherwise would have difficulty exporting mainly from lack of knowledge about foreign markets. A government also seeks to avoid using scarce foreign exchange for imports and to avoid the uncertainty of making independent exports. The market is thereby circumvented through direct or quasi-barter. Barter is usually thought of as the direct and immediate exchange of goods for goods, with each party directly using the goods so gained. In counter-purchasing, the exporter may have no particular use for the items offered in exchange but accepts them with the understanding that he will sell them to a third party at the best return he can get. Multiple exchanges may be required, with several countertrades needed to complete the transaction; this is done by trading companies with extensive knowledge of markets around the world. In each transaction, the market is not the dominant mechanism for making the exchanges, though it is anticipated that some market eventually will be used to dispose of the products traded. Therefore the market is still a limiting factor.

Clearing agreements are a more formal means of balancing trade; they require offsetting exports and imports between two countries over a fixed period of years, so that little foreign exchange is needed to meet payments. Specific items to be covered by the arrangement are agreed to in advance.[10] A "buy-back" agreement arises when a government uses a foreign direct investment inflow to increase exports. In this case, the investor or licensor (offering technology) agrees to accept local goods as payment for dividends or royalties; it must then market these outside the host country to obtain the desired foreign exchange—as with Pepsi-Cola's entry into the U.S.S.R., all of these types of transactions are considered "countertrade," thus offering many more alternatives in exchange than simple barter.[11]

It has been estimated that trade under such bilateral arrangements ranges from 5 to 20 percent of total world trade and will rise to between 20 and 50 percent by the year 2000 because of an increased concern over equity (as compared to efficiency).[12] Besides the volume, what is significant about these activities is that they seek to gain a participation in the investment/production or in the trade/exchange process that would not have been available to a country through the market. Consequently, they are seen by neoclassical economists as "distortions" of the market. This distinction on "distortion" is somewhat useless; "distortions" occur when the basic situation is (or could be) undistorted and aberrations arise that would upset this "undistorted" situation. Since all markets are imperfect and governments do intervene in many markets, there are no undistorted markets around the world. It is arguable, therefore, that the effects of coproduction and countertrade could bring a "normally distorted" situation closer to what might have occurred under undistorted market decision making.[13] However, it would be difficult to trace out the events necessary to prove this proposition. In any case, the purpose of governmental intervention is to achieve a result that is different from (and more acceptable than) market or imperfect-market solutions.

These arrangements are concrete examples of nations trying to achieve a more equitable distribution of costs and benefits (distributive justice) through unilateral rules or international agreement. For the purposes of policy analysis and an assessment of future policies necessary to move toward managed trade, an assessment is required of how each of these new activities works to satisfy the objective of equity in the process of economic growth and international trade. They are undertaken because of shortages of foreign exchange, lack of marketing information or expertise, development of selected sectors, or distrust of markets. Each of these situations is seen by developing and socialist countries (in which most of the countertrade takes place), as inequitable and requiring correction by direct action outside of the market.

Countertrade is a reversion to the bilateralism of the 1930s with even greater constraints. Consequently, those seeking more open economies argue against it, as have the GATT and OECD Secretariats—asserting that the world would be better off *in the long run* using market mechanisms. Classical economics was based on a concept of equilibration of long-run forces, emphasizing that "almost anything can happen in the short run" and that it is impossible to trace out the causal factors in short periods. John Maynard Keynes, however, observed that "In the long run, we are all dead" and that corporate and government policies are mostly directed to the short run. Pressures for countertrade are predominantly short run, leading both companies and governments to initiate such transactions.

Bilateralism in the 1930s was an attempt to balance the international accounts between two countries that had little reserves of foreign exchange but sought to trade without significant restrictions on specific commodities. The aim was to let exports and imports be determined by market conditions (usually altered by tariff or other barriers) but to constrain the size of deficits between two countries. Each country had a series of clearing arrangements, giving rise to bilateral credits or debits, but it was seldom the case that the bilateral balances were made available for use in meeting balances with third countries. In the post-World War II world, a number of bilateral agreements were negotiated, but principally among the countries who were not members of the IMF or the GATT. A number of such arrangements were made by Western European and developing countries with the Soviet bloc, and many remain today. Such agreements also exist between the U.S.S.R. and Eastern European countries, binding the latter by forcing exports to the U.S.S.R. which these countries would prefer to market in Western Europe.

Most types of countertrade go a step further by attempting to balance specific export and import transactions. The initiative is often taken by the exporter of goods seeking a market in a developing country or one that has a scarcity of foreign exchange. The purchasing country may want the goods, but the lack of foreign exchange (or the unwillingness to commit foreign exchange for that particular purpose) gives rise to a counter offer to buy on condition of acceptance of commodities or future buy-back of output in payment. The valuation of the commodities is negotiable, with the recipient attempting to obtain as much as he can to increase profits or cushion the losses which occur from resale in third markets. In some cases, the original seller can use the goods himself and can, therefore, determine the real value more readily.

The practice of countertrade is principally among developing countries or between them and some of the advanced countries, especially the Soviet bloc. Some 50 developing countries in Africa, Latin America, and Asia have either established rules for mandated or permitted countertrade.[14] However, it does not appear that more than 20 of them have actually completed significant countertrade exchanges; there are difficult problems of valuation of goods involved. Countertrade has taken place even among the advanced countries, but principally in the aeronautical or military equipment sectors. The United States has a special regulation permitting imports of materials from developing countries for its strategic stockpile in exchange for surplus agricultural products.[15] The strong principles of the U.S. government against such bilateral trade are violated when it comes to the national interest.

Countertrade appears to amount to no more than 10 percent of the trade *among* the developing nations and 30 percent of LDC trade with the Eastern European countries. Overall, the OECD estimates that the maximum volume is around $80 billion or some 5 percent of world exports.[16] Although this is not a large volume, it does seem to be increasing as the result of the attempts of developing countries to pay for international debts and needed oil imports, and conversely the need of the oil-producing countries to sell oil surpluses without directly driving down the

price on world markets. Thus, both the oil producers and
the non-oil developing countries are seeking to sell commodities at higher prices than they would gain on the world
markets, by exchanging them on a barter basis, so the *real*
terms of trade *may* be no better than on the market *but* the
certainty of trade at known prices is seen as greater.

There are other reasons for countertrade, including
mere market expansion. Even General Motors and Chrysler
reportedly accepted bauxite from Jamaica in exchange for
trucks and cars in 1982; the U.S. government also reportedly acquired bauxite for its strategic stockpile, exporting
powdered milk and butter oil to Jamaica. Pepsi Cola has
taken vodka from the U.S.S.R., which it sold at a profit. In
1984, Boeing reportedly sold aircraft to Pakistan, taking 20
percent of the value in local products, and McDonnell-
Douglas sold aircraft to China, promising to promote tourism as part of the exchange. According to a U.S. government
report, the single most important product grouping involved in countertrade during 1980–81 was "aerospace
products."[17]

The closing of foreign markets through exchange controls and import restrictions have induced capital equipment exporters in the advanced countries, particularly, to
seek to hold those markets by accepting commodities in exchange. The initiative, therefore, is not always on the side
of the developing country or one with low foreign-exchange
reserves.

An immediate question arises—if the recipient of the
goods can dispose of them on the international market,
why cannot the producing country do so and use the exchange to purchase the imports it wants? The answers are
found in the lack of information on the part of the exporting
country, in the absence of a distribution network, and in
the unfamiliarity of purchasers in third countries with that
particular source of supply. Many importers around the
world want to know personally those from whom they are
buying and to rely on them to assess quality and service-
ability of products. Known intermediate agents or distributors are important in establishing networks for countertrade.

Some countries—such as Japan, the Netherlands, Britain, and West Germany—have sizable trading companies

that are the intermediaries for exports and imports around the world. They may produce nothing themselves but simply handle transactions for others. Their advantage is that of having the network of information and the contacts which permit ready disposal of goods in many directions. They are also able to undertake trilateral and multilateral deals through currencies that are otherwise somewhat restricted. The United States has encouraged the formation of such companies, but only a few were established and they are without all the necessary abilities that Japanese trading companies have. Two strong efforts—Sears and Citibank—failed. If the United States is to enter this arena, it probably will require government assistance to catch up.

These bilateral deals are deemed necessary or desirable in order to redress what at least one party considers to be an unacceptable distribution of the gains from trade. Trade theory indicates that the larger gain from an exchange in international trade goes to the country having greater specialization, key resources, demand patterns that give it an advantage, a more advanced economy (having gone further along the learning curve and therefore having lower costs), stronger currency, fewer competitors, an advantageous distribution of factors of production, or an early start in a particular industry. There is nothing in free-market determination of trade that indicates that the gains from the exchange are equally or even equitably distributed. Therefore, in mercantilist fashion, each country is seeking to push the exchange in its own favor. And under countertrade, the importing country is seeking to exchange items that it otherwise would not be able to export under the given market conditions (including its own ignorance of market opportunities).

Even if information were made more readily available and it could be appropriately interpreted throughout each country, the question of equity in the distribution of gains would still remain. There is nothing in market exchanges that automatically provides for an equitable division of benefits. And even if such a balance could be achieved in real terms (based on comparative advantage, productivity, scale of production, technology, factor cost, etc.), a disruption in the balance of gains could still occur through shifts in exchange rates on world markets, unrelated to any given transaction between any two countries. Shifts in exchange rates alter the list of goods in which a country has a comparative advantage and alter the demand for specific commodities, redirecting the gains. Bilateral deals can protect against such adverse shifts, by being insulated from shifts in demand or exchange rates; thus, they can provide certainty if not greater equity.

Therefore, countertrade is used to obtain two of the "criteria of acceptability" noted in Chapter 1—equity and stability. Progress is also gained, though probably not in the most efficient manner. Even if markets were perfect, countries would not likely be satisfied with the results, since all want to impose "socially-acceptable" (equity) criteria on market-determined results. To date, *there is no economic or other theory that reconciles the market mechanism with what is considered socially acceptable.* And it will be difficult to form an acceptable theory since both efficiency (effectiveness) and equity are non-quantifiable in socio/economic/political terms. Until such a reconciliation exists, tension will exist between the two goals of efficiency and equity.[18] And increasing attention has been paid over the past several decades to equity, arising from the fact that governments are asked to take more responsibility for the welfare and development of national economies. No government takes a position that would sacrifice the interest of the nation, even in a relative sense. Such sacrifices are acceptable only when a larger community of interest exists such that mutually offsetting sacrifices are anticipated, even though not quantified, and are seen as balanced over the long-run. If bilateral mechanisms constraining trade and investment are to be avoided, ways must be found of achieving both equity and efficiency in the same system, plus the desired stability and acceptable participation of nations to begin to build a world community.

NOTES TO CHAPTER 16

1. For the distinctions and differences in countries' policies, see Robert E. Driscoll and Jack N. Behrman (eds.), *National Industrial Policies* (Cambridge, MA: Oelgeschlager, Gunn and Hain, 1984).

2. The concept of mobile industries was earlier presented during 1972 in discussion between business, academic, and government officials who were considering the feasibility of creating an "International Industri-

alization Institute." The group was concerned with the shifting patterns of industries internationally and how this might be guided in the most effective manner to maintain world economic growth. (See National Academy of Science and National Academy of Engineering, *Meeting the Challenge of Industrialization*, Washington, DC, 1973.)

3. See, for example, Robert Reich and Ira Magaziner, *Minding America's Business* (New York: Harcourt, Brace and Jovanovich, 1982); also F. Gerard Adams and Lawrence R. Klein, *Industrial Policies for Growth and Competitiveness: An Economic Perspective* (Lexington, MA: Lexington Books, 1984).

4. President's Export Council, *Industrial Targeting* (Washington, DC: Dept. of Commerce, Dec. 1984).

5. Some proposals along cooperative lines for Europe and other regions are provided in Jack N. Behrman, *Industrial Policies: International Restructuring and Transnationals* (Lexington, MA: Lexington Books, 1984); see also William Diebold, Jr., *Industrial Policies as an International Issue* (New York: McGraw-Hill, 1980).

6. See J. N. Behrman, *Multinational Production Consortia: Lessons from NATO Experience* (Washington, DC: Dept. of State, Office of External Research, August 1971).

7. *Loc. cit.*

8. Assembly of the Western European Union, "Joint Production of Armaments," Recommendation 108 (June 24, 1964), p. 3.

9. Arnold Kramish, "Atlantic Technological Imbalance: An American Perspective," *Defense Technology and the Western Alliance*, no. 4 (Aug. 1967), p. 11.

10. A comprehensive study of post-World War II clearing agreements was made by Raymond F. Mikesell and Jack N. Behrman, *Financing Free World Trade with the Soviet Bloc* (Princeton: Princeton University International Finance Section, study no. 5, 1960).

11. There are multiple types of agreements, varying by provisions and duration; virtually every agreement is unique. (See, Group of Thirty, *Counter-trade in the World Economy*, New York, 1985.)

12. See the OECD study on *Countertrade: Developing Country Practices* (Paris, 1985), and that by the Group of Thirty, *op. cit.*

13. This is the position taken by Rolf Mirus and Bernard Young in "Economic Incentives for Counter-trade," *Journal of International Business Studies* (Fall 1986), pp. 27–39.

14. See K. W. Elderkin, and W. E. Norquist, *Creative Countertrade* (Cambridge, MA: Ballinger, 1987); also, Stephen S. Cohen and John Zysman, "Countertrade, Offsets, Barter, and Buybacks," *California Management Review* (Winter 1986), pp. 41–56.

15. International Economic Studies Institute, *Raw materials and Foreign Policy* (Washington, DC, 1976), p. 29.

16. OECD, *Countertrade*, p. 12.

17. U.S. International Trade Commission, *Assessment of the Effects of Barter and Countertrade Transactions on U.S. Industries* (Washington, DC: USITC Publication 1766, Oct. 1985), p. xiii.

18. A strong move in this direction is made in Amitai Etzione, *The Moral Dimension: Toward a New Economics* (New York: The Free Press, 1988). For a more traditional economist's view of the matter, see Arthur Okun, *Equity and Efficiency: The Big Tradeoff*, (Washington, DC: Brookings Institution, 1975).

CHAPTER 17

Leadership in the World Community

There have been numerous calls for new leadership in the world economy for the purpose of achieving a closer community of interest among the nations, particularly among those that are more wealthy and powerful. Some of the recommendations have called for a revision of the GATT, an expansion of the World Bank, a return to the Bretton Woods Agreements, a return to the gold standard, acceptance of free trade around the world, the removal of specific barriers, the construction of a network of bilateral agreements, and in late 1987, U.S. Secretary of Treasury Baker suggested the formation of a monetary standard based on a package of commodities including gold—an idea that has been in the literature for over 50 years and known as a "Commodity Reserve Currency."[1] None of these have seemed to satisfy the criteria of acceptability that governments require of major new proposals for closer interdependence (discussed in Chapter 1).

NEED FOR NEW INITIATIVES

Most of these calls for new initiatives are vapid: they suggest no way in which initiatives would be taken and they offer no specifics on how they would meet the multiple criteria of acceptability. Nor do the proposals address the obstacles faced in applying new techniques or creating new institutions. Further, they are not in line with the sweep of economic history, which is toward more integration of economic units into larger communities of interest. Yet, the world is not ready for global unification. The world has progressively integrated into larger groups: from the nuclear family to the tribe and tribal nation, to the city and the city-state, to the nation-state and to several regional associations. The attempts after World War I to jump the step of regionalism into international cooperation through the

401

League of Nations (mainly countries of Europe and North America) and after World War II to jump to global cooperation through the United Nations have proved to be inadequate. The underlying community of interest necessary for success was not established first. The calls for world federalism and for the demise of the nation-state were too early and were not moves that strengthened community ties, since the nation-state would be weakened. All sound moves toward larger communities of interest have occurred through the formation of new central entities that would carry out the communal activities and trade-offs *with* the participation of the lower governmental units. It is impossible to move from the individual or subnational units directly to world federalism. The nation-state must be used as a building block. Indeed, the combining of nation-states through regional associations and the institutionalization of economic relations therein is probably a prerequisite to the formation of a world community of interest. It is necessary to learn first *how* to accommodate national interests in a more cooperative setting.

At the same time, more and more ties are being formed through the opening of the world economy, as described earlier. The formation of a strong intermediate step of the establishment of *regional* communities is needed next. And this step requires leadership from new sources around the world with a better understanding of the means of using the resources available for different kinds of development. A key technique in meshing regional economies and beginning to open them to worldwide free trade is the *sectoral* (or "free-trade corridor") arrangement.[2]

The formation of a wider community of interests requires leadership to make the trade-offs and adjustments required in the changed relationships that will emerge.[3] During the Pax Britannica of the nineteenth century, Britain performed the role of the hub country with the British Commonwealth being the association of nations which was large and stable enough to absorb the shocks of changes in the world economy. Given its wealth and power, Britain was able to maintain a relatively peaceful world for nearly a hundred years. The duration was intimately tied to the fact that the spread of technology and industrialization was slow enough not to give rise to serious alternative claimants for the leadership role. The Pax Americana, of the mid-twentieth century, was based essentially on the strengthening of the United States as a result of the two world wars. The United States became a large net creditor nation from 1920 through 1980, but trade deficits increased rapidly from 1970 to 1990, running the United States into a net debtor position by the mid-1980s. By 1970, the United States had already shifted from a position of economic dominance to one of *relative* decline in the world economy, exacerbated by large federal budget deficits and low rates of saving.

During the Pax Americana, the United States fostered the freeing of trade under the Reciprocal Trade Agreements Acts and the GATT. Under the Bretton Woods Agreements, the World Bank, the IMF, and the GATT formed the basis for a more open world economy—at least for the so-called "free-world." The decline of U.S. leadership began with the heavy costs of the Vietnam War and of the "Great Society," fostered by President Johnson. Since the U.S. government was unwilling to raise taxes to support both of these endeavors, inflation rose at home and an excess of dollars flowed into the world, which led eventually to the removal of the dollar from its link to gold and its devaluation. The United States relinquished its hegemonic role by failing to keep its economy strong; it actually asked other nations to "take over" the burdens of economic leadership. Consequently, the 1970s and 1980s were decades of uncertainty as to leadership in the world economy, with no other country coming to the fore. A primary question at the end of the 1980s was where world leadership would come from.

The United States continued to urge a return to the Bretton Woods Agreements, but these were unacceptable to the rest of the world, as well to the United States in practice, though not in principle. The relative rise of European countries and those in the Far East, including Japan and the "Four Tigers," meant that the world economy was more important than any single national economy in determining the changes in national growth rates or the patterns of trade and investment.

After World War II, the United States stood as the only major country not devastated by the war, with its capital assets and its personnel largely intact and in a position to assert industrial leadership. Significant portions of the male populations of Britain, France, Germany, the Soviet Union, and Japan were lost in the war. Japan and Germany showed the most rapid development of post-war leadership. Each country required construction of a new, modern capital base and appeared to call forth the better qualities of the people, who in each case had a culture infused with a "work ethic." Since 1960, the quality of leadership in France, Britain, and the United States has not been stellar, with few top officials recognizing the changes that were forming a new world economy and altering the relative positions of major countries.

In the immediate postwar period, the United States produced nearly 50 percent of world GNP (combining U.S. domestic production and its ownership of production overseas), and the trends then indicated that it would produce 60–70 percent by the year 1990. Obviously, this did not occur. On the contrary, its assistance to the rest of the world and other countries' own determination brought higher rates of growth elsewhere, causing a *relative* decline in U.S. GNP to less than 30 percent of the world's GNP in 1980, with a projected drop to around 15 percent by the year 2000. The United States will remain the largest country, but it will be challenged by the positions of Europe, Japan, and only later by the U.S.S.R. and China.

Rather than a bipolar world, a multipolar world now exists, with the United States merely "first among equals." This position does not give it a right (nor is it expected) to dictate the rules of the international game. In the absence of the Bretton Woods system, the world has been seeking a new set of rules—and a new ordering principle. The difficulty of establishing them rests, as discussed earlier, in the complexity of the criteria of acceptability and the absence of any theoretical construct to explain how to make the trade-offs among these criteria. (As in political-risk analysis, several academic disciplines need to be drawn on to address the different criteria, and it is extremely difficult to bring them together in the formation of a single model or theoretical framework.)

With the international economy driving the various national economies—meaning that each of the national econ omies adjusts to the world economy—the trend is toward greater interdependence among nations despite the fact that they seek to maintain a high degree of independence. The pull of technology, markets, and TNC strategies is toward integration, while the pull of governments is in the opposite direction. National governments, therefore, are taking an inappropriate stance, expressed virtually everywhere in neomercantilism.

Contrarily, what is needed is a policy for carrying the inevitable integration in directions and modes that are more acceptable. This requires moves to the formation of a world community of interest that permits trade-offs and adjustments to be more readily made. To achieve such a community requires a set of strategies at the corporate and governmental levels aimed at establishing the necessary framework and achieving the criteria of acceptability. This is not being done, and it appears that the ability (or will) to do so is low—as seen in the absence of leadership, the predominance of neomercantilism, and the repeated disputes over the distribution of benefits.

The fundamental and unrecognized problem in international economic relations is that of the distribution of benefits.[4] This is a problem not just in economics but in the political arena as well, and it is not resolved simply by putting economic decisions into markets. In fact, it has been the lack of acceptance of the distribution of benefits through market decisions that has caused interferences in markets by TNCs, by governments, by labor unions, and by other groups.

The world economy is therefore in a period of turbulence and uncertainty which offers opportunities for building new institutions. The groundwork is being laid for new initiatives simply by the destruction of old relationships, including the dominance of the U.S. economy. It is likely that some significant shifts will occur that will facilitate formation of the needed community of interest and the institutions that it will require. What is needed is some forethought to what would be the most appropriate system and what strategic decisions are necessary to get there?

One of the givens in the formation of such strategies is that the nation-state should be the building block for the next stage of international cooperation, and a second is that we should not skip the stage of regionalism. Rather, it should be used in the more ready formation of communities of interest, so that the trade-offs are not so difficult. If we do not move to regional cooperation, the alternatives are bilateral cooperation or worldwide cooperation. The latter is exceedingly difficult, given the complex criteria of acceptability of new arrangements; and bilateralism is too short-term and limited in scope to be a basis for the structure desired for the longer term. National industrial policies also are inadequate because they lead only to greater protection, where transnational coordination is necessary. Such coordination is required to prevent industrial policies from becoming protectionist, but the proposed agreements must focus on the issues of sectoral development and look toward opening key sectors to membership wider than merely regional. Greater coordination will arise when a larger community of interests exists (as in the NATO experience), such that mutually offsetting sacrifices are anticipated (even though not quantified precisely) and are seen as balanced over a given long-run period. If bilateral mechanisms constraining trade and investment are to be avoided, ways must be found of achieving both equity and efficiency in the same system, plus the desired stability and acceptable participation of nations to begin to build a one-world community.

STRUCTURED INVESTMENT AND FREE TRADE

To set a new direction for the role of TNCs in the world economy—one that is acceptable to governments and therefore meets the seven criteria of acceptability discussed in Chapter 1—three stages must be achieved; they are the same for any substantial social change: the recognition that the present situation is unacceptable, presentation of a vision for improvement, and an understanding of the ways in which the vision may be accomplished. Dissatisfaction with the existing situation must be so great that society is willing to make substantial efforts (even sacrifices) to achieve a better situation. This is precisely what happened after the "Cultural Revolution" in China; the situation was so bad that virtually everyone realized that substantial changes were necessary. Mikhail Gorbachev in the U.S.S.R. did not have such a critical signal, but he is betting that the people are sufficiently dissatisfied to be willing to make substantial changes. There is, however, a question as to whether or not this is the case; the Soviet people may be able to suffer the present economic stress *without* making substantive changes.

In the present condition of the world economy, there is sufficient wealth so that those having it do not seek radical change, or even reform, accepting only marginal improvements—mostly toward enhancing their share of the benefits. There is insufficient recognition that the continued disagreements over the distribution of benefits prevents higher levels of efficiency and more progress for all. There are solutions available that would radically improve the welfare of the world both materially and psychologically, but they would require significant changes in behavior. The changes in the U.S. role seen in its loss of hegemony and international competitiveness should have made it willing to make substantial adjustments, but the presidential campaign and election of 1988 indicated that this was not yet the case.

One of the measures of dissatisfaction is a comparison between what exists and what is feasible in an improved future. Not to see what could be done through more cooperative approaches within the world economy is not to have a basis for comparison between the present and a potential future condition. Therefore, the enunciation of a vision is itself a means of focusing dissatisfaction with the present situation. The emergence of increased industrial, technological, financial, and even cultural integration in the world economy is binding nations more closely together—despite the fact that they are psychologically (and even intellectually) unprepared. From developments in many aspects of life, there is evidence that the new vision must be one involving closer cooperation, unification of attitudes, and harmonization of principles of conduct, law, and order. Pressures from the environment; the wasting of resources; the existence of poverty, hunger and disease; changes in technology; the shift from a bipolar to a multipolar world; and so on, point to a new paradigm of greater communitarian approaches instead of the conflict-competitive ones of the past.[5]

This vision does not fit with the main thrust of U.S. society, which remains adversarial between business and government and competitive in the private sector. A number of groups and networks have adopted a more communitarian approach and increased their questioning of the value of competition in society.[6] Even within companies, there is a move toward greater participation in management and in decision making on the shop floor. Some efforts are being made to balance competition with greater cooperation.

In the world economy, the development of strategic alliances and complex linkages is leading to more cooperative ties among companies, both private and public. Governments have forced some of these cooperative arrangements through a number of "performance requirements" and through negotiations on investment and trade patterns. Underlying economic pressures to form cooperative arrangements also arise from the complexity of developments in science and technology, the shifting comparative advantages that leave specialization to occur at the margin rather than among whole sectors of economic activities, plus an integration of markets, through the reduction of barriers to trade and FDI and the globalization of financial markets. The interest in increased standards of living and national welfare is encouraging economic integration (through TNC activities and new technologies) at a time when governments are also seeking to enhance the benefits for their own countries, therefore altering the processes of investment and production as well as the flow of trade. A new vision is needed of how to meld efficiency and equity to the benefit of all players—particularly the TNCs and governments. This vision is difficult to arrive at without an understanding of *how* it might be achieved.

The mechanism for achieving such a vision is the TNCs themselves. The TNC is able to meld within its own operations the criteria of both equity and efficiency since it is located in many countries and is able to move the site of production, the utilization of technology, and the pursuit of R&D activities among different countries. It thereby alters comparative advantages in production and trade. Realization of this fact by governments has led to their guiding the TNCs in more desirable directions. The TNC is able sometimes to respond to these incentives and disincentives without serious damage to its own objectives, but more often the most efficient strategy is altered. The complex affiliations through strategic alliances of TNCs is a response to the government initiative and the underlying economic changes. In the process, the TNCs have accelerated the growth of and altered the comparative advantages in a number of countries—within Europe, in the Southeast Asian nations, as well as Japan. They can be encouraged to continue to do so. Any new mechanism for utilizing the capability of the TNCs should seek to avoid damage to their efficiency in production but should move toward a more equitable distribution of benefits. This requires that a high level of competition remain in the production and physical distribution of goods and services into various markets, with more attention to the equitable distribution of the location of economic activities and the benefits from specialization.

At present, the strategies of TNCs are altered by each individual government insisting on the location of certain production within its borders—plus the utilization of high technology, the export of final products, or support of depressed areas as the price of being permitted to serve the domestic market in the country or obtaining access to certain factors of production (viz., natural resources, labor, capital, or technology) through the bargaining process. Each government then enters into bilateral negotiations with the TNC, which must consider trade-offs among the several bilateral arrangements in an attempt to form a more global international strategy out of the multi-bilateral bargains. Bargaining theory is of particular use in determining how the bargain should be reached. It is a technique that can be honed more or less well through experience and learning. But it is less the process and more the content of the negotiations that is important in meeting the criteria of acceptability of any new arrangement. And the TNC can be brought through a new negotiating orientation on the part of governments to meet most of these criteria.

The fundamental change that is required is that governments recognize that nationalistic policies are reducing the efficiency of the TNCs and their networks by interfering in location decisions and activities in serving the world's markets. At present, in order to achieve *equity* (i.e., to gain *more* of the benefits), they are reducing *efficiency*. The reduction of efficiency is occurring mostly in the intervention in the patterns of trade but also in affecting the location of production sites and various activities associated with production. The most efficient combination of production sites is not permitted the TNCs, despite the fact that it is able to separate specific phases of production without losing efficiency—since the division of labor is now quite readily achieved at the margin of production processes and within and among components rather than between major sectors. What is now feasible is to move away from merely *national* negotiations with TNCs to international (or regional) cooperative negotiations among participating governments, so as to enhance both efficiency and equity.

Present *national* industrial policies are protectionist and reduce the efficiency of TNCs—particularly that of the efficiency-seeker and the network seeker, including transactions among them and with the resource and market seekers. No agreement can be achieved by these policies on an equitable distribution of benefits among nations.

If governments could begin to see the TNCs as entities whose characteristics and abilities could be used for the purposes of meeting the seven criteria of acceptability, new integrative mechanisms could be put in place. The mechanism that is available essentially is a move to international or regional industrial policies. These policies would be aimed at achieving an equitable location of economic activities among the members with a freeing of trade thereafter. The objective would be to structure investment and production locations so as to achieve an equitable distribution of employment, technology applications, and abilities to export and then to let the TNCs pursue their competitive roles to achieve maximum efficiency in trade.

Given the abilities of TNCs to divide production stages and to locate production of components in different sites, a structured arrangement of investment would not necessarily harm economies of scale in the production process. In fact, TNCs are already designing products so that they can be readily produced in different stages among different locations, as is demanded by governments or is induced by economic and competitive factors. What is sought in a new mechanism is the agreement among participating countries that the basic benefits of economic growth are to be distributed equitably and that the markets will be free from interferences—leading to free trade. A concerted set of policies aimed at "structured investment with free trade" would result.

Joint action among countries has been undertaken at the sectoral or project level by NATO, by Airbus Industrie, and various other consortia to establish an agreed pattern of production and trade. To achieve equity, any region could, in principle, establish a scheme for allocating production to its member countries under a complementation agreement. But it would have to involve both governments and TNCs, avoiding the errors of the Andean Pact, ALADI, and ASEAN (as discussed in Chapter 12). Intraregional agreements are feasible, to permit integration ("complementation") among company affiliates in the region. But, since the goal of efficiency requires competition, it would be better to maintain several competitive sources of supply and help open both entry and exit for different companies within the agreed sector.

Such regional agreements would function much as the U.S./Canada Automotive Agreement. This arrangement permitted TNCs to offer patterns of investment and production location between the two countries for governmental approval and left trade in automotive vehicles and parts between the two countries free of barriers. Both efficiency and acceptable benefits were obtained. This bilateral accord has provided a basis for "rationalized" production of automotive products between the two nations for over 20 years, with free trade in the sector. Rather than assigning specific products to one or another of the countries, the agreement calls for a review of the impacts on the balance in trade of total automotive vehicles and parts, with production to be adjusted by the companies in ways they deem best.

Future sectoral agreements would set the broad guidelines for investment patterns and let companies make offers of how it would satisfy the guidelines so as to be permitted freedom of trade between the countries or regions. Such an agreement at the level of the OECD or the United Nations is

far less likely, given the number of countries that would insist on participating, given their differing levels of development (and different policy goals), and given the lack of a
sufficient community of interest among members of the
OECD or UN. However, since production is the key to economic development, attempts at multilateral agreement to
redistribute the costs and benefits of TNC production will
undoubtedly continue; they can be successful initially only
on a bilateral or regional basis.

The complexity of the agreement necessary to achieve
application of this vision is such that it would probably be
reserved for a limited number of companies in any given
agreement. Thus, it should be started on a regional basis
and focus on a few industrial sectors. More than one sector
would be desirable so as to permit trade-offs among the
member countries and among the different sectors so that
none felt it was left out in the process of industrial advance.

The mechanism proposed builds on the moves toward
coproduction and countertrade in that it emphasizes the
importance of *investment* in coproduction and attempts
to remove the pressures that have lead to interferences
in trade (e.g., countertrade). Rather than adopting "managed trade," which is inherently inefficient, the move is toward restructuring of investment in a cooperative fashion;
this can be done readily without inefficiencies because of
the networking abilities of TNCs. The mechanism would
create dynamic comparative advantages (giving nations new
opportunities) rather than managing trade out of static
comparative advantages, which are seen as inequitable or
unacceptable.

In order to achieve an agreement on a complex coproduction arrangement, experience indicates that about 15 is
a maximum for the number of countries involved. An agreement involving 14 countries was successful under NATO. To
implement such an arrangement, a group of countries (preferably within an established regional association) would
ask a number of TNCs to propose individually a structure of
production that each would like to have in the region showing the use of local suppliers among the member countries
and the expected patterns of production and trade.[7] The

member governments would assess the various proposals—just as in the U.S./Canada Auto Agreement—requesting some adjustments for equity. Upon approval, governments would step aside and let the various TNCs compete freely without interference. Governments would still be responsible to maintain a competitive structure in the markets—that is, to prevent cartels or anticompetitive agreements. A later need on the part of any TNC to close a particular plant, to alter significantly the level of production, or to change the product line would simply be signaled to the governments involved. If desired, negotiations would then occur as to what activities would be substituted and what "compensation" would occur among the members through new investment or trade adjustments—just as compensation is required for changes in tariff negotiations through the escape-clause provision.

It has been objected that such arrangements would be too difficult to negotiate. This objection is hardly valid given the extensive (and often fruitless) negotiations required in tariff reductions, monetary affairs, international debt settlements, energy policy, population control, and so on. The objective of more efficient and equitable production among the participating countries is so valuable that it would be well worth the difficulties of negotiations. In any case, similar negotiations have already taken place among the NATO countries and within the European Community. One of the difficulties within the European Community (and an obstacle that broke several of the other regional complementation arrangements) was the inability to find a way of balancing interests in the location of the particular industrial activities as well as agriculture. The continuation of subsidies to agriculture is a reflection of an unwillingness to adjust the location and *structure* of agricultural investment so as to make it more equitable among a larger community. The world is paying a heavy price for attempts at internal equity within a nation and for fears of dependence internationally—especially in the agricultural sector. This can be changed once it is recognized that the cost is reducible by equitable means. It is to be hoped that the desire to retain specific industrial sectors does not lead to high levels of subsidization before we accept more rational approaches.

SOURCES OF LEADERSHIP

Can we find leadership toward regional and sectoral arrangements from any country at present? The United States has adopted free-market principles that are unacceptable to major countries; it may not now be able to reframe them. Given the strength of Japan, is it possible for that country to assume leadership? Japan is itself mercantilistic, imbued with national goals that are more economic than social or political, and it appears to have no desire to lead the world. Although it recognizes the need to become internationally responsible, it is uncomfortable with this role. Contrarily, its primary and overriding objective remains to make the world safe for Japan. It faces the difficult issue of the distribution of the benefits of growth domestically and internationally, while being drawn into an increasingly interdependent and more competitive world, for which it is not wholly prepared. It lacks an internal leadership sufficiently attuned to the international obligations that are required of major countries; it has little concept of international sharing, though it is responding to urgings by other nations to aid LDCs. In addition, Japan faces significant economic needs domestically (particularly infrastructure and welfare to raise the standard of living), and it is being pushed by the United States and Europe to accelerate its domestic growth (as distinct from its export growth) to help increase its imports. But, given its historical isolation, Japan has not yet learned how to extend its cultural concept of obligation among Japanese also to the international community. Thus, it is not likely that Japan can soon step into a role of world leadership.

Even in the absence of economic dominance, the United States has some characteristics that could cause other countries to accept its leadership *if* offered in ways that are mutually advantageous. The United States is the most open economy of the world, with factors of production more mobile than others and with fewer regulations on foreign investment or trade. Its market is highly consumer-oriented and continues to grow. However, its assertion of leadership is hampered by the continuation of an adversarial relationship between business and government, and by too-close ties among economic/political/ military objectives and policies that mix these in ways not acceptable to other countries. It retains a high orientation to its own national interest while extending humanitarian and other aid to foreign countries. There is an underlying isolationism in the country (a preference to be "left alone" by the world), with a heavy moralistic and legalistic orientation to relationships with others/nations.

While it is important to have value-based policies, the morals espoused by the United States for others are not always adhered to by the U.S. government or people. On the matter of law, the United States has become highly technical and unyielding, while most of the world will accept a slippage in the interpretation of legal documents and agreements to accommodate changed circumstances or achieve equity (justice with mercy), compared to justice by technical compliance. These elements of U.S. rigidity make others wonder about the realism of U.S. leadership. In addition, U.S. leaders have not shown a high degree of understanding of the world's problems and the effects of the decline in U.S. hegemony. The United States faces a much higher degree of international interdependence than in the past, but it still flirts with protectionism in times of economic pressure, rather than seeking new initiatives in the pursuit of a more integrated world economy.

It can be noted, however, that the United States historically has proven to be the most flexible of nations in the twentieth century, rebounding from war, depression, and lesser setbacks with remarkable resilience. It was the United States that put billions of dollars into the reconstruction of Europe after World War II helping to move those countries into a regional community. It was the United States, along with Canada, that took initiatives toward a regional agreement in automobiles and parts (1965), and a larger free-trade agreement (1988)—and that continues to pursue linkages with Mexico on a sectoral basis. Further, the United States is pragmatically changing its practices, while continuing to adhere to its one-world, free-trade principles. It is this resiliency that makes the United States home to the plurality of TNCs that exist today and an attractive host country to virtually all of the others. It is conceivable, though very far from assured, that the United States could define and pursue an acceptable leadership position toward the objectives of regional and sectoral integration, using TNCs as the key vehicle. The beginnings could lie in the discussions of "industrial strategy," but much revision of perceptions of the world economy and the U.S. role therein will be required before the United States can come forward with a more acceptable program of international economic integration.

If one looks around the world for the sources of leadership, the search produces little. Britain is not in a position to assume the role; France finds it difficult to identify consistent leadership within its own country—as does Italy; Germany refuses to step forward in assuming burdens of the world economy, having enough on its shoulders to carry some of the adjustments to the reunification of Germany and within Europe itself. Europe must first achieve its own integration and identity before it can lead in world affairs. Perhaps the increasing unification of Europe in 1992 will enable and induce it to take a larger share of world leadership, but to do so it must avoid turning inward.

There is no significant economic leadership coming out of Eastern Europe, except their search for closer ties to the West. And the Soviet bloc is no longer a model for economic or political development elsewhere in the world. The Latin American region remains fractured in reality despite formal integration agreements. India is unable to rule itself. South Africa, at one end of the African continent, and the Middle East at the other remain in turbulence and instability. None of the East Asian countries are large enough to provide leadership, though South Korea may well develop into a model for the merging of Eastern culture and Western science. This is the basic marriage which is occurring around the world—the Western countries adopting more of the Confucian and Buddhist orientations to personal and social obligation, while the Eastern are seeking economic progress without succumbing to gross materialism.

Economic ideologies have also lost their attraction, with fascism in disrepute, socialism essentially a failure everywhere, communism merely a dream, and capitalism so radically changed by its adherents that it no longer should bear the name. On the one hand, American capitalism is seen by some critics as heavily welfare oriented (socialistic); by others, it is seen as significantly regulated by the government (fascistic). Its underlying value of individual responsibility has been so attenuated as to alter significantly the rights and obligations within the system, making it attractive mainly to those who seek mere economic (material) growth for its own sake.

There do not appear to be persons on the horizon who show the characteristics of leadership needed in the present phase; rather, events appear to rule, with governments and TNCs reacting only to pressures that eventually require a response. This is not necessarily bad, since we seem to learn only by facing extreme situations. But it does mean that bad or undesirable situations must become intolerable before we will act to correct them. Therefore, a decline into "unbearable" conditions is a cause for optimism. Mankind is not *supposed* to be so irrational and is *supposed* to be able to "think ahead" and reduce the impacts of adversity or impending dangers. But we hardly act so intelligently. (A new concept is arising, however, within the quality circles in Japanese companies—that of "activities to foresee dangers." It is potentially more important in a rapidly changing world than "just-in-time" inventory control.)

The TNCs themselves are a potential source of leadership, but presently they function mainly at the pragmatic level—that is, they are most able to discover and apply "what works" in achieving market efficiency and economic growth. They are presently unlikely to carry into their decision making any other values than the pragmatic one of efficiency. Regardless of whether they should be permitted to restrict their attention to such a single value, they have done so principally in the past. If the TNC is to step into a leadership role, it must evidence an understanding of the other criteria of acceptability that lead to greater equity within and among countries, greater participation of all involved, greater opportunities for creativity, greater stability, appropriate autonomy, and an acceptable protection of the environment. Without evidence of understanding and pursuit of these criteria, legitimacy for the TNC in exercising its power and influence will be withheld or reduced. To lead, they must demonstrate that they have fully in mind the interests and concerns of those who follow and are able to achieve mutual goals in appropriate ways.

Unfortunately, managers are not necessarily educated to be leaders, nor do their career paths necessarily produce such leaders. To move from the role of manager to that of leader requires an understanding not only of the situation, which is difficult enough (as illustrated by prior chapters), but also of other peoples and countries and their goals, and of themselves (meaning one's abilities, limitations, and purposes). Leadership requires an identification of high purpose, to which others can become attached or identified and effectively used in its pursuit. George Bernard Shaw observed that "Happiness lies in being used in a cause which one recognizes as greater than one's self."

Leadership involves the communication of the cause and the effective use of followers. This can be done internationally only if there is adequate cross-cultural education of potential leaders, only if they accept the responsibility to address the concerns of society, and only if they are able to display a high level of individual discipline and commitment. That is, only if they show an ability to achieve self-regulation and actualization can they show the way to others. TNCs in general have not yet produced or achieved this level of leadership, and any attempt at present to assert it collectively would be suspect. Yet, some few concerned managers of TNCs are visible; those who can should step forth as leaders.

Consequently, we face a period of development and preparation, which will inevitably be unstable and somewhat turbulent. Our leaders must identify high purposes and pursue them in order to prevent the overall situation from deteriorating into broader alienation and terrorism. The period is one in which competition will remain and may even be intensified among countries and companies, but it also should be one in which international collaboration is extended along avenues not yet traveled.

During this period of turbulence, we will need to arrive at a new vision of relationships among companies, among governments, and between TNCs and governments. This new set of concepts must be buttressed by new relationships between management and labor that expand the participation of both in a cooperative fashion, between management and the communities in which they operate, between management and government, among companies within industrial sectors, and among the leadership of TNCs—all must recognize a high level of interdependence in a more integrated world economy. Each of these relationships will need to be balanced in ways that do not leave either party in a position that is unsatisfactory over the longer term. Minority positions in the short term must be acceptable, simply because trade-offs are required in specific situations. But dominance of one group over the other for any lengthy time will not be acceptable.

If the managers of TNCs and government officials can grasp these concepts and mold their own strategies within them, they will have a better chance of assuming leadership roles at a time when both governments and firms appear to be floundering in the face of the world's problems.

The firms need the legitimacy to survive and grow, which comes from acceptability in government policy, while the governments need TNCs to promote economic development and facilitate even equity in distribution of benefits. Leadership requires an understanding of these issues and an awareness of how best to negotiate mutually acceptable goals, achievable through appropriate participation.

NOTES TO CHAPTER 17

1. Benjamin Graham, *Storage and Stability* (New York: McGraw-Hill, 1937). Frank D. Graham, *Social Goals and Economic Institutions* (Princeton: Princeton U. Press, 1942), chap. 5.

2. Why and how the U.S. government or TNCs should take the initiative on regional association and sectional agreements is argued in J. N. Behrman, *The Rise of the Phoenix: The US Role in a Restructured World Economy* (Boulder, CO: Westview Press, 1987).

3. A call for "new leadership" also comes from Japan, see Takatoshi Ito, "A Layman's Guide to Understanding Japan," *The International Economy* (Mar./Apr., 1988), pp. 40–43.

4. This issue is at the base of the questioning of free trade by John M. Culbertson, "The Folly of Free Trade," *Harvard Business Review* (Sept.-Oct. 1986), pp. 122–8.

5. George Lodge and Ezra Vogel argue that the countries with a more communitarian orientation have been the ones that have been more internationally competitive, compared to those that have maintained a conflict-competitive orientation in their social-economic systems. See *Ideology and National Competitiveness* (Boston: Harvard Business School, 1987).

6. See the descriptions of over 100 communitarian groups in C. McLaughlin, and G. Davidson, *Builders of the Dawn* (Walpole, NH: Stillpoint, 1985). Over 400 such groups are described by Jessica Lepnack and Jeffrey Stamps, *Networking* (Garden City, NY: Doubleday & Co., 1982).

7. How these agreements might be arranged among and between specific regions is further developed in J. N. Behrman, *Industrial Policies: International Restructuring and Transnationals* (Lexington, MA: Lexington Books, 1984).

Selected Bibliography

Aganbegyan, A., and T. Timofeyev. *The New Stage of Perestroika.* Boulder, CO: Westview, 1988.

Baker, James C., John K. Ryans, Jr., and Donald G. Howard, eds. *International Business Classics.* Lexington, MA: Lexington Books, 1988.

Ballance, Robert H. *International Industry and Business: Structural Change, and Industrial Policy and Industry Strategies.* London: Allen and Unwin, 1987.

Behrman, Jack N. *National Interests and the Multinational Enterprise.* Englewood Cliffs, NJ: Prentice-Hall, 1970.

——. *U.S. International Business and Governments.* New York: McGraw-Hill, 1971.

——. *The Role of International Companies in Latin American Integration.* Lexington, MA: Lexington Books, 1972.

——. *Conflicting Constraints on the Multinational Enterprise: Potential for Resolution.* New York: Council of the Americas, 1974.

——. *Decision Criteria for Foreign Direct Investment in Latin America.* New York: Council of Americas, 1974.

——. *Toward a New International Economic Order.* Paris: Atlantic Institute for International Affairs. 1974.

——. *Industry Ties with Science and Technology Policies in Developing Countries.* Cambridge, MA: Oelgeschlager, Gunn and Hain, 1980.

——. *Industrial Policies: International Restructuring and Transnationals.* Lexington, MA: Lexington Books, 1984.

——. *The Rise of the Phoenix: The U.S. Role in a Restructured World Economy.* Boulder, CO: Westview Press, 1987.

——, J. J. Boddewyn, and A. Kapoor. *International Business-Government Communications.* Lexington, MA: Lexington Books, 1975.

——, and W. A. Fischer. *Overseas R&D Activities of Transnational Companies.* Cambridge, MA: Oelgeschlager, Gunn and Hain, 1980.

————, and W. A. Fischer. *Science and Technology for Development: Corporate and Government Policies and Practices.* Cambridge, MA: Oelgeschlager, Gunn and Hain, 1980.

Bergsten, C. Fred. *America in the World Economy: A Strategy for the 1990s.* Washington, D.C.: International Economics Institute, 1988.

————, Thomas Horst, and T. J. Moran. *American Multinationals and American Interests.* Washington: Brookings Institution, 1978.

Bertin, Gilles Y., *Multinationals and Industrial Property: The Control of the World's Technology.* Atlantic Highlands, NJ: Humanities Press International, 1988.

Bertsch, Gary K., ed. *Controlling East-West Trade and Technology Transfer: Power, Politics, and Policies.* Durham, NC: Duke University Press, 1988.

Blake, David H., ed. *The Multinational Corporation.* Philadelphia: American Academy of Political and Social Science, 1972.

Boarman, Patrick M., and Hans Schollhammer. *Multinational Corporations and Governments.* New York: Praeger, 1975.

Boddewyn, J. J., and A. Kapoor. *International Business-Government Relations.* New York: American Management Association, 1978.

Brown, C. C., ed. *World Business: Promise and Problems.* New York: Macmillan, 1970.

Centre on Transnational Corporations. *Transnational Corporations and Transborder Data Flows: Background and Overview.* Amsterdam: North-Holland, 1985.

————. *Transnational Corporations in World Development* (periodic surveys). New York: United Nations, 1983, 1988.

Coolidge, P., G. D. Spina, and D. Wallace, eds. *The OECD Guidelines for Multinational Enterprise: A Business Appraisal.* Washington, DC: Institute for International and Foreign Trade Law, 1977.

Colloques Internationaux. *La Croissance de la Grande Firme Multinationale [The Growth of the Large Multinational Corporation].* Paris: Editions du Centre National de la Recherche Scientifique, 1973.

Coombe, G. W., Jr. *Multilateral Codes of Conduct and Corporate Accountability.* New York: American Bar Association, 1980.

Debold, William, Jr. *Industrial Policy as an International Issue.* New York: McGraw-Hill, 1980.

Destler, I. M., and H. Satoh. *Coping with U.S.-Japanese Economic Conflicts.* Lexington, MA: Lexington Books, 1982.

Dicke, D. C. ed. *Foreign Investment in the Present and a New International Economic Order.* Boulder, CO: Westview, 1988.

Doz, Y. L. *Government Control and Multinational Strategic Management.* New York: Praeger, 1979.

Driscoll, R. E., and J. N. Behrman. *National Industrial Policies.* Cambridge, MA: Oelgeschlager, Gunn and Hain, 1984.

Dunning, John H., ed. *The Multinational Enterprise.* London: Allen and Unwin, 1971.

———. *Economic Analysis and the Multinational Enterprise.* London: Allen and Unwin, 1974.

———, and Mikoto Usiu, eds. *Structural Change, Economic Interdependence and World Development,* vol. IV. London: Macmillan, 1987.

Dymsza, William A. and Robert G. Vambery, eds. *International Business Knowledge: Managing International Functions in the 1990s,* New York: Praeger, 1987.

Ettinger, J. van. *The Need for Industrial Restructuring by Industrialized Countries.* New York: United Nations Development Program, 1980.

Fayerweather, J. *International Business-Government Affairs: Toward an Era of Accommodation.* Cambridge, MA: Ballinger, 1973.

———. *The Mercantile Bank Affair.* New York: NYU Press, 1974.

———. *International Business Policy and Administration: A Compendium.* New York: The International Executive, 1976.

———, and A. Kapoor, *Strategy and Negotiation for the International Corporation.* Cambridge, MA: Ballinger, 1976.

Feld, Warner J. *Nongovernmental Forces and World Politics: A Study of Business, Labor, and Political Groups.* New York: Praeger, 1972.

Franko, L. *European Industrial Policy: Past, Present, and Future.* Brussels: The Conference Board in Europe, European Research Report, February 1980.

———. *The European Multinationals.* Stamford, CT: Greylock, 1981.

Furino, Antonio, ed. *Cooperation and Competition in the Global Economy: Issues and Strategies.* Cambridge, MA: Ballinger, 1988.

Gadbaw, R. M. and T. J. Richards. *Intellectual Property Rights: Global Consensus, Global Conflict?* Boulder, CO: Westview, 1988.

Ghadar, F., S. J. Cobrin, and T. H. Moran, eds. *Managing International Political Risk: Strategies and Techniques,* Washington, DC: Ghadar and Associates, August 1983.

Giersch, H., ed. *Reshaping the World Economic Order.* Tübingen FRG: J. H. Mohr, 1976.

Gilpin, Robert. *The Multinational Corporation and the National Interest.* Washington, DC: U.S. Government Printing Office, 1973.

Gladwin, T. N., and Ingo Walters. *Multinationals Under Fire.* New York: John Wiley, 1980.

Glickman, Norman J., and Douglas P. Woodward. *The New Competitors: How Foreign Investors Are Changing the US Economy.* New York: Basic Books, 1989.

Goldberg, Walter H. *Governments and Multinationals.* Cambridge, MA: Oelgeschlager, Gunn and Hain, 1983.

Granstrand, O., and J. Sigurdson, eds. *Technological and Industrial Policy in China and Europe.* Lund, Sweden: Research Policy Institute, Occasional Report Series, no. 3., 1981.

Grosse, Robert P. *Foreign Investment Codes and the Location of Direct Investment.* New York: Praeger, 1980.

Grub, Phillip D., F. Ghadar, and D. Khambata, eds. *The Multinational Enterprise in Transition.* Princeton, NJ: Darwin Press, 1986.

Gunter, H. *ILO Research on Multinational Enterprises and Social Policy: An Overview.* Geneva: International Labor Office, 1982.

Guisinger, S., and Associates. *Investment Incentives and Performance Requirements.* New York: Praeger, 1985.

Haendel, Dan. *Foreign Investments and the Management of Political Risks.* Boulder, CO: Westview, 1979.

Haririan, M. *State-Owned Enterprises.* Boulder, CO: Westview, 1989.

Hieronymi, Otto, ed. *The New Economic Nationalism.* London: Macmillan, 1980.

Hoffman, K., and Rafael Kaplinsky. *Driving Force: The Global Restructuring of Technology, Labor, and Investment in the Automobile and Components Industries.* Boulder, CO: Westview, 1988.

Hood, N., and Stephen Young. *Multinationals in Retreat: The Scottish Experience.* Edinburgh: University Press, 1982.

International Center for Settlement of Investment Disputes. *Investment Laws of the World.* Dobbs Ferry, New York: Oceana (loose leaf service, continually updated).

International Labor Office. *Multinational Enterprises and Social Policy.* Geneva: International Labor Office, 1973.

Jackson, John A. *International Competition in Services.* Washington, DC: American Enterprise Institute, 1989.

Jackson, Richard A. *The Multinational Corporation and Social Policy.* New York: Praeger, 1974.

Johnson, C. *Japan's Public Policy Companies.* Washington: American Enterprise Institute, 1978.

Joint Economic Committee. *The Mercantilist Challenge to the Liberal International Trade Order.* Washington, DC: Committee Print, 97th Congress 2nd Session, December 29, 1982.

Kapoor, A. *International Business in the Middle East: Case Studies.* Boulder, CO: Westview, 1979.

———. *International Business Negotiations: A Study in India.* New York: NYU Press, 1970.

———. and Phillip Grub. *The Multinational Enterprise in Transition.* Princeton, NJ: The Darwin Press, 1972.

Kindleberger, C. P. *American Business Abroad.* New Haven: Yale University Press, 1969.

Kline, John M. *International Codes and Multinational Business.* Westport, CT: Quorum Books, 1985.

———. *State Government Influence in U.S. International Economic Policy.* Lexington, MA: Lexington Books, 1983.

Kobrin, Stephen J. *Managing Political Risk Assessments: Strategic Response to Environmental Change.* Berkeley: University of California Press, 1982.

Kojima, K. *Japanese Direct Foreign Investment.* Rutland, VT: Charles Tuttle, 1978.

Korth, C. M., ed. *International Countertrade.* Westport, CT: Quorum Books, 1987.

Krayenbuehl, Thomas E. *Country Risk: Assessment and Monitoring.* Lexington, MA: Lexington Books, 1985.

Lall, S. J., and P. Streeten. *Foreign Investment, Transnationals and Developing Countries.* London: Macmillan, 1977.

Lauter, T. P., and P. M. Dickie. *Multinational Companies and East European Socialist Economies.* New York: Praeger, 1975.

Levcik, F., and J. Stankovsky. *Industrial Cooperation between East and West.* White Plains, New York: M. E. Sharpe, 1979.

Levitt, K. *Silent Surrender: The American Economic Empire in Canada.* New York: Liveright, 1971.

Liebowitz, R. D., ed. *Gorbachev's New Thinking: Projects for Joint Ventures.* Cambridge, MA: Ballinger, 1988.

Lispson, C. *Standing Guard: Protecting Foreign Capital in the 19th and 20th Centuries.* Berkeley: University of California Press, 1985.

Machlup, F., ed. *Economic Integration: Worldwide, Regional, Sectoral.* London: Macmillan, 1976.

Magaziner, Ira C., and T. N. Hout. *Japanese Industrial Policy.* London: Policy Studies Institute, no. 585, January 1980.

Mahini, Amir. *Making Decisions in Multinational Corporations.* New York: Wiley, 1988.

Mattelart, A. *Transnationals and the Third World: The Struggle for Culture.* South Hadley, MA: Bergin and Garvey, 1983.

Mautner-Markhof, F. *Processes of International Negotiations.* Boulder, CO: Westview, 1989.

Mazzolini, R. *Government Controlled Enterprises: International Strategic and Policy Decisions.* New York: John Wiley, 1979.

Meade, J. E. *The Theory of Customs Union.* Amsterdam: North-Holland, 1975.

Mikesell, R. F. *Foreign Investment in the Petroleum and Mineral Industries.* Baltimore, MD: Johns Hopkins University Press, 1971.

————, and others. *Foreign Investment in the Petroleum and Mineral Industries: Case Studies of Investor-Host Country Relations.* Baltimore, MD: Johns Hopkins University Press, 1971.

————, ed. *U.S. Private and Government Investment Abroad.* Eugene, OR: University of Oregon, 1962.

Modelski, George, ed. *Multinational Corporations and World Order.* Beverly Hills, CA: Sage Publications, 1972.

Moran, Theodore H., ed. *Multinational Corporations: The Political Economy of Foreign Direct Investment.* Lexington, MA: Lexington Books, 1985.

————. *Multinational Corporations and the Politics of Dependence.* Princeton: Princeton University Press, 1975.

Negandhi, A. R. *Multinational Corporations and State-Owned Enterprises: A New Challenge in International Business.* Greenwich, CT: JAI Press, 1986.

Newfarmer, R. *Profits, Progress and Poverty: Case Studies of International Industries in Latin America.* Notre Dame: University of Notre Dame Press, 1985.

Novak, M., and Michael P. Jackson, eds. *Latin America: Dependency or Interdependence?* Washington DC: American Enterprise Institute, 1985.

OECD. *Selected Industrial Policy Instruments.* Paris: Organization for Economic Cooperation and Development, 1978.

Paquet, G., ed. *The Multinational Firm and the Nation State.* Don Mills, Ont.: Collier-Macmillan Canada, 1972.

Pentland, C. *International Theory and European Integration.* New York: The Free Press, 1973.

Ponter, T. A. *Multinational Enterprises and Government Intervention.* New York: Saint Martin's Press, 1985.

Prahalad, C. K., and Yves Doz. *The Multinational Mission.* New York: The Free Press, 1987.

Raddock, D. M. *Assessing Corporate Political Risk.* Totowa, NJ: Rowman, 1986.

Ramesh, J., and C. Weiss, Jr., eds. *Mobilizing Technology for World Development.* New York: Praeger, 1979.

Report of the Task Force on the Structure of Canadian Industry. *Foreign Ownership in the Structure of Canadian Industry.* Ottawa: Queen's Printer, 1968.

Robinson, J. *Multinationals and Political Control.* London: Gower, 1983.

Robinson, Richard D., ed. *Direct Foreign Investment: Costs and Benefits.* New York: Praeger, 1987.

Said, Abdula A., and Luiz R. Simmons, eds. *The New Sovereigns: Multinational Corporations as World Powers.* Englewood Cliffs, NJ: Prentice-Hall, 1975.

Sampson, Anthony. *The Seven Sisters: The Great Oil Companies & the World They Shaped.* New York: Viking Press, 1975.

————. *The Sovereign State of ITT.* New York: Stein & Day, 1973.

Sauvant, Karl P., and Farid G. Lavipour, eds. *Controlling Multinational Enterprises: Problems, Strategies, Counterstrategies.* Boulder, CO: Westview, 1976.

Schnitzer, M. *U.S. Business Involvement in Eastern Europe.* New York: Praeger, 1980.

Schott, J. J. *More Free Trade Areas?* Washington, DC: Institute for International Economics, monograph 27, May 1989.

————. ed. *Free Trade Areas and U.S. Trade Policy.* Washington, DC: International Economics Institute, 1989.

————, and Murray G. Smith, eds. *The Canada-United States Free Trade Agreement: The Global Impact.* Washington, DC: Institute for International Economics, 1988.

Sethi, S. Prakash, and Jagdish N. Sheth. *Environmental Aspects of Operating Abroad.* Pacific Palisades, CA: Goodyear Publishing Company, 1973.

————— , and R. H. Holton, eds. *Management of the Multinationals.* New York: The Free Press, 1974.

Sigmund, P. E. *Multinationals in Latin America.* Madison, WI: University of Wisconsin Press, 1980.

Smith, David N., and Louis T. Wells, Jr. *Negotiating Third World Mineral Agreements.* Cambridge, MA: Ballinger, 1975.

Solomon, L. D. *Multinational Corporations and the Emerging World Order.* Port Washington, NY: Kennikat Press, 1978.

Stoever, W. A. *Renegotiations in International Business Transactions.* Lexington, MA: Lexington Books, 1981.

Tancer, S. B. *Economic Nationalism in Latin America.* New York: Praeger, 1976.

Ting, W. *Multinational Risk Assessment and Management.* Westport, CT: Greenwood, 1988.

Trilateral Commission. *Industrial Policy and the International Economy.* New York: Report of the Trilateral Task Force on Industrial Policy, 1979.

Truitt, J. F. *Expropriation of Private Foreign Investment.* Bloomington, IN: Indiana University Press, 1974.

Tugendhat, Christopher. *The Multinationals.* New York: Random House, 1972.

Tung, R. L. *Business Negotiations with the Japanese.* Lexington, MA: D C Heath, 1984.

Turner, Louis. *Invisible Empires: Multinational Companies and the Modern World.* New York: Harcourt Brace Jovanovich, 1971.

————— . *Multinational Companies and the Third World.* New York: Hill and Wang, 1973.

United States Senate, Committee on Finance, Subcommittee on International Trade. *The Multinational Corporation and the World Economy.* Washington, DC: Superintendent of Documents, 1973.

————— . *Multinational Corporations: A Compendium of Papers.* Washington, DC: Superintendent of Documents, 1973.

————— . *Multinational Corporations: Hearings, February 26–March 6, 1973.* Washington, DC: Superintendent of Documents, 1973.

Uri, Pierre, ed. *Trade and Investment Policies for the Seventies.* New York: Praeger, 1971.

Vaubel, R., and T. D. Willett. *The Political Economy of International Organizations.* Boulder, CO: Westview, 1989.

Vernon, R. *Sovereignty at Bay: The Multinational Spread of US Enterprises*. New York: Basic Books, 1971.

——. *The Economic and Political Consequences of Multinational Enterprise: An Anthology*. Boston: Division of Research, Graduate School of Business Administration, Harvard University, 1972.

——, ed. *Big Business and the State*. Cambridge, MA: Harvard University Press, 1974.

——. *Storm Over the Multinationals: The Real Issues*. Cambridge, MA: Harvard University Press, 1977.

Viner, J. *The Customs Union Issue*. New York: Stephens and Sons, 1950.

Waldmann, R. *Regulating International Business through Codes of Conduct*. Washington, DC: American Enterprise Institute, 1980.

Wallace, Don, Jr., ed. *International Control of Investment*. New York: Praeger, 1974.

Warnecke, S. J. *International Trade and Industrial Policies*. New York: Holmes and Meier, 1978.

Wilkens, Mira. *The Maturing of Multinational Enterprise: American Business Abroad from 1914 to 1970*. Cambridge, MA: Harvard University Press, 1974.

Zurawicki, L. *Multinational Enterprise in the East and West*. Netherlands: Sijthoff and Noordhoff, 1979.

Index